DATE DUE		
8.3.16		

DEMCO

What the Doctor Didn't Say

Jerry Menikoff
with Edward P. Richards

What the Doctor Didn't Say

The Hidden Truth about Medical Research

OXFORD
UNIVERSITY PRESS

2006

OXFORD
UNIVERSITY PRESS

Oxford University Press, Inc., publishes works that further
Oxford University's objective of excellence
in research, scholarship, and education.

Oxford   New York
Auckland   Cape Town   Dar es Salaam   Hong Kong   Karachi
Kuala Lumpur   Madrid   Melbourne   Mexico City   Nairobi
New Delhi   Shanghai   Taipei   Toronto

With offices in
Argentina   Austria   Brazil   Chile   Czech Republic   France   Greece
Guatemala   Hungary   Italy   Japan   Poland   Portugal   Singapore
South Korea   Switzerland   Thailand   Turkey   Ukraine   Vietnam

Copyright © 2006 by Oxford University Press

Published by Oxford University Press, Inc.
198 Madison Avenue, New York, New York 10016

www.oup.com

Oxford is a registered trademark of Oxford University Press

Library of Congress Cataloging-in-Publication Data
Menikoff, Jerry.
What the doctor didn't say : the hidden truth about medical research / Jerry Menikoff
with Edward P. Richards.
p. ; cm.
Includes bibliographical references and index.
ISBN-13 978-0-19-514797-1
ISBN 0-19-514797-9
1. Clinical trials.   2. Informed consent.   3. Human experimentation in medicine.
I. Richards, Edward P.   II. Title.
[DNLM: 1. Informed Consent—Popular Works.   2. Clinical Trials—ethics—Popular
Works.   3. Therapeutic Human Experimentation—legislation & jurisprudence—Popular
Works. W 20.55.H9 M545p 2006]
R853.C55M46 2006
610.72'4—dc22   2005054711

Portions of chapter 10 previously appeared in Jerry Menikoff, *The Hidden Alternative:
Getting Investigational Treatments Off-Study*, 361 Lancet 63 (2003), and are reprinted
with the permission of Elsevier Science.

Printed in the United States of America
on acid-free paper

We cannot know why the world suffers. But we can know how the world decides that suffering shall come to some persons and not to others. . . . For it is in the choosing that enduring societies preserve or destroy those values that suffering and necessity expose.
—Guido Calabresi and Philip Bobbitt, *Tragic Choices*

CAPTAIN RENAULT: What in heaven's name brought you to Casablanca?
RICK: My health: I came to Casablanca for the waters.
CAPTAIN RENAULT: The waters? What waters? We're in the desert.
RICK: I was misinformed.
—*Casablanca*

Acknowledgments

For reading and commenting on all or portions of various drafts of this manuscript I am grateful to the following people: Carl Coleman, Nancy Dubler, and Jesse Goldner, the nicest and most knowledgeable group of co-authors a person could ever wish for; Chris Crenner, my very supportive department chair; the always enthusiastic members of the Ethics Club, especially Don Marquis, Dick Silverstein, Russ Jacobs, Maureen Dudgeon, and Ron Stephens; and Mary Faith Marshall, whose presence is very much missed. And for helping me better understand the world of human subjects research: all of the dedicated personnel at the federal Office for Human Research Protections with whom I have had the great privilege and pleasure to work, particularly Michael Carome, Kristina Borror, Karena Cooper, and Pat McNeilly; Karen Blackwell, John Finley, Sharon Grable, Dan Voss, and the other hard-working people who protect research subjects at the University of Kansas Medical Center; and the many participants in the online IRB Forum, who are always coming up with new issues leading to fascinating discussions. And last, but far from least, a big thank you to Jeffrey House, Peter Ohlin, and Stephanie Attia from Oxford University Press for having endured the sometimes less than pleasant task (yes, it's true!) of putting up with my many requests, yet still making sure this book actually saw the light of day.

This book, like many others, owes a great deal to those have come before, particularly the lawyers, doctors, and ethicists who have reached for a better understanding of the differences between being a patient and being a research subject. Among that group, special mention is owed to Henry Beecher, Jay Katz, and Charles Fried.
—Jerry Menikoff

Many thanks go to Katharine C. Rathbun, my wife, for her unstinting support; and to John Costonis of the Louisiana State University Law Center, for his institutional and intellectual support and encouragement.
—Edward P. Richards

Contents

Introduction   xi

1 The Dilemma of Human Research   3

Part I   How Good Studies Can Be Bad Choices

2 The Nature of Research   15
3 A Case Study: The Difference between Being a Patient and Being a Research Subject   24
4 How the Law Protects Patients Who Get Nonstandard Care   37
5 The Weakened Legal Protections Given to Research Subjects   51
6 How Bad for the Subjects Can a Study Be?   61

Part II   Consent: What Are Subjects Told?

7 What Informed Consent Requires   83
8 The Anatomy of a Consent Form   94
9 The Good, the Bad, and the Ugly Research Study: From *Consent* to *Choice*   113
10 The Hidden Alternative   124

Part III   When Consent Can't Be Obtained

11 Incompetent Adults   145
12 Emergency Research   158

13 Children in Research: The Basic Rules   165
14 Can Children Be Enrolled in Studies That Are Bad for Them?   180
15 Research and Reproduction   190

Part IV   The Role of Money

16 Should Research Subjects Be Paid?   211
17 Compensating Researchers: Dealing with Conflicts of Interest   222

Part V   The Challenge for the Future

18 Where Do We Go from Here? The Paradox of Pediatric
Cancer Research   239

Notes   253
Index   313

Introduction

Pick up a newspaper on any random day, and there's a decent chance that you will find a new report raising concerns about the effectiveness or safety of some medical treatment. Hormone replacement therapy for menopausal women, we learn, causes heart attacks and strokes and makes dementia more likely. Painkilling drugs taken by millions, such as Vioxx and Celebrex, have perhaps actually killed tens of thousands by causing heart attacks. Antidepressants given to teenagers may be leading some of them to commit suicide.

The headlines reflect an important underlying truth: for many problems, in spite of the many wonders of modern medicine, there is still a great deal of uncertainty about what works and what doesn't work. There are often concerns about whether the benefits of a particular treatment outweigh the possible harms. Many people, upon reading these stories, are no doubt throwing up their hands and thinking, "What's a person to do?" They might be suspecting that too often, in choosing a medical treatment, there is nothing better to do than flip a coin and hope for the best.

While there are no easy answers, there are helpful ways to think about such questions. This book focuses on those instances in which uncertainty is greatest—the world of promising-but-not-yet-proven therapies, therapies that are still being evaluated in research studies—and shows that there is crucial information that a patient can and should use in making a best choice. There are ways to come up with the right answer to crucial questions: *Should I be treated with standard care even it isn't that good? Should I participate in a research study? And are there other treatment options I should be thinking about that my doctor hasn't mentioned?*

A New Role for Research Studies

More and more frequently, doctors are telling their patients that participation in a research study may be an excellent treatment option. By exploring how people should decide about whether to participate in such a study, this book will provide an insider's look at the world of "maybe" medicines, those that may or may not be good treatment choices. It will provide the information that a patient needs to make the best choice among treatment options, even in the face of uncertainty about the risks and benefits of particular treatments. No matter what the disease or what the treatment, there are certain common differences between receiving the usual type of treatment, receiving some innovative treatment directly from your doctor, and participating in a research study. This book will explain those differences. It will empower patients in a variety of ways, sometimes giving them information that can have life-or-death consequences.

The odds are great that most readers currently know little of this information. And that is perhaps the most fascinating part of the story. Forty years ago, Henry Beecher, Dorr Professor of Research in Anesthesia at Harvard Medical School, published an article in the *New England Journal of Medicine* describing how medical researchers had, in a number of instances, risked the health or the lives of their subjects. In most cases, the researchers had never even told them that they were participating in research. Beecher's article was a bombshell. He provided many details of outrageous things that doctors were doing to research subjects. His revelations were seen as a "devastating indictment of research ethics [which] helped inspire the movement that brought a new set of rules."[1]

We now live in a world in which those no-longer-so-new rules are operating, presumably to provide adequate protections to research subjects. And ours is a world in which such protections are more necessary than ever, given how much the role of research has changed since Beecher's day. "Clinical trials"—research studies in which some new treatment for a medical problem is being tested—are a key step in obtaining regulatory approval of drugs and devices generating hundreds of billions of dollars in profit each year. Millions of patients each year end up enrolling in these studies. And often they are under the impression that doing so is the best choice for treating their medical condition.

Telling Only Part of the Truth

Unlike in Beecher's day, it is the rare patient nowadays who will not at least be told that they are being asked to participate in a research study. The current rules actually provide patients with a great deal of information before they make a decision. But is it the right type of information? I (JM) have spent much of the past decade trying to answer that question. During that period I have reviewed thousands of consent forms and have become a nationally recognized expert on how this country tries to protect its research subjects.

This book reveals my conclusions: there is good reason to believe that in many thousands of cases, research subjects are not being given the information they most need in order to make good choices. This book will highlight not the rare headline-making unusual circumstance, but will instead present example after example demonstrating what is likely to happen to the average person as they are asked to participate in research. After explaining the nature of the relationship between patients and researchers, I (together with help from my coauthor, Edward P. Richards, who wrote chapter 17)[2] will show the specific ways in which consent forms commonly fail to provide crucial pieces of information. We give the details of real studies, providing a modern-day update of the information that Beecher provided forty years ago. Among many other things, we describe:

- the patient at the Cleveland Clinic who told his doctors he wanted to get treated with the newest chemotherapy, and who could have gotten it, but instead ended up in a research study and died without the treatment that would have saved his life;
- the thousands of women who are being offered participation in studies of drugs to prevent breast cancer, and who are told about the option of having both breasts surgically removed but not about the option of taking a low-risk drug that millions of women have already used to treat osteoporosis that also appears very likely to be active in preventing breast cancer;
- the patients who underwent a new form of colon cancer surgery, but who were not told that few of the surgeons performing the surgery would themselves have agreed to undergo it, nor why that was the case.

And we end this book with the rarely mentioned story of what is currently happening to the majority of children who develop cancer: how they are being enrolled in research studies under a type of arrangement that a former United States solicitor general and current Harvard law professor once described as "inhuman."[3]

Why Is Information Being Hidden—and Does It Have to Be?

The state of affairs revealed in this book is not an accident. Nor is it perhaps, as you might now be thinking, a conspiracy concocted by drug company executives in darkened rooms. In part it results from the actions of thoughtful, well-meaning people. Many experts are concerned that, if patients were fully informed about their medical treatment options, it would be harder to get them to enroll in research studies. Then, they fear, important research would not get done or would be delayed. The result would be that we would all suffer.

As we will try to demonstrate, those concerns are overstated. The sky will not fall as a result of giving patients the information they need to make good choices. We will show that there are ways to properly inform patients while continuing to get adequate participation in research. In contrast, deceiving people as a way of getting them to enroll in research studies is a destructive course of action. Not only is it unethical, but the truth about what is happening will eventually be revealed. The time to build confidence in a more open system is now.

What the Doctor Didn't Say

1

The Dilemma of Human Research

In the last decades of the twentieth century, there has been a growing attempt to portray participation in a clinical trial—a research study comparing some new treatment to the existing treatment—as often being a great choice for someone with a hard-to-treat medical problem. Such research studies presumably give people access to the best doctors at the best medical centers, provide them with far more medical attention than they would otherwise get, and also give them a chance to receive some cutting-edge treatment. Under this new reality, participation in research has become something to be sought after, replacing in peoples' minds the old image of a Dr. Frankenstein performing some frightening "experimental" procedure in a dank and dark laboratory.[1]

As Jane Brody, perhaps this nation's leading health writer, stated in 2002 in one of her popular *New York Times* columns: "At the very least, by joining a clinical trial, you will receive the best established therapy. At most, you will be among the first to receive a treatment that proves to be better, either more effective or less hazardous."[2] According to Brody's analysis, joining a clinical trial is likely to be a no-lose situation for a patient. And her viewpoint has been seconded by no less august an assembly than the doctors in charge of medical research on childhood cancers. They unequivocally have advised parents of children with cancer that "clinical trials are proven to offer children the best chance of survival."[3]

Thus, an article published in 2004 in the leading British medical journal, *Lancet*, came as something of a surprise to many. The article, written by a group of scholars at Harvard University, reviewed all previous published studies comparing the outcomes of cancer patients who participate in clinical trials to those of patients who did not participate.[4] Their conclusion? *There was no good evidence to show that patients who entered clinical trials did any better than those who did not.* They also cautioned that future patients should not be encouraged to participate in studies based on the unproven conclusion that doing so would be good for them.

Actually, the results of the Harvard study shouldn't have been all that surprising. Once a person understands the true nature of research, and how it is regulated in this country, it is easy to show—which we will do in this book—that in many instances a patient can do better by choosing *not* to participate in a research study. And for most people, that is a far more important point than what the Harvard scholars reported. Those scholars were concerned with what happens, *on average*, in certain types of research studies. But for someone who is considering participating in a particular research study, "on average" is not the piece of information that is most useful to them. They are far more interested in knowing whether being in *that particular* research study is a good choice.

This book attempts to explain how someone interested in making the best decisions about their health care should deal with the common scenario in which there is some uncertainty about the effectiveness or safety of the treatments being offered. One common situation in which that takes place is when a person is asked to be in a research study. The fact that choosing to be in the study is often a bad choice for a self-interested subject has a number of important consequences. That possibility of making a bad choice is at the heart of how we regulate the relationship between researchers and their research subjects, and how we determine what sorts of things we allow the researchers to do to those subjects. The simple truth is that while some research studies are a very good choice for someone who just wants to do what is in his or her best interests, many are bad choices. As we shall explain, it is in the very nature of research, as it is currently conducted, that there are *many* such "bad choice" studies.

Indeed, if there were no "bad choice" studies, research with human subjects would be a relatively straightforward endeavor. Participation in a study would always be a good thing for a subject, and so both society and the subject would benefit. Life would be simple.

But that isn't the world in which we live. Any society that wants to allow research with human subjects to be conducted faces a dilemma: if there are important research questions that appear to require such "bad choice" studies to be done, under what conditions can they be conducted? What decisions will a society make about how to get people into these studies?

The Myth of Altruism

It would be nice to think that we can rely heavily on altruism: that people will be stepping up to the plate in large numbers, willingly lining up to expose themselves to significant risks for the benefit of the greater society. To evaluate that possibility, consider events following the tragedy of September 11, 2001. In late October of that year, several weeks into the anthrax scare that followed the events of 9/11, a *Washington Post* headline read "Smallpox Vaccine Studies Swamped with Volunteers."[5]

From the headline, a reader might have guessed this to be an upsurge of patriotism stemming from the terrorist attack: people wanting to do their utmost, putting even their health at risk, to help their country develop the resources necessary to fend off a biologic warfare attack. No doubt these were the wonderful new stirrings of sacrifice-for-country that came in the wake of 9/11.

A few paragraphs into the story, the true motivation was laid out:

> Most volunteers are hardly motivated by altruism, they admit: They just want the vaccine. And they want it now.
>
> "I'm really worried about smallpox," said [Kathy] Tullier, a 46-year-old social worker [who "rushed to track down the nearest research center, 'ready, willing and able,' she said, to offer herself up as a guinea pig,"] "and I'd love to have my family protected. . . ."
>
> Only a few of the volunteers have professed an interest in helping science's fight against bioterrorism. . . . "Everybody's trying to protect themselves," [said a nurse recruiter at the University of Maryland.] "People are seeing this can benefit them."

There is a persistent belief that people often enroll in studies out of a sense of altruism, that they are motivated by a desire to benefit others. Yet many research experts have long disputed this claim, at least where there are significant health risks to participating in the study. As mentioned in the introduction, Henry Beecher is a famous Harvard physician whose 1966 article *Ethics and Clinical Research*,[6] detailing many examples of unethical studies, almost single-handedly forced this nation to redirect its efforts at improving research ethics. In that year he wrote that "excepting the extremely rare individual, the reality is, patients will not knowingly seriously risk their health or lives for a scientific experiment."

And there is an increasing amount of evidence, from studies of research subjects, dramatically confirming the commonsense truth of Beecher's words. Most prominently, researchers at the University of Chicago have for a number of years been studying why cancer patients enroll in clinical research studies. In particular, they have been examining "phase I" studies of new drugs, which are the earliest stage in testing a new drug, mainly performed to see how much of it can be given before it produces unacceptable side effects.[7] Participants are extremely unlikely to benefit from being in these studies. Indeed, their design makes it far more likely for them to be harmed than helped.

Yet when asked about why they chose to be in these studies, the great majority of the subjects indicated they hoped that they would have a cure or remission of their disease as a result of their participation. Most strikingly, *not a single person mentioned altruistic factors in answering this question!* As the researchers conclude in their study, as in previous ones conducted by other researchers, "altruism was not a motivating factor in subjects' decisions to participate in a phase 1 trial."[8]

This is not an especially surprising finding, when one thinks about it. As Beecher noted, people in general are not extraordinarily altruistic, at least not when altruism involves substantial risks to their health. Yes, there is the occasional newspaper story of the person who donates an organ to a perfect stranger—but that is the exception to the rule: it gets into the newspaper precisely because it is so unusual.[9] Most of the rest of us sit back in mild amazement at such stories, perhaps comforted that such exceptional people actually exist in a world more commonly full of Enron-like behavior. Indeed, until a few years ago, such donations were *not even permitted* in this country precisely because the organ transplant community suspected either that there must be some under-the-table (and illegal) payments involved, or else that the donor was insane. Surely, many felt, no sane person would engage in such highly altruistic behavior.

What Happened in the Past

Given the limits on altruistic behavior, societies have in the past used heavy-handed methods to get participants into studies. One option has simply been to order people into the studies at gunpoint, with a penalty of death for refusing. Consider Nazi Germany during the 1940s, when concentration camp inmates were forced to participate in experiments intended to help learn information about troop survival in adverse conditions. In high-altitude survival studies, subjects were placed in low-pressure chambers, and the simulated altitude was raised, causing the deaths of many subjects. In another experiment, subjects were kept in tanks of ice water for hours at a time, or kept naked outdoors in subfreezing temperatures. To study treatment of battlefield wounds, prisoners were injected with bacteria such as streptococcus and gas gangrene, while blood circulation was stopped by tying off blood vessels. In another case, poisons were secretly given to people in their food. If they did not die from the poisons, they were sometimes nonetheless killed immediately thereafter so that autopsies could take place.

Those events led to the creation of the Nuremberg Code in 1947, a statement of basic principles that were believed to make human subjects research ethical.[10] Even though Americans wrote the Nuremberg Code, it was not at that time (or even later) formally adopted as part of American law. And in the absence of any significant limitations on the conduct of researchers, a number of incidents occurred throughout the twentieth century suggesting the United States had its own problems about respecting the rights of the research subjects.

It was not until 1972 that an enterprising reporter exposed the "Tuskegee Study," in which black males with syphilis had been studied since 1932 by the U.S. Public Health Service—a study that was still taking place in the 1970s. The men had been lied to for years, never told that a cure for their disease, penicillin, had been discovered. A variety of other research "scandals" have occurred in this nation, including injection of live cancer cells into Jewish old age home residents, intentionally infecting institutionalized children with hepatitis (on the rationale that they likely would have gotten infected anyway), military experiments involving soldiers unknowingly consuming LSD, and government experiments in which thousands of Americans were exposed to radiation.[11]

A blue-ribbon panel's investigation into what happened in some of the government's radiation experiments has led to a number of lawsuits. Some of these studies, designed to help our military, are particularly chilling in a post-9/11 world where terrorism and weapons of mass destruction are now part of daily conversation:[12]

- During the 1950s and 1960s, the CIA ran a project called MKULTRA, which "was established to counter perceived Soviet and Chinese advances in brainwashing and interrogation techniques." The CIA funded 149 sub-projects at universities and research institutions to perform "research and development of chemical, biological, and radiological materials capable of employment in clandestine operations to control human behavior." The subjects in these studies were often enrolled in medical and psychological experiments without even knowing they were taking place. Among the "untoward results" were the deaths of two subjects.
- Between 1960 and 1972, patients suffering from inoperable cancer—most of them poor and uneducated African Americans—were exposed to "massive" doses of radiation as part of a study conducted by the Department of Defense. The subjects were specially selected so that they were not close to death, but rather were in good clinical condition—at least, before having portions or sometimes all of their body exposed to radiation in the study. They were not told they were participating in a study, but only that they were getting the radiation to treat their cancer. In fact, the Department of Defense was trying to find out what would happen to troops who were exposed to radiation following the explosion of an atomic bomb. As a report prepared for that department explained it, the study was designed to calculate "a baseline for determining how much radiation exposure is too much."
- During the 1960s, the Atomic Energy Commission funded a study on prisoners in Oregon to see how radiation affects male fertility. Healthy male prisoners were asked to volunteer to have their testicles irradiated and to then allow multiple biopsies of the testicles to determine how much their sperm had been damaged by the radiation. Due to the researchers' concerns about permanent sperm damage, a requirement of the study was that the prisoners agree to undergo vasectomy before leaving the prison "to prevent contamination of the genetic pool." As a federal judge described it, this was "the unkindest cut of all."

The publicity following the exposure of the Tuskegee Study did lead to efforts to clean our own house. Congressional hearings led to the passage in 1974 of the National Research Act and the appointment of a commission to evaluate how to ethically conduct research involving human subjects. That year also saw the enactment of the earliest form of the federal regulations now known as the "Common Rule," establishing the basic structure of the system by which ethical standards would be set for all federally funded—and even much privately funded—research. The commission issued a report in 1979, known as the Belmont Report.[13] That report established three principles—autonomy, beneficence, and justice—as the ethical foundation for research with human subjects. Subsequently, those principles were incorporated into modifications of federal regulations, adding new teeth to the bare bones structure that had previously been created.[14]

The regulations establish a federal agency, the Office for Human Research Protections, that interprets the Common Rule and tries to make sure that researchers throughout the nation are complying with it.[15] But the most important element of enforcement is built into the regulations themselves, which require institutions where research takes place to create (or hire) a review committee, known as an "institutional review board" or IRB, that must review every study to determine that it is in compliance with the regulations.[16]

There are thousands of IRBs in this nation, and they review tens of thousands of research protocols each year. And if a study is being conducted in a number of locations (e.g., patients being given a new asthma drug at university medical centers around the country), then in general a separate IRB at each location must review the study and determine that it satisfies the requirements of the regulations.

The regulations that constitute the Common Rule are somewhat complicated, and we will say much more about specific aspects of them in many other chapters of this book. But in simple terms, they require IRBs to enforce two basic principles that are essentially restatements of the two themes established a half century ago by the Nuremberg Code: (1) a study cannot be *too* risky: it must be designed so as to minimize risks to subjects, and the risks must be reasonable in relationship to benefits;[17] and (2) in most cases, the subjects must have given their "informed consent" to participate in the study.[18]

The Reality of Today

But the passage of these relatively modern regulations has done nothing to eliminate the underlying dilemma of needing to use subjects in studies that are bad for them. Consider several stories that made headlines near the end of the twentieth century:[19]

- On March 29, 1996, 19-year-old pre-med student Nicole Wan volunteered to undergo bronchoscopy—having a flexible tube threaded down her throat to collect lung cells—as part of a study at the University of Rochester to learn about how our lungs protect themselves from infection and pollution. Two days later, the previously healthy young woman died from a heart attack, apparently the result of having gotten an overdose of anesthetic during the procedure.
- On September 13, 1999, 18-year-old Jesse Gelsinger, who suffered from a relatively mild form of a genetic disease called ornithine transcarbamylase deficiency—his liver wasn't able to break down certain waste products produced in his body—was injected with a specially designed virus as part of a "gene transfer" study at the University of Pennsylvania. The study was not intended to help Gelsinger, but rather to gain information about how much of this virus could be safely given to new-born infants with a more severe form of this disease. Four days later he was dead.
- On May 4, 2001, Ellen Roche, a healthy 24-year-old who worked in the Asthma and Allergy Center at Johns Hopkins University, began participating

in a Hopkins research study in which she inhaled a compound called hexamethonium. She was given the compound with the intent that it would irritate her lungs, so researchers might better understand what happens in the lungs of people with asthma. Within five days of getting the hexamethonium, she ended up on a ventilator in an intensive care unit. She died less than a month after entering the study.

These are just a handful of headline-making studies. The far more important question is, what is happening in the "average" research study in which any of us might be invited to enroll? How likely is participation in such a study to be a bad choice for someone? What is it that might make participation a bad choice? And perhaps most important, how likely is someone to be given the information that will help him or her distinguish the "good choice" from the "bad choice" studies?

While these are questions that are highly relevant to people whose jobs intersect with the areas of human subjects research—researchers, administrators, and regulators—they are especially relevant to any of us who might one day be asked to become a research subject. For as the Harvard study on outcomes for cancer trials patients demonstrates, there is a great deal of confusion—perhaps intentionally maintained—about what really happens in research. The fact that the myth that "research is almost always good for subjects" has come into being without any real evidence supporting it—and in the face of very good reasons to doubt its truth—suggests something is very wrong.

And, most important, there is actually a much larger group of us who need to pay attention to these issues. The dilemma of wanting to make good choices about medical care in the face of uncertainty about how well a particular treatment might work is not unique to the person being asked to participate in a research study. Talk to any doctor and you will discover that a surprisingly large percentage of medical care involves decision making in the face of incomplete information. And many of the issues that confront a person who has been asked to participate in a clinical trial are similar to those that any person dealing with a decision about uncertain medicine should be thinking about. Perhaps there is a research study that is their best choice, but they haven't even been told about it. Perhaps they should consider being treated with some new type of medical care outside of a research study—and again, they haven't even been told about this option. Thus, an understanding of how a patient should decide whether or not participating in a research study is a good choice is relevant to a far larger group of people than those specifically asked to enter a study.

This book attempts to highlight that reasoning process by cutting through the cloud of confusion surrounding what happens to research subjects. We attempt to reveal the true nature of research and to use the rules we uncover to empower the average person, giving each of us a better opportunity to make informed decisions about our health care, inside or outside of the research setting.

We also hope, by exposing the research system to the light of day, to stimulate changes that will make it truer to its avowed goals of adequately protecting the subjects. And we attempt to accomplish that by a new approach:[20] by putting human subjects research under the lens of a particular type of microscope, the law of torts. Simply stated, tort law is what allows each of us to sue for damages when someone has harmed us. Whereas criminal law protects society as a whole, tort law is the remedy that protects each of us as individuals.

Malpractice is the one part of tort law that governs the relationship between doctors and patients. It spells out the duties our society imposes on doctors. But what does tort law say about the duties that a researcher owes to a subject? That is a subject that has received scant attention. Yet as we shall show, there are surprising differences between what the law allows a doctor to do to a patient and what that same doctor can do when the patient suddenly becomes a participant in a research study. Those differences are of crucial importance to anyone thinking about being a research subject, to people who are part of the research establishment, and to all of us as members of the public who benefit from the fruits of research.

The heart of our discussion will be developed in the first three parts of this book. In part I, we explain in detail the ways in which participating in a particular study may be bad for a subject. We provide a roadmap that someone could use in trying to determine whether a particular study is a "good" or "bad" choice for them. We demonstrate the ways in which researchers are permitted to do things to subjects that society does not allow doctors to do to patients outside of the research setting. We explore *how* bad for a subject participation in a study might be.

In part II, we explore the rationale that allegedly justifies having subjects participate in the "bad choice" studies. That rationale is *informed consent*: the notion that the subjects have been given enough information to make an informed choice about participating in the study and thus have done so willingly. We examine to what extent subjects are indeed given the information they need to make appropriate choices. As part of doing that, we demonstrate many holes in the current system and point out the pieces of information that a prospective subject—and, indeed, many patients who are facing similar types of decisions that are not related to participation in research—will often *not* get but that they should be asking for. And in part III, we explore those circumstances in which the current rules do not even require informed consent.

The Ethics of Deceit

In part IV we discuss the role of money in human subjects research before closing the book, in part V, with an exploration of a question that the entire book in essence poses: what will be the consequences of being more honest with subjects and permitting them to make better decisions about participating in research?

As we noted in the introduction, some in the research community seem to believe that if they told the truth to people, many patients—largely motivated by self-interest—would quickly decide not to become research subjects.[21] These researchers would say that it is a good thing that people who enroll in studies do not always fully understand the choice they are making, since otherwise there would be fewer people in studies and we would all suffer from the resulting decrease in medical knowledge.[22]

In effect, these views legitimize a system that involves deceiving people under certain circumstances, arguably for the greater good of society.

Some would likely prefer that this book were never written, or at least that few people ever read it. Perhaps they could take comfort in what Yale law professor Robert Burt said of a collection of essays that attempted to clear the air about another issue in bioethics—how the law defines when someone is dead so that organs can be removed from them—that raised similar concerns.[23] Professor Burt thought that letting the public actually understand the issues discussed in that book would be harmful. He acknowledged that he presumably should have wanted the book "to have been burnt in manuscript rather than published." But he was confident that it would, due to its depressing topic (death), only "sell a few thousand copies, almost all destined for library shelves, and then serenely sink from public view."

We freely admit that the information contained in this book, if it results in empowering people who are offered enrollment in studies, may indeed lead—at least in the short term—to a decrease in participation in research studies. But we don't think the only choice is between deceiving the public and having inadequate participation. There are ethical ways both to be truthful to people and to adequately encourage participation in research—perhaps even to create more participation than exists today. In part V, we show that our legal system is flexible enough to permit this result—though hard choices will have to be made.

But we are getting ahead of ourselves. Before moving to the "answer," we begin in part I with the main topic of this book: laying out the problem of why participation in many studies might be a bad choice for a self-interested subject and explaining the differences between "good choice" and "bad choice" studies. The decision-making rules we lay out there will empower many patients, even when participation in research is not an issue, who find themselves in the all too common scenario of confronting choices involving less-than-complete information about proposed treatments.

Part I

How Good Studies Can Be Bad Choices

2

The Nature of Research

[T]he issue in medical experimentation is the risking of lives to save other lives. . . .
—Guido Calabresi, *Reflections on Medical Experimentation in Humans*

Why is it that being in a research study may so often be a bad choice for someone who is primarily concerned with his or her own well-being? In this chapter we begin to explore the principles behind why that is so—even in many of the clinical trials that might generally be perceived as very good choices. The key lies in understanding the true nature of research—something that remains mired in confusion.

How the Health of a Research Subject is Subservient to the Goal of Answering the Research Question

The cover story for *Time* magazine on April 22, 2002, was an exposé of human subjects research entitled "How Medical Testing Has Turned Millions of Us into . . . Human Guinea Pigs."[1] In that story, the authors provided a list of six questions to ask your doctor if you are considering enrolling in a research study. The first of those questions was, *What is the primary purpose of the clinical trial, to help cure patients or to advance medical knowledge?*

Oddly enough, this is a dumb question, and the fact that one of this nation's most professional news magazines listed it as the "number one question to ask your doctor" says a great deal about the current state of confusion regarding the nature of research. *Time*'s question was dumb because a patient doesn't even need to bother to ask it. The correct answer is almost *always* going to be the same: the primary purpose of a research study is virtually *never* to treat the patients, but rather to advance medical knowledge. At least *some* things are done in *every* research study not for the primary purpose of benefiting the subjects but rather to help answer a research question: it is *doing those very things that causes the study to be a research study.* Indeed, we can consider this to be a simplified definition of research: research involves doing certain things ("research procedures") for the primary purpose of answering a particular research question.

Moreover, as we will later show, it is highly likely that in many if not most studies, at least some of those "research procedures" are *not* in the best interests of the subjects. These things may be trivial, for example, recopying some patient information in a second set of books; or they may be major, such as randomizing a person to get a surgical procedure and then not doing the "treatment" part of the operation (e.g., opening up their skull in preparation for an injection into their brain and then injecting a "useless" substance, salt water, into their brain). But at least some of them are probably things that, had patients been solely looking after what was best for themselves, they would have said "no" to.

In some cases, it will nonetheless be in a person's best interests to participate in a study. This will likely depend on why they are deciding to participate and what their other options are. Thus, to rephrase the question that *Time* magazine provided, subjects *should* be asking, "To what extent will being in this study possibly help cure me or make me feel better, and more important, how does that compare to my other options?" The portions of the study that advance patients' interests may be so good that they outweigh the study procedures they would prefer to avoid. The study may allow access to therapies patients can't get anywhere else. In other cases, it may not be in a patient's best interests to participate, but he or she may want to do so anyway, for altruistic reasons.

But across all the great variety of studies, it remains the case that in most instances, the study is *not* being conducted primarily to treat (or "do good things for" if you prefer that) the people who participate as subjects in the study. For some readers, this proposition is likely to generate a big yawn—while others are likely to do a double take, not believing what they read. Yet the statement is surely correct—and the fact that large portions of the public, the editors and writers at *Time* magazine, and, most important, many subjects who participate in research studies, might be surprised by this statement should be of concern to all of us.

Perhaps most surprising, even large percentages of the people running the studies don't understand this simple fact. A group of scholars at Harvard Medical School recently examined how well participants in studies, and the cancer researchers conducting the studies, understood what research is really about.[2] One of their conclusions, published in the prominent British medical journal *Lancet*, is quite startling: "Despite all [the people] surveyed being on the academic staff at research institutions, fewer than half recognized that *the main purpose of clinical trials is to benefit future patients*" (emphasis added) and not the patients actually participating in the studies. What makes this even more troubling is that the people (almost all of them doctors) questioned in this study—29.5% of whom said they were *unsure* of the right answer to this question, and an additional 24.6% of whom actually gave the *wrong* answer—were among the best of the best, working at three extremely prestigious Harvard-affiliated institutions: Dana-Farber Cancer Institute, Brigham and Women's

Hospital, and Massachusetts General Hospital (often considered the best hospital in the United States).

Even following the deaths of Jesse Gelsinger and Ellen Roche mentioned in chapter 1, the public appears to be getting a mixed message that contradicts this basic proposition. And the message surprisingly comes from the highest levels, people who are leading experts on research ethics. Dr. Greg Koski, a renowned researcher at Harvard Medical School, was brought in by federal regulators in 2000 to head the newly reorganized branch of the federal government that oversees the ethics of human subjects research, the Office for Human Research Protections. He became this nation's most powerful research ethics official, the leader in making sure that research is conducted in an ethical manner. In a special report that Johns Hopkins University published in its own magazine regarding changes in how research was being conducted there following the death of Ellen Roche, Dr. Koski made the following comments:

> The process for protecting subjects should not be an impediment to doing research. But we have to recognize where our priorities are. If we as a society are going to look to science for these benefits, and accept these benefits knowing that the only way we can get them is if we actually use people as subjects, then we have a moral and ethical obligation to make sure that we are looking out for their interests and well-being and rights. *That's got to be our first priority.* (emphasis added)[3]

Similarly, Secretary of Health and Human Services Tommy Thompson, in announcing the appointment of members of a new committee to advise him on ethical issues involving research with human subjects, stated that science and medical research should not take place "at the expense of the people who participate in . . . clinical trials."[4] And a report in the *New England Journal of Medicine* told about how the Association of American Medical Colleges, a group that speaks for most medical schools (and thus most major medical research institutions) in this country, had adopted new financial conflict of interest policies for researchers. Those policies made it clear that "the welfare of the patient is paramount" and must be "the top priority."[5]

All of these commentators are undoubtedly well-meaning. The primary purpose of their comments is certainly an important one: to emphasize that we should be doing more to make sure, *to the extent possible,* that we do not *needlessly* expose research subjects to harm. But that is *not* what they actually said: they make a much more compelling promise about the extent to which people will be protecting the well-being of the subjects. And that promise echoes a similar promise that even shows up in sections of the federal regulations, which talk about "ensuring the safety of subjects."[6]

These comments, simply put, are wrong. They send a message to people who might enroll in research studies that overpromises.[7] Doing research involves *intentionally* exposing persons to risks, and *not for the primary purpose of treating them or making them better,* but rather to answer a research question.[8] And, given the sorts of things that are commonly done in research studies, being a research subject in many cases will indeed be a bad choice for someone who is mainly concerned about his or her own best interests. Jay Katz, the Yale law professor who in 1972 authored *Experimentation with Human Beings*, the first law textbook in this field, noted that "[p]articipation in human research *always* involves an element of sacrifice, for subjects are asked to submit to interventions that expose them to *risks for the sake of advancement of knowledge.*"[9] Sometimes those extra risks may be very small. They might not lead to any harm, or might merely involve a small amount of inconvenience to the subject.

But in some situations, being exposed to these extra risks may lead to the subject being substantially worse off. The study in which Jesse Gelsinger participated clearly demonstrates this important point. As we noted in chapter 1, while Jesse suffered from a genetic abnormality, his symptoms were relatively well controlled, through diet and medications, when he entered a "gene transfer" study. Indeed, it was clear that this study was extremely unlikely to benefit him. The study was clearly designed and labeled as a "phase I" study: such studies are intended merely to determine how large a dose of the compound can be given before seeing significant side effects. As Arthur Caplan, this nation's most prominent bioethicist, and himself an ethics advisor to the research team conducting the study, stated with regard to gene transfer studies: "If you cured anybody, you'd publish it in a religious journal. It would be a miracle. The researchers won't say that. But I'm telling you. . . . All you're doing is you're saying, I've got this vector, I want to see if it can deliver the gene where I want it to go without killing or hurting or having side effects."[10] Caplan was actually not saying anything particularly controversial. Indeed, Jesse and his family had been told that the study was not designed to help him.

Yes, in retrospect, it appears that lots of corners may have been cut in doing the study. The researchers appear to have deviated from the protocol—they failed to follow the rules they set out for themselves in designing the study. And they do not appear to have fairly and fully disclosed to Jesse and his family all of the risks that might take place. But *even if all of those things were corrected*, the bottom line remains the same: this study was primarily not about helping Jesse Gelsinger. It was extremely unlikely to help him. It was far more likely to harm him than help him. And that doesn't mean that it was a "bad" or "evil" study. Rather, these conclusions are to at least some extent inherent in the nature of a phase I study. Our first rule of research is a fact of nature that we likely cannot change (at least given the current framework for conducting research), that shapes the nature of any modern-day research study. We can announce that "the welfare of the subject is paramount" all we want, but that won't change the facts: it isn't.[11] Answering the research question is what is paramount in a research study.[12]

And as we attempt to show in later chapters of this book, the study in which Jesse Gelsinger participated is far from unique in this regard. All studies—including all clinical trials, those very studies that are most commonly felt to be a good choice for someone with a medical problem—are governed by these general rules.

Enough said: it is very difficult to pursue two goals that will often be in conflict and yet always make sure that both of them are achieved. Doing research involves a similar clash of goals. The *primary* purpose of doing research is to perform certain research procedures on someone in a way that will *generate knowledge*. Doing what is best for the research subject therefore becomes, of necessity, a *secondary* goal that will sometimes give way to that primary goal. To a greater or lesser extent (depending on what the research procedures are—collecting data, doing surgery, etc.), doing research *is often* going to involve some level of risk to research subjects, risk that is *being imposed for a purpose other than for their benefit*. We can try to minimize that level of risk—and, indeed, the federal regulations require that to be done, as we describe in subsequent chapters—but we are extremely unlikely to eliminate it. The question is *how much* risk we are willing to permit a subject to bear for the sake of advancing scientific knowledge, and how to resolve the trade-off between risks to subjects and gaining that knowledge. We are back to a classic dilemma: society is regularly involved in determining how "suffering shall come to some persons and not to others."[13] These are the tragic choices involved in designing a system for research on human subjects.

Research Studies Are Not the Only Way Society Lets Sick People Get Access to Innovative Therapies

Now that we have shown the nature of what happens *in* a research study, it is important to recognize certain activities that can take place *outside* of a research study. To do that, let's return to the proposition that opened this book: the belief among many that being in a clinical trial is almost always a good thing. One of the reasons for that belief was that being in such studies gives the subject access to some cutting-edge therapy they couldn't get anywhere else. As *New York Times* columnist Jane Brody put it, you may "be among the first to receive a treatment that proves to be better, either more effective or less hazardous." If indeed this were true, then at least with regard to clinical trials—where patients with some illness are being randomized between standard care and a new treatment—perhaps the negative aspects of being in research studies wouldn't be that troublesome. Yes, things may be done to subjects purely for research purposes, but after all, they are getting access to the new treatment, so they really don't have much to complain about. There's a trade-off: you want the new treatment, you have to subject yourself to some risks so that medical knowledge can be advanced.

There's one problem with this line of analysis: it is based on a false assumption. A person doesn't always have to participate in a research study to get treated with some new form of cutting-edge therapy. Many new treatments are available directly from doctors, without any need to be in a study. And there are many reasons why people might want to get the treatment that way, avoiding those aspects of being a research subject that are contrary to their own best interests. The most obvious one is that being in a research study often means having your treatment chosen by randomization. If your goal is to be treated with a new type of treatment, why be in a study which gives you a 1-in-2 chance at that treatment, when you can get it outside of a study and be assured of getting it?

The failure to distinguish between participating in a research study and directly getting some "experimental" (in the sense of not yet fully proven) therapy outside of a research study has been around a long time, and still exists. This distinction is a hugely important one—particularly from the point of view of patients, trying to figure out what is best for their care—yet it is rarely spelled out clearly.[14] We shall demonstrate in later chapters of this book that failing to recognize this distinction can lead to horrible consequences for someone with a medical problem.

And it is important to recognize the natural tension caused by this distinction between a particular person's interests and those of the broader community. Each of us should be strongly in favor of there being as much research as possible about whatever "group" we belong to—a woman, a child, a person with breast cancer or Parkinson's disease or some exceedingly rare medical condition. But it doesn't follow that we would necessarily want to be a participant in a research study, even if we have a current medical problem for which there is no cure.

A man who has AIDS might well be thankful that as a result of the activism of the HIV/AIDS community, there are a variety of drugs that treat his condition. But if his symptoms are getting worse in spite of those drugs, it doesn't follow that he should want to enter a randomized study involving a comparison between standard care supplemented (1) by a placebo (essentially no treatment) or (2) by the hot new drug being studied. Ideally, he might be better off seeing if he can get that drug outside of the study and, only if it is not available in that manner, then considering enrolling in the study. In other words, his interests—wanting to get that hot new drug—are very different from the interests of the broader group of which he is a part (the AIDS community).[15]

Thus, the critical question should be, how often is it the case that a new treatment will be available outside of a research study? The honest answer is, no one knows for sure. Surprisingly, there are no comprehensive records kept, even by the federal government, of what studies are being conducted with human subjects. (It is often said—correctly—that there are much better records kept by the government about how many animals are in studies, and what is done to them, than are kept regarding humans.) But an educated guess would suggest that a substantial percentage of treatments being studied in clinical trials can be obtained outside of these research studies. And in some areas—such as cancer treatments—it may well be that in more than half of the studies the new treatment can be obtained that way.

The main situation in which a new treatment is usually hard to obtain outside of a research study is where a brand new drug, never before used in human beings, is being investigated. But that actually accounts for far fewer studies than most people would likely guess. Many studies involve using a drug that was approved by the FDA for a different medical problem than the one it is usually used for. And other studies involve using FDA-approved drugs in new combinations, or at higher strengths, or for longer treatment periods. We will discuss the significance of this phenomenon—technically called "off-label use"—in greater detail in chapter 10. The important point is that once the FDA has approved a drug for at least one use, doctors are permitted to use that drug for any reason they deem appropriate. And many treatments—such as a new surgical procedure—are not even subject to any FDA regulation at all. Thus, there would be no federal law preventing a doctor from directly providing such a treatment to a patient.

And even in the clearest case where it is hard to get a drug outside of a study—a drug that has not yet been approved by the FDA for any use—there still are sometimes ways of directly being treated with the drug. In that circumstance, the drug manufacturer is permitted to give that drug to people outside of the trial on what is commonly referred to as a "compassionate use" basis (though admittedly drug companies are reluctant to allow this).[16] An interesting example of the growing attention being paid to compassionate use of drugs was buried in the avalanche of publicity surrounding the company ImClone. ImClone was involved in testing a promising new cancer-fighting drug named Erbitux. It was the FDA's decision to not approve the sale of that drug that led to the drop in the price of ImClone stock and the controversies about Martha Stewart's possible insider trading. ImClone later supplied additional data to the FDA, and Erbitux was finally approved for use in cancer patients.

Erbitux had its true believers from the very beginning, including Frank Burroughs, whose daughter Abigail, a University of Virginia student, died while trying to get treated with the drug. ImClone had chosen not to provide the drug on a compassionate use basis, which was perfectly within the company's legal rights. As a result of these events, Burroughs has created the Abigail Alliance for Better Access to Developmental Drugs, which sued the FDA to get it to force drug manufacturers to implement compassionate use programs.[17] The compassionate use issue is just one of the examples of the availability of unproven treatments outside of research studies.

The Therapeutic Misconception

The fact that experimental treatments are often available outside of research studies allows us to expand our discussion beyond some of the examples we have discussed thus far—in particular, the studies in which Ellen Roche and Nicole Wan (see chapter 1) were enrolled—which are somewhat atypical in terms of what many people would consider the "average" research study. Those two studies, admittedly, did not involve any attempt to "treat" the participants, since they involved doing things to healthy people. In contrast, many—perhaps most—studies do indeed involve providing some sort of treatment to the people who enroll in them, often something different than they would have gotten from their doctor.

Much of the rest of this book focuses on such clinical trials, research studies performed on sick people and designed to compare different treatments for their illnesses. Participants in these studies have existing medical problems and no doubt usually hope that, by participating in the study, their medical problems will be cured or at least alleviated—and ideally in a more successful way than if they did not participate in the study. Thus, this argument goes, the comments about keeping the best interests of the patients "primary" may not be true of "nontherapeutic" studies such as those involving healthy subjects, but that is not the case for a study that does indeed involve treating a patient for a particular medical condition. Surely, the argument continues, where a study involves enrolling patients who have an existing medical problem, and the study involves giving them some sort of treatment, it is appropriate to say that their well-being must be of first importance.

In fact, that claim is wrong, even in such so-called "therapeutic" studies. Even using the terminology "nontherapeutic study" and "therapeutic study" is sometimes troublesome, since it tends to suggest that the primary purpose of at least a large class of studies—the therapeutic ones—is to treat the patients who enroll.[18] That is true of few studies. Again, recall the definition of research: something specific has to be done—a "research procedure"—for the primary purpose of answering a research question. That purpose may or may not coincide with doing what is best for the patient. And people should not confuse getting some new treatment with being in a research study. If they really want that new treatment, they might well be better off getting it outside of a research study, if that is an option.

The problem of research subjects misunderstanding the purpose of a research study, and thinking that every "treatment" decision in the study has been made with the intent to maximize the benefit to them, is so widespread it even has its own name: the *therapeutic misconception*. This term, coined over two decades ago, highlights the fact that people participating in research studies often fail to fully realize that "there may be major disadvantages" to them from being in the study.[19] And notice that this type of misunderstanding is the biggest problem not in studies that are clearly nontherapeutic, but rather in *precisely* those studies where the subjects are given some type of treatment for their medical problem.

Nicole Wan obviously was unlikely to think that getting a bronchoscopy was good for her, since she didn't have a medical problem that needed any treatment. Similarly, the person with asthma who enrolls in a study where the researchers will merely have him run on a treadmill to see how badly his asthma affects endurance is unlikely to be confused about the fact that being in the study is not going to do him any good. On the other hand, if he enrolled in a study where he was randomized between taking his usual medication or some new class of drugs, it may not be obvious to him how being in that study might be a bad choice.

What does our analysis thus far, when examined in the context of how people behave, tell us about the world of research studies? Perhaps the first thing to note is that it does not lead to a conclusion that participation in a research study is necessarily a bad thing for a particular person, even assuming that this person is seeking to do what is best for herself. Just because the primary goal of a study involves seeking an answer to a research question, it doesn't necessarily follow that the "research procedures" that take place in the study may not also end up being beneficial to the participant. Taking a particular action may end up serving two goals, even if it is only primarily intended to serve one of those goals. It depends on how much those two goals might actually overlap.

Thus, getting "extra" chest X-rays while participating in a study may reveal some aspects of the subject's medical problem that standard care would not have picked up. And even if some of the research procedures in a study do not end up benefiting the subject, it is still possible that the "whole package" involved in participating in a study may end up doing so: the study may give subjects access to a new therapy that they can't get elsewhere, and the benefits of that access may outweigh the downside of undergoing unnecessary and possibly harmful tests. And, finally, there may be a general benefit to participating in a study due to the fact that a great deal of attention is paid to study participants. As a result of that attention, study participants may end up getting, in at least some circumstances, better care than the "routine" clinical patient who risks being lost in the overworked, understaffed world of modern medical care.[20]

As is surely true, thousands of people have had their lives saved precisely because they enrolled in research studies. Our point is merely that for a subject with a medical problem who is solely looking to do what is best for treating that problem, participation in a research study is in many instances likely to be a far iffier proposition than choosing some other available option. All of the possible benefits mentioned above are just that: possible. While it is not quite right to say they are "coincidences," nonetheless it remains the case that research studies are not designed *primarily* to produce the best outcomes—more particularly, improvements over what standard care would lead to—for every subject who enrolls. Thus, there is indeed a "hit or miss" aspect to determining which research studies are, or are not, good deals for a patient.

Thus, from the point of view of someone being asked to be in a research study, a key issue is that person's being able to *distinguish* whether the study is a good choice or a bad choice. The mere fact that they are participating in a clinical trial, that they are being given some form of treatment for a medical problem, doesn't mean that the study is a good choice. So, our goal in the remainder of part I of this book is to highlight those specific things that may put a study on one or the other side of the good- versus bad-choice dividing line. And in order to provide those specifics, we need to first lay out the legal playing field: we need to explore the differences between what doctors are allowed to do to patients, as compared with what they can do to a subject in a research study.

3

A Case Study

The Difference between Being a Patient
and Being a Research Subject

Like the man who invented the better mousetrap, Dr. James Rowsey, a nationally renowned physician and chairman of the Department of Ophthalmology at the University of South Florida, thought he had a good idea. He had come up with a better way to perform a corneal transplant. By using a high-tech method that changed the shape of the corneal tissue that is sewn into a person's eye—adding "flaps" to that tissue—his transplant procedure could result in quicker and more effective healing. Rowsey predicted that the device required to perform his procedure might, if successful, generate sales of more than $112 million within a five-year period.

In the four years following his 1994 application for a patent on his new technique—it even had a catchy name, the "Tampa Trephine"—he apparently used this technique on more than 60 patients. Whether or not the Tampa Trephine produces better transplant results still remains unclear to this day. The results for Dr. Rowsey's career, however, were exceptionally clear, though very different from what he expected:

- By the year 1999, the University of South Florida had appointed a special panel to investigate his activities.
- On October 1 of that year, he resigned from the College of Medicine, giving up his positions as a tenured professor and as holder of a prestigious endowed chair, and entered private practice.
- The leading professional society for ophthalmologists, the American Academy of Ophthalmology, had suspended his membership for two years, citing ethical violations.

- By the year 2000, the primary federal agency charged with regulating research (the Office for Human Research Protections) was investigating both Dr. Rowsey's activities and the inadequacies of the University of South Florida's procedures for protecting research subjects.
- At least two of his patients who underwent the new procedure were suing him in Florida state court, claiming, among other things, battery, fraud, and child abuse.

The saga of Dr. Rowsey and the Tampa Trephine provides a stepping-stone for our exploration, in the chapters that follow, of the surprising differences between the legal protections given to patients compared to those given to research subjects.

The Standard of Care for Corneal Transplantation

Dr. Rowsey was not writing on a blank slate when he designed his new procedure, and so we begin our inquiry with the procedure that he was trying to improve upon. Corneal transplantation is, in some respects, the poor stepchild of the transplantation field. It doesn't save lives, and that may explain why it doesn't get the press coverage that goes to kidney, lung, and liver transplants. While it may not save a person's life, it can be the one thing that makes a person's life worth living, particularly when it brings sight to someone who was formerly blind. In excess of 40,000 corneal transplants are done each year, more than any other type of solid organ transplant.

And, as a general matter, corneal transplantation is quite successful. That is actually somewhat surprising, given that the cornea—the thin, clear sliver of living tissue that covers the fluid-filled front of our eyes—is a rather complicated thing.[1] The cornea is one of the few solid tissues in our bodies that is perfectly transparent—and making living tissue transparent is a very hard thing to accomplish. Although it is alive, and thus needs oxygen, no blood vessels flow through it, since that would interfere with its ability to transmit light. It "breathes," in essence, by absorbing oxygen from the air on its outer surface and from the fluids that bathe its inner surface.

For almost 150 years, it has been known that the cornea from someone who has died can be transplanted into a living person.[2] During the last half century, the technique has been refined to produce the current relatively high level of success. The great bulk of corneal transplants—which are done to correct a variety of corneal problems, though most relate to problems with the hexagon-shaped cells on the inner corneal surface and their ability to prevent fluid buildup in the cornea—are full-thickness transplants. Basically, a large portion of the central area of a deceased person's cornea is "punched out," including all of the layers from the outside to the inside of the cornea, and then is sewn into place in the patient's eye after a similar portion of the patient's malfunctioning cornea has been punched out.

While for a brief period in the very early days of corneal transplantation, the punched-out piece of cornea was square in shape, for the past several decades a circular piece of cornea has uniformly been used. Thus, it is common to use the term "button" to describe it: in both shape and size, it is not all that different from an ordinary button on a man's dress shirt. The usual corneal button is approximately one-third of an inch in diameter and about 1/50th of an inch in thickness. The device used to cut out the corneal button from the donor's eye is given the technical name "trephine," but it is in essence just a fancy razor blade in a circular shape. Imagine that the top of a metal sewing thimble was cut off, right near the end, and the cut edge on the thimble was then polished to razor sharpness: that is very close to what a corneal trephine is.

After cutting out the button of tissue from the donor cornea, a hole of just about the same size is cut out of the patient's own cornea. The donor button is then placed into position, and it is sewn into place, using very fine pieces of nylon suture material, so fine that they can barely be seen without using a microscope. While suturing techniques vary somewhat, they usually involve some combination of "radial" sutures, often combined with a "running" suture. The radial sutures, like the spokes of a bicycle wheel, are short sutures that run from the outer edge of the donor cornea to the adjacent portion of the patient's own cornea. Often these will number from four to sixteen. The running suture, in contrast, takes a zigzag path between the donor tissue and patient's cornea, going 360 degrees around the donor button and returning to its starting point, then being tied to itself. As you can imagine, the running suture has to be sewn very carefully—you certainly don't want it breaking near the end after you have spent quite a bit of time going around the cornea, carefully threading the suture pass after pass.

A Departure from Standard Care

All of the details you have just read about corneal transplants can be summed up in a single phrase: they describe the *standard of care* for performing such a transplant. That concept has a special significance in the legal system: when a patient goes to see a doctor, the law, subject to some limited exceptions, assumes that the doctor should —and *will*—provide the patient with standard care for their condition. Explaining the exceptions to this rule will be our main endeavor for the next several chapters. For now, we want to highlight that there are the two very different ways a doctor might come within one of the exceptions: one involves continuing to treat someone as a patient, while the other involves instead enrolling them in a research study.

To explain these differing categories, we need to return to our story about Dr. Rowsey and failing corneas. Corneal transplantation, while generally successful, is far from perfect. It takes months for the cornea to fully heal. During that period, the sutures need to hold the cornea in place while the patient's own cornea begins to form its own sufficiently strong connections to the donated button of tissue. The sutures can distort the gentle curves of the cornea, thus causing light rays to bend irregularly—called astigmatism—as they pass through it. In fact, the cornea plays a crucial role in focusing light onto the back of the eye: it actually has more focusing power than the lens in our eyes. The patient will often have blurry vision during this period, and beginning with a few months after the surgery, an ophthalmologist may start removing some of the sutures to reduce the astigmatism.

Dr. Rowsey's goal was to develop a method to shorten the period of healing following a corneal transplant and to reduce the amount of astigmatism.[3] To do this, he wanted to be able to perform transplants with fewer sutures yet still allow the donor cornea to remain firmly held in the correct position as the wound healed. He hoped to reduce the time needed for surgery from two hours down to a half hour. His innovative approach involved changing the shape of the corneal button. He would add six thin "tabs" to the edges of the top surface of the button. Then, before putting the donor cornea into position in the patient's own eye, he would cut small slots in the edges of the patient's cornea. After inserting the donor cornea into position, he would then gently put the tabs into the corresponding slots. In very simple terms, the procedure is similar to what children do in playing with paper dolls—using the tabs to hold something in place.

The tabs that Dr. Rowsey was designing were smaller than those on paper dolls, and they would be extremely thin. They would measure approximately 1/10th of an inch on each side, and their thickness would be a mere 1/500th of an inch (one-tenth the thickness of the entire cornea).[4] To accurately cut such small tabs, he needed a finely machined device. Luck was in Rowsey's favor, for at the time he was dreaming up his device, changes were taking place in the southern Florida economy, as a local nuclear weapons plant was being converted to domestic uses. More than a half million dollars of government funding ended up being spent on Rowsey's idea.[5] In the same plant where years before the government might have gone to obtain a miniature neutron generator as part of a nuclear warhead trigger, the engineers from Martin Marietta Specialty Components transformed the Tampa Trephine from idea to reality. And on August 12, 1994, Dr. Rowsey filed a patent on the trephine with the U.S. Patent and Trademark Office: "This invention relates to sutureless corneal transplantation and, more particularly, to a method and apparatus for transplanting corneas without the use of sutures."

He then began testing his device in the real world. Initially he used the trephine on pathologic specimens, to demonstrate that it could make the precise cuts needed. He then moved on to using it on cats, due to the similarity between the anatomy of cat and human eyes. While he was still in the midst of doing his cat studies, he began using the new technique on some of his patients. By his own reports, at least 34 patients underwent corneal transplantation using the Tampa Trephine technique between 1994 and 1996; at least 60 patients had undergone this technique by March of 1998.[6]

Oddly enough, this series of events came to light, at least in part, due to circumstances far removed from the world of corneal transplantation. Dr. Rowsey's dedication to patient care was apparently rivaled only by his dedication to God—in particular, the God of fundamentalist Christians. He told employees at the University of South Florida that he wanted to build the "best Christian ophthalmology department in the country." Angered by such practices as prayer sessions at weekly faculty meetings and better treatment of the "born-again" Christian members of the department, two faculty members sued the university, claiming that they were "coerced and intimidated" into following Rowsey's religious practices, in violation of federal civil rights laws. A third ophthalmologist settled his claim against the university for $125,000. And, even worse for Rowsey, another disgruntled faculty member began looking into Rowsey's questionable practices involving the Tampa Trephine.[7]

Distinguishing Research from Getting Nonstandard Care as a Patient

When people at the University of South Florida began learning that Dr. Rowsey had begun using the Tampa Trephine technique on his patients—and not just on cats—efforts were made to stop his work. Interestingly, these efforts were concentrated on demonstrating that Dr. Rowsey was improperly performing *research* and was thus in violation of various federal rules relating to how research was conducted. He had never acknowledged that he was doing research and had not filed to have his work reviewed by the university's institutional review board.

Ultimately, the Office for Human Research Protections, the federal agency that regulates most human subjects research in the United States, issued in the year 2000 a report concluding that "the activities involving the Tampa Trephine penetrating keratoplasty procedure for corneal transplantation under the direction of Dr. Rowsey *unequivocally* represented research involving human subjects." As a result of the university's failure to correctly regulate this research project, that agency required the University of South Florida to conduct an audit of all ongoing research projects and to demonstrate that each project was correctly being supervised according to federal regulations.

In addition, the university was required to send a letter to all of Dr. Rowsey's patients who underwent the Tampa Trephine procedure, informing them of their "unwitting participation in the research." Specifically, the letter told the patients that while Dr. Rowsey's device never actually touched their eyes,

> using [the Tampa Trephine] required changing your corneal transplant surgery from the standard surgery, because donor corneas cut out with the Tampa Trephine had a different shape in comparison to donor corneas cut out using the standard tool. It has been determined that (a) this type of surgery with the Tampa Trephine involved research; and (b) you should have been informed that you were a subject in the research and the surgery was experimental.[8]

At least two of Dr. Rowsey's patients did in fact end up suing him. (Interestingly, they hired the same Tampa attorney who had represented some of the doctors who had brought the civil rights complaints against the university. He was a personal injury lawyer who had a penchant for motorcycle cases—his 1-800 telephone number included the word HOGLAW, and his website came complete with spinning 3D motorcycles. For him, this was a venture into a new legal territory, the world of medical malpractice.) Apparently the Tampa Trephine was not as risk-free as Rowsey hoped it would be. A review of Rowsey's work by an investigatory panel at the University of South Florida had ultimately concluded that there were "significantly more complications than are normally found when using standard techniques."[9] Joanne Cassidy, one of the two patients who sued him, had eye surgery at age 9 and indicated in court filings that she had never been told that the surgery she received was experimental.[10] Her vision in her left eye allegedly never improved after the surgery.[11] Harry Rogers, an 85-year-old who in his youth was a "gifted athlete who ran against the fabled Jesse Owens," says he ended up becoming legally blind and unable to stand sunlight as a result of Rowsey's surgical procedure.[12]

Looking at this set of events, a question might occur: why was so much of the attack against Rowsey directed at demonstrating that he was improperly "doing research?" The people who were accusing him of wrongdoing probably recognized that his activities were somewhere in the borderline between two different categories. He might have been *a doctor treating a patient*, using a surgical procedure that was a departure from standard care. Or, he might have been *a researcher conducting research on a subject*. The important thing to understand is that these two categories have very different legal consequences, something the next several chapters will explore. But before we go on to understand those very different consequences—consequences that many people greatly misunderstand—we need to better define what activities put something in one category or the other.

The category that is easier to define is the concept of a patient getting nonstandard care. Simply stated, this takes place when a doctor provides some treatment that is not standard care to a patient *solely for the purpose of treating that patient*.[13] Imagine, for example, that Dr. Rowsey said the following to the first patient that underwent the Tampa Trephine procedure:

> You need a corneal transplant procedure. Now, there is a standard way to do this procedure, and I could perform that on you. However, it just so happens that I am working on a better way to do a corneal transplant! Thus far, I have only been doing it on cats, but I have had good results. I think that having this modified procedure will improve the likelihood that you will have a good outcome.

Let us suppose that the patient indicated she was interested and that Dr. Rowsey subsequently gave her substantial details about the special risks and benefits of this new procedure, including a special consent form to sign that spelled these things out in detail. If indeed Dr. Rowsey had no plans at that time to study how well it worked in this person (and thus was not doing any of the additional things we describe below that researchers do to answer research questions), let alone do it in other patients, then this would likely have involved merely *providing nonstandard care to a patient*. It would not have involved any *research*. There were no research procedures—things done *primarily* to help answer a research question—taking place.

What Is Research and Why Do We Care about It?

We now turn to that category more difficult to define: research. We have already given a simplified definition in chapter 2: research involves doing one or more things (research procedures) for the primary purpose of answering a research question.[14]

We might rephrase this as a question: is the activity specially designed to help us learn things that will be of interest to other people? In the medical field, for example, the question would be, "Will it help us better take care of the medical problems of future patients?"

Note the key difference in terms of *intent* between a doctor providing nonstandard care to a patient and a researcher doing research.[15] In defining the category "providing nonstandard care," we required that the doctor's purpose be *solely to treat the patient.* In that respect, providing nonstandard care is very much like providing standard care: the sole purpose of the endeavor is to benefit the patient. Indeed, in terms of standard medical ethics, the doctor should always be keeping the well-being of the patient as the primary goal. This fundamental concept is taught to medical students early in their training, and it finds support in numerous legal and ethical pronouncements. One prominent commentator has described it as "the paradigm of the physician who bears unreserved loyalty to the interests of his particular patient."[16] The leading code of medical ethics in this nation, written by the American Medical Association, states that "a physician has a duty to do all that he or she can for the benefit of the individual patient."[17]

But in doing research, a new goal is now being pursued, a goal that may conflict with doing what is best for the patient.[18] We have a classic conflict of interest situation on the part of the researcher-physician, and perhaps they can no longer be fully adherent to that basic ethical precept of keeping the patient's best interests foremost.[19] As we noted in chapter 2, by trying to learn more about the answer to the research question, things may be done to patients that are *not* necessarily in their best interests. And the time has come for us to begin to spell out exactly what these things might be.

The simplest thing that might be done that converts something from being "providing care" to "doing research" is to create a set of research records. In other words, the doctor might merely re-record the results of the patient's care in a second set of papers where the researcher can then compare the results of different patients to one another, hoping to learn more about how well the procedure works and perhaps how to modify it to make it better. For example, as discussed above, Dr. Rowsey might have been providing the Tampa Trephine procedure to patients, claiming that it was the best thing for them (even though it was not standard care). If he nonetheless wanted to use their results to refine his technique, then he should have been getting their permission for this "research use" of their results. He'd be asking a patient, "Mr. Smith, can I record some of the information from your medical chart and put it in another file, where I will compare it to the results of other patients who undergo this technique?"

But our primary concern in this book—and the primary concern for most research subjects—is not the risk relating to confidentiality breaches, but rather a qualitatively different type of risk, namely, health risks. Thus, we now turn to describing those "additional things" that might happen to a patient who enters a research study that can sometimes lead to adverse health consequences for the patient. For the remainder of this chapter, we assume—as the federal regulators did ultimately determine to be the case—that Dr. Rowsey was indeed performing research, doing at least some things primarily to answer a research question.

Under these circumstances, here are some of the things he might have might have wanted to do in conducting his research study. These are the sorts of things a researcher would commonly find useful in trying to answer a research question. In this discussion, we attempt to particularly highlight the ways in which the "research aspects" of the study might pose risks to the subjects' health.[20]

Directly Altering the Treatment Given to the Patient

Dr. Rowsey might have asked patients to undergo the Tampa Trephine procedure but to do so in the context of a research study. In other words, every patient who agreed to enter this study would undergo the Tampa Trephine procedure. Note the subtle but crucial difference between this scenario and our prior discussion where he was recommending the Tampa Trephine procedure as part of nonstandard care given by him as a doctor (not as a researcher). He is telling the patient *very different* things in these two settings:

- Nonstandard Care: "This *is* the best procedure for you."
- Research: "I *don't know* if this is the best thing for you. You might end up better off than with standard care, but you might not."

As highlighted in chapter 2, an important dividing line is crossed in moving from getting nonstandard care (not as part of a research study) to participating in research: the doctor is no longer necessarily providing the patient with a type of care that he is promising to be the "best thing" for the patient. And the patient is generally being asked to assume some risks to help produce knowledge that will benefit future patients.

Randomization

A special way in which patients entering a study might have their treatment altered from what would have taken place outside of the research setting is through the use of *randomization*. Given its popularity, and its importance in well-designed research studies,[21] this technique deserves special attention. Dr. Rowsey, for example, might have chosen to randomize participants in his study between the existing technique and the Tampa Trephine technique. Indeed, before he began actually using the procedure in people, he had proposed such a study and filed for its approval at the University of South Florida (though he ultimately never conducted it). Each time a patient came along who needed corneal transplant and also met whatever other eligibility criteria he had set up for participating in the study, that patient, assuming they agreed to be in the study, would have had a 50–50 chance of either getting the standard treatment or getting the new technique. Some type of randomization device—something as fancy as a computer program or something as simple as flipping a coin—would be used to determine which technique was used on each patient.

Randomization is a common technique in research studies where two or more different treatments are being compared. Indeed, it is generally considered the gold standard of how to do a research study. By randomizing patients, a researcher avoids the possibility of some form of bias taking place in selecting which patients get assigned to which treatment. Time after time, treatments that seem to be major improvements over standard care when initially given to a few patients are later proven to be no such thing when studied in a randomized trial. This happened to one of the most promising and well-publicized cancer treatments of recent years—the treatment of women with advanced breast cancer by use of high doses of chemotherapy followed by bone marrow transplantation. It also happened with the use of hormone replacement therapy in women as a way to reduce the risk of heart attacks—not only was it shown to not do that, but it actually increased that risk.

Some have argued that not only is randomization a wonderful technique for conducting a research study, *it is also in the best interests of the subjects or, at worst, does not cause them any harm.*[22] This argument is based on the idea that subjects will only be randomized between two different treatments when there is sufficient professional disagreement among medical experts about which of the treatments is better. (This idea is embodied in a technical term, clinical equipoise, which we discuss in detail in chapter 6.) Imagine, for example, that the two treatments were put on the two ends of a seesaw, which somehow magically weighed their respective net relationships between benefits and risks: ideally, studies would only be conducted where the seesaw was perfectly balanced, with neither side hitting the ground.

However, even if the collected judgment of medical professionals as a whole determined there was such a balance in a particular instance, it does not follow that in the eyes of specific patients with their own preferences about health care (and thus their own individual weighings of risks and benefits), there would also be such a balance. Thus, the argument about randomization virtually never causing any harm to the subject loses much of its credibility.[23] Even if there really is a dispute among medical professionals about which of the treatments is better, many patients, if they are adequately informed about the differences in the treatments, will have various reasons to prefer one or the other.[24] Consider the landmark studies in which women with breast cancer were randomized to get either breast-sparing surgery or more radical surgery, at a time when doctors were genuinely unsure about whether there was a difference in how effective these procedures were in eliminating the cancer. It was hard to get any women to volunteer for this type of study, precisely because— *even though there was a perfect balance according to the professionals*—the two treatments were different in so many ways, and those differences mattered a great deal to most women.

In most studies, the differences between the two treatments will not be so obvious, but nonetheless there are still likely to be various types of differences, differences that will matter to large numbers of patients. In later chapters of this book, we provide a variety of examples. Perhaps the most obvious "difference," and one that bears special mention at this point, is that in many cases there will be some tentative information about possible differences between the two treatments, based either on existing studies or on the scientific justification supporting the possible effectiveness of a treatment. Indeed, due to the way we prove the effectiveness of a drug, there is often a *great deal* of tentative evidence hinting one way or another before a large randomized trial is conducted.[25] Since only one of the treatments can be given, is it "good" for a patient that the tentative information be ignored, which is effectively what randomization does?

The simple answer—which any of us can no doubt confirm by our own medical experiences as patients—is generally *no*. Ask yourself: how would you feel if your doctor suggested—*not* as part of a research study—that he pick the treatment you get by flipping a coin? Very few of us, as patients, would accept this type of behavior. In real life, we rarely make decisions by flipping a coin. When there are complicated decisions to make, we do the best we can using the limited information we have. Ignoring relevant information, even if it is not very reliable, is rarely an ideal way to achieve a specific goal. And in the world of medical care, there will often be a great deal of such information that can lead a patient to want to opt for one treatment over another.

Standardization of Treatment

As part of Dr. Rowsey's hypothetical research study, he would have written a protocol explaining what he proposed to do to each research subject. That protocol would likely "standardize" various treatment events, by specifying rules regarding how to do numerous things to the participants in the study. For example, it might spell out exactly how to cut out the corneal button, how many sutures to use in sewing it in the subject's eye, what medications to use postoperatively, and how often to use those medications. From a research standpoint, it is important to have some degree of uniformity with regard to what is done to the participants in a study: the more that the treatment might vary from subject to subject, the less likely anyone will be able to conclusively determine an answer to the research question. All those little variations create "noise" in the data that may hide the effects of the single difference in treatment that the researcher is trying to study. And a study that is unlikely to answer (or at least help contribute to answering) the posed research question is generally considered unethical: subjects are being exposed to risks for no good reason. Thus, in Dr. Rowsey's case, were he to randomize patients between the standard corneal transplant and the Tampa Trephine technique, he would want to make sure that the people in each group underwent essentially the same treatments.

But from the point of view of a patient, being locked into a rigid regimen of treatment may not always be a good thing. In the world of treatment (as opposed to research), a doctor will usually look at numerous aspects of a patient's care—how well the wound is healing, how much pain they are having, and so on—and will vary types of medications, frequency of medications, and so forth, in order to do what is best for the patient. The doctor *personalizes* the patient's care. Admittedly, too much personalization can sometimes be a bad thing: where there is evidence that certain types of treatments provide better outcomes, it can be better for the doctor to follow the protocols adopted by the profession, which specify the proven rules that produce better outcomes. Thus, following a protocol with regard to some aspects of care can be a good thing. But even where proven protocols exist, there are often instances where patients' medical courses do not fit what typically happens, and thus the doctors make their best decisions about how to deviate from the recommended plan.

In almost all research studies, it is also accepted that there are instances in which, to protect the well-being of a subject, the protocol need not be followed and the subject's care can be individualized so as to do what is best for that person. But given the primary goal of answering the research question, research protocols often will restrict the ability to personalize a subject's care to a somewhat greater extent than takes place in the world of clinical care. Indeed, so important is it that doctors adhere to the rules laid out in the study protocol that the very terminology used for a departure from those rules—a protocol *violation*—effectively chastises the doctor for having done something wrong. Thus, by laying down strict protocol treatment regimens—stricter regimens than often exist in clinical treatment—a study may to some extent intentionally be subordinating the well-being of the subject to the goal of producing better research results.[26]

Nondisclosure of Interim Results

The goal of a research study is often to answer a question—for example, does expensive new drug A cure disease X more effectively than old (and very cheap) drug B—to a particular degree of certainty. If we are doing the study in order to alter how thousands of future patients will be treated, we want to be relatively sure of our results. If we are only slightly convinced that new drug A is better, then there is a substantial chance that telling doctors to switch to new drug A may do little to help future patients (and may even harm some of them), while it may also incur essentially useless increased costs.

For these reasons, a good research study is designed so as to enroll enough subjects, and to continue for a sufficient period of time, so that it is likely to produce a sufficiently certain result. This is often stated in terms of a degree of certainty under the laws of statistics; for example, we often seek to find a 95% level of statistical significance before saying that the new drug is better than the old. What this means is that the better results shown by the new drug in the study would in 95 chances out of 100 be due to the new drug really being better (as opposed to being due to chance, i.e., that for some odd circumstance the new drug seemed to work better in these patients even though it really isn't any better).

What the desire to obtain statistical significance means is that, as part of the study, it is necessary to ignore "interim" results prior to reaching the necessary level of statistical significance. Consider, for example, a situation in which half the number of subjects planned for a study have already been enrolled and begun treatment, and the interim calculations demonstrate that it is 90% likely that drug A works better than drug B.[27] We haven't yet reached the 95% level that we aim for in proving a difference between two drugs, but we are very close.

Based on that tentative information, the likelihood that drug B would eventually be shown to be superior to drug A would be approximately 1/50,000. This is an

extremely small number. What might the consequences be if we released this information to the subjects? If the drugs were being tested to see how well they treated a
serious medical problem, such as cancer, and if drug A were available outside of the
study, it is likely that all of the subjects would drop out of the study and make sure
they take drug A.

In this scenario, in most instances participants in the trial would not be told
these interim results, precisely because knowing that information would cause them
to end their participation in the trial. And if lots of participants were dropping out
of the trial, we would never enroll enough subjects to reach the end of the trial and
to produce the appropriate level of statistical significance. In other words, we would
never get beyond the interim results and never be sufficiently certain whether there
is adequate justification for putting thousands of future patients on the new and more
costly drug A. Again, there is a conflict between doing what would be best for the
participants in the trial—telling them the interim results, and letting those in the
"likely worse treatment" arm leave the trial and switch to the other treatment—and
letting the trial continue so as to produce the information needed to best lead to
well-informed treatment decisions for future patients.

Extra Tests and Procedures

It is not uncommon that a research study may involve additional tests that would
not be part of standard care. For example, the researchers may do a number of diagnostic tests at the start of the study—perhaps several imaging studies such as chest
X-rays or a CT scan or MRI of part of the body—to make sure that the person considering entering the study does not have some other medical problem that might
complicate the interpretation of what might happen to them in the study. Similarly,
part of the study might involve doing a biopsy of some body part; this might involve
a surgical procedure, or needing to snake an endoscope down into a body cavity,
such as the stomach. These tests and procedures may have risks, often minor, though
in some instances they may be substantial. And they are in some cases being done
solely for research purposes: the results will not alter the medical treatments provided
to the subjects. The tests and procedures are needed by the researchers, however,
because the information they provide will help them answer the research question
that they are trying to study.

How We Treat Research Differently

Thus, there are a variety of things a researcher might want to do in a study that could
be contrary to the best interests of the subjects. For this reason there are, as we noted
in chapter 1, special legal protections accorded to participants in research studies.
Our discussion of one set of protections—the need to get informed consent from
subjects—is deferred until part II. To understand what information we should be
giving to subjects, we need to first understand what things the law allows researchers to ask subjects to consent to.

What does the story of Dr. Rowsey tell us about those rules? The fact that so many bad things happened to Dr. Rowsey for violating the rules might initially be viewed as a strong endorsement of the existing legal protections for subjects. But that would be a premature conclusion. What happened to Dr. Rowsey happened because he *bypassed* the applicable rules. He never admitted he was doing research. He never filed his study with the University of South Florida's institutional review board. He was punished for blatantly ignoring the rules.

In this chapter we have used his story to illustrate how an innovative treatment— some form of nonstandard care—might be provided to someone in two very different settings: either as a patient or as a research subject. But we still haven't explained the laws that apply to these two different scenarios. Suppose that Dr. Rowsey *had* filed his study for review by his university's institutional review board: would he have been permitted to perform the Tampa Trephine procedure on his patients as participants in a research study? What are the actual protections that the law would have provided to those subjects? How protective are they?

To answer these important questions, we turn first in chapter 4 to answering a related question: would Dr. Rowsey have been permitted to perform the Tampa Trephine procedure on his patients *outside* of a research study? Only by contrasting the legal rules governing what doctors can do to *patients* can we understand what can be done to *research subjects.*

4

How the Law Protects Patients
Who Get Nonstandard Care

When we discussed Dr. Rowsey and his new form of corneal transplant procedure in chapter 3, we left an issue hanging: why was everyone so concerned about proving that he was "doing research"? Those who criticized what happened to his patients seemed to think that if he *wasn't* doing research, then it would have been hard to find anything wrong in his actions, as least from a legal point of view. Presumably the University of South Florida would then not have been able to discipline him. Thus, everyone spent a great deal of time and effort trying to prove that he was doing research and that he behaved improperly in failing to comply with the federal research regulations.

The growing concern among many has been that there is a gaping loophole in our system for regulating what "new things" doctors can do to patients. Yes (so the argument goes), we have an extensive set of protections that apply to a doctor doing research—the Common Rule and related federal regulations—but there is an easy was to avoid being subject to them: just make sure you are *not* doing research! Presumably, a doctor can merely provide patients with nonstandard care and not perform any of the extra activities that would make his actions cross over the line into "doing research." Maybe Dr. Rowsey was unsuccessful in taking advantage of this loophole—recall, it was ultimately determined that he was doing research—because he was a bit sloppy in policing his own actions that made it look like he was doing research. Perhaps the next Dr. Rowsey will be more careful—he won't write up a protocol, he won't present his results at major national research meetings, he'll intentionally try to avoid taking any actions designed primarily to answer a research question—and will be successful in avoiding being subject to the research regulations.

The concern about this gap in our rules has been boldly highlighted in a prominent article by Robert Truog, a leading Harvard anesthesiologist and bioethics scholar, who together with his colleagues wrote in the *New England Journal of Medicine*:

> Consider this paradox: if a physician reads a case report about a novel method of ventilation for critically ill patients and wants to try it in the next several patients with respiratory failure he or she treats, the physician may do so provided the patients have given general consent for treatment. On the other hand, if a physician is interested in performing a randomized, controlled trial to determine rigorously which of two widely used antibiotics is more effective at treating bronchitis, he or she must prepare a formal protocol, obtain approval from the institutional review board, and seek written informed consent from potential participants. In each case, the physician is performing an experiment. In each case, there is uncertainty about the best way to treat the patient. Yet in the context of clinical care, the experiment can be done with virtually no external scrutiny, whereas in the context of a clinical trial, the experiment is prohibited unless substantial hurdles are overcome. This is true even when the experimental therapy (e.g., a promising but risky method of ventilation) involves risks that are unknown or substantially different from those of the alternatives.
>
> To put it another way, physicians can do almost anything they want in the name of therapeutic innovation, but only if there is no attempt to gain systematic knowledge from the intervention. Or, . . . "I need permission to give a new drug to half my patients but not to give it to all of them."[1]

We now turn to this issue and attempt to demonstrate that these concerns about a gap in our system are to a large extent unwarranted.

While the law relating to this area is still sketchy, we will show that it is definitely *not* the case that physicians can do "almost anything they want in the name of therapeutic innovation." Rather, the claimed gap in the rules is filled by the part of our laws that people writing about medical research commonly ignore: the state tort laws relating to malpractice. It is certainly *not* the case that a doctor can legally perform virtually any procedure on a patient, no matter how bizarre and risky, as long as the patient has been informed of the risks and has consented. There are lots of things that *cannot* be done to a patient, even if the patient has (after getting full information) agreed to that treatment.

Only by examining these rules can we show that, in a very real sense, those who worry about the regulatory "hole" that lets doctors do too much in the way of "nonstandard care" have it absolutely wrong: not only is there no such "hole" on the nonresearch side, but to the extent there is a hole, it relates to what can be done to *research subjects*. By describing in this chapter how the law protects the well-being of patients, we can then go on in chapter 5 to contrast that to what happens to research subjects.

The Federal Limits on What Types
of Medical Care We Can Get

There are a variety of laws that regulate what kind of care a person can receive from a health care provider. While most of our attention in this chapter focuses on state laws and, in particular, the malpractice branch of tort law, we begin with a discussion of the national government's involvement in regulating health care. By and large, what happens between patients and health care providers is left for the states to regulate. But there is one big exception to that: the set of rules administered by the U.S. FDA.

The FDA indirectly controls the ability of doctors to use, and patients to get access to, a wide variety of things that are needed to diagnose and treat medical problems. In particular, it regulates the sale in interstate commerce of three broad categories of items: drugs, devices (e.g., cardiac pacemakers), and biologics (products made from biologic materials, such as vaccines or blood used for transfusions). Until the FDA has approved an item for at least one use, with some major exceptions, it generally is the case that a patient cannot get access to that item, even if their doctor thinks it is appropriate for their medical problem.[2] And, since getting FDA approval of a product is in most cases a massive undertaking, requiring years of testing done by a company interesting in manufacturing the product, and tens if not hundreds of millions of dollars, there are lots of possible treatments that do not have FDA approval and thus are in large part forbidden to be used.

Why do we have such laws that appear to blatantly trump the autonomy of doctors and patients and to override their ability to agree, among themselves, on what constitutes a "best treatment" in a particular instance? One major reason is *paternalism*, the much-maligned notion that the government knows (at least some of the time) what is good for us better than we do and that it needs to protect us from our bad decisions.[3] This is actually not that uncommon a thing for our government to do: many states have laws requiring the use of motorcycle helmets or seatbelts, regulating how safe a car must be before it can be sold to consumers, requiring that buildings be constructed according to certain safety standards, and so forth. All of these rules override the personal choices of individuals in various ways: a poor person may well be priced out of the market for housing and become homeless due to the added costs of meeting safety standards.

And, in the health care field, given the complexity of how our bodies operate and the horrible consequences that can occur if wrong decisions are made about what kind of treatment to get, government paternalism has played a major role. As we have seen, you can't always get access to any drug you want: the law may not allow it to be sold in this country, and even if it is, you may be required to first have a doctor determine that using the drug is in your best interest. If you need a particular medical procedure, you will likely be required to get it only in a facility that has received appropriate licensing, and it probably can only be provided by health care workers who are appropriately trained.[4]

One of the best illustrations of the extent of this paternalism comes from the controversy over Laetrile during the 1970s. During that period, this compound, derived from grinding up the seeds or pits of certain fruits such as apricots, was acquiring something of an "underground" reputation as a possible treatment for cancers that were otherwise incurable. People with such cancers were often desperate to get their hands on it. But it had never received the approval of the FDA, which, under the applicable laws, had to receive appropriate proof that the drug was both safe and effective for the intended use (e.g., that it treated specific cancers) before that agency would grant authority for this compound to be sold in interstate commerce in the United States. Some patients would go to Mexico, where Laetrile was readily available.

Eventually, a number of terminally ill cancer patients brought suit against the federal government to prevent it from interfering with their attempts to get Laetrile. They argued that there was little evidence showing that the drug was harmful to anyone. They are also noted that since they are dying of nontreatable diseases, it should ultimately be their decision as to whether or not to use this drug that may or may not be of any use. In effect, they were asking the courts to interpret the laws administered by the FDA as not requiring proof of both drug safety and efficacy where a patient wants to use the drug for a nontreatable terminal illness. The case made its way to the U.S. Supreme Court, which rejected the claims of the patients.

The Court, in a unanimous opinion, concluded that the law as written did not make any exceptions for terminally ill patients and that there were good reasons for Congress not to have wanted such an exception:

> Cancers vary considerably in behavior and in responsiveness to different forms of therapy. Even critically ill individuals may have unexpected remissions and may respond to conventional treatment. Thus, as the Commissioner concluded, to exempt from the Act drugs with no proved effectiveness in the treatment of cancer "would lead to needless deaths and suffering among . . . patients characterized as 'terminal' who could actually be helped by legitimate therapy." . . . If history is any guide, this new market would not be long overlooked. Since the turn of the century, resourceful entrepreneurs have advertised a wide variety of purportedly simple and painless cures for cancer, including liniments of turpentine, mustard, oil, eggs, and ammonia; peat moss; arrangements of colored floodlamps; pastes made from glycerin and limburger cheese; mineral tablets; and "Fountain of Youth" mixtures of spices, oil, and suet. In citing these examples, we do not, of course, intend to deprecate the sincerity of Laetrile's current proponents, or to imply any opinion on whether that drug may ultimately prove safe and effective for cancer treatment. But this historical experience does suggest why Congress could reasonably have determined to protect the terminally ill, no less than other patients, from the vast range of self-styled panaceas that inventive minds can devise.[5]

Thus, it is perfectly permissible for the government, within limits, for our own good to restrict us to choosing only from among drugs, devices, and biologics that have been appropriately been determined "safe" and "effective."

State Limits on Access to Medical Care

State laws regulating the type of health care that someone is permitted to get fall into two broad categories: *licensing laws,* which determine what qualifications a health care provider has to have in order to offer their services to the public, and *tort laws* (malpractice, to be specific), designed to provide a remedy to a patient when a provider fails to provide the appropriate level of health care. Both types of laws essentially try to do the same thing: assure that a patient going to a particular category of health care provider gets someone who is appropriately trained and who provides services consistent with the standards set by their profession.

While this system in many ways mirrors the paternalism theme of the federal FDA rules, it does allow some degree of patient choice. One aspect of that choice relates to a patient's ability to pick the "type" of health care provider they wish to go to. There is an increasing recognition in many state laws that patients should be able to choose "alternative" forms of health care.[6] These states have often carved out special rules authorizing people to practice these alternative forms of health care (within certain specified limits—we don't want the "herbal" expert to be doing abdominal surgery). Thus, there are state laws that permit health care services to be provided by, for example, naturopaths and homeopaths and acupuncturists. And there are similar laws regulating the practice of somewhat more mainstream practitioners such as chiropractors and massage therapists. In each instance, a state's laws may permit a person, usually after demonstrating appropriate training and competence consistent with the rules established by that field, to offer their healing services to the public.

It was long ago recognized that if you go to such an approved alternative healer, to some extent it is caveat emptor: you are assuming the risk that this alternative form of health care is not as effective as mainstream (often called "allopathic") medical care. Consider a case from almost a century ago, where a woman suffering from appendicitis, fearful of an operation, went to a Christian Scientist healer, who indicated that he could help channel the power of God in order to cure her.[7] When the religious treatment proved ineffective, she ended up suing the healer. But she offered no proof that he was doing anything different than any other Christian Science healer would do, or that he was attempting to cure a condition that other healers would not similarly claim was curable by their methods. The court rejected her claims, noting that a healer who truthfully holds himself out to patients as belonging to a particular "school of practice" (e.g., homeopathy or the "hydropathic" water cure) must be judged only by whether or not he properly followed the rules of that school.

While there is a growing interest in alternative forms of medical care, it nonetheless remains the case that most of us get the bulk of our medical care from "mainstream" practitioners (e.g., physicians and the various health care providers that work with them). More important from the point of view of this book, most medical research in this country is performed by such mainstream practitioners. So, in order to better appreciate the dividing line between nonstandard care and participation in research, we now turn to an examination of how these state laws apply to the mainstream medical practitioner. In particular, we attempt to show that these laws retain a high level of paternalism.

Indeed, the very rules we have just been discussing, when applied to a patient who goes to a mainstream practitioner, will similarly restrict that practitioner's ability to deviate from the standards established by her profession. Yes, a medical doctor will indeed, in certain circumstances, be able to provide "nonstandard" care. But an important rule will govern such deviations: *A doctor can provide a patient with nonstandard care only when doing so is reasonable and is in the best interests of the patient.*

In reality, this is merely a specific instance of the legal rules that apply to *all* interactions between doctors and patients: doctors are almost always supposed to be doing what is best for the patient. In the remainder of this chapter we flesh out this rule and demonstrate its consequences. And in chapters 5 and 6 we complete the picture by contrasting this to the very different rules that determine what can be done to a person participating in a research study.

The first set of restrictions that lead us to the rule stated above are state licensing laws. These laws are designed not to advance the ability of patients to choose different kinds of care, but quite the opposite: to make sure that a health care provider gives the type of care he or she is trained to provide. A good example of this is the case of Dr. George Albert Guess, a licensed physician who practiced family medicine in Asheville, North Carolina.[8] Dr. Guess often provided homeopathic remedies to his patients: he would give them something to swallow that included an extremely tiny amount of some natural substance, such as moss or nightshade plant. Because there is so little of the natural substance in these remedies, there is a negligible chance that these remedies might actually harm a patient. Indeed, there was no evidence that any of his patients were harmed, and several patients who had not been helped by conventional medicine claimed Dr. Guess's treatments did relieve their symptoms.

In a scenario reminiscent of the Laetrile saga, although none of his patients was complaining, Dr. Guess's fellow medical practitioners brought a complaint before the North Carolina Board of Medical Examiners. That group found that Dr. Guess was the only physician in North Carolina to use homeopathic remedies and that the use of such remedies was not consistent with the standards of practice for physicians in that state. The board revoked his license, although it agreed to "stay" that penalty and allow him to continue to practice as long as he refrained from using homeopathic remedies. The fact that many of his patients wanted these remedies was to no avail. Indeed, a subsequent lawsuit brought by those patients, claiming that the board's actions violated their rights under the U.S. and North Carolina constitutions to obtain the medical care of their choice was decided in favor of the board, though largely on narrow technical legal grounds.[9]

The Importance of the Standard of Care

The *Guess* case demonstrates that state licensing laws can and will be used to make physicians (and other types of practitioners) adhere to the standards established by their professions. And those laws are buttressed by the branch of law that we now concentrate on: medical malpractice (a branch of tort law). At the heart of medical malpractice law is the same notion we saw in the *Guess* case: that a patient who goes to a "mainstream" health care provider, a licensed physician, is entitled to the type of care that the profession has determined to be most appropriate for the patient's medical problem. This is what is known as "standard of care" under the law.

We introduced this concept in chapter 3: there was a standard of care for how to do a corneal transplant, involving using sutures to sew the donor corneal button into the patient's own cornea. It was this standard from which Dr. Rowsey departed. Simply stated, the standard of care occupies a privileged position within the law. As we noted in chapter 3, the law generally requires that doctors treat patients according to the standard of care. This requirement is enforced by state tort laws. Doctors who fail to provide their patients with standard care are usually committing malpractice, since they are assumed to have breached the rules requiring that they do what is best for their patients.[10]

Who makes the determination of what constitutes standard care? Under tort law, that determination is delegated to the medical profession as a whole. Thus, it is not the government (e.g., a state law) that spells out the treatment for any particular medical condition. Rather, in an informal and not well-defined process, doctors determine among themselves what constitutes the appropriate treatment for each possible medical problem. These determinations are not written down in any definitive single book or set of books; you won't find *The Standard of Care for All Forms of Disease* on any library shelf. It is often not easy to determine what the standard of care is for a particular medical condition. Nonetheless, such determinations are made thousands of times each year, as malpractice suits take place, each centering around a single question: *Did Dr. Jones adhere to the standard of care in treating Mr. Smith?* One way or another, a variety of doctors, allegedly "experts" who should know what the standard is (sometimes prominent scholars who teach and practice at the best hospitals and medical schools, and who perhaps authored leading textbooks on the disease in question), will testify in court about what the standard is. And the fact finder in that case—sometimes a jury, sometimes a judge—will weigh the testimony of the experts brought in for both sides, ultimately coming to a conclusion as to what the standard was and whether the doctor adhered to that standard.

Beyond Standard Care

While we have laid out the bare bones of malpractice law—that a doctor who deviates from standard care commits malpractice and can be forced to compensate a patient for the resulting injuries—we now need to flesh out those rules, concentrating on the cases at the margins where there are some modifications to this general principle. For although medical malpractice law is at its heart paternalistic, protecting patients from what is deemed "substandard care," it also recognizes that even in the world of medical care, it is not always the case that "one size fits all." Even within the world of standard care, choices are often permitted.[11]

Permitting any deviations from standard care is a relatively recent development. If a half-century ago a doctor had given a patient (even with that person's informed consent) a treatment that was not considered standard care, then the doctor would likely be found to have committed malpractice if the patient ended up having some adverse consequences from that treatment.[12] But in recent decades tort law has accepted to a greater degree the possibility that sometimes it is appropriate for doctors to deviate from standard care, and they won't be legally liable just because a bad outcome takes place.[13] And, as we noted previously in framing the rule governing these departures, the unifying theme is that such a departure must be *reasonable* when evaluated in terms of *the best interests of the patient*. Basically, the interests of the patient are generally the number one priority.

Among the relatively few court decisions addressing these issues is the 1978 opinion by the Indiana Supreme Court in *Brook v. St. John's Hickey Memorial Hospital*.[14] Twenty-three-month-old Tracy Lynn Brook had been diagnosed with a possible urologic disorder. To better determine the nature of her problem, she underwent an X-ray study that involved injecting her with contrast material that would help to outline her urologic system on the films. Dr. Warren Fischer, the radiologist, was unable to find a vein to use for the injection and therefore injected it into her calves. A few months later, her right leg became stiff and her heel began to lift off the ground. Her problem was determined to be due to a shortening of her Achilles tendon, which might have been caused by calf muscle damage attributable to the injection. The problem was eventually corrected, but she had to undergo two operations and to wear a leg brace for a time.

Her father sued the hospital involved and the radiologist, claiming that giving the injection in her calf was malpractice and had caused her problem. The FDA-approved instructions accompanying the contrast material stated that it should be injected into a patient's buttocks. Dr. Fischer, in his defense, noted that he had intentionally avoided using Tracy's buttocks because he remembered reading articles in medical journals recommending against giving injections into the buttocks of tiny children, since that could cause muscle damage. A jury found in favor of Dr. Fischer, and on appeal, the Indiana Supreme Court rejected the argument that a radiologist could only use a new procedure after it had passed through an "experimental" stage of testing.[15]

The court bolstered its conclusion by quoting from a legal reference work stating that "even where there is an established mode of treatment, the physician may be permitted to innovate somewhat if he can establish that, in his best judgment, that was *for the benefit of his patient* and *where the established modes of treatment have proved unsuccessful*."[16] Regarding the latter point, the court noted that Dr. Fischer had introduced articles from prestigious journals such as the *Journal of the Ameri-*

can Medical Association, warning of the paralysis that could result from making an injection into the buttocks of a small child.

In effect, the court was applying time-honored tort concepts to a "new" question: how do we determine the extent to which a physician is permitted to deviate from standard care? Just as the legal system looks to the medical profession to determine what constitutes the standard of care, so too must it look to the profession to determine when departures from standard care are appropriate—in other words, when a departure is in fact in the best interests of the patient. The court did not rely on Dr. Fischer's own words in concluding that it was best to make the injection somewhere other than in the buttocks; rather, it required him to present the same sort of evidence of expert professional opinion that would be needed in any malpractice case to justify a physician's conduct.

The Role of Waivers

Thus far, everything we have described appears consistent with a relatively narrow role for departures from standard care: they can be undertaken only when doing so is reasonably in the best interests of the patient. We now address a handful of important cases that seem to suggest a broader role for nonstandard care: that as long as the patient consents to the care provided, and specifically agrees ahead of time not to sue for malpractice, then that agreement (often called a "waiver" of the patient's right to sue) may be upheld by the courts. As we shall try to demonstrate, even these few waiver cases, properly understood, do not suggest anything different from the general rule we have articulated.

At the outset, we note that waivers of the right to sue for a departure from standard care are often viewed as against public policy, and thus in the usual situation, a patient's having signed such a document will not prevent the patient from successfully suing a doctor. The most famous case illustrating this principle involved a man named Hugo Tunkl, who was admitted to the UCLA Medical Center in 1956.[17] While Tunkl was being admitted to the medical center, he was asked to sign a form that all patients were required to sign, "releasing" the hospital from liability if its doctors or other employees were negligent.[18] This release form was intended by UCLA to change the rules that would otherwise apply to any medical center if a doctor employed by it committed malpractice: usually, the medical center could be successfully sued since an employer is in general responsible under the law for harmful things an employee might do as part of his job.

Tunkl did later sue UCLA and two of the doctors it employed, claiming that his treatment constituted malpractice. The California Supreme Court, in a 1963 opinion, determined that the release form Tunkl signed was to be ignored and could not prevent him from suing UCLA. The court noted that a California law declared agreements designed to exempt people or companies from liability for their negligent actions to be void if they related to the "public interest." It concluded that the relationship between a patient and a hospital was clearly one in which there is great public importance and thus determined the release form to be unenforceable.

As we have said, the *Tunkl* analysis is certainly the rule followed in almost all circumstances: an agreement to relieve a health care provider of her liability for malpractice will be given no legal effect.[19] We don't let people sign away the protection from malpractice that the law gives them. Consider the case of 52-year-old Barbara Rojas.[20] She wanted to get rid of the drooping skin that was hanging from her upper arms following her successful efforts to lose a large amount of weight. There was a problem, however: she couldn't afford to pay the fees that were being charged by plastic surgeons. By word of mouth, she learned of Guillermo Falconi, a physician from Ecuador who had never been licensed in the United States but nonetheless was practicing medicine in California. Ms. Rojas hired Falconi, who performed the surgery in the bedroom of her California home. She ended up dying a day later from blood loss, and Falconi was ultimately convicted of second-degree murder.

While these facts are quite outrageous, imagine if we changed them a bit. Even if the doctor had been licensed and fellowship trained in plastic surgery, even if he had fully told her about the special risks she was taking in having the cut-rate surgery performed in her bedroom and asked her to sign a paper absolving him of liability for harm that occurred to her as a result of those higher risks (as long as he performed the procedure correctly), that should not have mattered: he would still be liable for malpractice. Her consent would be irrelevant. Our society will not permit such risks to be imposed upon a patient, regardless of whether that patient is naive or desperate enough to consent to them.[21]

But surely there are other situations in which a particular patient may want, indeed *demand*, a deviation from standard care, perhaps based upon their own unique preferences. Surely the law does not forbid all such deviations. How do we decide when, if ever, such a deviation will not cause the doctor to be liable for malpractice? What effect, if any, might be given a signed statement by the patient that attempts to limit their ability to sue for malpractice? There are few court decisions addressing this type of situation, but thankfully two New York State decisions help us work through the legal analysis.

The first case, *Colton v. New York Hospital*, involved a kidney donation by Donne Colton to his brother, Dudley, in 1972, a time when kidney transplants were still somewhat new and thus did not yet constitute a "standard" procedure. Dudley died shortly after the transplant, due to liver problems that he had been suffering from even before the transplant. But the lawsuit generated by these circumstances related to what happened to Donne, the donor: he went into shock and acute renal failure as a result of the operation to remove his kidney, and also developed a life-threatening infection. The high doses of antibiotics he was given to fight the infection ended up making him deaf.

In Donne's subsequent lawsuit against New York Hospital, the key issue related to the legal effect of a document that he and his brother had signed prior to undergoing the operations. The document stated that New York Hospital and its doctors "wished to be absolved from any and all liability, damages, lawsuits and causes of action arising out of or in connection with" the operations, and thus Donne and Dudley each were required to promise not to sue the hospital or doctors due to the experimental nature of the transplant.[22]

The court ended up finding the agreement to be enforceable, but only in a limited way. Although the agreement attempted to prevent any type of lawsuit, the court said that lawsuits were barred only if the doctors performed the procedure in a "nonnegligent" and "proper" manner. In effect, it was saying that, regardless of the agreement, the law would still require that both the *decision* to perform the kidney transplant and the *manner* in which it was performed be appropriate. Thus, consistent with the general rules of negligence, both of these aspects of what happened to Donne had to be evaluated by the knowledge base of the profession. Even a "new" and "untested" procedure could end up being performed in a way that the relevant professionals would conclude was inappropriate. For example, perhaps Donne had been kept under anesthesia too long, or the blood vessels leading to his removed kidney were tied off using the wrong type of sutures or an incorrect type of knot.

Similarly, if the near-unanimous opinion of other kidney experts, on reviewing the facts relating to Dudley's illness, had been that a transplant had absolutely no chance of working, then presumably it could be concluded that the decision to perform the transplant was itself negligent (in which case Donne was needlessly exposed to the risks of the donor operation). And in such circumstances, public policy requires that a patient be permitted to sue, regardless of what documents were signed. Absent this rule, a patient would be prey to whatever screwball idea a doctor might come up with, and the law would stand by powerless to protect the patient as long as the appropriate covenant not to sue had been signed.

Imagine that a doctor, with no evidence to back him up, told a patient in heart failure that perhaps surgically removing the spleen would improve her heart function. The doctor has the patient sign a document like the one in the *Colton* case and then performs a technically perfect surgical procedure to remove the patient's spleen. Surely the *Colton* court would not conclude that the patient could not sue the doctor for negligently recommending the experimental procedure—any more than a court would have found blameless the doctor that performed the skin-reduction procedure on Barbara Rojas in her bedroom. Crucial to the *Colton* court's reasoning was the unstated conclusion that, based on professional opinion at the time, Dudley was a reasonable candidate for the experimental procedure.

The need for such rules is further illustrated by a second court opinion, that of *Schneider v. Revici*.[23] In 1981, Edith Schneider's gynecologist discovered a lump in her breast. A subsequent mammogram revealed a suspicious one-centimeter nodule. She was advised by a number of doctors that she should undergo a biopsy to determine whether or not it was cancer. She told those doctors that she did not want to undergo a biopsy and that she would find a doctor who would treat her without any need for surgery. On a radio program, she heard about Dr. Emanuel Revici, a physician and researcher who treated cancer patients with "nontoxic," noninvasive methods. When she went to see him, he concluded she did have cancer and agreed to treat her. He had her sign a consent form that included language "releasing" him from any liability to her, given that she recognized that the treatments he was using were unproven and that he did not guarantee any particular results.

He began treating her with selenium (a mineral that plays a role in normal human biologic functioning) and had her make various dietary changes. According to his records, after four months of this treatment, and on three later occasions, he advised her to have the tumor surgically removed. She later denied he ever suggested this. In any event, after fourteen months of his treatments, at a time when the tumor had spread to her lymph system and the other breast, she finally underwent surgery and chemotherapy at Memorial Sloan-Kettering Hospital.

In a subsequent malpractice action against Dr. Revici, which eventually was reviewed by a federal appellate court, the major issues were about the consequences of the consent form she had signed. The court held that the language in the consent form was not specific enough to constitute a binding agreement not to sue the doctor, and thus the rule created by the *Colton* case was no help to Dr. Revici. However, the court found a somewhat different doctrine, that of *assumption of risk*, more relevant. Under this doctrine, which is a part of the tort law of New York and most states, the fact that someone agrees to allow something to be done to them, having been fully informed about the risks that it will impose, can lead to a reduction (perhaps even down to $0) in the amount of money the patient might otherwise be entitled to in a tort lawsuit.

In accepting that the assumption of risk doctrine might protect the doctor from malpractice liability in this case, the court observed "that an informed decision to avoid surgery and conventional chemotherapy is within the patient's right 'to determine what shall be done with his own body.'" This phrase is key to the court's conclusion. As the court correctly notes, we all, as patients, have a right, likely protected by the U.S. Constitution, to refuse any medical care we don't want—regardless of whether that care is "standard care" or not. The facts of the case indicated that Ms. Schneider had been told by a number of doctors of the likely adverse consequences of that refusal and had nonetheless persisted in her initial refusal to have surgery.

Given those facts, we might well ask—applying our general rule about "reasonableness" in terms of a patient's best interest—what constituted reasonable conduct on the part of Dr. Revici when she arrived at his office? If a patient with cancer was refusing both surgery and chemotherapy, was it reasonable to offer her treatment with selenium and dietary changes? Ultimately, that would be a question for a judge and jury, a question that would need to be answered by providing the court with expert testimony from other doctors. Those doctors would indicate what they would have considered appropriate treatment under such circumstances. But given that Ms. Schneider was refusing the only treatments known to be effective (in 1981), it is certainly possible that professional opinion would back up Dr. Revici's treatment: there were no other effective treatments to offer her, and the treatment he offered her, while not proven, was at least very unlikely to harm her, and there was a slim possibility it might have some effect on her cancer.[24] Thus, while the court doesn't say anything about the need for Dr. Revici's conduct to have been reasonable under the circumstances, such a conclusion appears necessary in order for this case to be consistent with other aspects of tort law.

Applying the Reasonableness Rule to Departures from Standard Care

What we have attempted to show in this chapter is that when a doctor treats a patient, in the great majority of situations, the legal system and, in particular, state tort law will protect the patient by making sure that the doctor adheres to the "standard care" established by the other members of his profession. And, to the extent departures from that standard are sometimes permitted, those departures will need to meet the test that they are *reasonable choices in terms of the best interests of the patient.* As we saw in Ms. Schneider's case, sometimes what is reasonable depends on the applicable circumstances: a doctor needs to accept a patient's legitimate exercise of her legal rights, and so it can be reasonable to recommend minerals and dietary changes for a patient who is (consistent with her rights) refusing chemotherapy and surgery.[25]

On the other hand, we should be very clear about what would *not* be acceptable. When Ms. Schneider came to Dr. Revici, she had already decided to reject mainstream therapy, a fact that no doubt played a major role in the court's reasoning. Suppose another woman later came into Dr. Revici's office, one who had just felt a lump in her breast and had not yet consulted any doctor. Would it have been appropriate for Dr. Revici to even suggest to her selenium and dietary changes as the proper and *sole* treatment? Absolutely not—nor does anything in the court's opinion suggest otherwise. The standard care for this patient would be surgery and chemotherapy, and Dr. Revici would be under a duty to tell her that. Any suggestions on his part that such therapy was not appropriate would likely constitute malpractice on his part.

So, let us return to the "paradox" that Harvard anesthesiologist Robert Truog complained about at the beginning of this chapter: that if he hears about a "novel method of ventilation for critically ill patients" he can go ahead and depart from standard care and try it on a patient, as long as the patient agrees to it, with little malpractice risk. As this chapter has attempted to demonstrate, he would face a *substantial* malpractice risk: if something bad happens to his patient, he should be liable for malpractice unless in a court of law it is demonstrated that his fellow anesthesiologists would, in terms of what is best for that patient, also find it reasonable to depart from standard care and use that novel method.

We can apply this same analysis to the other types of things that might happen in research studies and ask whether the law would allow them in the setting of a doctor treating a patient. It would rarely be in a patient's best interest to be exposed to unnecessary procedures—X-rays, CT scans, spinal taps, surgery on their skulls—where such things are not totally risk-free and they are not being done to alter the patient's treatment. It would generally *not* be in a patient's best interest for a doctor's hand to be tied and his ability to modify the treatments he gives his patient limited, even though he thinks that such modification might make the patient more comfortable or improve the patient's outcome. It would *not* be in a patient's best interest for a doctor to agree to deny a patient access to information that the patient might find very important in deciding to change treatments. All of these activities, if done by a doctor who is engaged in treating a patient, would likely be malpractice: they deviate from the overriding principle that doctors treating patients are supposed to be making decisions based on what is best for the patient.

Finally, let us apply this analysis to Dr. Rowsey and his novel method for performing corneal transplants. Assume that he was doing this in each instance—as he himself claimed—*not* as part of a research study, but rather solely as part of the patient's clinical care. Let us also assume that he adequately informed the subjects of the substantial risks inherent in the new procedure and told them of the risks and benefits of the standard way of doing the transplant. Had all this taken place,[26] and had a patient consented to have the procedure performed, would Dr. Rowsey have been liable for malpractice? Or would the fact that he was *not* doing research have shielded him from liability, as many seemed to think? As we have attempted to show, his departure from standard care would likely raise a substantial question about whether it was a reasonable thing to do in terms of the best interests of the patients. And that is a question that would ultimately be decided in a court of law, based on the expert testimony of fellow ophthalmologists.

What facts would be relevant as those ophthalmologists reflected on this issue? The fact that there was a standard procedure that had been utilized for decades, with a known success rate and relatively known risks, would he highly relevant. It would likely also be relevant that, to a particular patient, the added benefits of Dr. Rowsey's procedure, even if it was as successful as he hoped it to be, might not be that great— and thus might be outweighed by the largely unknown risks. Cutting an hour off the surgery time and eliminating the need for adjustments of sutures in follow-up visits could indeed produce substantial benefits for tens of thousands of future patients. Adopting that new procedure as standard care would make a great deal of sense, but only *after* we have completed the needed research studies and know that those benefits are real and that the procedure rarely, if ever, produces any serious adverse outcomes. If you are the patient being exposed to the new procedure when those benefits are yet unproven and the risks are largely unknown, it seems a lot less reasonable to undergo the possible unknown risks in return for relatively modest (and still unproven) benefits. These are the sorts of concerns that might lead other ophthalmologists to conclude that having a patient undergo this new and substantially different procedure was not a reasonable thing to do—and might well have been malpractice.[27]

5

The Weakened Legal Protections
Given to Research Subjects

In the preceding chapters, we showed that the American legal system fairly vigorously protects patients from "substandard" care. Most of the time, patients are *required* to be given standard care. And even when there are departures from standard care, they are acceptable only when the nonstandard care provided to the patient, given the relevant circumstances, is nonetheless *in the best interests of the patient.*

We now turn from the situation of a doctor treating a patient to that of a person becoming a subject in a research study. And we come to spelling out one of the key reasons that participation in a research study may in many instances be a bad choice for a self-interested person: simply stated, *a participant in a research study is not given the legal protections we just discussed.* Things can be done to them that are *bad* for them. Things can be done to them that do not meet the "best interests of the patient" rule that applies to clinical care. Things can be done to them that would constitute *malpractice* if they were performed as clinical care and had not been done as part of a research study. But what are the rules that determine the limits of this? Just *how bad* can participation in a study be for a particular subject? This is exactly the issue that this chapter and the next discuss.

It is not as if there are no limits on what can be done to research subjects. The Nuremberg Code—though that document is not formally binding on the United States—listed a variety of such rules, including this one: "No experiment should be conducted where there is a priori reason to believe that death or disabling injury will occur; except, perhaps, in those experiments where the experimental physicians also serve as subjects."[1] A clear modern application of a similar rule involves the FDA's rules for approving antidotes to certain chemical or biologic weapons as relaxed after the tragedy of 9/11, allowing certain antidotes to be approved for use based on proof of *safety* in humans, but without proof that they are actually *effective* in humans.[2] For effectiveness, only testing in animals will be required.

This FDA rule was implemented precisely because of the ethical limits on research with human subjects. Imagine, for example, we took 50 healthy human volunteers, put them in a room, and exposed them to a nerve gas that is known to be 100% lethal within an hour, and then exposed them to the new drug that we are testing to see if it really counteracts the nerve gas. Such a study would generally be considered inappropriate:[3] we will not expose healthy people to a lethal agent, crossing our fingers that everyone will do well on the chance that the antidote really is 100% effective. Given our inability to ethically do that type of study, the FDA was forced to approve these agents with some lesser form of proof of efficacy—animal studies only.

On the other hand, by this point in the book it should come as no surprise that we *do* permit studies to take place that are significantly bad for the participants. Many studies are nontherapeutic, in the sense that they do not involve trying to treat someone for an illness or otherwise do anything that might benefit the subject. Thus, in almost all such studies, the risks to the subject—even if they are very low—likely outweigh the benefits. We routinely do things to healthy people—have them run on treadmills, have them take newly developed medications to test for side effects— that impose various kinds of risks. Some may be relatively benign, such as running on that treadmill at a modest pace. Others may pose more substantial risks, such as participating in a phase I drug study and being one of the first human beings to swallow a new drug that has thus far been tested only in animals. And in recent years, subjects have been asked to swallow small quantities of proposed new pesticides, to see if these compounds posed any risks to human beings.[4]

Similarly, even people in therapeutic studies, where they are being given a new therapy to see if it can help treat their illness, may be exposed to added risks, such as the extra CT scan, the spinal tap, or the bone marrow biopsy that is performed solely to help researchers collect additional research data (and will not change the treatment given to the patient). Clearly, these procedures are not required to comply with tort law's "best interests of the patient" rule that is imposed on the usual interactions between doctors and patients. And there may be far more significant risks from being in a study, risks that many might consider significantly life-threatening.

Consider a study in which people with peanut allergies, many of whom had in the past experienced near-fatal reactions, were invited to participate in a study of a new drug that might reduce such allergies.[5] Half of the participants in the study would be getting a placebo and yet would, as part of the study, be subjected to multiple injections of peanut flour under their skin. The researchers later observed that it "was a lot harder to recruit volunteers than we thought it would be."[6] Even though the exposure to the peanut compounds would be under conditions where emergency treatment was available, thus making the risk of serious injury relatively low, the subjects were "justifiably nervous" about being intentionally exposed to this life-threatening substance.

Admittedly, this was a relatively unusual study, specially chosen by us because of its special risks. The more important question, at the heart of this book, is: *What about the average clinical trial?* Our discussion of the applicable rules in this chapter is designed to lead up to a discussion in chapter 6 of what are in many ways the most typical "therapeutic" clinical trials: ones that randomize subjects between the current standard of care and some "new-and-possibly improved" treatment. This is the sort of study that comes to mind when most of us think about research studies. And this is often the sort of study that people may clamor to enroll in, to get the chance at that new (albeit unproven) treatment.

As we noted at the very beginning of this book, the impression that being in such a study is often a good thing is not limited to the public. It is worth noting again this comment by Jane Brody, one of this country's leading health writers, which appeared in her column in the *New York Times*: "At the very least, by joining a clinical trial, you will receive the best established therapy. At most, you will be among the first to receive a treatment that proves to be better."[7]

Of course, she is plainly wrong in suggesting that a person entering such a study faces a win–win situation. It may end up that the new treatment is worse than standard care, and thus the subject can indeed be worse off for being in the study—maybe a great deal worse off. That is not especially surprising, or even troublesome: after all, research does involve venturing into the unknown, and it would be wrong to expect that a subject can be guaranteed there is no possibility of an untoward outcome. And, just because it can happen that there is a bad outcome, it doesn't mean that choosing to be in the study in the first place was an unreasonable thing for a nonaltruistic subject to do.

But as we will try to show, in fact participating in such studies will indeed often be a *significantly* bad choice for a subject. In many instances—indeed, in a growing percentage of trials being conducted in recent years—it is probably known from the very start of the trial that entering the trial is *not* in the best interests of many or even most of the subjects. And by that, we mean that they will be exposed to significantly increased risks in the trials—in rare cases even life-threatening ones—that are *not* counterbalanced by possible benefits to them. Simply stated, even the therapeutic elements of a study—the things done to the subject to treat them—will not meet the rules that would apply to nonstandard treatments given to a patient *outside* of a study. Things can be done to a subject, for treatment purposes, that would not meet the "best interests of the patient" standard that governs the type of care that can be given to a patient not participating in a study.[8]

What are the criteria that allow us to impose significant life-threatening risks on people in research studies, even when those risks are not balanced by other advantages to the subjects? It is to the complicated set of rules governing this state of affairs that we now turn. In this chapter, we attempt to lay out the basic principles, while in chapter 6, we explore how they apply to several common types of study designs.

The Source of Legal Standards of Care for Research Subjects

The starting point for evaluating what sorts of "bad" things can be done to people in studies (in contrast to the "best interests of the patient" standard that applies in treating patients outside of a study) is the set of federal regulations known as the Common

Rule. Most research conducted in this country is required to comply with these regulations.[9] If a researcher or institution is subject to these rules and fails to comply, then the federal government may impose a variety of sanctions. Most significantly, it can force an institution to cease conducting federally funded research and thus turn off the spigot of federal research dollars that they were receiving. This is a potent weapon, particularly when applied to major research institutions. When this sanction was imposed on leading medical research centers such as Johns Hopkins and Duke, within days officials from those centers had met with federal officials and worked out conditions under which future research would be supervised, so that the flow of dollars could promptly restart.

From the point of view of a subject in a research study who ends up being injured in a study, however, the federal regulations do not provide any legal remedy to individuals.[10] Though this may come as a surprise, federal law does not give any of us a right to go to court and sue if we are injured in a research study. This is actually not that uncommon a situation: due to policy and political considerations, Congress will often think that some particular area needs regulation but decide that allowing lawsuits by individuals would be too disruptive. Thus, in diverse areas from suing HMOs to retaliating against people who send you pornographic spam, there may be extensive federal regulation yet very limited rights for injured people to get into federal court.

But here again, state tort law comes to the rescue. It does allow an injured subject to sue for money damages, and in so doing, it will play a growing role in determining what is or is not acceptable behavior on the part of researchers. There is relatively little very specific guidance about the application of tort law in this area, since few lawsuits have ever been filed, and even fewer have reached an appellate court that might provide guidance on these rules. Only recently have there been significant numbers of lawsuits based on alleged misconduct by researchers, and most of those have been settled before a judge has gotten to write an opinion.

Nonetheless, the general rules of tort law that we discussed in previous chapters let us lay out the basic roadmap of this area. As we attempt to show here, researchers (whether they are doctors or not) do have a duty to protect the well-being of subjects, but it is a different sort of duty than a doctor usually has to a patient.[11] Most important, it is a weaker duty, in the sense that while a doctor has to do what is best for a patient, a researcher has a much less demanding obligation.[12]

Precisely because so many "bad" things can be done to a research subject, we apply (or at least we should be applying) strict informed consent rules, much stricter than those we apply to clinical care. The subject should know exactly what they are getting into and how their well-being is no longer the number one priority. This change in legal status is acceptable, by and large, only because subjects *have agreed to be under* the weakened legal protections that apply to the relationship between subject and researcher.[13] Given the accepted policy in favor of conducting appropriate research in this nation, the legal system in effect allows a person to consent to this watered-down set of protections.[14] And in part II of this book, we examine whether or not those informed consent rules adequately let people know about the change in their legal protections.

But first we need to spell out those altered legal protections. Where do the guidelines that will be applied in a state "research malpractice" lawsuit come from? By and large, people who conduct research these days (particularly medical research) are considered to be part of a community that adheres to a variety of rules. Thus, as is true with the tort law applying to other types of professional activities, someone conducting research is likely to be held by the law to the rules of that professional community. The most obvious and important set of rules are the Common Rule and related federal regulations, which strongly influence the conduct of almost all research in the United States. Indeed, even for research that is not formally subject to the Common Rule, a court might well find that a researcher who violated some of the "core" requirements of the Common Rule was acting negligently if most other researchers under the same circumstances would nonetheless have considered it appropriate to follow those rules.

Thus, even though the Common Rule does not create a specific federal right allowing a subject to sue researchers, in a backhanded way it creates a set of standards that state tort laws will in essence incorporate, allowing lawsuits in state courts when they are breached.[15] And, in addition to the Common Rule itself, there are a variety of general principles discussed in the growing professional literature about how to do research that also create standards for conducting research, standards that in a similar way become legally binding for purposes of tort law.

The Federal Common Rule

As the discussion thus far has suggested, the starting point in determining what sorts of risks a subject can be exposed to is the Common Rule and related federal regulations. And as we have previously noted, the regulations embody a variety of rules designed to *protect* the subject. Thus, for example:

- Risks to subjects have to be minimized.[16]
- Subjects have to be selected in an equitable manner.[17]
- Adequate provisions have to be made to monitor the data for purposes of ensuring the safety of subjects.[18]
- Adequate provisions have to be made to protect the privacy of subjects and to maintain the confidentiality of the data that is collected.[19]
- Special additional safeguards have to be provided if any of the subjects are especially "vulnerable" to coercion or undue influence.[20]

While all of these items are important protections for the subjects, do they assure that being in a study is "good" for the subject and is in the subject's best interests? The simple answer is *no*. They are not even *intended* to do that.

Indeed, the regulations *specifically acknowledge* that a study need not be in the best interests of the subject. That key rule is buried in a rather convoluted sentence that merits our attention: "Risks to subjects [must be] reasonable in relation to anticipated benefits, if any, to subjects, and the importance of the knowledge that may reasonably be expected to result."[21] This mouthful of less-than-crystal clear guidance is essentially all that the Common Rule tells us (apart from the above list of specific criteria) regarding the sorts of risks to which a subjects can be exposed, and the relationship of those risks to possible benefits to subjects and to society. Surprisingly, given its importance, there is relatively little authoritative guidance about what this sentence really means and how its mandate should be applied in evaluating the acceptability of specific proposed research studies.

The history of the provision, however, and the comments of people involved in the deliberations that led up to the creation of this rule, does provide some helpful information.[22] In an earlier version, the federal regulation was actually somewhat clearer in providing a rule that essentially works out to the following mathematical equation:

$$(\text{benefits to the subject}) + (\text{benefits to society from new knowledge}) > (\text{risks to the subject})[23]$$

Note that this rule didn't require that the study be "good" for the subject. Due to the introduction of the "benefits to society from new knowledge" component, theoretically no matter how small the benefit to the subject, a large risk to the subject could be found acceptable if there were substantial enough benefits to society from learning something important. In other words, in some circumstances, the risks to the subject could vastly outweigh the benefits to the subject, and yet the study would still be acceptable.

Consider, for example, the Nazi study in which people were dunked in tanks of freezing water and ice. Presumably, if there was an urgent need to know what happens to people under such circumstances—perhaps it would play a major role in our current efforts to defeat a pending terrorist plot—then, if the other rules (e.g., making sure there is no other way to gain this information with lower risks to subjects) were met, this study might be acceptable. Similar issues are raised by our current post-9/11 environment. If there were a very serious threat that large portions of the U.S. population might be exposed to a highly lethal chemical weapon, the equation given above might justify exposing consenting subjects to that toxic agent, even if we knew that many of them might die in the testing.

Interestingly, the rule that was finally adopted, as quoted above, was actually designed to be *less* paternalistic, *less* protective of the well-being of the subject, than the "equation" we have just evaluated.[24] Note how instead of saying that the benefits side of the equation needed to outbalance the risks side, all the current rule says is that there must be "reasonableness" in terms of the magnitude of the risks and benefits. Thus, the benefits don't even have to outweigh the risks. Rather, the only requirement is the much vaguer one that that they are, in common parlance, "in the ballpark" of the magnitude of the risks.

To summarize, there are two distinct ways in which the current Common Rule accepts the possibility that participation in a study may be "bad" for the subject (with risks outweighing benefits): (1) benefits to society are included on the benefits side of the equation, and (2) in any event, benefits need not outweigh risks but only be in a "reasonable" relationship to them (whatever that means). Note there is not even any specific requirement that, *from the point of view of the subject*, there must be a particular relationship (even one of reasonableness) between risks and benefits.[25] This is a far cry from the "best interests" rule that applies to doctors treating patients.[26]

In any event, as this discussion demonstrates, the rules describing the acceptable relationship between risks and benefits to subjects are rather vague. To get a better understanding of how they are actually applied and to what extent they significantly protect the well-being of subjects, it is necessary to explore specific types of study designs that are commonly conducted. That task is undertaken in chapter 6.

Why Vague "Study Design" Rules Have Such Huge Consequences

Before we turn to the specifics of study design, it is worth a brief aside to explain why the rules we have just outlined have such a huge impact. To understand this conclusion, we need to highlight the two distinct ways that researchers might do something wrong in conducting a study:

1. They might *design* the study incorrectly. In other words, their plan for the study (formally called the protocol) might be defective in one way or another.
2. Their plan for the study might be fine, but they might fail to adhere to appropriate standards *in implementing that plan.* In other words, they might not be appropriately careful in carrying out that plan.[27]

An example of the type of misconduct described in category 2 is what happened to Nicole Wan in 1996.[28] As we mentioned in chapter 1, the healthy 19-year-old sophomore at the University of Rochester and her boyfriend had volunteered for a study at the school's medical center about how smoking and air pollution affect the lungs. The study paid $150, and the two young people decided to participate in order to have some extra spending money. During the study, a narrow tube (a bronchoscope) was snaked down her throat and directed into her lungs, where lung cells were collected. This is a standard procedure that is often performed as part of person's clinical care if they have certain lung problems. Nicole, being healthy, had no need of it.

There are certain well-accepted standards for how to safely perform this procedure on a patient, including how much anesthetic a person can be given. There would usually be no reason that someone performing the procedure in a research study, solely to collect research data, should not be held to the same standards of care that would apply in the clinical (nonresearch) context. In Nicole's case, they ended up trying to collect a large number of samples of her cells and gave her more anesthetic than the protocol permitted any subject to be given. Immediately after the procedure she was weak and in great pain, and two days later she died when her heart stopped, apparently due to an overdose of the anesthetic lidocaine.

In the ensuing storm of criticism, it is noteworthy that the researchers were *not* criticized for having performed the bronchoscopy in the first place. Apparently it was considered acceptable, in terms of the rules we just described relating to the risks and benefits of a study, to expose healthy subjects to a single competently performed bronchoscopy examination. (And undergoing a bronchoscopy, while relatively safe, is not all *that* safe: approximately 1 in 300 bronchoscopy patients develop a "major" or "life-threatening" complication, such as a collapsed lung or an abnormal heart rhythm.[29]) The problem was that Nicole got exposed to higher risks that those she expected (and had consented to undergo): she underwent a *negligent* examination, one with too much anesthesia, one that failed to adhere to the established standards for how to perform a bronchoscopy.

Determining whether or not there is a category 2 error—failure to adhere to a well-designed plan—is not very different from the sort of question that is resolved in most malpractice and similar tort lawsuits. We already have a "plan" to look to; the major issue is how much the researchers deviated from that plan. In essence, the research protocol serves the same purpose as the "standard of care" does in the usual malpractice case: it is a benchmark against which the questioned conduct must be judged.

On the other hand, errors in *designing* a study present much more open-ended questions. In such cases, there is no "accepted" plan for comparing what happened: the very fact at issue is whether or not the plan is acceptable, whether it complies with the risk–benefit rules for studies. To explore the sometimes blurry line between these two types of errors, consider what happened to Patricia Vodopest. She was a nurse who enjoyed climbing mountains, and in 1989 she came across an article in *The Mountaineer* magazine by Rosemary MacGregor, a woman who shared both Vodopest's vocation and avocation.[30] MacGregor's article, "Breathe Like a Sherpa at High Altitudes," described a recent expedition on Mount Everest where MacGregor conducted a preliminary study to see if a biofeedback breathing technique might help in preventing high altitude sickness. The article noted that the technique required weeks to months of training and discussed a second expedition that was planned for 1990.

The article invited anyone interested in the expedition to contact MacGregor, and Ms. Vodopest did just that after reading a second article about the upcoming trip. She subsequently joined the new expedition to the Himalayas. On that expedition, MacGregor was accompanied by Merrill Hille, an associate professor of zoology at the University of Washington, and they submitted a research proposal describing the study to the institutional review board (IRB) at that school, which was approved.[31] They also had all subjects sign a form saying that the subjects released the researchers "from all liability, claims and causes of action arising out of or in any way connected with" their participation in the trek. The University of Washington IRB subsequently (and correctly) determined that this release was a violation of federal regulations, which do not permit participants in research studies to give up any legal rights as a condition to participating in a study.[32] The researchers failed to mention the IRB's actions to any of the climbers, however.

Vodopest traveled with the other subjects to Phakding, Nepal, in March of 1990 and began the trek up the mountain. At 8,700 feet she began to have various symptoms, such as headaches, dizziness, and an inability to eat or drink. She was not urinating and became exhausted and dazed. MacGregor was aware of these symptoms but told her that they weren't due to altitude sickness. They continued to climb. At

11,300 feet Vodopest felt very ill, but MacGregor told her that if she continued to breathe correctly, then she would be fine. She wasn't: her symptoms became possibly life-threatening, with terrible headaches, a racing heart beat, loss of balance, and nausea and vomiting. She failed a simple neurologic test administered by another trekker who was a nurse.

Vodopest was sent down the mountain the next day. She had developed swelling of her brain (cerebral edema) due to altitude sickness and, allegedly, has suffered permanent brain damage. In her subsequent lawsuit against MacGregor, she claimed that the researcher had behaved negligently in "promoting the use of her breathing technique, rather than advising Vodopest to descend to a lower altitude, as a remedy for her symptoms of high altitude sickness." While the lawsuit doesn't specify what the protocol actually said, we can nonetheless consider two ways it might have been written:

1. It might have said that the moment a subject appeared to be developing any symptoms of altitude sickness, the person would be treated appropriately and allowed to go back down the mountain.
2. It might have said that a subject would be allowed to develop early symptoms of altitude sickness, but she would be kept in the study until more severe symptoms developed, to see if the breathing method would help those early symptoms go away.

Note how the difference in these two possible versions of the protocol might lead to differences in analyzing whether or not MacGregor was negligent. Under protocol version 1, we have a relatively straightforward "failure to adhere to protocol" question. A sufficiently trained nurse, experienced in mountain climbing and leading expeditions, should or should not have been able to conclude that Vodopest was developing high altitude sickness. This is very similar to a standard malpractice question. And by allowing a subject to proceed on the trek only until they might be developing altitude sickness, the subject would not be subject to any higher risk than if they were on that trek purely for recreational purposes.

On the other hand, protocol version 2 raises a question that is far more difficult to answer.[33] It is certainly much riskier for the subjects to allow them to begin developing symptoms of high altitude sickness and to then hope that the breathing technique would reverse those symptoms. This is not the sort of risk that the average person climbing a mountain is exposed to; presumably, they get appropriate treatment (including ending their ascent) when symptoms begin. Is this new risk one that we should allow subjects to consent to, assuming that, fully informed, they are willing to undertake it? We don't have any obvious "standard" to compare this risk to. In other words, the far riskier study, paradoxically enough, becomes the one that is more likely to meet the standards of the regulations.

For another example of such issues, consider what happened to Michelle Payette during the summer of 1990. The 27-year-old was a summer research intern at Rockefeller University, looking forward to shortly beginning medical school at the University of California at Davis, when she agreed to participate in a research study at Rockefeller.[34] The study, intended to see how three types of diets might alter a person's "good" (HDL) cholesterol level, involved, among other things, hospitalizing her for several days and injecting her with radioactive iodine on a number of occasions. During the following fall, back in California, she felt fatigued, discovered her hair and skin were dry, and gained weight. She was diagnosed with an enlarged thyroid and hypothyroidism.

Her lawsuit, filed in 1993, claimed that she developed hypothyroidism as a result of the injections she received during the research study. She argued, among other things, that the study had a "negligent design." Her lawsuit doesn't make it clear exactly what these design problems were: perhaps she contended that the study involved too many injections of iodine, or they were too close to one another. Note how much more complex an issue this is compared to what happened to Nicole Wan. An appropriate analogy would be if Nicole Wan's family had not sued based on the bronchoscopy having been negligently performed, but rather claimed that it was inappropriate for Nicole to undergo even a "competently performed" bronchoscopy. That argument—like deciding whether Patricia Vodopest should have been permitted to intentionally develop significant symptoms of high altitude sickness—poses difficult questions relating to what levels of risks subjects can be exposed to in a particular study. Was it really acceptable for Nicole to be subjected to the significant risks of a bronchoscopy, even if it had been done without any negligence?

Why is the vagueness of the standards for determining "research design" so important? Because many of the greatest risks that subjects are exposed to in studies will likely raise design issues. What happened to Nicole Wan—researchers basically performing a standard procedure in a negligent manner—is a relative rarity. If we look over the various reports of bad things happening to research subjects, almost all of them seem to involve at least some, or even mainly, issues relating to study design: was it acceptable to expose Ellen Roche to the breathable form of hexamethonium?[35] Should the relatively healthy Jesse Gelsinger have been enrolled in the University of Pennsylvania study, as opposed to infants with more severe forms of his disease who were highly likely to die in any event?

As long as there are relatively vague criteria for assessing how risks and benefits factor into study design, it will be relatively hard to conclude that there is anything wrong with a variety of studies, in spite of their imposing a great variety of risks on subjects. So it is now time to examine, in chapter 6, the specific way the rules relating to risks and benefits are applied to the major types of studies and to see exactly how they are (or perhaps are *not*) protecting subjects.

6

How Bad for the Subjects Can a Study Be?

Experimentation has its victims, people who would not have suffered
injury and disability were it not for society's desire for the fruits of
research. Society does not have the privilege of asking whether this
price should be paid; it is being paid.
—President's Commission for the Study of Ethical Problems
in Medicine and Biomedical and Behavioral Research, *Compensating
for Research Injuries*

In chapter 5, we saw that the major rule relating to the risks and benefits of a permissible study doesn't actually prevent studies from being significantly "bad" for subjects. And yet, as we saw from the beginning of this book, many very smart people, ranging from leading health writer Jane Brody to the top-notch pediatricians who treat childhood cancers, have no trouble concluding that participating in perhaps the most important type of study—clinical trials to test some new treatment—will generally be in a patient's best interests.

The obvious question is, how are they coming to this conclusion? Are they merely confused? If the applicable rules, as we discussed in chapter 5, do not require that study designs be so attentive to the well-being of the subjects, why is it that these very smart people believe and actively profess that being in studies is so commonly a good choice for a subject? Is it mere coincidence? Is it that researchers voluntarily impose on themselves rules that are much stricter than those in the regulations? Or is it something else?

The likely response these believers would probably give refers to the concept of *clinical equipoise.* This mysterious concept, while nowhere explicitly mentioned in the Common Rule or in any regulations, is nonetheless well recognized both by the federal government and by most experts in research ethics as a requirement that must be met in clinical trials.[1] And it is likely that they would point to clinical equipoise as the ultimate protector of the well-being of subjects, the concept that transforms an undefined relationship between risks and benefits into one in which the benefits of participation outweigh the risks. We now turn to examining this mysterious concept and to evaluating whether it indeed provides much of a safeguard to the well-being of research subjects.

Providing Subjects with an Unproven Treatment Instead of Standard Care

The requirement of clinical equipoise initially came into being as an informal requirement in conducting the classic type of clinical trial, one where a person with a particular illness is randomized between standard care and some new type of treatment. Under this rule, it is in most cases[2] considered unethical to conduct a study unless the subject gets either standard care or some other treatment that is in "clinical equipoise" to standard care.

What does it mean for a treatment to be in "clinical equipoise" with standard care? The concept of clinical equipoise was initially created by a Canadian bioethicist named Benjamin Freedman, who wrote about it in a now-classic 1987 paper in the *New England Journal of Medicine*. As Freedman explained it,[3] clinical equipoise exists when there is "genuine uncertainty" among members of the professional community about which of two treatments is better.[4] It doesn't matter whether the patient's own doctor, or a handful of researchers, thinks one or the other treatment is better. What matters is whether there is sufficient uncertainty among the group of physicians that regularly treat the medical problem being studied. That "group uncertainty" determines if a new treatment is in clinical equipoise with standard care.

An example is helpful. Assume that a researcher wants to test whether chicken soup alone is a good treatment for patients with severe pneumonia. Would it be ethical to do so? No, because chicken soup would not be considered to be in clinical equipoise with standard care for severe pneumonia, which involves using high doses of relatively powerful antibiotics. If we asked physicians who treat pneumonia whether they think that chicken soup might work as well as antibiotics, we would likely find very few (if any) who answer yes to that question. Nor would our researcher likely be able to come up with evidence (from a journal article, e.g.) convincing many of these doctors to change their minds. Thus, there is virtually *no* uncertainty about the fact that antibiotics are better than chicken soup. Antibiotics and chicken soup are not in clinical equipoise as treatments for severe pneumonia. Therefore, giving a subject in a study chicken soup as the sole treatment would be exposing that subject to a treatment that is substantially inferior to standard care and to a significant risk of death. Thus, this would be unethical and presumably in violation of the regulations.

While clinical equipoise requires there to be "uncertainty" among the relevant group of physicians about which is the best treatment, we need to be careful to note what it does *not* require. It does not require there to be a split in what treatments doctors are *actually using* to treat a condition. For example, there is no requirement that about 50% of the patients are currently getting treatment A and the other 50% are getting treatment B in order to conclude that there is clinical equipoise. Indeed, there can be clinical equipoise even if *no* patients are currently getting the new treatment. Obviously, if we didn't allow such a rule, then we would never be able to test that new treatment on the very first subject.

All there needs to be is "some evidence" that the new treatment might be better,[5] with that evidence being sufficient to generate among the applicable group of physicians uncertainty about which treatment is better. The rule does not specify what that evidence must be—how rigorous it needs to be, or how substantial—nor does it specify how many physicians have to be open-minded about the possible benefits of the new treatment. (It can't just be one or two, but it doesn't have to be most of the physicians—only a "reasonable minority" is needed, itself a vague concept.) As long as enough physicians will sometimes conclude, "Gee, based on what you have shown me, I think there is a decent chance that new treatment B *might* really be as good as currently accepted treatment A," clinical equipoise can exist even if none of those physicians is yet willing to take the risk of trying treatment B on their patients.

Thus, in a real sense, the clinical equipoise rule is not all that demanding. There is often a great deal of uncertainty in the world, and given that fact, it may not be that hard to conclude that we are not sure which of two treatments might be better. Consider how Marcia Angell, a former editor-in-chief of the *New England Journal of Medicine*, described the clinical equipoise requirement:

> An essential ethical condition for a randomized clinical trial comparing two treatments for a disease is that there be no good reason for thinking one is better than the other. Usually, investigators hope and even expect that the new treatment will be better, but *there should not be solid evidence one way or the other*. If there is, not only would the trial be scientifically redundant, but the investigators would be guilty of knowingly giving inferior treatments to some participants in the trial.[6]

Angell's description of the clinical equipoise requirement clarifies that it should often not be very difficult to satisfy: many things can suggest the possible superiority (or equivalence) of some new proposed treatment, and there will rarely be preexisting "solid" evidence negating that possibility.

The Protection Clinical Equipoise Doesn't Provide

It is time to ask the key question: how much protection does the clinical equipoise requirement really provide for a subject? In particular, does it assure that participation in a study is in the best interests of the subjects? The answer from some leading scholars,[7] and the apparent published position of the FDA,[8] appears to be that yes, the clinical equipoise rule does assure just that. After all, so the argument goes, we are treating the subject either with standard care or with something that, for all we know, might be as good as standard care (or even better). As indicated by the quotation from Jane Brody earlier in this chapter, even knowledgeable commentators perceive such studies to be almost universally "a good deal" for the average subject.

In fact, that perception is plainly wrong. The clinical equipoise requirement provides much less protection to a subject than one might initially think. Not only does it permit studies to take place that might be a bad choice for some of the prospective subjects, but it even allows studies to take place where we *know* from the outset that participation is likely to be a bad choice for the great majority of people who are asked to be in the study. In spite of the clinical equipoise requirement, researchers can enroll people with a serious illness—perhaps life-threatening—in a study that may randomize them to a treatment that is significantly riskier than standard care, without a likely compensating benefit to the subjects. And, in fact, this set of circumstances is quite common.

The best way to explain this circumstance is to provide a prominent real-life example. The Clinical Outcomes of Surgical Therapy (COST) study, funded by the federal government, was conducted in part to determine whether someone with colon cancer should have the tumor removed by the usual sort of surgery involving a large incision in their abdomen (so-called "open" surgery) or by the new "keyhole" (small-incision) surgery where most of the procedure is performed while looking through a narrow tube called a laparoscope. Specifically, the primary goal of the study was to determine whether the length of disease-free survival and overall survival are the same for both types of surgery. From the beginning of the study, few experts appeared to think that the small-incision surgery can produce *better* results. Indeed, there was tentative evidence suggesting a risk that, due to the way the cancer is rubbed against other tissues while being pulled out through the small incision, cancer may redevelop along that incision because cancer cells were deposited there.[9] This is a risk that does not appear to exist in the standard large-incision way of doing the surgery. Thus, the main question posed by the study was whether, in terms of cancer recurrence, the small-incision surgery can produce results *as good as* the large-incision surgery.

It doesn't take much thinking to figure out that until we *resolve the uncertainty*, until we know whether or not the two surgeries produce an equivalent chance of curing a patient's cancer, it probably isn't a good thing for an average patient to undergo the small-incision surgery. After all, the possible advantages from that surgery—getting out of the hospital a day or two sooner, perhaps getting back to work a bit earlier—are likely not enough to justify being exposed to a possibly increased risk that the cancer was not cured. And this commonsense conclusion had been reached way back in 1994—the same year the COST study was begun—by the surgeons who specialize in this kind of surgery. The American Society of Colon and Rectal Surgeons then issued a policy statement telling surgeons that the new laparoscopic procedure "*should not be performed* [on patients] outside of a randomized clinical trial."[10]

Of course, we might then ask, why was it acceptable to perform it on the people who would be getting the laparoscopic procedure *inside* the clinical trial? During this study, nearly 1,000 patients were enrolled, and half of them were randomized to receive the laparoscopic surgery. And there was little reason to think that it was any less risky for those subjects than it would have been if someone got the surgery outside of the study. Thus, people participating in the study were being exposed to a possibly increased risk of death (the chance of not having the cancer adequately treated), one not likely fully counterbalanced by any significant benefits.

Did this study comply with the current regulatory standards? In particular, were the two types of treatment in clinical equipoise throughout the study? Even under the strictest view of clinical equipoise, the answer would appear to be yes. No one knew whether the two treatments are equally good at treating a patient's cancer. Throughout the study, there was genuine uncertainty about which of the two types of surgery is better. Clinical equipoise existed from the outset of the study up until the results were evaluated. (And it is worth noting that, if it didn't exist, many people—the researchers, the NIH, which funded the study, and the journal that published it—would be violating their own rules against being involved with studies that are not conducted according to applicable ethical rules. Thus far, no one has raised any concerns about the study being unethical due to lack of clinical equipoise.) But what about the question we posed: is being in the study *good* for a subject? The answer, at least from the viewpoint of the "reasonable" subject, a person with the usual views about a possible increased risk of cancer returning, clearly seems to be *no*.

How can this be the case? The answer is that the existence of clinical equipoise merely requires the answer to a question about what we might learn *in the future* from conducting a study: is it possible that a new treatment might be shown to be better than standard care? But a person, making a decision right now about what treatment to get, is confronting a very different choice. They need to decide before the uncertainty about the two treatments is resolved. And that uncertainty needs to be taken into account in making their decision.

Simply stated, *in deciding whether participation in a study is good thing, a subject needs to compare the benefit and risks of participating—including factoring in any uncertainty—to the known benefits and risks of standard care.* This is the equation that is at the heart of distinguishing "good choice" and "bad choice" studies. The existence of clinical equipoise tells us very little about the outcome of that comparison in any particular study. It doesn't tell us whether participating in the study is good for almost all subjects, a substantial number of subjects, only a few subjects, or almost none of the subjects.

Moreover, if we really wanted to impose a requirement that clinical trials comparing new treatments to standard care needed to be good for the subjects, we already know how to do that. The federal regulations already impose such a requirement on certain studies involving children, on the theory that since they can't really consent for themselves, they shouldn't be enrolled in studies that might be significantly bad for them.[11] But there is no such similar restriction imposed on studies involving competent adults—and requiring clinical equipoise doesn't produce that result, either.

Applying the risk–benefit analysis to the colon cancer study, most people would not find it in their best interests to take on an increased risk of their cancer coming back in order to get a chance—and only a chance—of getting out of the hospital a day or two sooner.[12] As we noted, way back in 1994, the professional society for these doctors reached the same conclusion and announced that it would be inappropriate for doctors to be using this type of surgery to treat patients with colon cancer.[13] And this finding was repeated in a 2001 editorial in the *Journal of the American Medical Association* (*JAMA*), a leading medical journal, accompanying a report of initial findings from the colon cancer study indicating that the benefits from the small-incision surgery are relatively modest.[14] It just isn't a reasonable thing for most patients to trade an increased risk of death for a chance at a benefit that is so very small.

But—and this is a *big* but—this conclusion doesn't mean that there isn't a good reason to find out whether or not the laparoscopic surgery cures cancer as well as the large-incision surgery. That's all the clinical equipoise requirement really tells us: that yes, from the viewpoint of society, this is a reasonable question to try to answer. It is reasonable to impose the risks of participation on the subjects, given the possible social benefits. If we really knew that the two surgeries were identical in terms of cure rates, and the laparoscopic surgery did indeed let people leave the hospital sooner, with less pain, then all future patients—and society—would benefit by shifting to doing only laparoscopic surgery. (Imagine summing up the benefits over tens of thousands of future patients, each perhaps getting out of the hospital two days earlier than would otherwise have been the case, having less discomfort, etc.) Thus, it makes a lot of sense, from the point of view of society, to resolve the uncertainty. It therefore makes a lot of sense to conduct the randomized study. And, in fact, the colon cancer study produced just such a result: it proved that there was no increased risk of the cancer returning, and that it is a good thing to be performing laparoscopic surgery on colon cancer patients.[15]

The same analysis could be applied to Dr. Rowsey's Tampa Trephine method for performing corneal transplants described in chapter 3. After he had completed testing the procedure in animals, and before he began using it in humans, there was presumably a legitimate possibility that it might produce better results than the standard way to perform the surgery. Thus, the new procedure was likely in clinical equipoise with the standard procedure. And if the new procedure fulfilled all of its promise —for example, if it cut the time for the procedure from one or two hours down to fifteen minutes, and if it enabled a patient to see 20/20 on the second postsurgical day instead of having a month or two of blurry vision while sutures were being cut from time to time, the benefits to society could be *huge.* Imagine tens of thousands of patients, each one gaining an extra two or three months of better vision and also saving the financial costs of 90 minutes of operating room time.

And yet—as we showed in chapter 4—until we *resolve* the uncertainty about whether in fact these benefits exist by actually finishing the research, there are substantial arguments supporting the conclusion that this procedure was most likely *not* in the best interests of most patients who would otherwise be eligible for the standard form of corneal transplant. The *possibility* that the new treatment would get a subject out of the operating room sooner, and *might* give them better vision a month or two sooner, than standard care might not outweigh the risks that the new treatment may create some unknown problems and could lead to visual results that are substantially worse than those of the tried-and-true decades-old surgery. It might well have even been malpractice to provide the new procedure to a patient outside of a research study. On the other hand, it still could be reasonable to want to evaluate the Tampa Trephine in a research study—and that study might well have been approvable under the risk–benefit analysis required by the regulations.[16]

An AIDS Example

Another example of this phenomenon—how even if equipoise exists, participating in a study can still be a very bad choice for the average subject—comes from what is perhaps the most-discussed series of studies in recent times. In 1994, it was proven that use of the drug AZT (zidovudine), when given to a pregnant woman who is infected with the HIV virus, can substantially reduce the likelihood that her child will end up being infected.[17]

While this discovery has had a substantial impact in the United States, with the use of AZT rapidly becoming standard care for HIV-infected pregnant women, it had little impact in the many undeveloped countries in Africa and Asia where the virus is far more common than in the United States. One of the major reasons for this outcome was the high cost of AZT: both the people and the governments in these countries were poor, and neither could afford to pay for this drug. So a question was posed: was there a much cheaper way to substantially reduce transmission of the virus from mothers to children? One idea was to use AZT but at a much lower dose (e.g., 1/10 of the dose used in the United States).

Based on this type of reasoning, prominent researchers in the United States, including branches of the U.S. government, worked together with officials of some developing nations to design studies that would answer these questions. In these studies, women were randomized between getting a placebo—something known to have no effect, such as a sugar pill—and getting the "low-dose" AZT. These studies eventually were conducted and proved that using low-dose AZT could indeed prevent HIV transmission to infants at a significantly reduced cost. However, these studies also generated a huge amount of controversy, for a number of prominent American critics labeled them as unethical.[18]

What was the source of that claim? It centered around whether, in judging the acceptability of the studies, the standard of care in these countries for preventing HIV transmission should be considered to be the use of AZT—which, due to the cost considerations, virtually no one actually got—or no treatment at all, which in fact was the reality. The critics of the studies claimed that even though AZT was rarely used in these countries, the ethics of the study had to be evaluated by taking account of the best treatment known, even if it was available only in other countries. And if indeed AZT was considered as standard care in the undeveloped countries, then conducting a randomized trial with a placebo as one arm would be considered unethical: it would violate the clinical equipoise rule, since we know that AZT is very effective, and thus we know that assigning a woman to no treatment—namely, giving her a placebo—is much worse than giving her standard care. Thus a placebo would not be in clinical equipoise with standard care, and thus no one can be given a placebo in such a study. (Recall our chicken soup example above—in this case, giving placebo to some people is like giving chicken soup to some people with severe pneumonia.)

It is far from clear that the critics were correct in concluding that standard care should be determined on an "international" scale for such a study.[19] But regardless of how one resolves that issue, it is interesting to evaluate the alternative study that these ethics sticklers proposed: instead of having the low-dose AZT compared to placebo, they *wanted a randomized study which compared "normal-dose" AZT to low-dose AZT*.[20] In effect, they were saying that such a study *would* be ethical and *would* comply with American standards for research ethics. In particular, it would certainly meet the clinical equipoise test: we wouldn't yet know (before doing the study) that the low-dose AZT would be any worse than the normal dose.

So, let us think a moment about this "more ethical" study, the one the critics—those who were arguing for a *very demanding* interpretation of the American research ethics rules—*wanted* to be conducted, the one that would meet the clinical equipoise requirement. Imagine that such a study were to be conducted in the United States. Would participating in this study be a "good thing" for patients? More particularly, is the possibility of being assigned to the low-dose AZT (which will happen half of the time) a good thing for them? Or, restating that question as we did with the colon surgery study, would it be reasonable for doctors, outside of a study, to offer the low-dose AZT to patients in the clinical setting? Imagine Dr. Jones says to her patient: "Laura, we don't yet know if a low dose of AZT will work as well as the standard dose in making sure that the HIV virus is not transmitted to your baby. But I'd like to suggest you try the lower dose. It will likely have fewer side effects. And it will save you quite a bit of money! And, again, for all we know, it *may* indeed work as well as the high dose."

Simple reason tells us it would not be acceptable for a doctor to offer this to a patient, outside of a research setting. It would surely be malpractice, under the "best interests of the patient" rule that the law imposes on doctors treating patients. The additional risks, due to the uncertainty about whether the low dose works as well as standard care, far outweigh the possible benefits to a woman.[21]

On the other hand, is this a worthwhile study for society to conduct? Absolutely! If indeed the low-dose AZT did work as well as the high dose, then it would be of great benefit to switch to the low dose for all patients. The cost savings alone, summed across thousands of patients, would be substantial, perhaps in the tens of millions of dollars. And there might indeed be some reduced side effects. So again, we see that the clinical equipoise requirement does little to assure participation in a study is in the best interests of the subjects.

How Rare Are "Bad Choice" Studies?

So, it is clearly the case that clinical trials can take place, in full compliance with both the regulations and the clinical equipoise requirement, and yet be a bad choice for most people who are merely trying to do what is best to treat their medical problem.

But how often does that occur? Have we merely chosen a few oddball studies, when in fact the chance of a patient encountering such a bad choice study is as rare as a blue moon?

We think not. A substantial percentage of current studies—particularly those involving testing a brand new drug—are likely to fit into the "bad for the subject" category. Consider what the *Wall Street Journal* wrote in a 2002 four-part series on the pharmaceutical industry: "[T]hese days, launches of breakthrough drugs . . . are few and far between. . . . Many of the industry's most productive labs have managed to remain so by frequently launching drugs that are only slightly better than those already on the market. Then they charge a premium for these incremental improvements."[22] Thus, for many patients enrolled in drug studies, the "new" drug, even if it fulfills all its potential (a big if), will offer modest benefits over already-approved drugs: perhaps you only need to take it once a day instead of twice, or perhaps it causes milder or fewer side effects.[23] Until we know exactly how well it works, is it in a subject's best interest to assume the risk that the new drug is not as effective as standard care, when the possible benefit to the subject (which may or may not even exist) is relatively modest? Where the subject has a serious medical problem, this will in many instances not be a reasonable trade-off, and such studies will fit into the "bad choice" category.

And there is another broad range of studies that also fit into this category. These days, we are often likely to be studying treatments designed to temporarily relieve symptoms from a chronic condition, such as arthritis or asthma. Subjects are often given the medication only for a relatively brief period of time—several weeks or months—and may not be able to get it thereafter. Is the trade-off of possibly better temporary relief of symptoms against the risk of being one of first people exposed to a new drug, a reasonable one? The risks of being one of the first to try a new drug are not insubstantial—particularly if the drug is not merely a slight variation on prior drugs, but a new type of chemical that has not previously been used in human beings. Indeed, even after a drug is approved, there are sometimes significant undiscovered risks, since in getting FDA approval the drug only was likely tested on at most a few thousand people. That relatively small number can detect only common risks. In other words, we *know* that the approval process is not very likely to detect relatively rare risks. It isn't even designed to pick up those small risks. (This is the trade-off our society makes in wanting to not wait too long for a drug's approval, since meanwhile people are being denied the possible benefits from the drug.) Thus, there can be "hidden" risks that will not become known until the drug starts being used by much larger numbers of people, after its approval.[24]

For this reason, some physicians recommend staying away from relatively new drugs until they have been used by lots of patients. In effect, they are suggesting that the smart patient should let the initial users of these drugs be the guinea pigs:

> One after another, blockbuster-selling drugs are being yanked off the market for killing and injuring Americans. . . . Should a savvy patient ever swallow a new medicine until it's been sold for a year? After all, that first year of sales often is when bad side effects are spotted.
>
> "I sure wouldn't," said Dr. Raymond Woolsey, a leading drug-safety expert and cardiologist at Georgetown University. "I don't personally, and I don't usually prescribe it unless I have to."
>
> Even the Food and Drug Administration's commissioner urges consumers to be cautious. It's advice Dr. Jane Henney says she'd follow

herself: closely question when your doctor wants to switch to a brand-new remedy.[25]

All of these concerns about being an "early" user of a new drug are multiplied when we are talking about being a subject in one of the first studies of the drug, prior to FDA approval: instead of there having been tens or hundreds of thousands of prior users, thus giving many chances for possibly serious side effects to reveal themselves, you might be merely the tenth or fiftieth human being to be exposed to this drug. Seen in that light, getting—at best, if the drug lives up to its promise—some temporary benefit doesn't seem like such a great deal.[26]

Telling the Subjects If a Study Is "Good" or "Bad" for Them

As we have attempted to show, in the most common category of studies, the "gold standard" clinical trial in which a subject is randomized between standard care and some new treatment, there are many instances in which the study will be a bad choice for subjects who are solely interested in their own well-being. In particular, if giving some new treatment outside of a study is bad for someone, then a study in which subjects are randomized to get that new treatment is also likely bad for the subject. And some of the "hottest" new treatments, according to the editorial commentary in leading medical journals, fit into that "too risky to be given to patients" category. Consider the following:

- Regarding new ways to treat aggressive breast cancer by modified versions of the high-dose chemotherapy approach (which we discuss in detail in chapter 10), an editorial in the *New England Journal of Medicine* noted that such investigational treatments "can neither be justified nor supported outside of clinical trials."[27]
- Regarding the keyhole surgery for colon surgery, discussed above, a *JAMA* editorial specifically advised surgeons to resist the demand to provide this procedure to patients, while at the same time recommending the surgeons be more vigilant in getting patients into research studies.[28]

Clearly, these commentators—writing in the two leading medical journals—are right to conclude that there are instances in which some treatment should not be given directly to patients but where society should be willing to impose the risk of that treatment on subjects in a study. We allow subjects in studies to have greater risks imposed on them because doing so benefits society by adding to our medical knowledge. Nor is this necessarily anything to be disturbed about: after all, we are talking about adults, and they can make their own choice whether or not they wish to enroll in the study. The fact that some people are willing to altruistically accept risks in order to help others is something we should celebrate. And presumably the risk–benefit relationship from the point of view of the average subject will not be *too* extreme; otherwise, the study would likely be found to be inconsistent with the federal regulations. Finally, some of the subjects may have preferences that differ from those of the "average" person, such as putting a high value on getting out of the hospital a day early, and for them participation may indeed be a good thing.

But shouldn't the consent forms clearly tell a prospective subject being invited to participate in a study whether the risk–benefit relationship is so *very* bad that relevant experts (and perhaps even the editorial board of a leading medical journal) have issued an opinion on this issue? (This is particularly true given the well-demonstrated phenomenon of the therapeutic misconception, discussed in chapter 2: patients being asked to enroll in a research study by a doctor tend to mistakenly believe that being in the study must be good for them.) Shouldn't the subject be told that the experts in this field, the professionals who actually perform this type of surgery (or whatever the relevant treatment is in the study), think that it is so bad that it should not ever be offered directly to a patient? We address informed consent issues in part II of this book, but the studies we are discussing raise this issue so starkly that it merits some discussion here.

Consider again the study on small-incision surgery for colon cancer. Since 1994—even prior to beginning that randomized study—the American Society of Colon and Rectal Surgeons (ASCRS) has continuously maintained the position that this type of surgery should not be performed outside of a research study, since it is too risky. And proof of how risky many surgeons thought it to be was evident from surveys of what they would want done if *they* had colon cancer. A presentation at the 1994 ASCRS annual meeting by a Cleveland Clinic colorectal surgeon gave the results of a survey sent to all members of that group: "Although nearly 75 percent of surgeons would gladly use the laparoscope to treat their patients, only 6 percent would have the same technology applied to themselves."[29] A follow-up study presented in 1998 showed a slight growth in the acceptability of the procedure, but again with relatively few members willing to have it performed on themselves (between 9% and 15%, depending on where in the colon the cancer was located).[30]

What were the subjects who enrolled in this study told about this issue? Based on the consent form (which is the only objective way to verify this), they were told that the study was designed to see if "the new way of removing the cancer-containing bowel is as good as the traditional way." They were told that there was a possible benefit from getting "smaller incisions and faster recovery." Regarding the increased risk of the cancer coming back, the Risks section of the consent form described that in what might charitably be described as a rather subtle way: "Even though the new technique only affects HOW the colon is removed, it is possible that the new technique may change the way the tumor grows back after surgery if it does." We leave it to the reader to decide whether this sentence is blatantly deceptive in terms of adequately informing someone that they may be facing a greater chance that the cancer will return.

Did the consent form say anything that put all this information together and actually *compared the risks to the benefits of participation*? This one didn't say a word on that issue. (And, as we shall see in part II, this actually isn't that unusual a failing.) Thus, even though there was an explicit statement from a professional body saying that the relationship of risks to benefits was a very bad one, sufficiently bad that a doctor shouldn't actually offer this to treatment a patient (outside of a study), subjects were not informed of this fact. Nor were they informed of the surveys of colorectal surgeons, demonstrating that few of them would have the procedure performed upon themselves.

It would not be very hard to actually include this sort of information in the consent form:

> The expert opinion of surgeons who do this type of surgery is that the risks to you from participating in this surgery significantly outweigh the benefits from participating. This is because the benefits from participating are relatively minor, while there is a risk that this surgery may lead to a greater chance for the cancer coming back than is the case for the standard large incision surgery. Indeed, a professional group has told surgeons that due to this possibly increased risk, this type of surgery should *not* be performed upon anyone outside of a research study. Thus, if you are enrolling in this study, you should probably be doing so because of your desire to help future patients, and not because being in this study is likely to be in your own best interests. In fact, unless you are a person with somewhat unusual values, *being in this study may likely be a bad choice for you, at least in terms of your own health.*

And it would be appropriate to also include the information that so few surgeons would want the procedure performed upon themselves.[31]

Consider the following hypothetical dialogue between a prospective subject who was offered enrollment in the colon cancer study, having read only the consent form that was actually used:[32]

SUBJECT: Gee, doc, I like the idea of this keyhole surgery. But being in the study, I only get a 50–50 shot at having it. How about I pass on the study, and you instead just give me the keyhole surgery?

DOCTOR: Oh, I couldn't do that. It would be too risky for you. In fact, I was just reading an editorial in a recent issue of a leading medical journal, *JAMA*, noting how I should be resisting the demands of patients like you to be given the keyhole surgery. After all, we don't know how safe it is or if it cures the cancer as well as the large incision procedure. Indeed, the professional society I belong to has formally adopted that position since 1994. We hope that, by having people like you participate in this study, we will find out the answer to how good the keyhole surgery is.

SUBJECT: Wait, maybe I'm missing something here. You tell me it would be too risky for you to just go ahead and give me the keyhole surgery. But you are asking me to be in the study. And if I am in the study, there is a 50% chance I will end up getting the keyhole surgery. Is the keyhole surgery less risky if I get it while I am in the study than if I got it from you just as a patient, outside of the study?

DOCTOR: Well, no, the risks are the same either way. I would do the exact same operation in either situation, and I would do the same follow-up tests.

SUBJECT: So, if I understand you, being in the study isn't in my best interests. After all, I have a 50% chance of being assigned the keyhole surgery, and you tell me that procedure's risks outweigh its benefits to me, based on what we currently know about it.

DOCTOR: Well, I suppose, looked at that way, you're right. Narrowly speaking, being in the study isn't in your best interests, if you compare risks and benefits. But you forget that by being in the study, you are helping us determine whether or not the keyhole surgery is indeed as effective as the large incision surgery. That is what makes exposing you to these risks ethical.

SUBJECT: I'm going to have to pass on the study, Doc. I'm as willing as the next guy to help out with medical research, but not when it means exposing myself to a possibly higher risk of the cancer coming back—that's a risk that most reasonable people wouldn't think is outweighed by the benefits from being in the study.

Placebos

Thus far, we have been concentrating on what is considered one of the more "benign" types of study: taking people with a medical problem and giving them either standard care or something that we hope (and have at least some tentative evidence to suggest) will at least be as good as standard care. And we have shown that these new treatments are perhaps not as benign as some would suggest. Now we turn to studies that appear, at first glance, *to be far riskier*: studies where there is an effective treatment for a condition, yet some of the subjects *are denied that treatment and instead given a placebo* (e.g., a pill with no active ingredients). Imagine, for example, a study in which subjects with a treatable medical problem are randomized, 50–50, to get either some new unproven treatment or a placebo.

Placebo studies play an important role in modern medical research, since they are designed to deal with a difficult problem that arises in testing whether a particular new treatment actually works. In many types of illnesses, convincing a person that you are giving them an effective treatment can produce a substantial improvement in their symptoms. If you are feeling weak, have a headache, are suffering from assorted aches and pains—in each case from legitimate, accurately diagnosed "real" illnesses—then if a doctor gives you a pill and tells you it will work, there is a good chance that you will feel better afterward even if the pill had no actual "working" ingredients. In effect, our minds do indeed play a strong role in how we feel. Being told that something will help us feel better often does indeed produce exactly that outcome. This is what is commonly known as the "placebo effect" of a treatment.[33]

If we just gave a new drug to a large number of people with the specific medical problem it is being tested on, the odds are rather high that a substantial percentage of them will indeed feel better afterward. To eliminate this placebo effect—to test whether it is really the new drug and its active ingredients that produce the health improvement—we traditionally randomize the subjects so that half of them get the new drug and the other half get a placebo (e.g., a sugar pill). The two types of pills appear identical, and the subjects are not told which they got (a so-called "blinded" study). In this way, even if there is a placebo effect, and people feel better just because they have been told they are getting a pill that might work, that same effect should apply equally well to the 50% of the subjects who get the new drug and to the 50% who get the sugar pill. If the result of the study shows that the people who got the new drug had *better* outcomes than those who got the sugar pill, we can be relatively confident that this is due to the drug itself and not to the placebo effect. Doing the study in this way doesn't eliminate the placebo effect, but rather allows it to cancel itself out, since the people in both arms of the study will have the same placebo effect.[34]

Such studies would initially appear to violate the clinical equipoise rule. If there is a standard treatment for a particular medical problem, then presumably it is generally accepted that the treatment does indeed really do something to help alleviate or even cure that medical problem.[35] Under those conditions, we can be relatively confident that a placebo would not work as well as standard care, and thus *a placebo could not be considered to be in clinical equipoise with standard care.* And therefore you could not ethically assign any of the subjects to get a placebo. Recall our chicken soup example: randomizing people with the pneumonia to get antibiotics or chicken soup would be considered unethical, since the existence of the chicken soup arm violates the clinical equipoise rule.

In fact, placebo studies regularly generate a great deal of controversy, precisely because it seems as if we are requiring the subject who is assigned to the placebo arm to undergo such huge risks: being deprived of the known benefits of standard care. In recent years, there has been a great debate between the United States, where placebo use remains common, and much of the rest of the world, where its use has been strongly discouraged. One of the leading international codes for conducting research, the Declaration of Helsinki, for a long time appeared to prohibit the use of placebos in situations where doing so would violate clinical equipoise: "In any medical study, every patient—including those of a control group, if any—should be assured of the best proven diagnostic and therapeutic methods."[36] This statement, if taken at face value, might indicate a huge gulf between what is done in the United States and what is done elsewhere.

But even in the United States, the use of placebos in such circumstances is well circumscribed. It is commonly accepted that placebos should *not* be used in studies where there would be serious consequences to nontreatment of a patient's medical problem.[37] Indeed, even though the FDA is often given the blame for promoting the rule that every new drug or device must be tested against a placebo, there is little evidence that the agency adheres to such a strict rule.[38] If you hunt around, you are unlikely to find many research subjects who are given placebos in studies involving serious illnesses where there are already highly effective treatments. You won't find people who just had a heart attack being randomized to a placebo arm where they are given no treatment. You won't find someone who was just diagnosed with a severe life-threatening infection being randomized to placebos. It is accepted that such studies would be unethical.

In what sorts of studies is a placebo arm considered ethical, in spite of there being a "proven treatment"? *Only when not getting the proven treatment poses relatively small risks to a person.* And there are lots of medical problems that satisfy this condition. Assigning people with headaches to take a placebo is not particularly troublesome, since it is common for people not to bother taking a pill every time they have a headache. People with early symptoms of Parkinson's disease often intentionally delay beginning medications for the disease (which only help with symptoms and don't slow the progress of the disease). Thus, it is similarly considered acceptable to randomize them to a placebo.

Admittedly, there are still a variety of issues to be worked out in drawing the line between "acceptable" and "unacceptable" placebo studies. Obviously, people can have differing opinions on what they consider serious harm.[39] But regardless of how that debate is resolved, one thing is worth noting: those studies that fit into the category of "acceptable placebo studies" are not likely to be very high risk. After all, we generally have quite a bit of information about what happens to someone when they are not treated for a particular medical problem. If we know that this causes seriously bad things to happen to the person, and there is a treatment that prevents those bad things from happening, then we will not be allowing a placebo to be used in a study of that illness. In fact, the U.S. position on placebo use appears so reasonable that the anti-placebo provisions of the Declaration of Helsinki have recently been relaxed to duplicate rules similar to those in the United States.[40]

Given this situation, let's now compare what happens in the "allowable" placebo studies to what happens in the type of study discussed in the preceding section, namely, one where a subject is randomized to either standard care or some new treatment (commonly referred to as "active control" studies). In the placebo-controlled study, the classic complaint was that subjects being assigned to the placebo arm are exposed to too much risk. But as noted, we in general have very good information about the risks of nontreatment of a disease and only allow placebo studies to take place when nontreatment is acceptable. Thus, we have a relatively well-defined upper bound on the risks to which someone will be exposed in a placebo study. Granted, that person won't get any benefits, but the relationship of risks to benefits can't be that bad, since we have an upper bound on risks.

Now look at the "active control" study, where someone is randomized between standard care and some new form of care. These studies are not subjected to the form of "weeding out" we apply to the placebo-controlled studies: in these studies, we don't eliminate diseases where nontreatment or failure to adequately treat might lead to truly horrible consequences to the subjects. Thus, there is no "upper bound" on the risks to which a subject might be exposed. For example, in the study of keyhole surgery for cancer, it might have worked out that the keyhole surgery produces a significantly higher risk of cancer recurrence than the standard therapy.

Viewed in this way, perhaps we shouldn't be worrying so much about the ethics of placebo-controlled studies. The current rules effectively put a cap on how bad such studies can be for the subjects. However, in the relatively noncontroversial active control studies, we currently do not impose any similar cap on the risks to subjects. Perhaps it would be appropriate for us to pay more attention to the active control studies, or at least be far more upfront in letting prospective subjects know to what extent a particular study is good or bad for them.

Sham Surgery

One of the more controversial types of studies is the so-called "sham surgery" study. Historically, most surgical procedures have never undergone the type of gold standard randomized testing that is required to demonstrate effectiveness of other types of treatments, such as new drugs.[41] Perhaps this was at least partly due to the belief on the part of surgeons that they could tell whether or not a particular procedure was effective, and thus there was no need for such testing. But more and more, modern medical care is dealing with the consequences of slowly progressing diseases, and it becomes far harder to tell whether a treatment for that type of problem, even if it involves surgery, is effective. Moreover, growing health care costs in recent years have increased pressures to make sure medical treatments really are effective, and even surgical procedures have gradually been forced to undergo randomized testing. And—no great surprise—they have often been found not to live up to their billing. Surgeons are no more omniscient than are other types of doctors in "knowing" that a particular procedure really works.

Thus, there are a growing number of surgical procedures that are being subjected to randomized testing and often being proven ineffective, or at least less effective than previously thought. Radical mastectomy—removing a woman's entire breast and underlying muscles—used to be a routine treatment for most cases of breast cancer. Only after conducting studies in which women were randomized between very extensive and less extensive forms of surgery was it shown that the far less disfiguring procedures were equally effective in many women.[42]

But while the utility of performing randomized trials to study surgical procedures has now been well demonstrated, there remains a special problem in some cases. As we discussed in the previous section, medical treatments often produce a substantial placebo effect: a person may feel better just because they know something is being done to treat them and not because the treatment really had a specific effect on their illness. This raises an interesting question: to what extent is the placebo effect a problem in the world of surgery? How many "approved" surgical techniques are currently being done in which the patients feel better afterward not because of the specific things done to them in the operating room, but merely because the vivid reality of having undergone a surgical procedure has convinced the person they should feel better? If we don't make an attempt to account for that effect, we may end up never realizing that many allegedly effective operations are actually producing no health benefits other than a placebo effect.

If we really wanted to see how powerful the placebo effect might be in the world of surgery—particularly in surgical procedures where the outcome is largely measured by how much better the patient "feels"—we should ideally be doing studies that eliminate that placebo effect by comparing the real thing to a placebo. But recall a key feature of the usual placebo study involving testing a new drug: it requires the subjects in both arms to be equally unsure of whether or not they are getting the "real" treatment. If the group that got the sugar pill, for example, were able to figure out that they got the sugar pill, then presumably the placebo effect might be smaller for them than for the other group. As a result, we might incorrectly interpret the difference in outcomes between the two groups as demonstrating the effectiveness of the new drug. In drug studies, it is usually relatively easy to manufacture an inactive pill that looks and tastes identical to the new drug.

In the surgical situation, as you can readily imagine, it is often very difficult to arrange things so that a person doesn't really know whether or not they have undergone surgery. Yet in the 1950s, a Seattle cardiologist named Leonard Cobb conducted such a landmark study and demonstrated the existence of a surgical placebo effect in a compelling manner.[43] At the time, there was a popular treatment for angina—chest pain caused by decreased blood flow to the heart—that involved making two small incisions in the chest wall and tying sutures around two arteries so that some blood would be rerouted to go to the heart. Nearly half of the people who underwent the procedure indicated that they had improvement of their chest pain. A quarter of a million people had the procedure, called internal mammary artery ligation, performed on them. Cobb, who with other doctors was concerned that perhaps the procedure was being overpromoted, randomized patients in his study so that half of them underwent the actual procedure, while in the other half the chest incisions were made but the arteries were not tied off. The subjects did not know whether or not they were getting the "real" procedure.[44] His results were startling: there was no difference in the relief of pain or other benefits between the two groups. Dr. Cobb's study demonstrated that all of the symptom relief that patients were getting from these surgeries was due to the placebo effect and had nothing to do with redirected blood flow to the heart.

Cobb's study did not lead to many others doing such "sham surgery" studies, but in recent years, perhaps due to efforts to control health care costs, this type of study has seen an upsurge. One important reason has been that both the National Institutes of Health and the FDA have been promoting it, viewing it as an important way to prove the effectiveness of certain types of surgical treatments. Among the more recent uses of sham surgery was a attempt to determine whether osteoarthritis of the knee—the common type of arthritis that comes from aging—is made less painful by undergoing arthroscopic lavage, a procedure where a flexible scope is threaded inside the knee and used to cut loose "debris."[45] Here is how *The New York Times* described what took place in surgeon J. Bruce Moseley's operating room as he conducted his sham surgery study:

> All 10 [subjects] would be dispatched to the recovery room and sent home
> from the hospital by the next morning equipped with crutches and a
> painkiller. But there the similarities ended. For while two of the men
> would undergo the standard arthroscopic surgery for their condition—the
> scraping and rinsing of the knee joint—and three would have the rinsing

alone, five would have no recognized surgical procedure at all. Their surgery would be a placebo, an exercise in just pretend.

> Moseley would stab the placebo patients' knees three times with a scalpel—to make it feel and look real, there had to be incisions and later, scars—but that was it.[46]

And the result of his study showed that all subjects—whether they got the real surgery or the fake surgery—had about the same amount of improvement after the procedure. Thus, a procedure that was being performed about 650,000 times a year, at a cost of $5,000 a pop—costing society over $3 billion annually—was ineffective. The pain relief was due to the patient's belief in the effectiveness of the treatment and not to the removal of tissues from inside the knee.

A common criticism of such studies is that they seem to expose subjects to inappropriately high levels of risk, given that the sham procedure they undergo is of no benefit to them.[47] But that criticism fails to draw a meaningful line between sham surgery and other types of procedures that are regularly permitted in research. As the previous chapters of this book have demonstrated, lots of things are done to research subjects solely for research purposes, and these things expose them to at least some harm. Some may be relatively low risk, such as getting being exposed to additional X-rays. But others have substantial, even life-threatening risks. Consider some of the studies discussed in chapter 5: exposing people with peanut allergies to injections of peanut flour; Nicole Wan undergoing a bronchoscopy; Michelle Payette getting injections of radioactive iodine.

No doubt we have a visceral reaction to someone's body being cut open, but that in itself doesn't mean that sham surgery is particularly high risk, or even any riskier that other nonbeneficial things done to people in research. Indeed, in the knee arthroscopy study, the actual "surgical" part of what happened to the placebo group —three half-inch incisions in the skin—was relatively benign. Which is not to say that all sham surgery has such low risk. The most controversial category of recent sham surgery studies involve attempts to treat patients with Parkinson's disease by treating the area in their brain that has been injured by the disease.[48] In one such study, the actual treatment being studied involved drilling holes through the skulls of the subjects and injecting fetal cells (obtained from aborted embryos) into the appropriate part of the brain.[49] For the placebo subjects, holes were drilled completely through the skulls, but the brain was not entered.

This obviously involves greater risks than in the knee surgery study, but perhaps the most important thing to note is that these risks are relatively well understood. Thus, sham surgery studies, like the studies where a person is given a placebo instead of standard care, enable us to have a relatively well-defined upper limit on the risks that subjects can be exposed to. The more difficult question is what that upper limit shall be, but that is a question that is not unique to sham surgery. Hopefully, over time, the federal regulations will be revised to put more specific limits on what are appropriate risks in sham surgery (and, indeed, in all research studies). For example, in both the knee study and the Parkinson's disease study, the subjects who got the sham surgery were not exposed to general anesthesia, which has very low but not insignificant risks of serious consequences, including death. In other Parkinson's disease sham surgery studies, the subjects *have* received general anesthesia. And in some of those studies, the sham surgery subjects have had catheters placed inside their brains for a period of months, to bathe the brain cells with a placebo solution instead of the growth hormone that was given to the "real surgery" subjects.

While we need to develop clearer and more uniform standards that are consistently applied to sham surgery studies, the ability to usually know the extent of the sham surgery risks ahead of time means that these studies should not be especially hard to conduct in an ethical manner. Being able to specify what the risks are makes it much easier to get truly meaningful informed consent: the subject can decide if they are willing to accept, for example, the 1-in-10,000 chance that they will die as a result of anesthesia, or the known consequences of having a hole drilled through their skull. The difficult part remains drawing a line between risks that can and cannot even be offered to subjects—what specific risks are we willing to let a person accept when there is no possibility of benefit to them? How do we determine the relationship of the importance of the research to the level of allowable risk? And these questions are no different than those for most other nonbeneficial things we do to subjects. It is important to remember—as our above discussion of clinical equipoise indicates—that it is often the risks we can't quantify ahead of time that are most troublesome. In the deepest sense, a subject can never knowingly consent to unknowable risks, and thus informed consent is least helpful there.

In the Parkinson's disease study where fetal cells were injected into the brains of subjects, it was eventually discovered that cells can grow too much and lead to uncontrollable movements. And since the cells were in the middle of a person's brain, there was no way to stop this side effect, as there might be if, for example, a person was getting an experimental drug. Here is how Dr. Paul E. Greene, a Columbia University researcher who helped conduct the study, described the "absolutely devastating" results to a *New York Times* reporter:

> "They chew constantly, their fingers go up and down, their wrists flex and distend," Dr. Greene said. And the patients writhe and twist, jerk their heads, fling their arms about.
>
> "It was tragic, catastrophic," he said. "It's a real nightmare. And we can't selectively turn it off."[50]

There is a somewhat ironic twist to what happened in this study. As is not uncommonly done in studies, once the new treatment is shown likely to be effective, subjects previously assigned to get placebo are often then permitted to get the real treatment. This is an option sometimes built into sham surgery studies, since it obviously makes recruiting subjects a great deal easier. In the Parkinson's disease study, fully 70% of the subjects who were assigned to get the sham surgery later asked to undergo implantation of the fetal cells. (At the time, the initial results of the study appeared to be promising.) None of the 20 subjects who received sham surgery appeared to suffer any serious side effects from that procedure. But of the five people who developed the "devastating" involuntary movements, two of them had been sham surgery subjects who opted to later get the real surgery.

Part II

Consent: What Are Subjects Told?

7

What Informed Consent Requires

In part I of this book, we showed that the current rules for human subjects research allow researchers to conduct studies that in many instances may not be in the best interests of a self-interested subject. Researchers are given relatively wide leeway, under the law, to do things to a subject that a doctor would not be permitted to do to a patient. Moreover, many of the studies that someone might think are generally good choices for a subject with a difficult-to-treat medical problem—clinical trials involving cutting-edge treatment—may in fact be rather bad choices.

What legitimates enrolling subjects in these bad choice studies? What makes it ethical to expose subjects to substantial risks so that society may add to medical knowledge? What is it that permits research subjects to be accorded substantially weaker legal protections than those given to patients? In most instances, the justification lies in the concept of *informed consent*: the idea that the subjects, after being given appropriate information, have voluntarily and freely *agreed* to be part of this dramatically altered legal regime. Informed consent, then, shoulders a great deal of weight: the legitimacy of much of our system of human subjects research in large part turns on how good a job we are doing in obtaining informed consent. Thus, in part II of this book, we now evaluate that important job. In the process, we also highlight the information a person should make sure to obtain before deciding to enroll in a study. And in several important respects, this will be the same type of information that all patients should be using in picking the best treatment options in the face of imperfect information about risks and benefits, even if they are not contemplating participation in a research study.

Decades of Change

As noted in the introduction, in 1966, a prominent professor at Harvard Medical School named Henry Beecher published a landmark article in the *New England Journal of Medicine*.[1] He was interested in examining whether studies involving human subjects were being conducted in an ethical manner. He came up with a method that, in retrospect, seems both obvious and brilliant: he merely read through a variety of recent medical journals, documenting various things he came across that appeared troublesome. The things he found were so troubling that in spite of being a well-known Harvard professor, he still had trouble convincing the *New England Journal* to publish his findings.[2] Indeed, to avoid possible legal problems, he ended up writing the article in a way that did not specifically identify the studies and who conducted them.

But his article, entitled "Ethics and Clinical Research," was nonetheless a bombshell—no doubt helped by his having contacted the major newspapers and television stations ahead of time and giving them a heads up on what his article would reveal. He documented a variety of studies that appeared to be "truly unethical" and that could be found just by leafing through recent journals. He described, for example, a study in which a treatment known to be effective for typhoid fever was denied to some charity patients: 22.9% of them died, compared to less than 8% of those who got the drug. In another study about human physiology, people undergoing minor surgery were exposed to enough carbon dioxide to cause ventricular arrhythmias lasting up to 90 minutes, with the risk of a stroke from reduced blood flow to the brain.

While Beecher documented a variety of ethical problems in the studies he described, the predominant problem he was concerned with was informed consent. He noted that among the 50 studies, only two even mentioned getting informed consent of the subjects. Some of them even specified that the subjects were *not* told what was happening to them; for example, in a study in which subjects were denied the best known method for preventing the development of rheumatic fever following a throat infection, "a medical officer stated in writing that the subjects were not informed, did not consent and were not aware that they had been involved in an experiment." More than 500 men were denied penicillin, and they ended up having a significantly higher rate of rheumatic fever, which could lead to life-threatening heart problems.

And even in the studies where it was never mentioned what efforts, if any, were used to get the informed consent of the subjects, Beecher concluded that, given the risks involved, it was highly unlikely that genuine informed consent had been obtained: "Ordinary patients will not knowingly risk their health or their life for the sake of 'science.' Every experienced clinical investigator knows this. When such risks are taken and a considerable number of patients are involved, it may be assumed that informed consent has not been obtained in all cases."[3]

Of course, Beecher's article was written at a time when there were no federal regulations requiring informed consent in research studies. Indeed, the concept of informed consent, even in the nonresearch setting, was still in its infancy. So, we might ask: *How much have things changed in the forty years since Beecher's landmark article?* In the current world of federal regulations, institutional review boards, and the threat of lawsuits, are we now doing a good job in terms of getting the informed consent of research subjects?

By any standard, it must be recognized there has been a *massive* change with regard to informed consent, and all for the better. The federal regulations require that in almost all studies involving some significant degree of risk, the subject has to agree to participate in the study after being given an appropriate amount of information about the study. Usually, that information has to be provided not just orally but also in the form of a written consent form, which the subject should be given time to read and ask questions about. The consent form is required to include specific categories of information, including a discussion of the benefits and risks relating to participating in the study, and the alternatives to participation. In retrospect, the problems that Beecher wrote about—people being enrolled in studies without their even knowing they were in a study—seem to be from a very different world.

Recognizing that we are now living in a world that properly imposes relatively demanding standards with regard to obtaining informed consent, our goal in this and the next three chapters is to explore how well the current system is complying with those standards. To be sure, the problems today relating to lack of informed consent are likely to be of substantially less importance than those that took place in Henry Beecher's day: then it was failure to even be told about a study, and today it is more likely to be failure to provide a particular piece of information about the study. Nonetheless, given the importance of informed consent in protecting the interests of prospective subjects, it is worth applying a critical eye to current practices.

And looking at the studies that have made national headlines at the turn of the twenty-first century, it is striking that in almost every case, one of the alleged problems has been the lack of adequate informed consent.[4] Such claims were made not just in the studies in which Jesse Gelsinger[5] and Ellen Roche[6] died, but also in studies involving having children in Baltimore live in homes contaminated with lead paint;[7] randomizing pregnant women likely to give birth to premature babies to two types of drug treatments;[8] giving people with malignant melanoma, an often-fatal form of skin cancer, an experimental vaccine;[9] using an artificial heart, where the patient's widow later said that "[h]e would have been better off dead";[10] and new treatments for leukemia and breast cancer studied at the world-renowned Fred Hutchinson Cancer Research Center.[11]

What do these headline-making events tell us about what is happening in research studies in general? The fact that only a handful of claims about inadequate consent have made the front pages of newspapers might be viewed as reassuring, given that millions of people are participating in research studies each year. To explore this issue further, in this and the following three chapters we attempt to evaluate the state of informed consent not for the headline-making studies, but rather for the run-of-the-mill study. In this chapter we attempt to lay out the legal rules behind the concept of informed consent, and in chapters 8–10 we apply those rules to determine how good a job we are routinely doing in getting informed consent that fully complies with the letter and spirit of those rules.

Our conclusions are not that reassuring: it appears that there are practices for obtaining consent that are commonly accepted, both by researchers and by government regulators, that lead to troubling "defects" in a substantial percentage of studies, likely involving hundreds of thousands of subjects.

The Legal Standards for Informed Consent

How do we determine what information subjects must be given in obtaining their informed consent? As we show in chapter 8, although the federal regulations spell out certain requirements—such as disclosing information about risks, benefits, and alternatives—the regulations are nonetheless relatively vague.[12] To truly understand what subjects need to be told, we again turn to tort law. As we have previously noted, tort law ends up playing a growing (and crucial) role in regulating research, since both the Nuremberg Code and the federal regulations do not themselves give any of us, as research subjects, a right to sue if we are injured or otherwise harmed while participating in a research study.[13] Only tort law provides that crucial protection.

There is relatively little specific guidance in tort law about the standards for getting informed consent of a person to participate in research.[14] Only a handful of states have passed any specific statutes dealing with this issue. And, until recently, there were few lawsuits brought against researchers, so the courts have had little opportunity to comment on these issues.[15] Thus, to explain what standards courts will likely apply (and *should* apply) as lawsuits begin to be brought against researchers, we need to initially turn to a related area of the law. We need to examine what is required in getting informed consent in the context of clinical medical care, outside of the research setting.[16] To do that, we'll undertake a brief historical tour of legal developments during the twentieth century.

If a patient went to a doctor in 1900, there probably wouldn't have been much of an attempt by the doctor to involve the patient in treatment decisions. Doctors were viewed as mysterious, godlike figures, and medical paternalism ruled the day: it was the doctor that made all the decisions. One of the first cracks in that edifice came in a 1914 lawsuit. In January of 1908, Mary Schloendorff had gone to New York Hospital suffering from a disorder of the stomach.[17] Ms. Schloendorff was told by her doctors that they had detected a lump inside her body. To better determine what kind of lump it was, she needed to undergo an examination under anesthesia (ether). She allegedly told the doctors that they could go ahead and do the examination, but that they were not to perform any operation. She wanted to hear the results of the examination before agreeing to any treatment of her condition. The examination did take place, and while she was under anesthesia, a fibroid tumor was surgically removed. As a result of the operation, she developed gangrene in her left arm, several fingers had to be amputated, and "her sufferings were intense."

The New York Court of Appeals determined that, if Ms. Schloendorff's account of what happened was true, she had indeed been wronged. Justice Cardozo's description of that wrong remains one of the most-quoted statements in American health law: "*Every human being of adult years and sound mind has a right to determine what shall be done with his own body; a surgeon who performs an operation without his patient's consent, commits an assault, for which he is liable in damages.*" But the *Schloendorff* case was only an early step toward recognizing what is currently understood as "informed consent." It didn't say anything about a doctor needing to give certain information to a patient before treating them. It merely determined that if a doctor performs an operation that he never got the patient's permission to do, then he is committing a type of tort (specifically, a battery—an unwanted "touching") and can be successfully sued by the patient. Of course, those stark facts are less frequently the case in most modern-day disputes about informed consent. A physician, we would hope, will rarely go ahead and do something without asking in one way or another for her patient's permission. Rather, the controversy these days is more likely to relate to the issue of *how informed* was the patient's consent to the treatment: was the patient given the appropriate information to enable an informed decision?

The law's movement from the simple concept of *consent* to the more complicated concept of *informed consent* took an additional forty years. In 1954, Martin Salgo was a very unhealthy 55-year-old who was increasingly being troubled by cramping pains in his legs that caused intermittent limping.[18] When he was examined at Stanford University Hospitals by a leading vascular surgeon, his calves and thighs were found to be atrophied with barely detectable pulses. His right leg was blue. Dr. Gerbode concluded that Mr. Salgo had serious circulatory problems including a likely blockage somewhere in his abdominal aorta, and he would probably need surgery to replace part of the aorta. To help determine the exact location of the blockage, the surgeon advised Mr. Salgo to undergo aortography, a procedure in which a radio-opaque dye is injected into his aorta and X-rays are taken. Mr. Salgo agreed to the procedure, and it took place without any apparent complications. However, when he awoke the next morning, he discovered that his legs were paralyzed.

In his subsequent malpractice lawsuit against his doctors and Stanford University, one of the issues raised on appeal related to the appropriate jury instructions about what he should have been told about the aortography test. Note that, under the *Schloendorff* test, it would be hard to conclude that the doctors done anything wrong: Mr. Salgo had said "yes" to undergoing aortography, and that is exactly what was done to him. However, the appellate judge created a duty to disclose that seemed to significantly extend prior law: "A physician violates his duty to the patient and subjects himself to liability if he withholds any facts which are necessary to form the basis of an intelligent consent by the patient to the proposed treatment." The judge said little more about what must be disclosed to meet this standard—noting merely that one need not disclose every risk, "no matter how remote," since that would unduly alarm the patient, and that "discretion" must be employed in disclosing risks, based upon a particular patient's "mental and emotional condition." Nonetheless, subject to that discretion, a physician was to provide a "full disclosure of facts necessary to an informed consent."

The *Salgo* case thus began what is currently understood as the modern doctrine of informed consent to medical care. And it is important to note the differences between the basic legal claim in the *Salgo* case—that the doctors behaved in a *negligent* way—and the battery claim in the *Schloendorff* case. In a battery claim, the only issue is whether a doctor did something that the patient had not given permission for. In contrast, in a negligence action, there is a new and more complicated issue— did the doctors disclose the *right amount* of information?[19]

What Negligence Law Teaches Us about Informed Consent

How does the law determine what is the right amount of information? Recall what we discussed in chapter 4 about malpractice law: negligence generally takes place when a doctor fails to adhere to the standard of care. And that standard is established by the medical profession. So, it would make sense that the standard for determining what information to provide a patient would also be set by the profession. Under that reasoning, a doctor performing gall bladder surgery would need to conform to the amount of disclosure to patients generally provided by other gall bladder surgeons, just as he would need to be guided by those colleagues in determining how to actually do the surgery.

What we have just described is often called the *professional standard* for determining the content of informed consent. This was the general rule for determining the contents of informed consent, at least until 1972. In that year, a landmark case suggested a new approach.[20] Jerry Canterbury had been a 19-year-old clerk-typist working for the FBI when he developed back pain. He ended up being referred to Dr. William Spence, a neurosurgeon in Washington, D.C., who ordered special tests. A myelogram, where X-rays were taken of Canterbury's spine after injecting him with a dye, indicated a "filling defect" in part of the spinal column. Dr. Spence determined that there was probably a ruptured disk and recommended spinal surgery—specifically, a laminectomy—to correct it. Canterbury agreed to the procedure. During the operation, Dr. Spence discovered a swollen spinal cord with unusual-looking blood vessels surrounding it. He made an attempt to release the pressure on the spinal cord by "enlarging the dura—the outer protective wall of the spinal cord—at the area of the swelling."

Although Canterbury appeared to be doing well during the first day after the operation, he subsequently discovered that he could not move his legs. He developed paralysis from his waist downward. While he later recovered some function, he ended up requiring crutches for walking, suffered from urinary incontinence that necessitated his use of a "penile clamp," and had "paralysis of the bowels." He sued Dr. Spence for malpractice, and lost that case. The trial judge noted that there was no evidence that Dr. Spence had been negligent in how he performed the surgery. As long as a doctor follows the appropriate standard of care, he is not negligent, even if there is a horrible outcome for the patient.

But there was a separate issue: was he perhaps negligent in how he obtained Canterbury's consent? The appellate court noted that Dr. Spence had failed to tell his patient that in any laminectomy operation, there is a small risk of paralysis, about one chance in 100. Note that under the then-existing standards for informed consent (the professional standard), Dr. Spence would have been under a duty to tell Canterbury about this fact only if other doctors were similarly conveying such information. There was no evidence that such was the case. But the court determined that the professional standard is not the right way to determine what information should be given to a patient. After all, it reasoned, the law allows members of a profession to establish the standard of care because they have the special expertise needed to determine what constitutes appropriate care.

But, as the court noted, no special training or skills are needed to determine what pieces of information a patient would need to know in deciding whether or not to undergo a particular medical treatment. Thus, the court created a new standard for disclosure, the so-called *reasonable patient* standard: the patient should be given the information that any reasonable patient, in those circumstances, would have wanted to know. In a malpractice trial, the decision on whether disclosure was appropriate could thus be determined by the judge or jury, based on their own views of what a patient would want to know. This was a dramatic change from what happened with the professional standard rule, where doctors would be brought into the courtroom as expert witnesses, and they would describe what information other doctors would commonly tell patients.

Sadly, this change did little for Jerry Canterbury. While it was later determined that he should have been told about the risk of paralysis, the court had also created a "causation" rule for determining when someone has been harmed as a result of not being told of a risk. Under that rule, the patient is considered to have been harmed only when a reasonable patient, had they been told the withheld information, would have decided not to undergo the operation. A court eventually concluded that, under this standard, a reasonable patient would have undergone the back surgery even if told of the rare risk of paralysis. It did not matter what Jerry Canterbury would have done with that piece of information (or even what he claimed he would have done), and so he still ended up losing the malpractice case.

The case of *Canterbury v. Spence* did, however, end up dramatically altering the landscape of informed consent law in this nation. Gradually, over time, more and more states—since as we have noted, tort law is state law, and its specific rules depend on the state you are in—ended up switching to the reasonable patient standard. Today, approximately half the states still follow the professional standard, and the other half follow some version of the standard created by the *Canterbury* court.[21]

From *Consent to Care* to *Consent to Research*

Let us now see if these concepts have any relevance not just to doctors taking care of patients, but researchers enrolling someone in a study. Although there are few court cases about research that give us much guidance,[22] does the basic tort law about informed consent in clinical care tell us what standards should apply for getting informed consent in research? In particular, should the law be holding researchers to merely a professional standard—one where they need only provide the information that other researchers would generally provide—or the more demanding standard of giving the information that a reasonable person considering enrolling in that research study would likely want to know?[23] The answer to this question could make a huge difference in the protections any of us will be given as research questions.

Oddly enough, there is no specific guidance on which, if either, of these two very different rules should be applied in interpreting the disclosure required under the federal regulations. One possible answer might be that the standard depends on the state in which the research is taking place, since the federal regulations defer to state law for other purposes (such as determining when a person is a legally authorized representative for another incompetent person).[24] But deferring to state law merely ducks the question, since even at the state level, we would have the same issue in terms of a particular state's tort law. For example, assume we were in a state that applied the professional standard for determining the contents of disclosure in the clinical care setting. Should that same rule necessarily also apply to the research setting? Given the paucity of court opinions discussing research issues, it is not surprising that virtually no court has addressed this issue.[25]

To help evaluate this issue, let's use as an example what happened in July of 1953, shortly after Daniel Burton was born prematurely in a Brooklyn hospital. At that time, there was a great deal of uncertainty about how best to treat premature infants. Half of such children typically died while they were infants, while many of the survivors had brain damage.[26] Many others suffered from a form of blindness, retrolental fibroplasia (now called retinopathy of prematurity). Since this form of blindness appeared to be becoming far more common after doctors started using aggressive new treatments to keep premature infants alive, questions arose whether some of the new treatments might themselves be causing the blindness. In particular, some doctors wondered whether giving infants high levels of oxygen might be playing a role. New York Hospital (coincidentally the same place where Ms. Schloendorff had been treated 45 years earlier), where Daniel was transferred shortly after his birth, had conducted its own small study that suggested that increased oxygen might indeed be the culprit. On the other hand, it was also felt that the oxygen helped these premature infants survive and avoid brain damage.

Dr. Lawrence Ross, the pediatric resident who was assigned to take care of Daniel, being familiar with the tentative results of the in-house study, wrote orders that Daniel's oxygen level should be gradually reduced if he appeared able to tolerate that. Daniel seemed to be doing fine, and his oxygen level was soon lowered, without any apparent problems developing. However, only two days after he was admitted to New York Hospital, that institution agreed to participate in a large randomized study in which premature infants in the study would be assigned to get either "low oxygen" or "high oxygen," in order to definitively find out if oxygen levels played a role in causing retrolental fibroplasia. Dr. Mary Engle, another member of the hospital staff, apparently following orders from the head of the Department of Pediatrics about finding babies to be in the study, had Daniel placed in the study. He was assigned to the "high oxygen" arm. This took place even though Dr. Engle was not directly involved in his care. His parents were not even told about any of this.

The results of the nationwide study became available in September of 1954, demonstrating that high levels of oxygen did indeed cause blindness and that reducing the level of oxygen to the lowest level that they appeared to need would eliminate the blindness problem yet not cause an increased risk of premature death or brain damage. This was too late for Daniel, who had developed retrolental fibroplasia within the first month of his life. He was totally blind, barely able to detect light in his left eye, and not even that in his right eye. As he grew up, his eyes became painful and began to shrink. To eliminate the pain, he would need to have both eyes surgically removed and replaced by prostheses.

When his malpractice lawsuit reached a New York appellate court in 1981, the court found in his favor, based on a lack of informed consent. But in reaching this decision, the court had to strain a bit: New York courts had not recognized any legal duty to obtain informed consent, even for standard medical care, until 1965, twelve years after the events in question. While this court nonetheless found that such a duty did exist in 1953, in part because New York Hospital had created its own internal standards for getting informed consent, the court's reasoning seems to be especially influenced by the unique consequences of what happens when someone is enrolled in a research study.[27]

One can't help suspecting that, at least in the nonresearch setting, informed consent was likely not very rigorously followed back in 1953. Thus, given that there was indeed substantial uncertainty about whether oxygen was good or bad for premature infants, what actually happened to most such children depended on the best guess of their pediatricians. One pediatrician might have chosen to give an infant high oxygen, figuring that failure to do so would have increased the risk that the child might die or develop brain damage. Another pediatrician, treating a child who appeared identical in all respects, might have looked at the tentative evidence about high oxygen levels and chanced that keeping the child on lowered oxygen would decrease the risk of blindness without otherwise harming the child. Both pediatricians were making educated guesses, and neither one could likely be found liable for committing malpractice, since there was a genuine dispute about what to do. But what happened to Daniel was in a sense worse than what would have happened to either of those children: as the court noted, by being enrolled in the study, Daniel was denied his physician's "best judgment" and "clinical knowledge."

Of course, we currently live in a world where informed consent is now a bedrock requirement, both in clinical care and in research. And it is now well recognized among commentators, albeit not yet much addressed in court cases, that informed consent is a *much more important concept* in the research setting than in the world of clinical care.[28] Participants in a research study are entering an arrangement where they are agreeing to give up many of the protections that they would have had as a patient, such as generally being assured of getting standard care. And they are agreeing to a situation where the person treating them is under a conflict of interest, doing some things to serve the research goals and not only the best interests of the patient.[29] Thus, a core feature of the federal regulations, and of virtually every international code of research ethics, is a very strict informed consent requirement: persons should be participating in a research study only if, after being given sufficient information, they make a voluntary and informed decision to forgo those usual protections and enter into this unique arrangement.

We normally hear about how important it is that a doctor treating a patient obtain that patient's informed consent. But in a sense, *compared to the research setting, informed consent to clinical care isn't all that important.* After all, even if there were no informed consent, the patient would end up getting standard care, the care that almost all patients get, the care that the medical profession has judged to be the best. Yes, it is possible that this patient may be the rare person who might have wanted to refuse standard care, who might have had some special concerns leading him or her to want a unique variation from standard care. These, however, are the *unusual* situations. Most of the time, even if the informed consent of the patient is not adequately obtained, what happens to the patient would be exactly what they would have wanted. In contrast, in the world of research, by definition we are *always* doing things to the patient that are, to a greater or lesser extent, a deviation from what would happen in clinical care. Thus, getting informed consent in most instances has to be the key to making a subject's participation permissible.[30]

The Importance of the "Reasonable Subject" Rule

What does this discussion tell us about the question we are trying to answer: what is the proper rule to apply in deciding what information to disclose to research subjects when obtaining their informed consent? Should we apply a professional standard or a reasonable person standard?

This is an easy question to answer: the appropriate standard for determining disclosure in the research setting should always be the reasonable person standard. Whatever justification the professional standard continues to have in the patient care setting—and that justification is itself rather shaky—that rule appears totally inappropriate in the research setting, given the huge consequences that turn on a person changing his or her role from that of a patient to that of a subject.

Imagine, for example, that the professional standard rule had been applied to Daniel Burton's situation, but those events took place in the present day. Suppose the researchers had told his parents about the randomized research study they proposed to enroll him in and had said that there were two methods of treating premature infants, noting that doctors weren't sure which was better. Suppose they *never* mentioned that there was a recent study done at that hospital suggesting it is reasonable to lower the oxygen level and that doing so would not have any bad effects on survival or brain development. Suppose they further *never* mentioned that doctors at the hospital, for infants who were not in the study, would opt for lowering the oxygen level.

Would this level of disclosure be acceptable? *Should* it be? As we show in the chapters that follow, when we explore in detail what information subjects are typically given these days, under the professional standard it would likely be perfectly acceptable for the researchers *not* to tell Daniel's parents about the recent study at that hospital or about how they would have treated him if he were not in the study. After all, under that standard, all that needs to be demonstrated is that such items of information are often *not* disclosed by well-trained researchers. And, in fact, that would not be very hard to demonstrate, even today (sad as it may be to admit). In contrast, under the reasonable subject standard, the question is more demanding: would reasonable parents want to know about the results of the recent study? Would they want to know about what the doctors *would have done* to the child if he weren't in the study?

As this example demonstrates, applying the professional standard to informed consent in the research setting ignores the key reasons why we have special rules governing research: that research subjects surrender the usual protections afforded to patients, that they agree to have things done to them for the benefit of others, that they permit the researchers to be acting in a way that creates a conflict of interest between the research goals and the goal of doing what it best for the patient. Giving the researchers the ability to control the content of disclosure in effect creates the position of the "fox guarding the henhouse." Without denying that researchers are genuinely concerned about the welfare of their subjects, we can nonetheless also acknowledge that, given their conflicting interests, they are not in the best position to be determining the content of disclosure. And if the reader is not yet convinced, we will provide example after example in the next several chapters of current consent practices that are common—and thus would be perfectly acceptable under a professional standard—and yet that the average person would find troubling.

On the other hand, are there any good arguments against using the reasonable subject rule, a rule that works quite well in the nonresearch setting? Imagine that, in a particular case, there is general agreement that the average subject would indeed want to know a particular piece of information, for example, in the New York Hospital situation, the fact that doctors were then treating premature infants with lower oxygen levels. Is there any justification for *not* giving that information to subjects?

Not giving them information that they would want under conditions where we acknowledge that there is a special duty to make sure consent is truly informed smacks of hypocrisy. In point of fact, failing to disclose information in the face of a clear duty to do so, with the intent to have a subjects enroll when they might otherwise not have done so, deserves an appropriate label: this is *fraud*, plain and simple. It has no place in the world of medical research, in a system with high ethical aspirations.

Thus, the reasonable subject standard clearly is the appropriate one for determining the proper scope of disclosure. And in using it, we need to remember that we are actually not applying an especially rigorous standard. After all, in more than half the U.S. states, this is already the same standard that is applied in getting consent to everyday medical care, a scenario in which informed consent plays a much less demanding role. Yet, as we show in chapters 8–10, current standards for informed consent regularly fail to meet even this relatively undemanding criterion.

8

The Anatomy of a Consent Form

What we've got here is failure to communicate.
—*Cool Hand Luke*

In the space of a few weeks during separate discussions with two of this nation's leading bioethicists, both prominent figures in research ethics, I (JM) each time heard comments to the effect that, "Of course, consent forms are to a large extent irrelevant." This is part of the new approach coming from many in the research ethics community: getting informed consent is a *process*, involving not just the consent form, but also discussions (sometimes extensive) between the subject and the investigators, designed to help the subject understand what will happen to him if he decides to participate in the study. Under this view, the consent form is a relatively *minor* element of this process, and perhaps even irrelevant.[1] As one of these experts noted, it is the integrity of the investigator that ultimately protects the subject, not the consent form.

While encouraging researchers to engage in a more extensive discussion of consent issues with subjects is surely important, the newly popular notion that the consent form is a *minor* part of this process is troubling. For if the purpose of the informed consent process is to give a prospective subject certain information—the type of information that, under the legal standard we laid out in chapter 7, a reasonable person would want to know before making a decision to participate—how can we best assure that the subject was indeed given that information? While we could record and later analyze the actual discussions between researchers and their prospective subjects, that would be a costly and time-intensive process that few institutions have the ability to undertake.

In our society, we routinely use written documents as an efficient means by which to accomplish two important purposes: to *convey* information and to *verify* that someone entering into a transaction was given the required information. Imagine you were

94

buying a new house and had to reach an agreement with a bank about the mortgage and with the seller about the terms of sale. How comfortable would you be if the banker and the seller asked that you merely shake on the deal—after all, they tell you, they are both people of high integrity—and that there was no need to put anything in writing? In the United States, we frequently put important things in writing: that is the major way we verify, before two people agree to a joint undertaking, that both of them have a similar understanding of what is going to happen. The written document embodies that understanding, the so-called "meeting of the minds." In legal terms, we are talking about *the law of contracts*, a foundational element of our legal system and one of the first concepts taught to first-year law students.

In the world of standard medical care, contract law doesn't actually play that much of a role.[2] As we showed in part I, tort law substantially ties the hands of doctors, protecting patients by forcing doctors in most cases to give them standard care. Thus, to a large extent, there really isn't a great deal for the doctor and patient to bargain over, and there's not much need for a contract to be signed. Consistent with this notion, the type of consent form used in clinical care, such as for a surgical operation, is usually a "boilerplate" document, often only a single page, with blanks for filling in the name of the doctor performing the procedure and the name of the procedure to be performed. The rest of that page consists of a variety of legal warnings, none of which are unique to the specific procedure to be performed.

Contract law becomes important in such circumstances mainly when the doctor and patient have intentionally chosen to *depart* from standard care. A good example of this is the odd-but-true "Case of the Hairy Hand,"[3] a staple of the first day of many law school contracts courses, as immortalized in a scene from *The Paper Chase*:

> Professor Kingsfield picked a name from the seating chart. . . .
>
> Without turning, he said crisply, "Mr. Hart, will you recite the facts of *Hawkins versus McGee?*"
>
> When Hart, seat 259, heard his name, he froze. Caught unprepared, he simply stopped functioning. Then he felt his heart beat faster than he could ever remember its beating and his palms and arms break out in sweat. . . .
>
> His voice floated across the classroom: "I . . . I haven't read the case. I only found out about it just now."
>
> Kingsfield walked to the edge of the platform.
>
> "Mr. Hart, I will myself give you the facts of the case. *Hawkins versus McGee* is a case in contract law, the subject of our study. A boy burned his hand by touching an electric wire. A doctor who wanted to experiment in skin grafting asked to operate on the hand, guaranteeing that he would restore the hand 'one hundred per cent.' Unfortunately, the operation failed to produce a healthy hand. Instead, it produced a hairy hand. A hand not only burned, but covered with dense matted hair."[4]

As Professor Kingfield's comments suggest, contract law is relevant in this case precisely because the doctor *departed* from standard care. Absent that departure, contract law would have been largely irrelevant to the outcome: the doctor would have provided whatever care doctors generally gave for this type of injury. Assuming he did it competently, the boy would not have been able to get any damages from him, regardless of how the hand turned out.[5] But in this case, the doctor and the boy entered into a special agreement, and the rules of contract law played a major role in determining how this agreement would be interpreted and enforced.

In a similar way, contract law concepts become very relevant in the setting of a research study precisely because the person who participates in a research study is *always* agreeing to have at least some things happen to herself—some "research procedures," broadly defined (which may range from merely recopying data on the patient's clinical outcome in research log books, to doing a brand-new form of major surgery)—that are a departure from what would otherwise have taken place. The spelling out of what these differences are, and a subject's agreement to submit to them, is very much like entering into a contract. And where, if not in the consent form, would there be documentation of *exactly what* the subjects agreed to have done to them?[6] In the clinical setting, such a document is far less necessary, since we already generally know that the patient is going to get standard care.[7] But as we showed in part I, research subjects surrender at least part of the usual set of legal protections that they would benefit from as patients. So it is especially important that there be documentation of exactly what it is that the subject is agreeing to and that both the subject and the researcher have a common understanding of what will happen.

In the end, however, much importance is put on the "process" of obtaining informed consent; presumably, there is certain specific information that should be conveyed during that process. Where, if not in the consent form, do we lay out what that information is? Those who discount the importance of the consent form fail to provide any answer. It is as if the actual content of what the subject gets told does not matter, and the only important thing is that the researcher has integrity: "Trust me," she says. Which is a puzzling point of view, given that the whole point of the research study is to do something that involves a *departure* from doing everything solely for the patient's benefit. Trust her to do *what*? What are the terms of this agreement between research and subject: what does the contract say will be done? It can't be to *only* do what is best for the patient.

It is for that reason that the federal regulations generally require a special consent form to be prepared for each study, spelling out various details regarding what will happen in that study. The major pieces of information that must be disclosed under the regulations are as follows:

- A statement that the study involves research
- An explanation of the purposes of the research
- A description of the procedures to be followed
- Identification of any procedures that are "experimental"
- A description of any reasonably foreseeable *risks* or discomforts to the subject
- A description of any *benefits* to the subjects or to others that may reasonably be expected from the research

 • A disclosure of appropriate *alternative* procedures or courses of treatment, if any, that might be advantageous to the subject[8]

While, as previously noted, the regulations might be criticized for being vague, at least they appropriately recognize that the information needs to be conveyed in writing, in a consent form.

The National Cancer Institute (NCI) has itself correctly described such consent forms as "the foundation" of the consent form process.[9] Admittedly, there is evidence that these forms currently play a relatively small role in the decision-making process of many people who decide to enter research studies.[10] But that in itself is likely a reflection not of the futility of conveying important information through a form, but rather of how poorly currently used consent forms are written (as we try to demonstrate below).[11] There is no reason to think that the concept of using written documents both to convey information and to provide an easily verified objective record of what people have agreed to, a key element of modern society, somehow becomes unworkable when it comes to asking someone to participate in a research study. Printed words, appropriately chosen and highlighted, matter.[12] And so, in this chapter and in chapters 9 and 10, we turn to an examination of what consent forms commonly *do* tell subjects, and what, based on the applicable legal standards laid out in chapter 7, they *should* tell subjects.

Communicating the Truth about What Research Involves

You have the right to remain silent. Anything you say can and will be
used against you. . . .
—The *Miranda* warning

Some doctors view the process of obtaining the informed consent of a patient as if they are being forced to give a "medical" version of the *Miranda* warning used by police before interrogating suspects. Critics of this approach have correctly noted how wrong this is. Getting informed consent to *treatment* should not be viewed as if there is an adversarial relationship between doctor and patient: on the contrary, the two parties are working together toward a single goal, that of making the patient feel better.[13]

When dealing with a person contemplating entry into a research study, however, the analogy to the *Miranda* warning actually makes a lot of sense. The *Miranda* warning came about because of the U.S. Supreme Court's determination that a suspect being interrogated by a police officer might not fully realize that talking to the police can be harmful, and that the best thing might be to shut up and wait until a lawyer arrives. In other words, in spite of what common sense might tell us—that even the dumbest suspect should know that the police are pursuing their own goals, and those goals are diametrically opposed to the suspect's goals (staying out of jail)—our society has erred in favor of scrupulously protecting the legal rights of the suspects.

Compare this set of concerns to the research setting. As we have shown, the main reason there are special regulations relating to research is precisely because the researcher has a conflict of interest: the researcher is pursuing a goal, that of answering a research question, that may conflict with the best interests of a patient who is also a research subject. Patients would normally expect that everything their health care provider is doing has the primary purpose of treating their medical condition: in the research setting, this is not going to be the case.

Thus, just as it makes sense for a person arrested by the police to be warned—in a clear, explicit, and formal manner—that the police are not going to be doing everything possible to protect her legal rights, so it similarly might make sense to warn someone contemplating entering a research study that the researcher's primary goal will not always completely coincide with that of doing what is best for the patient. Indeed, such a warning is *even more necessary*, given that the health care setting is one where—unlike the suspect confronting a police officer—*the patient has every reason to believe her well-being is the number one priority of the doctor*. And it would not be that hard to include such a warning, perhaps in bold red print, at the beginning of consent forms for research studies. Such a warning might read something like this:

> This is a research study. It is important that you understand what that means. In general, when a doctor treats you as a patient, the doctor is required to always be doing what is best for you. But the primary purpose of a research study is to find the answer to a particular research question. If you participate in a research study, your well-being will come second to trying to answer the research question. In other words, if you participate in this research study, the doctors will no longer be required to always do what is best for you. Some things will be done to you that may not be in your best interests. Among these things are:
>
> [Mention specific aspects of study, such as randomization, extra tests, need to adhere to protocol, nondisclosure of interim results, etc.]
>
> It may still be in your best interests, overall, for you to enroll in this study, depending on what your other options are. Or you might nonetheless want to participate in this study out of a desire to help others, by helping the advance of medical knowledge, even if being in this study isn't in your own best interests.
>
> This study has been designed, and will be conducted, in a manner so as to make sure that risks are not unnecessarily imposed on you. But it has not been designed to eliminate those risks, risks that are being imposed on you not to help you but rather to help answer a research question. In deciding to be in this study, you should understand and think about the important difference between being a patient and being a participant in a research study. You should carefully evaluate your other options before deciding to participate in this study.

But you'll virtually never see that type of language in a consent form. In the rest of this chapter, we try to give a sense of what *is* found in the average consent form.

Dissecting a Gold Standard Consent Form

How well, then, do consent forms nonetheless convey the important information about what is happening in a research study? To allow you to judge for yourself, we include an example of what is clearly one of the best consent forms currently being used. The National Cancer Institute (NCI) put together a group of experts to study how best to write consent forms. It ended up producing very explicit directions on how consent forms should be written for cancer studies. In addition, it gave several examples of consent forms, one of which we have reproduced in the appendix at the end of this chapter (page 105).

At the outset, it should be noted that the NCI model consent forms are vast improvements over the sorts of consent forms used in the past. Indeed, they still are much better than a large percentage of other consent forms currently used. Thus, by examining this form, you are looking at an example of state-of-the-art in terms of consent forms. Ideally, to give you a sense of the *full* spectrum of consent forms being used, we would let you read a wide variety of consent forms currently being used and let you decide for yourself how good a job they are doing. As lawyers, it seems to us that a substantial percentage of the forms being prepared by researchers and study sponsors (e.g., drug manufacturers) today don't disclose the information the law requires—the information that a reasonable person would want to know. There are a wide array of problems, ranging from failing to disclose that randomization is taking place in the study to failing to describe what standard care is and how being treated in the study differs from standard care, to probably the most common (but far from least significant) failing, writing a consent form that is mind-bogglingly dense and incomprehensible to anyone other than the person who designed the study. To let you see that we are not making this all up, we would ideally refer you to hundreds of web pages where you could see these various types of problematic (but very real) consent forms.

But that is, surprisingly, hard for us to do—which is actually somewhat odd. The government, pharmaceutical companies, universities, and researchers all are actively engaged in trying to get more people to sign up for studies. With the Internet, they make a great deal of information available about such studies. They *want* people to know a lot about their studies, so that they will think about enrolling in them. There are web sites that list tens of thousands of trials, such as www.centerwatch.com (on behalf of the clinical trials industry) and www.clinicaltrials.gov (on behalf of the federal government). However, the thing you will rarely find on the web is the one document specifically designed to give someone almost all the information they need to know before agreeing to be in the study: the consent form for the study. And while we could reprint lots of consent forms on our own pages on the web (since putting them in this book would no doubt make your purchase price far too high), it is far from clear that the law would let us do that without getting the permission of the people who wrote those consents forms. Those people would perhaps not be happy to have this type of extra publicity for the consent forms they are using.

And so, we will have to make do with a few examples, beginning in this chapter with that much-better-than-average NCI form,[14] a copy of which appears at the end of this chapter. The study it describes is for women with breast cancer that has spread (metastasized) outside of the breast. A woman participating in the study would be randomized between two treatments: (a) a type of standard care, namely, getting two drugs commonly used as chemotherapy for breast cancer (doxorubicin and cyclophosphamide); or (b) those same two drugs, plus a newer anticancer drug called Taxol.[15] Given what we know about why there are special rules to protect research subjects, let us ask some basic questions about how well this form satisfies the reasonable subject standard for disclosure.

What Research Is About

The NCI consent form begins by forthrightly telling the subject that this is a research study. Indeed, the federal regulations require that this fact be disclosed.[16] But note what it does *not* say: it does not provide *any* information to the subject explaining what it means to be in a research study, or how it differs from getting care outside of a research study. In other words, regarding all of the issues discussed in part I of this book—the dramatic legal changes that take place in what can be done to a research subject as compared to a patient—essentially nothing is said.

Earlier in this chapter we provided a hypothetical warning that a consent form might include, briefly letting the subject know about these key issues in three or four paragraphs. What we said there bears repeating here: you won't ever find this sort of disclosure in consent forms.[17] It is not in the NCI consent form. All that matters, according to both the federal regulations and common practices in writing consent forms, is that the subject be told that they are being invited into a research study, as if the difference between being a patient and being a research subject is obvious to anyone.

Specific Aspects of the Study That Might Be Disadvantageous to the Subject

Being in a study involves having things done to you that are not done primarily for your benefit. Some of these things may, in fact, harm you. How well does the NCI consent form disclose these specific possibilities?

Extra Tests

In the paragraph on page 105, under the heading "Medical Tests," the consent form discusses the medical tests that will be done to the subject. It points out that "they are routine." Note the possible misinterpretation by the potential subject: that these are exactly the same tests that would be performed as part of taking care of the subject's illness. But that is not what "they are routine" always means in this context: the phrase is sometimes merely used to reassure the patient that these are the sorts of well-established tests that are done to patients (not specifically to patients with this medical problem) for some purpose or other, as opposed to being some brand-new type of test that the doctors cooked up just for this study. It does *not* always mean that each of these tests would have been performed on the subject as part of standard care.

Further below under the "Medical Tests" heading, the form does point out that some of these tests may be done more frequently than would be the case if the subject merely got standard care. It does not bother to say which tests it is referring to, or how many "extra" times they will be given. What it also does not point out is that the extra testing may be taking place solely to give the researchers extra information to answer the research question, as opposed to taking better care of the subject. The potential subject is left to guess which of these is true. In addition, the point that extra testing might be harmful to the subject—extra radiation exposure (from a mammogram, a bone scan, a MUGA scan, a chest X-ray), extra pain, the risk of something going wrong (e.g., an allergic reaction from a drug given to the patient in one of these studies)—is not mentioned. Indeed, even in section titled "What Are the Risks of the Study?" that appears later on in this form and is supposed to discuss such risks, there is no mention of any of this.

Randomization

In the section on page 106, "Randomization (Assignment to a Group)," the form does clearly describe what happens in randomization. It does not state, however, why the subject should perhaps be concerned about having the treatment chosen by randomization. A fuller disclosure might tell potential subjects, for example, that if they are very concerned about doing all they can to wipe out the cancer and are willing to risk unnecessary side effects, it would make sense to choose to get Taxol plus the chemotherapy outside of the study; or, vice versa, if they are especially concerned about minimizing the side effects from treatments, they might wish to avoid the study and just get standard chemotherapy, without the Taxol. In other words, essentially no guidance is provided to the potential subject about possible reasons for preferring one treatment to the other.

Adherence to Protocol

Not a word is mentioned anywhere in the consent form about the fact that, in treating the subject, the doctors will no doubt have to follow a set of instructions (the protocol) that limit what they can do in terms of varying the treatments; in other words, their hands are tied somewhat in terms of otherwise being able to do what might be best for a particular patient.

Admittedly, protocols will build into their procedures some permitted changes when it appears that doing something will be harmful to a particular subject. But, in the end, that is far from complete protection. Following a protocol, as opposed to doing what a doctor, in her own best judgment, might have thought best for the patient can lead to very different outcomes.[18] A protocol may, for example, specify a particular (high) dose of a drug that a subject is to be given. The subject may have a bad reaction to that drug, a reaction that causes permanent medical problems. Thus, the possibility of altering what treatments a subject gets after a problem develops isn't always all that helpful.

Interim Results

In the final sentence under "What Are My Rights as a Participant?" on page 110, the form indicates that subjects will be told about "new information" resulting from the study that may affect the subjects' health or their "willingness to stay on this study." In fact, this sort of paragraph—commonly labeled a "New Information" section—appears in most consent forms.

This language paradoxically seems to be incorrectly reassuring the potential subject and giving a highly deceptive picture of the true state of affairs regarding one especially important type of new information: things that are learned from the initial stages of this very study. In most studies, while such interim results will indeed be examined from time to time by an independent committee (commonly called a data and safety monitoring board), that committee will in general *not* terminate the study or authorize telling the subjects what the interim results are, unless those results are extraordinarily remarkable in demonstrating that one arm of the study is better than the other. Thus, in the usual case, even if there is relatively strong evidence that one arm is better than the other, the subjects will *not* be told of this. The study will normally be continued until the appropriate level of statistical significance has been reached.[19]

An example may be helpful.[20] Imagine that a randomized study is comparing a new drug to the current "standard care" drug for preventing people from dying from some deadly disease (e.g., some degenerative neurologic disorder). The study will take four years, and during that time subjects will not know if they are on the new drug or standard care. The usual "cut-off" point for determining statistical significance of a result is when the "p-value" (probability) is less than the 0.05 point; in other words, to be relatively sure that one of the drugs is better than the other, scientists traditionally require a high level of proof, meaning that there should only be 1 chance in 20 (or 0.05) that the evidence from the study might be due to chance, as opposed to being due to a real difference between the two drugs. Another way to say this is that we require 95% certainty (19 chances out of 20) that the evidence from the study demonstrates a real difference.

Imagine also that the study has run for two years and that half of the eventual number of subjects have been recruited and have been participating in the study. An interim analysis of the study's results thus far is done by the monitoring committee, and it demonstrates that the new drug A seems to be better than the old drug B, but this is only with a p-value of 0.10—only 90% certain; in other words, the difference between the two drugs has not reached the level of statistical significance (0.05) needed to appropriately demonstrate that one is better than the other.[21] We haven't yet reached the 95% level that we aim for in proving a difference between two drugs, but we are very close. Common sense would tell us that proof of drug A's superiority over drug B (i.e., the likelihood that we will reach that 95% level if the trial continues to the end) is looking very likely at this point: if we were at the race course, we'd no doubt be betting on drug A.

But the rules of statistics often override common sense. Based on those rules, there is still an excellent chance—more than an 83% chance—that by the end of the completed study, the result will be that *neither drug is shown superior to the other*. In fact, here are the odds on the three possible outcomes, if the study is conducted till the bitter end:

- A is proven better than B (at the required 95% certainty level): 16.9%
- B is proven better than A (at the required 95% certainty level): 0.002%
- Neither drug is proven better: 82.9%

These numbers tell us, on the one hand, how important it is, from the point of view of medical knowledge, to continue the study until the end: even though A was look-ing much better than B at the halfway point, that result will change most of the time, and it will usually be shown by the end of the study that there is no difference be-tween the drugs. From the viewpoint of society, it would be very wasteful to switch perhaps thousands of future patients to drug A, which is likely much more expen-sive than the old drug B, if drug A is not any better than drug B.

On the other hand, if you are a patient, trying to get the best drug (particularly if the study is about some life-or-death condition, and thus there is only one shot at being treated), and you learned about these results at the halfway point, you would be foolish not to want drug A. The chance that drug B is going to be proven to be better than drug A is 2 out of 100,000, similar to the chance that someone would win the lottery, whereas drug A has about a 1 in 6 chance of being proven better than drug B. Choosing drug A over drug B is an extraordinarily good bet. (How often have you turned down a bet where the odds were more than 8,000 to 1 in your favor?[22]) If we revealed these interim results to the participants, and if the new drug was available outside of the study, obviously a large number of them would drop out of the study to make sure they are getting the new drug, and thus we would never determine if either drug is better.[23]

What makes this state of affairs both ethical and legal is that the subjects have presumably *consented* to not being told this information.[24] But where, exactly, does this disclosure show up in consent forms? If you read through the consent form for the NCI breast cancer study, you will see that there is no language suggesting any-thing about not being told interim results from the study. To the contrary, the only relevant language would appear to be in the "What Are My Rights as a Participant?" section, which says, "A Data Safety and Monitoring Board, an independent group of experts, will be reviewing the data from this research throughout the study. We will tell you about new information from this board or other studies that may affect your health, welfare, or willingness to stay on this study." Not only does this lan-guage *not* provide the warning that would make this practice ethical, but it appears to do *just the opposite*: to affirmatively commit the researchers to disclosing interim results that, if patients knew about them, might affect their willingness to be in the study. Thus, the consent form appears to actively deceive the subjects, incorrectly reassuring them of something (being told of interim results) that will in fact usually *not* happen.

Appendix: National Cancer Institute
Sample Consent Form

Reproduced on pages 105 through 112 is one of the sample consent forms that accompanied the 1998 report produced by the National Cancer Institute's group of experts.[25]

A RANDOMIZED TRIAL EVALUATING THE WORTH OF TAXOL FOLLOWING DOXORUBICIN (ADRIAMYCIN)/CYCLOPHOSPHAMIDE (CYTOXAN) IN BREAST CANCER

This is a clinical trial (a type of research study). Clinical trials only include patients who choose to take part. Please take your time to make your decision. Discuss it with your friends and family.

You are being asked to take part in this research study because your breast cancer has spread to one or more of your underarm lymph nodes.

WHY IS THIS STUDY BEING DONE?

> The purpose of this research study is to find out whether adding the drug Taxol (paclitaxel) to a commonly-used chemotherapy is better than the commonly-used chemotherapy by itself at preventing your cancer from coming back. The study also will see what side effects there are from adding Taxol to the commonly-used chemotherapy.
>
> Taxol has been found to be effective in treating patients with advanced breast cancer. In this study, we want to see whether Taxol will be a useful addition to the treatment of patients with early-stage breast cancer and to see whether the side effects seem to be worth the possible benefit.

HOW MANY PEOPLE WILL TAKE PART IN THE STUDY?

> About 2,450 people will take part in this study.

WHAT IS INVOLVED IN THE STUDY?

> Please refer to the diagram on page [112].
>
> **Medical tests:**
> The following tests must be done to make sure that you are eligible for this study. None of these tests are experimental. They are routine. Depending on when you last had them, you may need to repeat some of these tests:
> • Mammogram
> • Blood tests
> • Chest x-ray
> • Gynecologic exam
> • Electrocardiogram
> • Bone scan
> • A special x-ray to study the heart (MUGA scan)

Many of the tests will also be repeated during the study. If you participate in this study, some of these tests may be done more frequently than if you were not taking part in this research study.

Procedures (treatment):
If you are eligible and agree to take part in this study, you will get two commonly-used chemotherapy drugs called Adriamycin (doxorubcin) and Cytoxan (cyclophosphamide).

These drugs will be given into your vein while you are in the doctor's office or clinic every 21 days for 4 visits. The procedure will take about 2 hours. The doses of the drugs may be changed if you have side effects. You will not need to be hospitalized unless you have serious side effects.

If you are older than 50, you will also take tamoxifen pills daily for 5 years. If you are younger than 50, you will get tamoxifen if your tumor has a positive estrogen or progesterone (ER/PR) hormone receptor test.

The Adriamycin and Cytoxan plus tamoxifen are usual treatments that would likely be given whether or not you are on this study.

Randomization (assignment to a group):
After completing the chemotherapy with Adriamycin and Cytoxan, you will be randomized to one of the study groups. Randomization means that you are put into a group by chance. It is like the flip of a coin, and assignment is done by a computer. Neither you nor the researcher choose what group you will be in. You will have an equal chance to be placed in either group.

> Group 1: Does not get Taxol.

> Group 2: Gets Taxol
> > Taxol is given by vein over 3 hours in the clinic or doctor's office every 21 days for 4 visits.

HOW LONG WILL I BE IN THE STUDY?

Your chemotherapy will last 4 to 8 months and the tamoxifen therapy will last for 5 years. Every 6 months you will come in for follow-up blood tests. We would like to keep track of your medical condition for the rest of your life to look at the long-term effects of the study. The researchers can take you off the study early for reasons such as:
• The treatment does not work in your cancer.
• Your health gets worse.
• You are unable to meet the requirements of the study (for example, you do not return for follow-up visits).

WHAT ARE THE RISKS OF THE STUDY?

While on the study, you are at risk for these side effects. Most of them are listed in this form, but they will vary from person to person. There may be other side effects that we cannot predict. Other drugs will be given to make the side effects less serious and uncomfortable.

Many side effects go away shortly after the drugs are stopped, but in some cases, side effects may be serious and/or long-lasting or permanent. Some may be life-threatening. Talk with the researcher about this. You may also want to talk to your regular doctor and/or read more about the drugs on the sheets attached to this form.

Reproductive risks: You should **not** become pregnant while on this study. You should not nurse your baby while on this study. Also, some of the drugs may cause sterility (make you unable to have children in the future). Ask for more information if this applies to you.

Side effects of treatment:
Groups 1 and 2
Adriamycin and Cytoxan (commonly-used chemotherapy)

Very likely:
- Lowered white blood count that may lead to an infection
  (If you get an infection or your white blood count becomes very low, you will get daily shots of G-CSF (Neupogen). G-CSF helps your white blood cells multiply to fight infections. Some patients get pain in their bones with the G-CSF.)
- Lowered platelets count which may lead to an increase in bruising or bleeding
  (If count gets too low, you may need platelet transfusions.)
- Lowered red blood cells count may cause anemia, tiredness, shortness of breath
  (If count gets too low, you may need blood transfusions.)
- Nausea, vomiting, or diarrhea
- Complete hair loss
- Skin and nail discoloration
- Irregular or permanent stoppage of menstrual cycles
- Mouth sores
- Time away from work

Less likely:
- Blood in the urine
- Heart damage (very rare at these doses)
- Irregular heart beat (may occur right after drug is given)
- Skin damage due to leakage of drug
- Acute leukemia (very rare at these doses)

Tamoxifen (part of commonly used anticancer drug regimen):
While on Tamoxifen you should have an annual pelvic exam. If you have abnormal vaginal bleeding, pelvic discomfort (pressure or pain), or other changes, report this to your regular doctor or the researcher as soon as possible. These might be related to changes in the uterus. Changes to the lining of the uterus can sometimes turn into a cancer of the uterus.

Very likely:
• Hot flashes
• Vaginal dryness or discharge

Less likely:
• Eye problems, increased risk of developing cataracts (clouding of eye)
• Uterine cancer
• Ovarian cysts or endometriosis (spillage of uterine cells outside the uterus)
• Blood clots (may be life-threatening)
• Inflammation of the liver

Side effects of the study drug (Taxol):
Group 2 only

Taxol
Many of these side effects occur with Adriamycin and Cytoxan that you will already have received as part of the commonly-used chemotherapy. This study will determine whether Taxol increases the severity of these side effects.

Also, three drugs will be given before the Taxol to control an allergic reaction that might occur. These are:
• A steroid similar to cortisone (dexamethasone [Decadron])
  (A brief, vaginal tingling sensation is possible when this drug is given.)
• An antacid (metoclopramide [Reglan]).
• An antihistamine (diphenhydramine [Benadryl]).

Very likely:
• Lowered white blood count may lead to an infection.
• Lowered platelets may lead to an increase in bruising or bleeding.
• Lowered red blood cells may lead to anemia, tiredness, or shortness of breath.
• Nausea, vomiting, or diarrhea
• Complete hair loss
• Irregular menstrual cycles or permanent menstrual stoppage
• Numbness or tingling in fingers or toes
• Pain in muscles and joints

Less likely:
- Allergic reactions (may happen during injection)
- Inflammation of pancreas and large bowel
- Irregular heart beat
- Inflammation of the liver

For more information about risks and side effects, ask the researcher or your regular doctor or contact _____.

ARE THERE BENEFITS TO TAKING PART IN THE STUDY?

There may or may not be direct medical benefits to you from taking part in this study. The expected benefit of taking part in the study is predicted to be similar to that of getting commonly-used chemotherapy without being in the study. Although Taxol has been shown to be effective in women with advanced breast cancer, it is unknown whether the addition of Taxol to commonly-used chemotherapy will improve the outcome for women with less advanced breast cancer.

The information learned from this study should help future patients with breast cancer.

WHAT OTHER OPTIONS ARE THERE?

Instead of being in this study, you have these options:
- Chemotherapy with Adriamycin and Cytoxan
- Chemotherapy with other drugs that are as effective as Adriamycin and Cytoxan
- Tamoxifen
- No chemotherapy

Discuss these options with your regular doctor.

WHAT ABOUT CONFIDENTIALITY?

Efforts will be made to keep your personal information confidential. We cannot guarantee absolute confidentiality. Your personal information may be disclosed if required by law.

Organizations that may inspect and/or copy your research records for quality assurance and data analysis include groups such as:
- The National Cancer Institute
- The Food and Drug Administration
- The National Surgical Adjuvant Project for Breast and Bowel Cancer
- Bristol-Myers Squibb Company, which is providing the study drug Taxol without charge

What Are the Costs?

Taking part in this study may lead to added costs to you or your insurance company. Please ask about any expected added costs or insurance problems.

In the case of injury or illness resulting from this study, emergency medical treatment is available but will be provided at the usual charge. No funds have been set aside to compensate you in the event of injury. You will be charged for continuing medical care and/or hospitalization at the usual rate.

You will receive no payment for taking part in this study. You may be charged for the drugs other than Taxol that are used in this study. The researcher will explain the policy at this institution.

What Are My Rights as a Participant?

Taking part in this study is voluntary. Your decision about taking part in the study will not affect your medical care at this institution.

If you agree to take part and then decide against it, you can withdraw for any reason. If you decide to stop taking part in the study, you should talk to the researcher so it can be done safely. Leaving the study will not result in any penalty or lost benefits to which you are otherwise entitled.

A Data Safety and Monitoring Board, an independent group of experts, will be reviewing the data from this research throughout the study. We will tell you about new information from this board or other studies that may affect your health, welfare, or willingness to stay on this study.

Whom Do I Call if I Have Questions or Problems?

If you have questions about the study, or if you think you have had a study-related injury, you should call ___RESEARCHER___ at ___TELEPHONE NUMBER___.

If you have questions about your rights as a research participant, call ___NAME OF CENTER___ Institutional Review Board or Patient Representative at ___TELEPHONE NUMBER___.

WHERE CAN I GET MORE INFORMATION?

You may call the NCI's **Cancer Information Service** at
1–800–4–CANCER (1–800–422–6237) or **TTY: 1–800–332–8615**

Visit the NCI's Web sites…
cancerTrials: comprehensive clinical trials information **http://cancertrials.nci.nih.gov.**

CancerNet™: accurate cancer information including PDQ
http://cancernet.nci.nih.gov.

A copy of the protocol (study plan) will be available at your request.

Please read the additional information provided with this form. Checklist of attachments.

SIGNATURE

I agree to take part in this study.

Participant _____   Date _____

Adjuvant Breast Cancer Study Plan

Breast Cancer Surgery

Adriamycin + Cytoxan
by vein every 21 days for 4 visits
Tamoxifen* for 5 years

Randomize

Group 1
Taxol by vein
every 21 days for 4 visits

Group 2
No Taxol

*For patients 50 years or older and those less than 50 years with ER positive or PR positive tumors

9

The Good, the Bad, and the Ugly Research Study
From Consent *to* Choice

In chapter 8, we examined how good a job consent forms do in informing subjects about the differences between being a research subject and being a patient. Now we turn to the other goal of informed consent: enabling a subject to determine whether enrolling in a particular research study is a good or bad choice for that person. To what extent do consent forms give subjects enough information to adequately distinguish "good choice" and "bad choice" studies?

Unfortunately, not very well at all. To demonstrate this, in this chapter we first give examples of certain types of information that are commonly omitted from consent forms. There is nothing particularly unique or unusual about the examples we describe; indeed, they have been chosen precisely because they are very common. Moreover, in most of the following examples, the language used in the consent forms is consistent with the type of disclosure suggested or even encouraged by the state-of-the-art rules for writing consent forms recommended by the National Cancer Institute (NCI) described in chapter 8. And we end this chapter by showing how these specific gaps in consent forms are actually representative of a much bigger failing in our system.

What Do We Already Know about the New Treatment?

When a study involves some type of new treatment, should the subject be provided with at least some background information about what is known about whether or not that treatment might be effective? There is currently no requirement to provide this information.

Study 1

In a major federally funded study, women with breast cancer that had spread beyond the breast to only a few (between one and three) lymph nodes under their arm were randomized to receive either radiation or no radiation treatment. The consent form's entire discussion of why the study was being done said merely that it was "to find out whether [radiation] treatment after chemotherapy will reduce the risk of breast cancer recurrence and thus help patients to live longer." Not a word more was said about the role of radiation in treating breast cancer.

In fact, there is a great deal known about its role in treating these women. Radiation, for women with four or more nodes containing cancer, is very effective in extending the lives of women—so effective that it is standard care. Here is what the protocol—the lengthy document that describes the study for the doctors who recruit patients into it, a document that subjects are generally not permitted to see[1]—says about this issue: "[I]t appears that postmastectomy radiotherapy not only improves local-regional control, but also impacts upon disease-free and possibly overall survival by reduction of breast cancer deaths." The protocol goes on to observe that "some have questioned" whether there is quite so much of a benefit in women with only a few lymph nodes (between one and three) with cancer.

The *New York Times* even ran a lengthy story on the front page of its Science section discussing the controversy over whether to use radiation in these women.[2] It discussed the arguments doctors used for and against using radiation. Among the pieces of information the article provided was that "there is no question that if given radiation, these women would further reduce the rate of recurrence [of the cancer] by two-thirds, bringing it down to 3 to 5 percent. But whether that translates into a survival benefit—and how much of one—is not known." The article also noted that "[m]ore and more [doctors] are now referring their patients to get radiation treatment." As noted above, none of this information—not even a single word about how it was *known* that the radiation would indeed decrease the likelihood of the cancer coming back—was provided in the consent form.

Study 2

In this study, women with vulvar cancer and involved nodes were randomized between getting radiation therapy alone or radiation therapy combined with cisplatin chemotherapy. The consent form notes merely that "[t]his research is being done because adding cisplatin to radiation treatments *in other similar cancers*, such as cancer of the cervix, has been shown to improve control of the cancer and survival."[3] The protocol not only confirms the statement about use of chemotherapy in similar cancers (noting that there is "a mounting body of evidence *all* supporting the benefits"[1] of using concurrent chemotherapy in similar cancers) but also indicates there is even evidence about the possible benefit of chemotherapy in vulvar cancer itself:

> While *the optimal dose and schedule and combination of enhancing drugs have not been defined*, various drugs and schedules have demonstrated benefit. In advanced vulvar cancer, . . . a phase II study has demon-

strated that concurrent 5–FU and platinum with modest dose irradiation *significantly* reduced the necessity of radical surgery or exenteration.[4]

Study 3

Patients with cancer that has spread to between one and three areas of their brains were randomized between getting either radiosurgery alone (a type of radiation applied just to the specific areas of cancer in the brain) or radiosurgery combined with whole-brain radiation therapy. The consent form has one sentence merely noting that "we do not know" which of these options is better. The protocol discusses the results of a number of prior studies that explored this issue, in addition to summing up the considerations that might favor one therapy over the other:

> Even if there is no survival advantage [to adding whole-brain radiation], quality of life may be improved and treatment may be cost effective, due to avoiding the psychological distress of brain recurrence and the future need for subsequent salvage therapy. On the other hand, the potential side effects of [whole-brain radiation] . . . may result in a decreased quality of life for the patient.

Even if it is not yet known for certain whether or not a particular treatment is effective, many prospective subjects would likely want to know relevant background information in deciding whether to participate in the study. The fact that there is not yet enough information for the medical profession to *definitively* choose which of two treatments is best for patients in general doesn't mean that most people might not want to use that tentative information to decide what is best for them. Yet as these examples demonstrate, it is quite common for consent forms, even in research scenarios involving life-or-death issues (e.g., cancer treatments), to fail to provide much (if any) specific information regarding what is already know about how well the new treatment might work.

Often, all the consent form says is that it is not known whether it works as well as the current standard treatment. Indeed, this practice appears to be specifically encouraged by the gold standard NCI model consent form.[5] The NCI template for writing consent forms specifically notes that the reason for doing a study should be explained in only "one or two sentences," and it gives the example: "We do not know which of these two commonly used treatments is better." Nowhere else does its model consent form require, or even suggest, the presentation of any specific information about previous studies relating to the "new" treatment.

What Is the Risk from Not Getting Standard Care?

Often a medical condition will already have a quite effective treatment, and a study thus might be intended to prove that a new treatment also is effective for that condition. Would a reasonable person want to get some basic information about the risk that the new treatment might be less effective than standard care?

Study 4

Persons with certain types of hospital-acquired pneumonia were randomized between getting intravenous followed by oral forms of a standard antibiotic that is usually used to treat this condition or intravenous and oral versions of an unproven antibiotic. The consent form describes the purpose of the study as being "to find out the effects of a new medicine." The protocol is far more specific in stating that the purpose of the study is to demonstrate that the new drug is merely "at least as good as" the usual drug combination. The consent form highlights, as a benefit from participation, the fact that "all patients will receive active medication." It nowhere says anything about the fact that standard care would be highly likely to fully cure the patient's problem. The risks section of the consent form never mentions the risk that the new drug might not work as well as standard care, nor does it state what the consequences to the patient might be if that happened.

Study 5

Patients undergoing cardiac surgery who were at a high risk of hemorrhage were randomized between getting an FDA-approved fibrin sealant to control bleeding during the surgery or an experimental fibrin sealant. The risks section of the consent form discusses numerous risks, such as the possibility of viral transmission from *both* of the sealants, but does not mention the risk of the experimental sealant being less effective than standard care or the health consequences to the subject if the experimental sealant is less effective in controlling hemorrhage.

These examples demonstrate three pieces of information that are commonly missing from consent forms: (1) how well *standard care* works, (2) the fact that the *new treatment* might not work as well as standard care, and (3) what the *consequences* are if the new treatment doesn't work as well as standard care.

The fact that consent forms frequently fail to even mention how well standard care works is puzzling. Presumably defenders of this practice would argue that the doctor would of course have discussed standard care with the patient. But surely it is odd that consent forms, the documents that are supposed to provide the key information that the subject should be thinking about in deciding to participate in a study, frequently don't even include a single sentence about how well standard care works. A subject who is being asked to try some new treatment is facing a very different decision if standard care is effective in 999 out of 1,000 cases, versus only in 1 case out of 1,000.

An equally puzzling circumstance is that the possibility of the new treatment being less effective than standard care is frequently not even mentioned in the Risks section of the consent form. After all, in many studies, that is likely to be the biggest risk relating to participation, perhaps far greater than the risk of getting some obscure side effect from the new drug. Near-compulsive attention is given in most consent forms to providing a subject with lengthy (and often mind-numbingly confusing) lists of possible side effects. Indeed, this is the one area of the consent form that the FDA often pays special attention to, requiring that certain side effects be listed. Yet it is apparently considered appropriate to not even mention this major risk of "lesser effectiveness" in the Risks section.

Furthermore, even if that risk is mentioned, consent forms will frequently not explain what might happen to subjects if that risk became a reality. Yet there is no reason to think subjects have the background to appreciate the possible consequences. For example, how important is it that the fibrin sealant works well during cardiac surgery? Does an ineffective sealant merely mean that the surgeon has to wipe away a bit of extra blood and the surgery takes a few seconds longer? Or instead might that mean that a major blood vessel springs a leak and the subject can bleed to death in a minute? Does getting substandard treatment for your infection mean that the researchers just switch you to another antibiotic, or might it mean that your infection becomes harder to treat, requiring extra days in the hospital and perhaps risking your life?

What Are the Possible Benefits from Participating in the Study?

It is well recognized that a consent form must describe the possible benefits a subject may obtain as a result of participating in a study.[6] To meet this requirement, should a consent form be required to say anything more than that "benefits are uncertain"?

Study 6

Subjects with high cholesterol who are already taking an approved "statin" cholesterol-lowering drug were randomized to receive, in addition, either an investigational drug that decreases LDL ("bad") cholesterol and increases HDL ("good") cholesterol, or placebo (an inactive substance). The subjects would be treated for an eight-week period and would not be able to get the study drug after that period. The Benefits section of the supplied consent form states, "You may have a good response to treatment. . . . It is possible that you will receive no direct health benefit from your participation in this study."

This type of vague language is extremely common. Indeed, the NCI recommendations on writing consent forms encourage such language.[7] Here is the language that the NCI recommends for the benefits section of consent forms in cancer studies: "Taking part in this study may or may not make your health better. While doctors hope [procedures, drugs, interventions, devices] will be more useful against cancer compared to the usual treatment, there is no proof of this yet."

What is particularly interesting about this language—as was true of the language from the cholesterol study—is that a person *need not really know much, if anything, about the study* in order to write the benefits section: all you need to do is fill in the brackets with a few words identifying the treatment that is being studied. As a consequence, a statement such as "participation may or may not make your health better"—or the commonly used language "no benefit is guaranteed"—ends up being minimally informative to the subject:[8] it can equally correctly be used in studies where the researchers are relatively confident ahead of time that there is a *very high* chance of there being a benefit to the subject, and in studies where it is *very unlikely* that the subjects will benefit.

Note that even apart from the failure to give any indication about the possible "likelihood of benefit," this language also fails to state *what* the hypothetical benefit might be, assuming it indeed did take place. In many cancer studies, researchers probably would have minimal difficulty in accurately predicting that it is unlikely that the subjects will benefit, and that any benefit will be, at most, a shrinking of the tumor that will have little or no effect on the subject's survival. And in the cholesterol study described above, we can be rather certain that temporarily lowering a subject's cholesterol for eight weeks is extremely unlikely to provide any long-term health benefits.

It is indeed appropriate, as the NCI determined, to not "overstate" benefits. But it would not be overstating benefits to add some genuine information about how *unlikely* the subject is to benefit, or how minimal that benefit is likely to be, so as to counteract a subject's natural tendency to overestimate the likelihood of benefit.

A Case Study: Consent Forms in Phase I Studies

To better explore the issue of how to appropriately describe benefits, let us provide a hypothetical example from outside of the health care arena. Imagine that following an economic downturn, large numbers of people began investing in used cars, incorrectly thinking that they could make thousands of dollars per car by reselling them in a few years. Congress, concerned about this, passes the Used Car Buyer Protection Act. This law requires used car dealers to give purchasers appropriate information about the likely resale value of a car in five years.

Assume that a particular car dealer's best predictions about the resale value of a particular car (from looking at similar models in past years) suggest that 95% of the buyers will end up having a *loss* when they resell the car. Moreover, of the 5% that have a profit, the amount of profit will usually be below $500, although a rare car may end up reselling for several thousand dollars. Under these conditions, one dealer plans to tell his customers, "You may or may not profit when you resell the car," or to perhaps say, "I cannot guarantee you a profit when you resell this car. Your possible profit is impossible to predict." Should such statements be viewed as meeting the car dealer's obligation under the law?

This scenario is actually a representation of exactly what is taking place in phase I drug studies in cancer patients. In the classic phase I study, a few people (e.g., three) are given a specified dose of the new drug being tested, to see what side effects, if any, are caused. (This is usually the first time that any human beings have ever been given this drug.) If they don't have any serious side effects, then the next group of three people will be given a higher dose, and so forth, until people begin to have serious side effects. In this way, we can determine the maximum tolerated dose of the drug. Then, knowing that information, we can begin to study (in phase II and III studies) if the drug actually is effective in treating a particular medical problem. By giving people in those subsequent studies the "highest tolerated" dose of the drug, as determined in the phase I study, we make sure that we don't inadvertently fail to find a beneficial effect of a drug by having given people too low a dose.

Researchers have long acknowledged that the chance of a subject benefiting from participation in a phase I study is "extremely low," whereas since the drugs being tested are often known to be toxic (that is how they usually work, by destroying cells), "the risks may be substantial and the possible harms severe."[9] In spite of these facts, survey after survey has demonstrated that people who enroll in such studies have astoundingly unrealistic expectations that they will benefit from participating.[10] In one survey of cancer patients at Philadelphia's Fox Chase Cancer Center, 45% of the patients enrolling in phase I studies indicated they believed that being in the study would extend their life by at least two years.[11] Yet the truth is that this virtually never happens: it is so rare that people commonly point to only one phase I study in recent years where people did actually get a substantial benefit.[12]

Thus, one question has arisen: to what extent is the "delusional thinking" on the part of people enrolling in these studies due to problems with the consent forms? To answer this question, the prestigious ethics branch of the federal government's National Institutes of Health reviewed hundreds of consent forms, and their findings were published in the *New England Journal of Medicine* in December of 2002 as a "Special Article."[13] The conclusion of this study: surprisingly, consent forms are *not* a big part of the problem. To quote the authors, "Although there is room for improvement, the substance of these forms is unlikely to be the primary source of misunderstanding by subjects in phase I oncology trials."

How did they come to this conclusion? In reviewing the consent forms, they determined that these forms "almost never promise direct benefit to subjects, rarely mention cure, and usually communicate the seriousness and unpredictability of risk." In other words, had the consent forms actually promised benefits to the subjects, for example, this would have demonstrated that the consent forms were part of the problem. But the forms they collected didn't do that: indeed, only 1 of the 272 forms said that the subjects were "expected" to benefit.

It is interesting, however, to dig beneath the surface of the data they collected. In 255 of the forms (94%), the benefits section "communicated uncertainty about benefit." The authors provide no further details about what they mean by this, but presumably these consent forms contain language somewhat similar to that used in most consent forms (and encouraged by the NCI, as discussed above), such as telling a subject that they "may or may not" benefit or that a "benefit is not guaranteed."[14] But a phase I study is not your average type of study. As noted above, and as the authors of the article readily admit, we know that the statistical likelihood of a subject benefiting from such a study is, in their own words, "extremely low."

So, the obvious question is, if we know that the chance of getting a benefit is "extremely low," and that piece of information is rarely given to subjects, aren't the consent forms failing to give subjects a very important piece of information? A leading commentator on this issue is Dr. Matthew Miller, a medical oncologist and current Harvard faculty member who used to be in charge of phase I cancer trials at the Harvard-affiliated Dana-Farber Cancer Center.[15] Very troubled by the circumstances under which he enrolled subjects in these trials, he developed guidelines for the language to be included in consent forms. In the Benefits section, he would add this sentence: "Based on prior experience, the chance that you will feel better or live longer as a result of participating in this study is almost zero."

But for the present, you are unlikely to find such a truly informative sentence in a phase I consent form. It would be interesting to see what would happen if half of the subjects being recruited for a phase I oncology study were given a consent form that contained that sentence, in large, bold red print in a square on the front page, and the other half were given the type of consent form that is currently used, merely noting in the middle of the form, with no special emphasis, that the subject "may or may not" benefit. That would be a good way to test the conclusion of the federal government's own ethics experts that failing to specifically tell a subject the very low likelihood of benefit is not a "primary source" of the misunderstanding by subjects.

Consider again our hypothetical car dealer disclosure law: if we required disclosure of car resale prices, should a dealer be permitted to take advantage of the fact that there is never certainty about a particular car's resale price—that one time in a thousand, perhaps, the car may end being resold at a high price—to merely tell all customers that "it is impossible to predict your profit"? And if that is unacceptable, how should we react, in the face of federal regulations mandating disclosing information about benefits, when similar obfuscation takes place in the far more important scenario of life-and-death decisions made by seriously ill patients?

Do Consent Forms Tell Subjects How to Make a Choice?

Although discussions about research with human subjects frequently emphasize the importance of getting a subject's *consent*, the examples provided in this chapter suggest that it may be appropriate to focus instead on a different word: the idea of informed *choice*. Our purpose in telling a prospective subject about a study is, in the end, not so much about securing their participation in the study but about allowing that person to make an informed choice: perhaps to be in the study, but perhaps to choose a different option, such as obtaining standard care, or even getting some new treatment outside of a study.[16]

The examples we have shown tend to highlight one common circumstance: that consent forms commonly fail to include the most important pieces of information needed to actually *help a person make a choice about whether or not to be in the study*. They often don't include the very information that a person needs in deciding if this is a "good choice" or "bad choice" study for them. Is a woman, choosing what course of action to take for her breast cancer (study 1 above), making an "understanding and enlightened" decision—a phrase used by the Nuremberg Code more than fifty years ago—when the key document designed to educate her essentially provides *no* information to help her evaluate how effective each of the two treatments might be in keeping her breast cancer from returning? She is effectively being given less in-formation about this possibly life-or-death decision than she would get in buying a new refrigerator. She is getting much less information than a *New York Times* story on this medical problem would have given her. Is this even minimally acceptable?

Consent forms virtually never contain even a brief discussion suggesting that there might be reasons for choosing one arm over the other. Most consent forms seem designed to narrowly provide the required categories of information and not to give the subject relevant guidance about how to use that information in thinking about whether or not to be in the study. Lists of risks, benefits, and alternatives—which are all that most consent forms provide and all that the federal regulations require—are not very helpful without advice on *how to think about* these isolated pieces of information. A decision to be in a study cannot be based on merely know-ing the possible benefits from participating or the possible risks from participating. Rather, the subject should be looking at the *relationship* of the benefits to the risks. And even that piece of information isn't enough, since that risk–benefit relation-ship for being in the study needs to be *compared* to the same piece of information for each of the major options available outside of the study.

As we have shown in this chapter, consent forms rarely supply this type of use-ful information. Moreover, researchers have an incentive to minimize the amount of information given to prospective subjects. There is evidence suggesting that sub-jects tend to enroll in studies at *decreased* rates when they are given *greater* amounts of information about the study.[17] This finding is supported by common sense: a subject who is merely told that we don't know which of two arms in a study is better has no reason to prefer one to the other. Providing more specific information—how well standard care works, the preliminary results favoring the new treatment, spe-cific facts about the possible benefits from participation—gives a patient a possible "hook" for preferring one option to the other.

The categories recounted in this chapter may help also explain the phenom-enon of the therapeutic misconception (which we discussed in chapter 2), whereby subjects tend to misperceive the extent to which participating in a study will be di-rectly beneficial to them. It has remained puzzling that subjects will frequently indi-cate they are entering a study out of self-interest, when it is clear that the study is unlikely to benefit them.[18] Perhaps in some cases this is not so much of a puzzle—or due to an "inherent" psychological phenomenon by which a person tends to paint for herself an overly rosy picture of the benefits from a study—but rather due to a more mundane explanation: consent forms, in a variety of ways, routinely deny a subject information that will enable them to determine that participation may not be in their best interests.

It is somewhat amazing to realize that in a document designed to help someone make an informed choice, *it is rare to find even a sentence or two actually explaining why a person (depending on their personal preferences) might be better off opting to not be in the study.* Yet as we have shown, many studies will indeed be bad choices for a person who is trying to do what is best to treat a medical problem. And the need for giving that person clear information about this situation is highlighted by the fact that it is often patients' doctors who are asking them to enroll in a study: patients are unlikely to imagine that their doctors would be asking them to do something that is not the "best thing" in terms of treating their medical problem.[19]

Although people often correctly complain about how consent forms are becoming lengthy documents of legal boilerplate, which confuse subjects, it would not be hard to design a relatively brief "front page" on consent forms[20] that tells the subject the key things they should be thinking about in deciding whether or not to enroll in a study. Even in a very complicated study, this need not be very long. Consider what this might have been for the breast cancer study (study 1) described above:

> We don't yet know if adding radiation to chemotherapy in women such as yourself, with one to three positive nodes, is helpful in letting them live longer. We *do* know that it is helpful in women with four or more nodes: for such women, the radiation treatment causes the cancer to take longer to reappear and it lets them live longer, and we routinely recommend that such women get radiation. In women with fewer positive nodes, such as yourself, we *do* know that the radiation does significantly decrease the likelihood that the cancer will come back. But we are not sure if it also enables them to live longer. Since radiation has substantial side effects, its benefits in such women might not outweigh its risks. This study is designed to answer that question, by randomly assigning women (like flipping a coin) to either get radiation or not get radiation.
>
> There are some important things you should think about in deciding whether or not to be in this study:
>
> 1. You may be the sort of person who wants to do everything possible to make sure the cancer doesn't come back. You might be willing to undergo a treatment that accomplished that even if it is not yet known for certain that it will enable you to live longer, and even though it can cause substantial (but rarely life-threatening) side effects. If this describes your feelings, you probably will want to go ahead and get the radiation treatment from a doctor, instead of participating in this study (where there would be a chance of being assigned to *not* get the radiation).
> 2. You may be the sort of person who is very concerned about unnecessary side effects: you don't want to undergo a treatment with serious side effects unless it is very certain that it is going to benefit you by extending your life. If you are that sort of person, you should think about having your doctor treat you without any radiation, instead of being in this study (where there would be a chance of getting assigned to *get* the radiation).
> 3. You may be the sort of person who doesn't have very strong feelings about either of the situations described in items (1) or (2). If so, being in this study may be a very reasonable choice for you.

In effect, this is the missing piece of most consent forms. In a large percentage of studies, there usually are very valid reasons why a person might prefer one treatment or another, instead of being in the study. Not very many people are going to find themselves in perfect "personal equipoise," finding themselves without any reason for preferring one treatment to the other. And yet subjects are rarely told that information in a form that lets them make meaningful decisions. Under the law's reasonable person standard for disclosure, this discussion would certainly appear to be a required part of a consent form: a reasonable person would indeed want to have this information. Of course, providing this missing piece highlights the ways in which being in a study may not be the best thing for a relatively nonaltruistic person. And the result will likely be fewer subjects choosing to enroll in research studies. We encounter again the dilemma posed in chapter 1: to what extent are we willing to be less than fully truthful to subjects to get them to enroll in studies?

10

The Hidden Alternative

fraud 1 a : DECEIT, TRICKERY; *specif*: intentional perversion of truth in
order to induce another to . . . surrender a legal right **b** : an act of
deceiving or misrepresenting: TRICK.
—Merriam-Webster's Collegiate Dictionary, Eleventh Edition

As we showed in chapter 9, informed consent is at its heart about choice: letting
persons who are being asked to enroll in a study decide whether or not they really
want to be in that study. Depending on the type of study, that decision may or may
not have important consequences for a person's health. There is one very common
type of clinical trial that most starkly ups the ante in terms of health consequences:
a study in which subjects will be randomized 50:50 between some "new" treatment
and standard care (which may not be very effective). People often do not realize that
the new treatment in many such situations could be obtained directly from a doctor. In such circumstances, the patient has a choice among three options: (1) standard care (perhaps largely ineffective), (2) being in the study (which gives them a
50% chance of getting the new treatment), or (3) directly getting the new treatment
outside of the study.

Curiously, however, consent forms will, in many instances, never let the patient
know that they even have any such choice. Often, the option of getting the new treatment outside of the study is never disclosed. In this chapter we explain how this
surprising state of affairs came about and explore the legality and ethics of this practice. As background to understanding the issues at stake, we begin with a story about
one of the more controversial cancer treatments of recent history.

Breast Cancer and High-Dose Chemotherapy

Our story begins in 1979, with researchers trying to come up with a better way to
treat women with breast cancer that has spread outside of the breast.[1] While there

were a variety of chemotherapy drugs used to fight this condition, none of them worked all that well. Only about 10–15% of women treated with them achieved remission of their disease, and even the remissions did not often last that long.

A common method for improving cancer treatments was to use stronger chemotherapy, such as higher doses of a drug. There were limits on this approach, however: chemotherapy drugs not only destroy cancer cells; they also destroy other healthy cells in a person's body, particularly those that divide rapidly. This is why cancer patients commonly lost their hair after chemotherapy. While losing your hair was not life threatening, loss of other types of cells—particularly those in the bone marrow—was. Thus, destruction of the bone marrow was viewed as a constraint that prevented doctors from giving chemotherapy stronger than a particular dose.

But in 1979, a "rebel" researcher began exploring a new idea: if the problem with the "high-dose" chemotherapy is that a person's bone marrow is destroyed, can't we somehow treat that problem? In fact, it is possible to replace a person's bone marrow by transplanting a donor's marrow. This was commonly done as a treatment for patients who had cancers that affected the bone marrow itself, such as leukemia. These patients would intentionally be given very toxic drugs and radiation designed to kill off all of their bone marrow, after which the transplant would be performed. The new bone marrow would sometimes not regrow, or the patient might die from the chemotherapy, but if everything worked, the patients would be cured of their cancer.

The researcher, Dr. Gabriel Hortobagyi, came up with the idea of using higher doses of chemotherapy to treat breast cancer and then performing a bone marrow transplant in the woman to replace the bone marrow that had unintentionally been destroyed by the chemotherapy. Since the woman's bone marrow was not itself cancerous, her bone marrow could be removed and saved before she received the chemotherapy and then "transplanted" back into her body after the chemotherapy. In this way, the likelihood of the bone marrow regrowing was greater than was the case for patients who received transplants of bone marrow from some other person: a person's immune system is relatively unlikely to attack or "reject" her own bone marrow. Since transplanting someone with her own tissues is described as an "autologous" transplant (*auto* meaning "self"), this entire treatment was given the somewhat unwieldy name of "high-dose chemotherapy followed by autologous bone marrow transplantation," or HDC-ABMT for short.

Back in the 1970s, bone marrow transplantation was a very risky thing, and thus proponents of HDC-ABMT initially were met with a lot of skepticism from their colleagues in oncology. And, indeed, even though the initial patients on which they tried the procedure were selected to be young and relatively healthy (apart from the breast cancer), about 20% of them died just from side effects of the highly toxic chemotherapy drugs. But as time passed, it appeared that they were getting very high rates of remission from this treatment: 50–60%, compared to the 15% achieved with the standard "low-dose" chemotherapy.

News of these successes spread, and more and more doctors began offering women with metastatic breast cancer HDC-ABMT as an option. As this was taking place, there had not yet been any authoritative proof that the new treatment was any better than (or even as good as) existing treatments. Research studies were starting to take place, in which women would be randomized between the currently used "low-dose" chemotherapy and the new HDC-ABMT, having a 50% chance of being assigned to either treatment. But many doctors were directly offering HDC-ABMT, and many women were choosing that option. In 1989, only 271 women received the treatment. In 1991 that number had tripled to 749, and by 1997 the number had grown to 2,853.

One of the reasons for the growing popularity of HDC-ABMT was financial: the new treatment was a big money-maker, with a high profit margin. In the early years it cost about $150,000–200,000, and for-profit companies discovered they could make large amounts of money by becoming very efficient in providing this treatment and charging less than the competition. Thus, a company such as Response Oncology made profits of $128 million in 1998, most of that amount from HDC-ABMT. And the university medical centers also noted the profit potential and joined the bandwagon. As one breast cancer expert noted, doctors who perform bone marrow transplants "are kings. . . . They usually get a higher salary, they usually get more money."[2]

Perhaps the greatest obstacle to the growth of this treatment was not the medical profession, but rather the insurance industry, which was initially footing the bill. Insurance companies have long recognized that there is a problem if they are required to pay for every untested treatment that comes along: all of us, as consumers of medical services, will end up paying for a great deal of ineffective care by means of rapidly increasing insurance premiums. So insurance contracts typically have provisions that exclude coverage of "experimental" or "investigational" treatments. And when women began to demand payment for HDC-ABMT, the insurers refused to pay, claiming it was not a covered treatment.

Over the past decade, numerous lawsuits were brought against the insurers. While they won some of the initial cases, over time they began to lose more and more of them, sometimes being forced to pay very high verdicts. The many court opinions make fascinating reading. Even the judges who ruled in favor of the insurance companies were troubled by their decisions, indicating their personal views with comments such as "sadly, I find that"[3] or "the court has sympathy for the plaintiff's situation."[4] The judges seemed to sense that, even if the treatment was not yet proven, it was the only chance these women had and that denying it to them was somehow wrong.

Consider what one judge said in dealing with the case of Judith Harris, a divorced 51-year-old rural letter carrier for the U.S. Postal Service. She had first noticed a bruise on her breast that would not heal. After a positive biopsy, she ended up getting a modified radical mastectomy combined with four cycles of chemotherapy. Since her cancer had metastasized beyond her breast, she was facing only a 20–40% chance of being alive in five years. Her doctor recommended HDC-ABMT, but her insurer, Mutual of Omaha, determined that this treatment was not covered due to the exclusion for experimental treatments. She brought a lawsuit in federal court; here is what the judge observed in ruling against her:

> Despite rumors to the contrary, those who wear judicial robes are
> human beings, and as persons, are inspired and motivated by compas-
> sion as anyone would be. Consequently, we often must remind ourselves

that in our official capacities, we have authority only to issue rulings within the narrow parameters of the law and the facts before us. The temptation to go about doing good where we see fit, and to make things less difficult for those who come before us, regardless of the law, is strong. But the law, without which judges are nothing, abjures such unlicensed formulation of unauthorized social policy by the judiciary.

Plaintiff Judy Harris well deserves, and in a perfect world would be entitled to, all known medical treatments to control the horrid disease from which she suffers. In ruling as this court must, no personal satisfaction is taken, but that the law was followed. The court will have to live with the haunting thought that Ms. Harris, and perhaps others insured by the Mutual of Omaha Companies under similar plans, may not ultimately receive the treatment they need and deserve. Perhaps the question most importantly raised about this case, and similar cases, is who should pay for the hopeful treatments that are being developed in this rapidly developing area of medical science?[5]

The judge noted in the end that the result was not "personally satisfying."

Other judges, so moved by these scenarios that they were unwilling to be the apparent cause of denying a woman possibly life-saving treatment, went to extraordinary lengths to reach decisions that seemed to blatantly conflict with the underlying law. Grace Rodela Fuja was 37 years old, and her cancer had spread to her lungs.[6] She was given a negligible chance of survival—only a few months of life—by her doctors at the University of Chicago if all she continued to receive was the standard "low-dose" chemotherapy. Although the doctors recommended HDC-ABMT, the University of Chicago Hospital refused to provide that treatment—which would cost $150,000—unless she demonstrated that the treatment would be fully paid for. The combination of her $21,000 billing clerk salary and her husband's $17,000 shipping clerk salary was nowhere near the amount needed. In spite of the fact that she ended up enrolling in a research study that had been approved by the Institutional Review Board at the University of Chicago, and signed a consent form clearly stating she was participating in a research study, the trial court determined that this was not research for purposes of the insurance contract, which had exclusions for coverage of treatment received as part of research.

As the insurers began to lose increasing numbers of court cases, they were also losing another battle: that of public opinion. Having a young but dying woman on the front page of a local newspaper, flanked by her loving family members and her caring doctor, all of them bemoaning the fact that her insurance company was refusing to pay for the one treatment that would save her life, was not exactly favorable publicity for the insurer.[7] So, over time, the insurance companies changed their positions and agreed to pay for the treatment. And state and local governments also got involved, with various laws being passed that required HDC-ABMT to be covered.

But there is one more piece of the puzzle that remained to be uncovered. For while lots of women were receiving this treatment from their doctors (and increasingly having less of problem getting it paid for by insurance), there were still some researchers out there trying to complete the "gold standard" research studies in which women would be randomly assigned to either the "low-dose" chemotherapy or HDC-ABMT. The researchers, however, were confronting a growing problem: it was very difficult to get women to enroll in these studies.[8] After all, why would a woman who was even considering getting HDC-ABMT decide to instead opt for a randomized trial? Whether or not that new treatment worked, it was clear—as her doctors would tell her—that the alternative, "low-dose" chemotherapy was very unlikely to be of much benefit. And being in the randomized trial meant she faced a 50% chance of being denied the new treatment that might save her life. Thus, enrolling in such a research study appeared to be a rather poor choice to most of these women dying of breast cancer.

Over time, however, the researchers did manage to gradually enroll women in the randomized studies. It no doubt took a lot longer than it would have if women had to enroll in the studies to get access to HDC-ABMT. But eventually the studies were completed, and the results were quite compelling. Four of five studies showed that there was no benefit to HDC-ABMT over the standard "low-dose" chemotherapy.[9] And while the fifth study, conducted in South Africa, showed there might be some benefit to the new treatment, it was later disclosed that doctors conducting that study had fraudulently altered the data from that study.[10]

What lesson, if any, should be learned from this series of events? In an editorial accompanying the publication of the results of one of the studies,[11] the *New England Journal of Medicine* criticized the early claims of success for HDC-ABMT that had been based merely on giving it to patients without randomizing the treatments.[12] The alleged "astounding benefits" for high-dose chemotherapy never existed, and a "careful reading" of the early results would have demonstrated that fact. The journal's main conclusion was to emphasize the importance of having new treatments evaluated in "appropriately designed trials"—presumably, randomized trials in most cases.

While it is easy, in retrospect, to agree that it would have been better if we had learned sooner that HDC-ABMT is no better than standard care, it is not clear that the journal's desire is easily accomplished. After all, those trials were indeed taking place for HDC-ABMT. The main problem was not that there were no well-designed trials, but rather that *few women were willing to enroll in them.* And, even in retrospect, can we say that the women who chose to forgo a trial and instead get HDC-ABMT were making a mistake? What was Grace Fuja to do, being told she had only a few months to live and that standard care was likely to do nothing to change that prediction? Wasn't a chance at something that might work a better option than certain death—and wasn't a 100% chance at that new treatment better than a 50% chance of getting it in a randomized trial?

Indeed, even in the face of the growing evidence, there is still support for HDC-ABMT. (Which perhaps is not surprising, given how often "settled" medical issues are later found to have been wrong.) And given the role that federal judges played in this series of events—approving the insurance payments that helped make the treatment directly available to women—it is fitting to close this section with the comments of Marsha Pechman the day after Congress confirmed her elevation from Washington state judge to federal judge.[13] She was still alive in 1999, six years after being one of the earliest patients to receive HDC-ABMT. Asked about the new evidence that the treatment was no better than low-dose chemotherapy, she and her Seattle physicians—including the director of the transplant program at the prestigious Fred Hutchinson Cancer Research Center, where bone marrow transplantation had been developed—disagreed with that conclusion. The *Seattle Post-Intelligencer*, observing that "Judge Marsha Pechman knows how to weigh evidence," quoted her as follows: "You can do all the studies you want. . . . I don't have any doubt the procedure saved my life."

The Cleveland Clinic Study

The moral of the HDC-ABMT saga might be that we all benefit from having well-designed randomized studies take place. So it certainly makes sense that great efforts are being made to enroll subjects in such studies. But presumably those efforts should conform with the law and with ethics. And so we come to the primary question for this chapter: in recruiting subjects for a study that randomizes between standard care and some "experimental" treatment, is it appropriate to *fail to tell them* that the new treatment is available outside of the study? Imagine, for example, that a woman enrolling in the breast cancer trials, being randomized between HDC-ABMT and low-dose chemotherapy, was *never told* that she could get the high-dose chemotherapy directly from a doctor. Would this have been acceptable? In fact, failure to give this piece of information happens all the time, even today (and likely happened all the time in the HDC-ABMT trials). One example of this has even made its way to the courts, in a case that has been quietly settled and has surprisingly generated no newspaper headlines.

In March of 1990, 45-year-old Daniel Klais went to see his long-time family physician, Dr. Cheryl Weinstein, for a routine examination.[14] Up to that time, Dr. Weinstein, who worked at the Cleveland Clinic, had treated him only for relatively minor medical problems, such as high cholesterol. Klais had recently noted some swelling in his neck. He forgot to mention this to Dr. Weinstein, but her physical examination of him revealed a one-inch nodule on the left side of his neck. She told him it was probably a benign fatty tumor or cyst.

He again saw Dr. Weinstein two months later, to get the results of some other tests, when he told her about continued swelling in his neck. Her examination at that time revealed two new nodules, leading her to suspect that Klais had lymphoma. She referred him to another Cleveland Clinic doctor, who performed a needle biopsy of one of the nodules. The result showed cancer cells; they were not cancer cells indicating lymphoma (a cancer originating in the lymph gland itself), but rather cancer cells that must have migrated there from a cancer elsewhere in his body. Further examination of Klais's body led to the discovery of the initial source of the cancer, which was at the base of his tongue.

Klais was told that he had a very advanced form of squamous cell carcinoma and that he had only one chance in four of still being alive in five years. He was referred to Dr. David Adelstein, a Cleveland Clinic medical oncologist who was doing research on how best to treat these head and neck cancers. Dr. Adelstein told Klais of a research study that he was then conducting. Standard care for Klais's form of cancer was to use radiation on the tumor and to then surgically remove it, but this was not very effective. The study was designed to see whether adding two chemotherapy drugs, cisplatin and 5-fluorouracil (5-FU), would improve a patient's outcome. People who enrolled in the study would be randomized: they would have a 50% chance of getting standard care (the radiation and surgery) and a 50% chance of getting the experimental treatment (radiation and surgery plus the two chemotherapy drugs).

Klais told Dr. Adelstein that he really wanted to get the chemotherapy. The doctor told him that there were no "good data" demonstrating that the use of the chemotherapy would improve survival. He did not mention that he had performed several studies providing tentative evidence that chemotherapy might indeed be helpful. He also never told Klais that there were other doctors who would be happy to directly give Klais the chemotherapy. Klais ended up agreeing to participate in the research study. The consent form that he signed, which was approved by the institutional review board (IRB) at the Cleveland Clinic, said nothing about the growing evidence that adding chemotherapy might be helpful in treating his form of cancer. It merely stated that "the best approach is not known." In contrast, the protocol that Dr. Adelstein prepared for the study noted that "pilot data . . . strongly suggest the possibility that some combination of chemotherapy and radiation therapy will have a significant impact on the surgical morbidity common encountered in managing head and neck neoplasms."[15]

Regarding Klais's alternatives to participating in the study, the consent form stated that "surgery and/or radiation therapy are the standard treatments" and that "other treatments are considered experimental." It did not mention that he could get the two chemotherapy drugs from a doctor, outside of a study, and thus be sure of getting them (instead of the 50% chance of getting them in the study).

Klais ended up getting randomized to the arm that he was hoping *not* to be assigned to, the no-chemotherapy arm. Initially, things seemed to go well after his treatment. When he reached his five-year follow-up in July 1995, he was told that he had a very low risk of having the cancer return and could consider himself cured. But in January of 1996 he was told that X-rays showed cancer had been detected in his lungs and that he might have only a few months to live. He died in March of 1997 of metastatic cancer.

Prior to his death, he brought a lawsuit against Dr. Adelstein and the Cleveland Clinic alleging, in part, that they had not obtained his informed consent to participate in the study. As he stated in depositions, he had been "going for a cure" in enrolling in the research study. His attorney's attempt to clarify his purpose in entering the study is not as foolish as it might otherwise seem, given what we already know about the purpose of research studies. Indeed, a participant in that study *might* have answered as follows:

> Well, I was willing to make a bit of a tradeoff between maximizing my ability to be cured, and helping society to develop a cure for future

patients with this illness. Thus, I of course recognized that by entering the study I was only getting a 50% chance at the treatment—the chemo —that, in my view, had a better likelihood of curing my cancer (though I realize that no one then knew for certain which treatment would be better). That was OK to me, since society benefited from my participation in the study. Hey, you'll just have to call me a cock-eyed altruist.

But Klais didn't say that. If we believe him—and the facts give no reason to question this particular assertion—he wanted to get the treatment that, in his best estimation, would maximize his chance of living.

Had he known two relevant pieces of information—about the preliminary evidence that chemotherapy appeared to be effective in treating his form of cancer, and that he could have gotten the chemotherapy directly from a doctor—he presumably would have gone to get the chemotherapy and not participated in the study. Since it later was demonstrated that adding the chemotherapy did indeed substantially improve a person's survival following his form of cancer, he might now still be alive. The trial court initially rejected his lawsuit, but an appellate court determined that, assuming the facts were as he claimed them to be, he had indeed stated a legal claim for lack of informed consent. The case was sent back to a trial court, and the parties (after Klais's death) entered into a private settlement that resolved this dispute.

The Availability of New Treatments Outside Research Studies

While there may be a dispute about a number of facts in that case, one thing *is* clear: the IRB-approved consent form did not mention that he could get the experimental treatment directly from a doctor, assuring him of getting what he wanted. How common is what happened to Daniel Klais? As we shall try to demonstrate, the situation that Daniel Klais found himself in is not at all uncommon.

To reach that conclusion, we need to address an initial question: how common is it that a "new" treatment being compared to standard care in a research study can *legally* be given to patients outside of the study? We briefly addressed this question in chapter 2, and it is time to say more about it. Contrary to what many people might think, in a great variety of circumstances, doctors are quite free to provide such treatments. The legal restrictions against providing a new treatment are generally of two kinds: state malpractice and related laws (e.g., state licensing rules), and federal regulations (largely those administered by the FDA). We've already discussed the malpractice laws in part I (see chapter 4), showing that they do not prevent doctors from offering a patient treatment with nonstandard care when that is a reasonable thing to do in terms of the best interests of the patient. And many new treatments are likely to satisfy that standard: after all, they are often being studied as an alternative to standard care precisely because standard care is not very effective. This was certainly true in Klais's situation.

As for the *federal* rules that might limit what treatments a doctor can give a patient, the first point to note is that these rules apply only to the three categories of "treatments" that are specifically under FDA jurisdiction: drugs, devices, and biologics (e.g., blood products). Thus, for example, surgical procedures are generally outside of FDA jurisdiction. If a doctor decides to alter the standard operation for removing a gall bladder so that the incision on the person's abdomen is one inch higher than usual, the FDA has no authority to tell him he can't do that. As a result, in most studies involving an altered surgical procedure, there would be no federal regulations preventing a doctor from performing the new procedure on a patient outside of a research study.

When drug companies or inventors come up with new drugs or devices, in general they *do* have to get FDA approval to use those drugs or devices.[16] Initially, they will file an application with the FDA, known as an Investigational New Drug application or an Investigational Device Exemption. The FDA would then give them limited permission to use the drug or device, but for the most part only in a research study. In that circumstance, a patient wanting access to the new treatment would indeed most likely have to participate in a research study. Even this conclusion is not absolute, however, since there is authority on the part of drug and device makers to provide for a type of "compassionate use" of the new product. In other words, it can be supplied to some people who are not in a study. The rules relating to compassionate use are relatively vague, although they in general require that the person not be eligible for an ongoing research study. Thus, it can actually be in a person's interest to *not* qualify for a study: in the study they might only have a 50% chance of getting the new treatment, whereas if they qualify for compassionate use they do get that treatment.[17]

Let us assume, however, that our study involves a drug or device that *has already been approved* for at least one use by the FDA: in other words, that the drug has been shown to the satisfaction of the FDA to be safe and effective in treating some medical problem and is currently on the market. For example, recall the two drugs that were being studied at the Cleveland Clinic. Both of these drugs had received FDA approval for use in treating at least one form of cancer: cisplatin for bladder cancer and 5–FU for a number of cancers such as colon and rectal cancer. And once a drug has received such an approval, it is effectively already "on the market," and doctors can then use it to treat any condition they choose. Doing so—deviating from the specified labeling that accompanies the drug and that is approved by the FDA—is known as "off-label" use of the drug or device. The FDA is well aware of this practice, and acknowledges that it is perfectly legal and not in violation of any FDA regulations.[18]

How common is it that a research study may involve examining a use for a drug or device that is already FDA approved for some other use? While it is not easy to get a direct answer to that question, one crude estimate might be gotten from looking at how often doctors use drugs in an off-label manner in treating patients (i.e., outside of research studies). Off-label uses are extremely common in modern medicine. Estimates are that *hundreds of millions* of prescriptions each year are off-label, perhaps anywhere from 25% to 60% of the 1.6 billion prescriptions written in this country.[19] In the field of cancer treatment, off-label use is estimated to be even higher, constituting about two-thirds of the prescriptions. This actually makes a lot of sense: once it is discovered that a drug is good against one form of cancer, oncologists will begin trying it on all sorts of other cancers that don't have very good treatments. And, finally, one of the biggest areas of off-label use relates to the treatment of children.[20]

The Extent of Nondisclosure

It would probably be hard to put a percentage on it, but it nonetheless seems clear that what was true in Daniel Klais's situation is true in many other circumstances: the "new treatment" being offered in a randomized study could be obtained directly from a doctor, outside of the study. Oddly enough, however, telling the subjects in these studies that they could get the treatment outside of the study appears to be rather controversial. Thus, for a subject participating in a research study, it is rather hit-and-miss as to whether they will be told this rather crucial piece of information.

Indeed, at least certain branches of the U.S. government seem to be actively discouraging researchers from telling subjects about the off-study availability of a new treatment. Consider the National Cancer Institute (NCI) "gold standard" guidelines for writing consent forms, discussed in chapter 8. The instructions to researchers about what to include in the consent form indicate that the subject should be told about "the option of no anticancer treatment at the current time, or treatment with standard therapy, when appropriate."[21] There is not a single word suggesting any possible need to disclose nonstandard treatments or that the "new treatment" arm of the study is available outside the study.

While that language might be interpreted to be inconclusive, another provision in the NCI document is even more explicit. A template is provided for writing consent forms, where instructions are given with regard to filling in the following blank in the alternatives section of the consent form: "You may get _____ (study treatments/drugs at this center and other centers) even if you do not take part in the study." In further describing what should go in this blank, the document includes a limiting phrase indicating that only "noninvestigational treatments" should be used to fill in the blank.[22]

Confirmation of the fact that nondisclosure of experimental alternatives is common comes from what the U.S. government itself describes as "one of the largest breast cancer prevention studies ever": the NCI-sponsored Study of Tamoxifen and Raloxifene (STAR), comparing the efficacy of those two drugs in preventing breast cancer in women at high risk.[23] Tamoxifen has already been demonstrated to reduce the risk of developing breast cancer and is approved by the FDA for such use. Raloxifene is the same type of drug as tamoxifen and is currently FDA approved for treating osteoporosis, although it has not been approved for preventing breast cancer. In the double-blinded STAR study being conducted in the United States and Canada, 22,000 women at high risk to develop breast cancer are being randomized between the two drugs. For five years each of these women will take one of the drugs but will not know which they are taking.

With regard to the alternatives to participating in the STAR study, the sample consent form ("approved" by both the FDA and NCI[24]) states that:

> Instead of being in this study, you can decide to do one or more of the following:
>
> - Perform self-breast exams, have breast exams done by a doctor or nurse, and get regular mammograms.
> - If you live in the U.S., ask your doctor to prescribe tamoxifen for you.
> - Request surgery to remove both breasts.

There is no mention of the fact that a subject could perhaps find a doctor who is willing, outside of this study, to prescribe raloxifene to prevent breast cancer. That this possibility is far from hypothetical is demonstrated by an interesting source: a lawsuit by the manufacturer of tamoxifen against the manufacturer of raloxifene to prevent the latter company from inappropriately giving doctors information about the possible benefits of raloxifene in preventing breast cancer.[25] Evidence in that case included market research demonstrating that *more than one-third of the physicians surveyed* acknowledged that at least some of their prescriptions for raloxifene had been written for the primary purpose of breast cancer prevention.

Thus, women enrolling in the STAR study are told about going and having both breasts surgically removed (even though they *don't* yet have breast cancer in either breast), yet they are not told about the possibility of getting raloxifene, a pill with well-understood risks that has already being given to millions of women to treat their osteoporosis. The rationale for these differences in disclosure was that bilateral mastectomy has already been proven to substantially reduce the likelihood of such women developing breast cancer,[26] yet it was still not certain whether raloxifene can do that.

On the other hand, it was not as if there was no evidence that raloxifene might prevent breast cancer. In fact, there is quite a bit, which was why the very expensive STAR study was even taking place. In the initial study that had been conducted to determine whether or not raloxifene was effective in treating osteoporosis (and which led the FDA to give approval for such use), researchers coincidentally observed a substantial and highly statistically significant difference between the percentages of women developing breast cancer in the placebo group and the group that got raloxifene.[27] Getting raloxifene appeared to reduce the risk of developing breast cancer by 76%. While, for a variety of technical reasons, the results of this trial were not, by themselves, enough to convince the FDA to approve raloxifene for use in preventing breast cancer, they nonetheless were very promising. As an editorial in the *Journal of the American Medical Association* noted, this study was large and well designed and had shown that raloxifene "significantly reduced the risk for [certain forms of] breast cancer among postmenopausal women with osteoporosis."[28]

And there was a very good reason why many women might want to use raloxifene instead of tamoxifen to prevent breast cancer. Tamoxifen was known to increase a woman's risk of getting endometrial (a type of uterine) cancer. Raloxifene did not increase the risk of that cancer. Thus, for many women, tamoxifen was a two-edged sword, decreasing the risk of one cancer but at the possible cost of a different type of cancer. Raloxifene promised the possibility of preventing breast cancer without that down side. Yet in spite of this, the women being asked to enroll in the STAR study were not told about their ability to get raloxifene outside of the study.

When Is It Proper to Disclose Out-of-Study Availability of an Unproven Treatment?

The federal regulations relating to research specify that a consent form include a "disclosure of appropriate alternative procedures or courses of treatment, if any, *that might be advantageous to the subject.*"[29] Is obtaining, outside of a study, an investigational treatment that constitutes one arm of that study an "appropriate alternative" to participating in the study? Some commentators appear to think that it is not. Consider the comments of Dr. D. Lawrence Wickerham, a co-leader of tamoxifen studies such as the STAR study, who has been quoted in the *New York Times* as stating that "[a]t the moment, it's too early to use raloxifene to prevent breast cancer outside of a clinical trial [e.g., the STAR study]. . . . We don't yet know raloxifene's long-term benefits or risks."[30] Similar comments have been made with regard to the appropriateness of giving modified versions of HDC-ABMT, such as tandem transplantation or immune modulation, to women with breast cancer. As noted in a 2000 *New England Journal of Medicine* editorial, such investigational treatments "can neither be justified nor supported outside of clinical trials."[31]

These conclusions merit further scrutiny. As Dr. Wickerham correctly notes, there would be a degree of uncertainty about some aspects of the benefits, or risks, or both, of such an investigational treatment. Does that fact in itself mean that getting that treatment outside of the study is not an "appropriate" alternative for a prospective study subject? With regard to the risks side of the analysis, a person who opts to get the treatment outside of the study will in many cases be exposed to *exactly the same risks* as a person who is randomized to that experimental treatment after enrolling in the study. Thus, the fact that the risks of the experimental treatment are still not fully known does not appear to be, in all cases, a reason for arguing against getting the treatment outside the study.

With regard to the benefits side of the equation, the very fact that we are permitting the experimental treatment to be used as one arm in a study, with the other arm being standard care, means that there must be clinical equipoise: "an honest disagreement in the expert clinical community regarding the comparative merits of two or more forms of treatment for a given condition."[32] As we discussed in chapter 6, this requirement is actually less protective of the well-being of subjects than many experts suggest. Nonetheless, the existence of clinical equipoise does create a starting presumption that using the treatment for the stated purpose, although efficacy has not yet been fully proven, is not *that* unreasonable. Just because some researcher has a crackpot idea about testing a new treatment, it doesn't follow that the researcher will be permitted to conduct the study: the clinical equipoise requirement does at least provide some minimal criteria for attempting to assure that subjects are exposed only to sufficiently plausible treatments in clinical trials.

In addition, there may be definite benefits to some subjects from going outside the study. A subject may be trying to get into a study that randomizes between standard treatment X and unproven treatment Y precisely because *she wants to get a chance at treatment Y*. Indeed, this is likely to be the case for many, if not most, people who enroll in such a study. As the *New York Times* has noted, "few people sign on [to a research study] out of pure altruism. They want the experimental drugs a study provides, often regarding them as 'treatment,' even when their safety and effectiveness have not yet been proved."[33] Thus, from a benefits viewpoint, the perceived benefits to certain subjects may be substantially greater in getting the treatment outside of the study, where they can be certain to get the desired new treatment, and not merely the 50–50 shot at it that is provided in the study itself.

Given that there are in many instances no greater risks, and that there might be significantly greater benefits (at least as perceived by the patient), it would seem that the possibility of getting the new treatment outside of the study would be a very appropriate alternative for many subjects. Directly providing such an experimental treatment is in fact not that unique an event. The laws in the United States specifically provide doctors with a broad range of discretion in offering a patient an unproven treatment when the doctor thinks that doing so may be in the patient's best interests.[34] Accordingly, prospective subjects in the study should be advised of this alternative.

The actual wording of such a disclosure in the Alternatives section of a consent form will likely vary from study to study, but it need not be more than a sentence or two in length. It should, however, be more specific than a generic statement such as "all treatments in this study may be available outside of this study." In the STAR trial, for example, an added sentence could mirror the language that was used to discuss the tamoxifen alternative (as quoted above): "If you live in the U.S., [you can] ask your doctor to prescribe raloxifene for you." In many cases, it might be appropriate to more specifically highlight off-study availability in its own paragraph, in bold print: "If you are considering enrolling in this study mainly to get the 50% chance at being assigned treatment X, you should be aware that you could instead be certain to get treatment X by obtaining it directly from a doctor, without participating in this study."

There are, no doubt, circumstances in which the use of a certain medication or procedure in an unproven manner outside of a formal clinical trial would be inappropriate. In some instances, it may be clear that subjects getting the new treatment outside of the study would be exposed to a much higher risk than if they got it as part of the study. The researchers may be using special techniques for monitoring for side effects that are not available to the average private practitioner, for example. In such a situation, it would perhaps be appropriate to not advise a prospective research subject of a highly risky off-protocol alternative. And, in some situations, the new treatment may be so risky, or the likelihood of its working as well as currently available treatments so uncertain, that a doctor would be acting against the best interests of the patient, and perhaps even be committing malpractice, by offering it to a patient. Such situations do exist, as we demonstrated in discussing "bad choice" studies in chapter 6. But as a general matter, we should be *requiring disclosure* of such options to prospective subjects, *absent specific facts indicating the impropriety* of such an out-of-study option.

The arguments we've presented do not require consent forms to disclose every possible alternative to participating in the study, no matter how implausible. We need merely apply the same standard used for other disclosures in the consent form, namely, asking whether this is information that a hypothetical "reasonable person" would likely want to know. Thus, for example, in a trial involving chemotherapy for a form of cancer, there should be no need to list various herbal treatments for the cancer, absent substantial evidence that such treatments are indeed reasonable alternatives to the options being evaluated in the study.[35] In contrast, such evidence automatically exists when a person enrolls in a study where a particular experimental treatment is compared to standard care. As noted above, it would likely be improper of the researchers to be offering the experimental arm if it indeed were not a plausible (though unproven) possible treatment, since then clinical equipoise would not exist between the experimental arm and standard care.

Applying these concepts to the STAR study, we can imagine a hypothetical osteoporosis patient who is contemplating entering that study. She is particularly intrigued by the idea of taking raloxifene, a drug that might prevent breast cancer, improve her osteoporosis, and yet (unlike tamoxifen) not increase her risk of endometrial cancer. She knows that if she enters that study, she has only a 50% chance of ending up getting raloxifene, and she won't even know whether or not she is getting it. How is she any "worse off" if she instead goes to a doctor and that doctor gives her raloxifene for the next five years? The testing done in the STAR study consists of semiannual breast exams and an annual routine blood test. Her private doctor can equally easily do all of this. The risk to her appears identical, whether she gets the raloxifene in the study or outside of it. On the other hand, given the fact of her osteoporosis, the benefits to her might well favor being certain of getting the raloxifene. If the study is stopped at any point due to compelling early results, her doctor will learn those results in exactly the same way that doctors participating in the study do. Under these circumstances, it is difficult *not* to conclude that getting raloxifene outside of the study is a perfectly appropriate alternative for her, and thus that option should be disclosed to her.

The "Too Risky for Prime Time" Alternative

These arguments should demonstrate that, in many research studies, it is quite reasonable for a doctor to be offering the new treatment directly to a patient outside of the study, and thus that option should be disclosed to a person who is considering enrolling in the study. But let us play devil's advocate and assume that we are dealing with one of those few studies where it would not be appropriate for the doctor to be providing that new treatment to his patients. For the sake of simplicity, let us assume (although we obviously believe otherwise) that this was the case for the STAR study. What if Dr. Wickerham was correct in stating that "it's too early to use raloxifene to prevent breast cancer outside of a clinical trial"? What if such a doctor was indeed doing something that was against the best interests of his patient?

We discussed this possibility in detail in chapter 6, where we explored under what circumstances participating in a particular type of study may actually be a significantly bad decision for a patient looking after his own best interests. And it is worth applying that same reasoning to this study: if it is *not* in the best interests of a woman who is at high risk for breast cancer to be treated with raloxifene to prevent that cancer (as opposed to getting a proven treatment, such as tamoxifen, or having both breasts surgically removed), then presumably it also wouldn't be in that woman's best interests if the doctor flipped a coin and, if it came up heads, gave her raloxifene. In other words, a 50–50 chance at getting treated with raloxifene still has to be bad for her. It may not be *as* bad as definitely being given raloxifene—after all, she still has a 50% chance of getting appropriate (proven) care—but it still is bad and against her best interests.

Of course, if this is true, then we must conclude that her participating in the study has to be a significantly bad choice for her (ignoring altruistic motives). This conclusion doesn't mean there is anything wrong with the study, or that it is somehow not consistent with the legal or ethical rules for conducting studies: after all, lots of studies may not be in the best interests of the participants. But there is a consent issue: the woman considering enrolling in the study should be informed that being in the study is so clearly not in her best interests. And, as we noted in chapter 6, we can confidently predict that in getting the informed consent of the woman, *no one is currently ever telling her any such thing.*

In the end, the critics of disclosing that the new treatment can be obtained outside of the study can't have it both ways. Either it is reasonable for doctors to give that treatment outside of the study—and that fact should be disclosed—or the patient should be clearly warned about the extent to which they are sacrificing their own best interests to help others.

Being a Doctor versus Being a Researcher

The scenario we have been discussing highlights the distinct differences between the role of a doctor in treating a patient, and the role of a researcher in conducting research with a subject. We can sharpen that comparison by addressing one additional issue. Let us assume we are indeed dealing with a study where the researcher has agreed that it *would* be reasonable for a patient to be given the new treatment outside of a study, and therefore the consent form discloses that fact to the subject. We have not yet addressed one interesting issue: *What if the subject asks the researcher if he would be willing to give the new treatment to her, outside of the study?* This is of course an obvious and reasonable question: for the patient who does indeed want to get the new treatment, and knows that it is available (or at least may be available) outside of the study, why not just get it from the doctor she trusts, the doctor with whom she already has a relationship?

As a legal matter, although there is little definitive guidance on this issue, the doctor probably does *not* have any obligation to provide the new treatment outside of the study.[36] The legal system is relatively paternalistic, as we have discussed in chapter 4. One way that paternalism is expressed is through the concept of standard of care: in most instances, it is expected that a doctor will provide a patient with care that conforms to this standard. While doctors are *permitted* to deviate from that standard when doing so may reasonably be seen as being in the best interests of a patient, the law will probably not *require* them to provide such nonstandard care. In effect, a doctor is given discretion as to whether or not to comply with a patient's request for such nonstandard care.

Thus, a physician-researcher probably has the legal authority to say "no" when the patient asks to get the new (nonstandard) treatment outside of a study. But taking that action will highlight for the patient the difference between the role of a physician and the role of a researcher. Imagine the following hypothetical dialogue between a doctor and his patient, whom she had invited to participate in the study:

PATIENT: You know, doc, I really am interested in this new treatment. So, instead of being in the study, and just getting one chance in two at it, how about you give me the new treatment, as your patient?

PHYSICIAN: Well, Laura, I'm not providing the new treatment outside of the study.

PATIENT: But, why not?

[Note: an honest researcher *cannot* at this point answer that it is *too risky* to provide the treatment off-study. Recall that we are assuming that the consent form discloses the possibility of getting the treatment off-study precisely because that would be a reasonable choice for the subject. If it was too risky for that to be done, we would be in the other category, a "bad choice" study, as we discussed in chapter 6). So, our honest researcher should be answering as follows:]

PHYSICIAN: Well, Laura, I'm trying to help answer an important question about whether or not the new treatment really works. If I provide the new treatment outside of the study, then there are some patients who might otherwise decide to be in the study who will get the treatment from me outside of the study. It will take me longer to complete the study, and thus future patients, who might benefit from our knowing if the new treatment really works, will be harmed. It is better that we answer this question sooner, instead of in effect continuing to take "best guesses" when doctors treat thousands of patients like you, not really being sure which treatment is best.

PATIENT: Gee doc, on the one hand you are telling me, that from my point of view, it would be very reasonable for me to want to directly get the new treatment, instead of being in the study. But then you turn around and tell me that you won't give it to me outside of

> the study. It seems to me that you are putting me, as your pa-
> tient, in a second-class position, behind your attempt to com-
> plete your study.
>
> PHYSICIAN: Now that you put it that way, Laura, I suppose I'd have to agree
> with you. I am doing just that. But I don't think there is anything
> wrong with that. For when I am doing research, I am often, in
> one way or another, doing things that conflict with the best in-
> terests of my patients.

This Socratic dialogue again highlights the very different rules that apply to a doctor
acting as a researcher, as compared to a doctor dealing with a patient outside of the
research setting, who is bound by the "best interests of the patient" rule.

Protecting the Patient versus Protecting
Medical Research

As demonstrated, "protecting the patient" often does not hold up as a legitimate
reason for justifying the practice of not disclosing out-of-study availability of an
investigational treatment. Even if an experimental treatment is not yet fully proven,
it still may be in a patient's best interests to directly get that treatment. Often a particular patient—perhaps dying of some fatal disease or facing irreversible changes
from disease progression—will have only one shot at making the correct choice.
In that circumstance, it is quite reasonable to play the odds and choose an experimental treatment that only tentative evidence suggests is better than standard care,
particularly if standard care is known to be relatively ineffective. Ignoring the preliminary evidence, and having a treatment picked by randomization, may not be
in the patient's best interests. In retrospect, it may end up that a patient who gambles
on a risky new treatment has made a bad choice. But as long as the law permits doctors to directly offer the experimental treatment to a patient, modern society accepts
that the choice of which route to take should be the patient's, not the researcher's.

Perhaps for that very reason, there is difficulty in recruiting patients for some
research studies, as occurred in the attempt to study bone marrow transplantation as
a treatment for breast cancer. At least some patients are already aware that they can
sometimes get experimental treatments outside of a study, and they are acting on that
information. This may explain, for example, why only a small percentage of patients
eligible for clinical studies of cancer treatments enroll in such studies.[37] Indeed, even
the STAR study has been having some difficulty in recruiting patients in certain re-
gions. As the director of a high-risk breast program noted, "The sense in the community was, 'Well, I can just take raloxifene. Why do I have to be in a trial?'"[38]

The fact that many people appear to be directly getting experimental treatments,
and bypassing randomized studies, must at the least make us suspicious that some—
perhaps many—of those who enter the trials have done so based on a misperception:
they wanted the new treatment and thought that the 50% chance offered in the study

was the only way to get it. This was exactly what apparently happened to Daniel Klais, who ended up being randomized to a "no-chemotherapy" arm in the Cleveland Clinic study we discussed above. In spite of knowing his desire to get the chemotherapy, his doctors allegedly stood by and never told him that he could directly go to a doctor and choose that option, avoiding the chance of being randomized to standard care.

Assuming Daniel Klais's claims are true, the doctors' actions in that case come very close to *fraud*: an "intentional . . . nondisclosure for the purpose of inducing another . . . to surrender a legal right."[39] And whether or not most other prospective subjects are quite as forthright as Klais in telling investigators why they might be choosing to enter a study, we already know that the desire to get the new treatment is a common reason for many of them. So if we fail to disclose off-study availability, and idly stand by suspecting they would go elsewhere if they knew that fact, we are at best on the type of shaky ethical ground that politicians in recent years have stood on as they defended themselves from perjury charges.

It is true that making the disclosures recommended in this chapter will likely further reduce the number of participants in research studies. There is, however, a solution for this dilemma: change the law so that when a treatment is being studied in a formal randomized clinical trial, a physician will not be able to directly provide that treatment to a patient outside of such a study. This is similar to what the law currently provides with regard to the initial approval by the FDA of a new drug. In this manner, society makes a binding determination that the interests of individual patients must come second to the needs of medical research. Following such a change, more patients will indeed enroll in studies: as is the case with trials involving drugs that are not yet FDA approved, patients who want an experimental treatment will recognize that a 50% chance to get it is indeed better than a 0% chance.

But absent such a change in the law—and we may well *not* want to make such a substantial alteration in the longstanding authority of physicians—we should not continue to have the burden of research borne disproportionately on the backs of the unsophisticated and ill informed. The research community prides itself on protecting the interests of vulnerable groups of subjects, such as prisoners, children, and pregnant women.[40] Perhaps we need to better recognize that those of us who are not particularly savvy about all of the available medical options are also vulnerable and equally need protection. *Every* prospective subject in a clinical trial deserves to be armed with appropriate knowledge, so that medical research gets conducted on an even, and fully ethical, playing field.

Part III

When Consent Can't Be Obtained

11

Incompetent Adults

The mere mention of experimental medical research on incapacitated human beings—the mentally ill, the profoundly retarded, and minor children—summons up visceral reactions with recollections of the brutal Nazi experimentation with helpless subjects in concentration camps, and elicits shudders of revulsion when parallels are suggested.
—*T.D. v. New York State Office of Mental Health*

In part II we illustrated the importance of getting informed consent. Informed consent is what generally makes it acceptable to enroll subjects in studies. It legitimates providing them weaker legal protections than those given to patients, and doing things to them that may not be in their best interests. Given that circumstance, it is perhaps surprising that the federal regulations approve of a variety of circumstances in which subjects can be enrolled in studies *without* their full informed consent, because the subjects are incapable of providing consent.

However, on some reflection, these exceptions to the informed consent requirements shouldn't be all that surprising. After all, we know there are "good choice" and "bad choice" studies. Sometimes the best treatment option for someone might involve participating in a research study—for example, a study that gives them a chance at getting a not-yet-approved drug for treating an otherwise fatal disease. If we had a black-and-white rule that prevented people from enrolling in studies unless they were able to consent, we would end up denying some people such treatment opportunities. Thus, there are good reasons for bending our rules to allow people to enroll in studies, even without consent, if we can determine that doing so is in their best interests.

But there is a second and much more controversial rationale used to justify enrolling incompetent subjects in research. As we noted at the beginning of this book, many important research questions may require conducting studies of the "bad choice" variety. If we don't do these studies, we may never learn how best to treat the people who are afflicted by certain types of medical problems. Does that justify enrolling people in "bad choice" research studies without their consent? And if so, how bad can such studies be? The chapters in part III discuss how the current rules deal with these contentious issues.

We begin in this chapter with the case of incompetent adults.[1] Research on such subjects has generated more than its share of controversy.[2] The quotation that begins this chapter is from a lawsuit brought in the 1990s by patients who had been involuntarily hospitalized in various psychiatric facilities in New York State. They claimed that they were improperly being enrolled in medical research studies and being exposed to a variety of risky procedures that might cause stroke, heart attack, convulsions, hallucinations, or other diseases and disabilities, including death. Such allegations conjure up images of nefarious doings hidden behind brick walls—a charge that resonates with some historical events, such as the infamous Willowbrook study, where from the 1950s to the 1970s institutionalized children were intentionally infected with hepatitis.[3] The New York courts ended up agreeing with the patients, though mainly on technical grounds: it was determined that the wrong agency had enacted rules that described the conditions under which such people could be enrolled in studies. But the controversy over what the right rules should be is so great that almost a decade later, no new rules had been implemented in New York.

Who Decides about Participating in Research?

To examine the question of when incompetent subjects can be enrolled in a study, we start with a real controversy. In early 2000, the federal Office for Human Research Protections (OHRP) received an anonymous letter complaining about what happened in one particular study. From 1995 to 1999, researchers at 32 medical centers in the United States were conducting a study funded by the federal National Institutes of Health (NIH) to determine if the female hormone estrogen might be effective in slowing the progression of Alzheimer's disease in women.[4] There had been some tentative evidence from a variety of previous studies that this might be the case, but the previous studies had involved small numbers of subjects and had tested the effect only over a few weeks. In this study, 120 women with mild or moderate Alzheimer's disease were randomized to receive over a one-year period a low dose of estrogen, a higher dose of estrogen, or a placebo.

The results of the study—which showed that estrogen did nothing to slow the progress of Alzheimer's disease—were published in the *Journal of the American Medical Association* in February of 2000. Several weeks later, officials at OHRP[5] opened the following letter:

> A recent article published in the *Journal of the American Medical Association* raises major concerns about the adequacy of protections for human subjects enrolled in a multicenter NIH-funded research project.
> The [study] . . . enrolled subjects with "mild to moderate" Alzheimer disease with Mini-Mental Status Exam scores "as low as 12."[6] Thus, the subject population must have included a significant number of subjects with markedly impaired mental capacity at the start of the trial, with

subsequent deterioration in mental capacity in most subjects during the course of the trial. Despite this, the article states "written informed consent was obtained from all participants."

How can legally effective informed consent, as required by [the applicable federal regulations], be obtained from subjects with such impaired mental capacity? Many such subjects would not have the capacity to make an informed decision regarding participation in such a complex research study, and if "consent" was obtained from such subjects, it should not be considered valid. In addition, if the article is inaccurate and informed consent was obtained instead from a family member or caregiver, such consent should also be considered invalid under the federal regulations, because many of the states where this research took place do not have laws that authorize a family member or caregiver to consent on behalf of another to participate in research.

I request that your office investigate the conduct of this research at each of the following participating study centers: [There then followed a list of all the centers where the study took place, which included some of the nation's leading academic medical centers such as Yale, Columbia, Massachusetts General Hospital, and Johns Hopkins.]

. . . I request that you assess . . . the capacity of the subjects at each site to understand information provided in the consent process, and the conditions under which the local and state laws for each site would authorize another individual to serve as a subjects [*sic*] legally authorized representative to consent to participation in research on behalf of the subject [and were those conditions followed]. . . .

Sincerely,

A concerned advocate

When Is Someone Able to Make a Decision about Being in a Research Study?

Our "concerned advocate" raises a number of interesting and important questions. The first of them is: *how do we determine whether or not a person is capable of making a decision about participating in a study?* This is obviously a crucial issue, for if the person is capable of deciding, then his "yes" or "no" should determine if he is in the study. On the other hand, if we decide that someone is *not* capable of making a decision, then his saying "yes" should not be enough, and we would need some separate set of rules for determining if he should be enrolled.

The federal regulations give no guidance at all on this question.[7] But this lack of guidance doesn't mean that the federal government isn't concerned about how researchers and study centers are resolving this issue. In response to the letter from the "concerned advocate," the compliance division of OHRP quickly opened an investigation into that study and sent letters to all of the institutions that participated, requiring them to respond to a number of requests. One of those requests was the following: "[Provide a] description of any procedures approved by the [institutional review board] for assessing subjects' cognitive status and capacity to provide initial and ongoing legally effective informed consent during the course of the trial."

The recipients of this letter were no doubt puzzling over what types of procedures they should be approving. There is in fact very little settled learning in this area, other than perhaps on the most general issues. Again, it is helpful to turn to decisions about health care. About all that people can agree upon is that a prior concept, "overall competency," is inappropriate. In the past, a person would in essence be determined to be either "wholly competent" or "wholly incompetent." If they were incompetent, then a guardian would be appointed for them by a court, and that guardian would in essence get to make almost *all* decisions for them, no matter what the issue was.

In recent decades, people have come to accept that this all-or-nothing approach is too crude and denies many people the right to make decisions about important aspects of their health care. The concept currently in favor to replace the disfavored competence approach is that of *capacity*: instead of asking whether or not a person is totally competent or totally incompetent, we should recognize that they may have the capacity to make decisions about some issues and lack the capacity to make decisions about other issues. Thus, we need to look at the specific question that the person is being asked and to evaluate that person's ability to understand that question and to make a reasoned decision about it. For example, even a very demented person may have the capacity to decide what flavor of ice cream she would like with dinner (or if she doesn't want any ice cream at all); on the other hand, that person likely would not be able to make a reasoned decision about participating in that double-blind research study involving the use of estrogen and placebos.

Consider the case of Rosaria Candura, a 77-year-old widow who apparently had mild Alzheimer's disease, being forgetful and confused about some matters. She was also suffering from gangrene in her right foot and lower leg, a condition that had not been cured by two prior operations. Her doctors recommended that her leg be amputated without delay, and when she refused surgery, her daughter went to court to declare her incompetent—a conclusion backed up by the doctors—so that the operation could proceed. A lower court granted that request, but a Massachusetts appellate court reversed.[8] The appellate court noted that there was no evidence that her "areas of forgetfulness and confusion cause, or relate in any way to, impairment of her ability to understand that in rejecting the amputation she is, in effect, choosing death over life." Yes, she was somewhat stubborn and irascible. Yes, she was making a decision that others might find to be unfortunate. But she understood what the decision involved, and ultimately it was she who would be experiencing the consequences of that decision. As the court noted, "the operation may not be forced on her against her will."

As Ms. Candura's case demonstrates, the switch to a more nuanced view of a patient's capacity to give consent, one that looks at the actual decision to be made and the patient's ability to reason, makes it harder to give objective criteria for concluding when a particular person's decision should be respected. In the past, some might have looked to a person's medical diagnosis—Mr. Jones has schizophrenia, Ms. Smith has advanced Alzheimer's disease—as the sole justification for concluding that someone lacked the capacity to make various decisions. Thus, all one needed to do was call in a psychiatrist to verify the diagnosis based on the stated criteria for diagnosing that mental disorder, and you would have an answer to whether the person is competent.

With the new emphasis on looking at the particular person's ability to reason, the psychiatric diagnosis fails to resolve the issue: you still need to talk with the person, see how much the person can understand, and see in particular how well that person can understand the issues that must be decided.[9]

Thus, determining a person's capacity to make a particular health care decision remains a somewhat fuzzy process, not easily spelled out with clear, objective criteria. And applying those fuzzy rules in the context of making decisions about enrolling in a research study gets even more complicated. At least, in the context of health care decisions, we are usually asking the person to think about consenting to something that, by societal standards, is considered to be in their own best interests, whereas in the research setting, that conclusion is far from a given. And as we have noted in previous chapters, the information given to prospective research subjects is often less than fully helpful in letting them understand whether being in a study is good or bad for them. These problems just get compounded when you are trying to enroll subjects whose ability to understand what they are being told is, at least to some extent, not as great as that of the average person.

Who Decides?

In any event, in one way or another, we do, in each study that involves enrolling people with mental disorders, have to specify those criteria that separate the competent to consent from those who are not competent to consent. In the estrogen study that the "concerned advocate" complained about, the people running the study applied a commonly used test called the Mini-Mental Status Examination to draw this line. This exam, which is a crude but quick way of determining how well a person's mind is functioning, involves asking the person to do eleven simple tasks; the person is given a few points for each task, with a possible high score of 30 if they get everything perfect.[10] A healthy adult in his early eighties would be expected to get a score of about 20. The people running that study apparently allowed people with scores as low as 12 to be considered capable of consenting to be in the study. The "concerned advocate" appears to be correct in noting that a person with a score of 12 would be in no position to be making a decision about being in a randomized study comparing the use of estrogen to placebo.

This gets us to the second important question about enrolling incompetent persons in research studies: *Who gets to make that decision?* The federal regulations do in fact address this question, in a manner that initially seems to be clear: they allow an incompetent adult to be enrolled in a research study when the "legally effective informed consent" of the subject's "legally authorized representative" is obtained.[11] And the clarification of what these terms mean is found in state law: in other words, you need to look at the laws of the state where the study is taking place to determine the identity of the appropriate decision maker.[12]

Determining the identity of the correct person is easier said than done. To explain why, we need to first explore how health care decisions are made for incompetent persons. And to do that, we turn to one of the most famous court decisions in recent legal history. On the night of April 15, 1975, while participating in a friend's birthday celebration at a tavern in Lake Lackawanna, New Jersey, 21-year-old Karen Ann Quinlan began to feel ill. She had apparently been drinking quite a bit and "popping whatever pills she could get her hands on."[13] She was taken home by a friend, where she collapsed into unconsciousness and stopped breathing for a period of time, requiring mouth-to-mouth resuscitation. An ambulance took her to a local hospital, where she was eventually diagnosed as being in a persistent vegetative state: due to the lack of oxygen to her brain, those portions of it responsible for thinking and feeling emotions had been permanently destroyed. However, since other portions of her brain were still functioning, she did not meet the legal definition of death in New Jersey.

Over many months following these events, her father fought a battle to turn off the respirator that was helping her breathe and to thus allow her to die in peace. His efforts were opposed by virtually everyone else involved in the case, including her doctors, the hospital, the local prosecutor, and even the State of New Jersey. Eventually, his legal battle made its way to the Supreme Court of New Jersey, which in a landmark ruling determined that Karen had a right to refuse the respirator, and that to allow her to exercise that right, it was appropriate to appoint her father to make decisions on her behalf. He subsequently did ask that the machine be turned off, and, to virtually everyone's surprise, Karen remained alive—still unconscious, a living body with no mind, but breathing on her own—for another 10 years. The diagnosis of persistent vegetative state was a new one back in 1975, and even experts in neurology didn't yet realize how long such a person could live.

While what happened to Karen Ann Quinlan raised complicated issues about refusal of life-sustaining care, her case also exposed a more mundane problem relating to everyday health care decision making for an incompetent person. If we look back at the common law—which might be described as the primordial ooze from which early legal concepts arise, before legislatures start enacting statutes—a surprising circumstance is evident: by and large, absent an emergency requiring immediate action, none of us is given any authority to make decisions for other adults, even if that other person is incompetent. Unless we are children—in which case our parents fit the bill— we have no "legally authorized representatives." This rule applies for all sorts of decisions, though of course our focus here is on health care decisions.

In essence, then, under the common law, there is a big "void" about how health care decisions are made for someone who is not in a position to consent to the treatment. Traditionally, the only way to fill this hole was to go to court, as happened in the *Quinlan* case, and to have a judge appoint someone as a guardian, authorizing that person to make health care (or other types of) decisions. But going to court is usually time-consuming and expensive. Thus, in the wake of the *Quinlan* decision, state legislatures began to pass a variety laws that simplified things.

The initial laws authorized people to fill out documents called "advance directives." Similar in concept to the ordinary will that people use to indicate who should get their property when they die, advance directives allow someone to indicate, in *advance*, what care they want if they should ever become incompetent. A person can either appoint someone else to make decisions for them (known as their agent under a power of attorney) or spell out specific treatments they would or would not want in various situations, or do both.

But since most people never get around to completing such documents (who wants to think about how decisions will be made when we are horribly sick?), many states have passed laws that automatically appoint a particular individual as a decision maker for someone who has become incompetent and who hasn't completed an advance directive. These laws try to make a "best guess" at who most people would have wanted to appoint as a decision maker, by using a "pecking order," where the person highest on a list who is available and willing to act as the decision maker gets appointed.[14] While such laws are very helpful, there are still many states that do not have such surrogacy laws or have laws that apply only in limited circumstances.

How might we sum up the laws about making health care decisions for an incompetent patient? As the group that specializes in developing model laws for states to enact in various areas has stated, there is a "fragmented, incomplete, and sometimes inconsistent set of rules."[15]

State Laws about Research with Incompetent Persons

So, we see that determining who is a person's legally authorized representative for purpose of making health care decisions is often rather confusing. Such a person may not even exist. And, as you can guess from preceding chapters of this book, answering the same question for the purpose of enrolling someone in a research study is even harder to do.

The biggest reason why this is so difficult is that most states don't have any laws that address the general question of when an incompetent person can be enrolled in a research study. Indeed, the best description of state laws in this area is that they look like Swiss cheese: there are a bewildering variety of laws that may very specifically describe what happens in one narrow scenario or another, but more "holes" than "cheese," given the lack of guidance for the uncovered scenarios. Thus, states may have laws describing who makes decisions about "experimental treatments" provided to an institutionalized "mental health" patient (Alaska), "experimental research" on someone with a developmental disability (Colorado), "experimental procedures" on the mentally retarded (Connecticut), "experimental research" on people who reside in residential care facilities (Iowa), and so forth.[16] We could likely fill up a book (and it would be a very confusing book to read, at that) if we attempted to give a complete description of all such relatively narrow laws.

What about the large number of people who fall into the "holes"? Imagine, for example, that you are in a state where there are rules for institutionalized retarded people, but the person you propose to study is a mentally retarded person who lives with his parents. Or the state law covers only the mentally retarded, but the person you wish to study has Alzheimer's disease. More generally, if there is no statute in a state specifically referring to how to make decisions about enrolling a particular category of incompetent person in research, how is such a decision to be made?

Recall the framework for making *health care decisions* for incompetent persons: we first look to an applicable advance directive, if the person filled one out; if there isn't such a document, then we see if the state has a law (or a judicial opinion) that automatically appoints a surrogate decision maker. Only if neither of these conditions is fulfilled, we need to get a court-appointed guardian. But there is an interesting and important aspect to both advance directive laws and the state laws that appoint surrogates: both of these sets of laws almost always refer to making "health care" decisions.[17] And that raises a complicated question that returns us to the core issues we have pursued throughout this book: when should enrolling someone in a research study be considered a "health care" decision?

Presumably, we can quickly eliminate studies that do not involve either diagnosis or treatment of a medical condition. But what about participating in studies that do involve treatment, such as a clinical trial where subjects are randomized between standard care or some new drug to treat a disease? As we have noted from the very first chapter, participating in such studies may or may not be a "best choice" in terms of treating a person's medical problem. And allowing a surrogate to make a "health care" decision would seem to require the surrogate to enroll the incompetent person only in those studies that are indeed the best choice for a particular person in terms of ways of treating the person's health problem.

Let's apply this to the estrogen study that the "concerned advocate" complained about to OHRP. If a person with Alzheimer's disease had never completed an advance directive discussing research studies, and that person lived in a state where there were no specific laws about research, should a family member that is authorized under state law to make health care decision be permitted to enroll the patient in this study? If the family member had concluded that getting estrogen was in the patient's best interests, the family member could have asked a doctor to prescribe it: estrogen is a marketed drug. Given that fact, there doesn't seem to be much justification for concluding that being in the study is a "best choice" from the point of view of the patient's health care. Thus, such a family member's decision to enroll the patient in the study would likely have been against the law, unless they were in a state that specifically gave legally authorized representatives authority to enroll people in research studies—and there are only a handful of such states.

The fact that these arguments are not considered frivolous is aptly demonstrated by the federal government's quick response to the letter of complaint. OHRP's letter to every one of the medical centers participating in the study—many of them among the nation's leading research universities—required them to describe, for any incompetent person who was enrolled in the study, "the applicable state and local laws that established [some other individuals] as the legally authorized representatives of the subject." OHRP was in effect acknowledging that in many states, it is questionable whether an incompetent person can be legally enrolled in many types of research studies.

The likely conclusion, not just about this study, but about a large number of other studies involving incompetent patients? It is probably the case that *incompetent persons are routinely enrolled in studies in violation of both the federal regulations and state law.* Indeed, leading authorities on research ethics have openly discussed this issue in major journals, sometimes in effect advocating a type of "civil disobedience," telling researchers to go ahead and violate the law by enrolling subjects under conditions where there has not been any consent by a legally authorized representative.[18] The estrogen study was neither especially risky nor especially controversial in terms of representing current practices for enrolling incompetent people in research studies. It was just that the "concerned advocate" effectively rubbed the nose of the federal government in this issue and forced it to take action.

Making Decisions to Enroll an Incompetent Adult in Research

There is general agreement among many that the current rules for determining when an incompetent person can be enrolled in a research study are both confusing and inadequate.[19] Indeed, although most of our discussion thus far has centered on deciding who has the authority to enroll an incompetent person in a study, we actually haven't even touched on what is perhaps the most complicated issue: assuming we have determined *who* gets to make this decision, *what standards* should then govern the exercise of that authority? This is the subtext of why many people are uncomfortable in interpreting the laws for health care decision making so as to extend those rules to research studies, for as we have shown, getting health care and being in a research study are somewhat different things.

But as we indicated at the start of this chapter, there are good reasons for allowing incompetent persons to be enrolled in at least some studies. Being in a particular study may indeed be in the best interests of a particular person. Thus, many ask, shouldn't we (1) make it clearer who can be the surrogate decision maker for an incompetent person, creating easier ways to designate such a person than going to court and getting a guardian appointed, and (2) at the same time, limit the authority of such decision makers by spelling out which sorts of research studies they would be able to enroll someone in?

One of the strangest aspects of the current federal regulations is that even though everyone recognizes that there is a need to limit the authority of people who make decisions about enrolling incompetent persons in research studies, the federal regulations give virtually no guidance on this issue. Incompetent adults are considered a "vulnerable class" under the regulations, and institutional review boards are given a mandate to take special measures to protect them. For other vulnerable classes, such as children, pregnant women, fetuses, and prisoners, there are entire subsections in the regulations that provide detailed rules spelling out what sorts of studies are permitted and which are unacceptable. Yet when it comes to incompetent adults, no special regulations have been enacted. And even on the state level, apart from the various specific-scenario statutes mentioned above, there are few sets of broad guidelines on this issue. In effect, when it comes to enrolling incompetent subjects in research studies, in many respects it is like the Wild West: anything goes. Once you have identified someone who has legal authority to enroll an incompetent person in a study, that surrogate decision maker can pretty much make such decisions on whatever grounds he or she chooses.

Oddly enough, it is not as if there has been a lack of effort to remedy this situation. As early as 1978, the group whose reports led to much of the current regulatory structure, the National Commission for the Protection of Human Subjects of Biomedical and Behavioral Research, provided specific recommendations for when incompetent subjects could be enrolled in studies. While their guidelines for a related area—enrolling children in studies—were implemented (and are discussed in chapter 13), an apparent "lack of consensus" led to a failure to adopt specific rules for enrolling incompetent subjects.[20] There have been a number of subsequent efforts to develop such rules, on both the federal and state levels. The most prominent work is that produced by the President Clinton's advisory panel on bioethics issues, the National Bioethics Advisory Commission, which in 1998 came out with a two-volume report and a full set of detailed recommendations.[21] On the state level, New York, in response to the high-profile lawsuit with which we began this chapter and that resulted in its existing rules for enrolling incompetent subjects being struck down as having been promulgated by the wrong state agency, created a task force to recommend new regulations.[22] The Office of the Attorney General in Maryland put together a working group on this issue, which came up with recommendations for a new statute.[23]

There is actually quite a bit of overlap among these three proposals.[24] They all agree that if a study could be conducted with people who are competent to choose whether or not to participate, then incompetent subjects should not be enrolled. They all agree that the concept of "assent" by the subject should be followed: even if a subject is incompetent, if the subject physically or verbally objects to something being done to them in a study, then that objection should be respected. They all are in favor of clarifying the laws governing advance directives, to make it clear that a competent individual can indicate, ahead of time, their willingness to be enrolled in various types of research studies at a later date when they might be incompetent.

Even on more controversial issues, there was still a great deal of agreement. Since few people fill out advance directives at present, the proposals acknowledge that we are not likely to have lots of people filling out directives in which they consent to future research. Thus, the three proposals agree that, under limited conditions, people appointed as surrogate decision makers for health care matters, either at the patient's choice (e.g., through a durable power of attorney for health care) or because of a state law that created a pecking order of automatic agents, should be permitted to enroll a person in certain types of research. They differed somewhat about what those conditions are. The National Bioethics Advisory Commission report was the most restrictive: it would allow subjects to be enrolled in studies only if they are low risk or if enrolling in the study actually appears to be in the subject's best interests. The two state reports would have also allowed surrogate decision makers to enroll someone in a study involving slightly more than minimal risk (specifically, a "minor increase over minimal risk"), even if that study had no possibility of benefiting the subject.

Apparently some things never change: none of these three proposals has been adopted. Indeed, the most high-visibility recent change regarding research on incompetent subjects does not involve *added* restrictions on the use of incompetent subjects, but rather *reducing* those restrictions. The State of California, chock full of major universities that get large amounts of funding to do all sorts of medical research, was concerned about the issue we discussed earlier: uncertainty about who is authorized to enroll someone in a research study. That confusion might have made it difficult to do certain types of studies; indeed, the University of California at San Francisco was cited by the federal government for improperly enrolling incompetent subjects in a controversial study about how to adjust ventilator settings for people with severe lung injury.[25] At the request of the University of California system, in 2002 the state legislature passed a law making it crystal clear that a variety of people would have authority to say "yes" to an incompetent person's participation in research.[26] The law created a pecking order, beginning with a person designated as an agent under an advance directive, and went on to include, among others, the person's spouse, adult children, adult brothers and sisters, adult grandchildren, and even any other available adult relative.

The law does put some limitations on the types of studies it authorizes. It applies only to studies relating to "cognitive impairment," "lack of capacity," or "serious or life threatening diseases or conditions" of a research subject. On the other hand, within those approved categories of studies, it doesn't make any distinction between those studies that might be a good choice in terms of the best interests of the subject, and other types of less beneficial studies. And nothing in the bill imposes *any* of the "risk level" restrictions that the three proposals described above had agreed were appropriate: presumably incompetent subjects in California can be enrolled in studies that impose substantial risks yet have no possibility of benefiting them.

For example, imagine a person with advanced Alzheimer's disease who also has metastatic lung cancer. That lung cancer was not caused by the Alzheimer's disease and has no special relationship to that disease. But regardless of that, because that person has a "life threatening disease or condition," the California law authorizes a surrogate decision maker, such as that person's spouse or adult daughter, to consent to the person's participation in research studies relating to lung cancer. And that consent is not limited to studies that are "good" for the patient. Consider the following possibilities:

- A phase I study of a new anticancer drug, in which participants will get only a single dose of the drug
- A study where the patient gets standard care for the lung cancer but also undergoes extra X-rays and blood tests to help researchers determine how lung cancer spreads throughout a patient's body
- The same study as above but that also involves more invasive procedures such as a spinal tap and a liver biopsy, also designed to gain information about how lung cancer spreads

- A randomized study comparing standard chemotherapy for the lung cancer to some new combination of drugs, where that combination could have been obtained outside of the study

These studies obviously differ from one another in the extent to which the patient is subjected to various levels of risk, and the extent to which there is an overall benefit from the patient's participation in the study. Some of them—for example, the second and third studies—are clearly not beneficial to the patient, and there is no particular need to perform such a study on an incompetent patient. There is no reason to think we could not find competent patients with lung cancer and get them to consent to be in the study. But the California law puts no limit on the participation of an incompetent person in any of these studies. Presumably, if the designated surrogate family member states that he or she thinks the patient would have wanted to be in the study, then that decision will be sufficient for enrolling the person. Of course, in failing to put substantive limits on what types of studies incompetent persons can be enrolled in, California's law is no different than that of most states or that of the federal government. It has merely clarified who gets to make the decision about enrolling an incompetent subject, a question that still is somewhat murky in many states.

The Bottom Line: Can We Involuntarily Enroll People in Studies That Are Significantly Bad for Them?

As we have demonstrated in this chapter, the existing laws relating to enrollment of incompetent people in research studies—both federal and state laws—are woefully inadequate. At the least, they should be clarified. It should be made very clear who can say yes or no to enrolling such a person in a study, and what types of studies such a person can be enrolled in.

But there is a remaining question: are there limits to what the federal or state governments might decide in passing statutes that clarify these rules? Is it acceptable to allow—as the proposals by the committees in New York and Maryland suggest—surrogate decision makers to enroll subjects in nonbeneficial studies that impose more than minimal risks? If so, how risky can those studies be? And when a surrogate decision maker is being asked to enroll someone in such a study, should there be especially high burdens of proof placed on that decision maker, justifying the decision maker's determination that the incompetent person would have wanted to be in the study?

The ultimate limits on what the government can do in this area—as in all other areas—lie in the U.S. Constitution and the constitutions of the various states. But there is little specific guidance regarding how those limitations will play out regarding research on incompetent persons. One of the few courts to address this issue was the appellate court that first reviewed the case with which we began this chapter: the lawsuit challenging the New York State regulations. That court found that various sections of the regulations—including those appointing surrogate decision makers who were not required to always act in a patient's best interests—violated the due process rights of incompetent patients under the Fourteenth Amendment of the U.S. Constitution and similar provisions of the New York State Constitution.[27]

Those findings, however, were ultimately thrown out by New York's highest court. That court noted that since there was another even clearer reason for finding the regulations improper—the fact that they had been promulgated by a state agency that did not have the power to issue such rules—there was no need to address the constitutionality of the rules.[28] That high court criticized the lower court for in effect issuing "an inappropriate advisory opinion." Nonetheless, the New York regulations were thrown out, and as noted above, the state has not yet adopted any replacement rules. Thus, New York is now in essentially the same position as many other states, with a great deal of ambiguity about the conditions under which research with incompetent subjects may be conducted. In an odd way, it is far from clear that an action intended to protect such subjects—the judicial determination that the regulations were not valid—really will produce that outcome.

In any event, as a result of the New York high court's ruling, the constitutional limitations on enrolling incompetent persons in research studies remain unclear. But as the state of affairs outlined in this chapter makes clear, it is not as if there will be a lack of future possible cases to be brought before another court. And in the next several chapters, we turn to additional examples in which thousands of legally incompetent persons are regularly enrolled as subjects in research studies: emergency research and research involving children.

12

Emergency Research

Often, someone who has suffered an acute medical problem—they just had a heart attack or a stroke or were in a car crash—will be unconscious or unable to think clearly in the initial moments when medical treatment is begun. There will often be no surrogate decision maker available at that moment. Under such circumstances, medical personnel are legally authorized to begin urgently needed medical treatment on a theory of "implied" consent. But can we enroll such people in research studies? Should we?

Until relatively recently, such emergency research was in fact nearly impossible to do, precisely because federal regulations required either consent of the subject (if competent) or that of a legally authorized representative. Special dispensation had to be obtained from federal regulators for such studies.[1] In the mid-1990s, medical researchers attempted to build a consensus around the need to relax the rules and regarding how that might be done while at the same time protecting the rights and well-being of the subjects.[2] Those efforts bore fruit in 1996, when the FDA adopted a change in its regulations that specifically allows such research under some relatively restrictive conditions.[3] That change made the front page of the *New York Times*, and it was not without controversy. While some people were "delighted" about the new rules, other experts felt it was "a fateful step" away from the core principle of research ethics and "an effort to make research more efficient at the expense of human rights."[4] We explore these competing views by initially describing one of the few studies that has thus far been conducted under the new rules.[5]

Treating Persistent Seizures before Getting to the Hospital

Status epilepticus, to quote the *New England Journal of Medicine*, is "a series of successive grand mal seizures lasting minutes or even hours, without the recovery of normal consciousness."[6] This disorder can result from a number of causes, ranging from a preexisting seizure disorder to head injury or use of alcohol or various medications, among others. Whatever the cause, the longer the person continues to seize, the greater the likelihood of permanent brain injury. There is a premium on stopping the seizures as soon as possible. Fortunately, there are two medications that are proven to be highly effective in doing this—diazepam and lorazepam—and their use in emergency departments to treat status epilepticus has been considered standard care for some time.

But often it takes quite a bit of time for a patient to arrive at the emergency department. Studies have shown that the average time between beginning to seize and starting treatment in a hospital emergency department can be several hours. Thus, over time, emergency medical service (EMS) systems in this country began to revise rules to allow their personnel to use these drugs when they encountered a patient who appeared to be in status epilepticus. By doing so, presumably the patient would get the benefit of earlier treatment, and thus the risk of permanent brain damage might be reduced.

In 1994, researchers at the University of California at San Francisco decided to study whether or not giving these drugs in the emergency setting was in fact a good thing.[7] They noted that there had never been any formal study comparing what happened to patients who got these drugs to the outcome for patients who did not. Also, they suggested some reasons why getting the drugs out in the field from EMS personnel might be harmful: the drugs can cause difficulty in breathing and worsen heart function, and an EMS worker might be incorrectly diagnosing that someone is in status epilepticus (and thus giving these drugs to someone who did not need them). In order to answer the questions they raised, they proposed a randomized study: when EMS workers in San Francisco came across a person whom they found to be in status epilepticus, that person would be enrolled in the study and would be injected with the contents of a syringe that contained one of the following: diazepam, lorazepam, or placebo (a salt solution). Thus, two-thirds of the people enrolled in the study would get one of the active drugs, and one-third would get the placebo.

Since the subjects would be seizing at the time they were enrolled in the study, and presumably there would rarely be a person around at that time who was legally authorized to consent on their behalf, the study was conducted under the new federal rules that allowed for the waiver of the requirement to get informed consent.[8] The new rules are rather detailed,[9] but the most significant requirements are that the person has to be in a life-threatening condition, with existing treatments being either unproven or unsatisfactory, and being in the study has to present the prospect of direct benefit to that person.[10] In addition, before the study was begun, there would have to be "consultation" with members of the community where the study would take place and with members of the group from which study participants would most likely be drawn.

One question to be answered about these new rules—the one that prompted the conflicting opinions about them that were quoted in the *New York Times*—is whether or not being involuntarily enrolled in a study is likely to be a good thing for a subject. The rules do seem to suggest that such needs to be the case, stating that "participation in the research [must hold] out the prospect of direct benefit to the subjects," due to prior studies demonstrating the possibility that the "intervention" has the potential to "provide a direct benefit" to the subjects. But what does this really mean? If it is merely saying something similar to the clinical equipoise requirement—that if we are not sure which of two treatments is better, it is acceptable to involuntarily randomize subjects to either treatment—then we already know from the discussion in chapter 6 that participation in such a study may well be bad for a subject. And, of course, in the scenario we are currently discussing, we aren't even getting the consent of the subject.

Let's apply this "direct benefit" rule to the seizure study. Was being enrolled in this study a benefit to the subjects? At the time that the study was begun, as the designers of the study themselves noted, "many" EMS systems were already letting their personnel give diazepam or lorazepam to patients who appeared to be having a seizure that would not stop. (Indeed, paramedics in the San Francisco area, where the study was conducted, had the authority to use diazepam.) Presumably, getting the drugs under those circumstances represented the best clinical judgment of both the people who were in charge of the EMS system and the actual health care provider who was treating the patient.

On the other hand, persons who were enrolled in the study had a one-third chance of being assigned to placebo. They would be denied the best clinical judgment of the person who was treating them and would have their care determined by the roll of the dice. Admittedly, it might have turned out that the treatment they ended up being assigned to was better than the one that their health care provider would have chosen. But as we have noted previously, most of us don't view being assigned a treatment randomly, and being denied the benefit of our doctor's best judgment, as something that is "good for us." Should the possibility of being assigned to get a placebo have been considered a benefit to these subjects?

To understand how some people interpret the "possibility of direct benefit" rule in the emergency research rules,[11] it is helpful to look at comments by Dr. Norman Fost, a leading bioethicist and pediatrician whose writings played a major role in getting the new rules adopted. He believes that for studies permitted under these rules, it will *almost always be the case* that the subjects, had they been competent, would have willingly enrolled in the studies anyway.[12] If that indeed were true, there would be very good justification for following these rules: we would both be doing what most people really wanted done anyway, and at the same time advancing medical knowledge so as to improve treatments for future patients.

Let us explore exactly how Dr. Fost comes to the conclusion that so many people would have jumped at the opportunity to be in these sorts of studies. Imagine a study in which a critically ill person is randomized between getting, in addition to standard care, either a placebo or some new but not fully proven therapy. This is what Dr. Fost says he would tell the patient if he later woke up after having been enrolled in the study, and complained about having been randomized to get the placebo:

> I am reasonably certain the standard treatment will not help. I don't know if the experimental treatment will help, but I think it is reasonable to try. If you were able to consent, I would offer it to you, and my best guess is that you would be interested in it and willing to try it. However, my own conscience tells me it would not be responsible to give it to you in an uncontrolled way, because neither you, nor I, nor future patients would ever know whether it helped or hurt. As part of a controlled trial, therefore, I am administering your treatment in precisely the same way that I would if you were awake. . . . [I presume that] a reasonable person would more than likely consent to such treatment, and I therefore also presume you would consent to a 50% chance of receiving such treatment. *If you tell me you would insist on receiving the experimental treatment, without being part of a well-designed study, then I regret to inform you that I cannot accommodate that request. I believe it is irresponsible to give potentially dangerous treatments, of unknown benefit, without appropriate review, oversight and efforts to learn from the experience, so that lethal mistakes will not be repeated.*[13]

Dr. Fost's final two sentences make it clear what he is *not* trying to do: *he is not trying to do what is best for this particular patient.* When it comes to a conflict between what the patient might likely want—getting the new treatment—and making sure the study can produce a result, Dr. Fost unequivocally opts for doing what is best *for the research.* Indeed, his complaint about the rules that existed prior to the 1996 change was that it was hard to do studies "because they seem to be crafted to allow a patient to receive experimental treatment when the physician believes it would serve a patient's interests."[14] That's an odd complaint, if viewed from the point of view of that patient: surely letting a doctor directly give a patient an unproven therapy, *when the doctor thinks that is the best thing for the patient,* can be a *very good* thing for that patient.[15]

Dr. Fost apparently believes that it is appropriate to subordinate the best interests of patients to the goal of getting the research done. This conclusion is also clearly shown in prior studies he has written about. In 1980 he was involved in a study where people who were suffering from brain swelling following traumatic head injury were randomized to one of three arms: getting the standard ("low" dose) of steroids, getting a higher dose, and getting a "highest" dose.[16] At the time, it was believed that steroids reduced brain swelling and made it more likely that a patient would avoid brain injury or even death. However, doctors speculated that giving higher doses of the steroids might be even more effective in preventing those bad outcomes and began the study to test that hypothesis. The only expected side effect of even the "highest" dose was getting a stomach ulcer, which could be treated and, in almost all circumstances, would not lead to permanent harm.

Is being enrolled in such a study without informed consent in the best interests of the subjects? Had subjects been magically able to wake up and participate in the consent process, it is highly unlikely that "almost all of them"—as Dr. Fost alleges—would have said yes to being in the study. The significant "down side" of getting the higher doses of steroid were relatively modest, the most significant being a risk of bleeding in the stomach. The "up side" of the higher doses appeared far more significant: a possibility of reducing the chance of brain damage or death. Certainly, many people presented with this scenario would opt for getting the higher doses and not for being enrolled in a study where they are randomized in a way that gives them a one-third chance of getting the "low" dose. And there would likely be no legal barrier to a doctor choosing to given a patient the higher doses.

Dr. Fost's conclusion that most people would have enrolled in these sorts of studies thus makes sense only if standard care is nearly worthless and if the promising "new treatment" *is not legally available outside of the study.* Yes, if your brain is swelling, and no proven drugs can stop the swelling, then most of us would leap at the chance of being in a study that gives us a 50% shot at getting a brand-new non-FDA approved drug *that isn't available outside of the study.* But the main reason that people would almost uniformly consent to be in that study is that it is the *only* way to get the new drug: that is what turns it into a "good choice" study. One such study involved a drug that had not yet been approved by the FDA for any purpose (and thus was not yet on the market), which was tested to see if it would improve brain function in comatose patients following a heart attack. The families and patients were debriefed after the study, and most were happy that "involuntary" enrollment had taken place. And why shouldn't they be happy: they got a 50% chance at something that wasn't otherwise available. Some of them even recognized the one thing that would have been a better option, expressing "a desire that the active drug, not the placebo, be given."[17] But that wasn't an option, due to the legal status of the new drug, which was not FDA approved.

So, the argument that people would have almost uniformly wanted to be in such studies—the main argument provided for legitimating the new rule—holds only in a limited range of circumstances. The discussion above illustrates one such circumstance: when standard care is relatively poor, the new treatment has the possibility of being much better than standard care yet has a minimal likelihood of any negative consequences, and that new treatment is not legally available outside of the study. Absent some such set of special circumstances, the argument about the likely wishes of possible subjects falls apart.

Oddly, however, the new rule *imposes no such limitation,* nor have most of the studies in which this type of analysis has been applied included such a restriction. Consider the seizure study: not only was diazepam legally available to be given to patients, but the San Francisco EMS system and many others had specifically authorized their paramedics to use the drug in appropriate circumstances. Perhaps some people would indeed opt to have been in that study. But it seems plainly wrong to conclude that virtually everyone would have thought it was a great opportunity. Surely a significant percentage would have said:

Gee, you tell me there is a drug that is effective in stopping seizures, and my brain might get permanently damaged and I might die if my seizures continue. And you want me to take a chance on not getting the drug because there is a possibility the paramedic might not be able to treat possible side effects of the drug? I'll take that chance—give me the drug! I *know* that letting the seizures continue is bad for me; I don't know that I will have any bad side effects from the drug, or that the paramedic is going to screw up in trying to treat them.

And, indeed, it worked out that being assigned to a placebo was very much a bad thing: the death rate for the people who didn't get the active drug was *two to three times higher* than those who received diazepam or lorazepam.[18] Eleven people who got assigned to the placebo ended up dying: the odds are that six or more of those people would have lived if they had been given one of the drugs. And had the study not taken place, there was a good chance that they would indeed have gotten those drugs, since the San Francisco EMS system allowed their use. In a very real sense, those subjects died so that we could learn whether or not the use of the drugs was indeed beneficial. The fact that people enrolled in studies may end up with bad consequences, and some may die, is itself not unusual. The special circumstance here, however, is that these subjects were never given the opportunity to consent to be in the study. And as we have demonstrated, it is not the case that almost all of them would have consented to be in the study, had there been an opportunity to ask them.

Perhaps it was felt by some that the special "public comment" features of the new rule assured the approval of only those studies where most subjects would indeed have wanted to participate, had they been given a chance to choose. The rule does require a type of public hearing involving the community of people who are most likely to be possible subjects in the study. But even that requirement does not assure that only "good choice" studies will be approved.

As we have noted previously in chapter 2, what is best for a particular community will often conflict with the interests of individual members of that community.[19] Members of a community may very much want a study to take place, so that the information is collected that will improve their own care. They may recognize that being in the study is not in the best interests of most subjects but may be hoping that they "luck out" and are not among those who end up participating in the study. Depending on how long the study will take place and how many subjects are needed, the odds may be good that they will not be a participant. Many patients with epilepsy might well have supported the San Francisco study, hoping that it would produce a result—and thus improve their own treatment—before they became one of the people whose care was randomized after EMS personnel were called to take them to an emergency department.

Ironically, there is currently an emergency research study that is getting quite a bit of criticism in the media—unlike the San Francisco study—and yet this study may be one of those "good choice" studies.[20] The study involves the use of an unproven blood substitute called PolyHeme. As part of the study, when EMS personnel encounter a person who has suffered massive blood loss after trauma and is in shock, they randomize the person to receive either fluid replacement (saline solution) or PolyHeme. The fluid replacement is standard care but does nothing to replace the ability of the lost blood to carry oxygen to parts of the body. Since EMS personnel do not routinely carry blood with them, participation in the study gives someone at least a 50% chance of getting a treatment that may well be proven to be much better than standard care, indeed, life-saving. And in this instance, since it is an unapproved product, that opportunity will come only from being in the study. Thus, there are much better arguments in this study—unlike the San Francisco study—for concluding that most people would indeed want to be participants, since it gives them a chance at a promising new treatment under emergency circumstances when other options are very poor.[21]

Acknowledging What the Emergency Research Rule Does

In summary, unless it is limited to a range of specific situations—and it isn't being so limited, nor does its wording or its procedures impose such a limit—the new rule for emergency research effectively does allow studies to be conducted that many people, given the choice, would choose *not* to enroll in. We may still want to do such research, and we may be willing to go ahead with these types of studies, knowing that many people are being enrolled even though they would have refused (given the opportunity), and that those people are being harmed to enable the rest of us to benefit from the medical knowledge gained in such studies.[22] Certainly, such harm took place to some of the people who were assigned to the placebo arm in the seizure study and were denied the drug that they would likely have been given were they not an involuntary participant in that study. It may indeed be the case that our society concludes that such harms are necessary in order to learn how to treat certain conditions and prevent vastly greater amounts of suffering by people in the future.

At the least, however, we should more openly acknowledge that this sort of tradeoff is taking place and not pretend that these are studies that virtually everyone would have wanted to say "yes" to. But, as we saw with the fact that there are still no federal regulations restricting what sorts of studies incompetent patients can be enrolled in, open acknowledgment of our willingness to use people in this way is not something that comes easily. So we may be more comfortable in just "using" these subjects, against their wishes in many instances, and not openly admitting that.

13

Children in Research

The Basic Rules

In chapter 11, we discussed the dilemma of enrolling incompetent adults in research studies. Although everyone acknowledges that these people are vulnerable and deserve special protections, no one has been able to get those protections written into law. In the meanwhile, there is almost an "anything goes" atmosphere surrounding such research.

In an unexpected way, research involving children presents a very different picture. A person below the age of majority—18 in almost all states—is considered to lack the ability to enter into many types of legal agreements, including consenting to get health care. There are only a few exceptions to this rule.[1] Thus, as is the case with incompetent adults, a minor's agreement to be in a research study is usually not legally sufficient to allow the minor to be enrolled in the study. The federal regulations specify that the consent of a "legally authorized representative" is needed. But while for incompetent adults, as we showed in chapter 11, it is often unclear who meets that legal standard, for most children there is usually someone who readily fits into that legal category—a parent. In addition, if the child is old enough to understand some of what will be involved in the study, the child's agreement to participate—referred to as their "assent"—is also usually required.

What types of studies can parents enroll their child in? Unlike the situation with incompetent adults, where there is essentially no definitive guidance, there actually is a set of federal regulations that attempt to resolve this issue for research with children. These regulations even specify what sorts of risks a minor can be exposed to for research purposes, and under what circumstances. The regulations create a set of "risk categories," requiring that all research studies conducted on children fit into one of these four pigeonholes.

Thus, one might think that these rules relating to doing research involving children are the long-sought-after Holy Grail in terms of enrolling subjects who can't consent for themselves. In this chapter and chapter 14, we explore those rules and whether they hold up to that promising buildup. We begin with a specific research study, one that has resulted in a prominent judicial opinion on the law and ethics of conducting research with children.

The Lead Paint Study

Like many other cities in the United States, inner-city Baltimore has long had a problem resulting from the historical use of lead paint in residential housing. Lead paint poses a clear health problem for young children, particularly those living in poorly maintained properties, since they can breathe in lead dust or swallow flaking paint chips. Once lead gets into the bloodstream of a young child, it can end up causing brain damage, permanently lowering the child's level of cognitive function.[2] The use of lead paint was finally banned in 1978 following the passage of a federal law, but lead paint that was applied prior to that date remains on the walls of hundreds of thousands of homes in the United States.

This problem was particularly acute in Baltimore when the Kennedy Krieger Institute, a prestigious nonprofit children's health care and research group affiliated with the Johns Hopkins University, decided to follow up on its prior groundbreaking studies on how to decrease the risk of lead poisoning in children. At that time—the late 1980s and early 1990s—approximately 95% of the housing in low-income neighborhoods in Baltimore was contaminated with lead paint. It was known that living in this type of housing posed substantial health risks for young children. But the lead paint predated the 1978 federal ban, and there were no federal or state laws as of the early 1990s that required landlords or homeowners to remove the old lead paint or, indeed, to do anything else to lessen the risk to children. Thousands of children lived in this type of housing. It was considered an unfortunate situation, but one without an easy (in particular, low-cost) answer. No one was expecting these poor families to suddenly pack up and move to better, and likely more expensive, housing. Even the government wasn't doing all that much to remedy the situation.

A major part of the dilemma was that the only proven way to get rid of the lead paint hazard involved a very expensive process of fully stripping the old paint from the walls. This process could cost tens of thousands of dollars per dwelling, an amount that exceeded the market value of most of these housing units. The property owners were thus rarely undertaking that effort—they would have been better off merely destroying the units. And, as noted, neither the federal nor state governments expected them to be undertaking this endeavor, nor did the law require it.

Against this background, researchers at the Kennedy Krieger Institute posed a question: perhaps there might be cheaper ways of reducing the lead paint hazard, ways that were cheap enough that they might actually be used in many if not most of these homes? These cheaper methods might not be as good as the "gold standard" method of fully stripping the old paint, but having most or at least a substantial part of the hazard eliminated would make more sense than having a "zero-risk" solution that is so expensive that virtually no one was adopting it. So staff at the Kennedy Krieger Institute designed a study to determine how much risk reduction might take place from several types of cheaper efforts to reduce the exposure of children to lead. This study ultimately made its way to the highest court in the State of Maryland, when the mothers of two children who participated in the study brought suit against the researchers (*Grimes v. Kennedy Krieger Institute, Inc.*).[3]

The study involved comparing, over time, the lead levels in children living in five types of homes (with 25 homes included in each group). Two of these groups were "control" groups, in which it was expected that the children would not have any exposure to lead: one control group involved children living in homes that had undergone the expensive gold standard "full lead abatement," and the second group involved children living in homes that were built after the ban on the use of lead paint (post-1980 homes). The part of the study that would later generate the controversy involved the three other groups, all of which involved children living in homes that were known to have preexisting lead paint, and the hazard had not been fully eliminated. In particular, the researchers went to landlords of such homes and provided funding (obtained from the government) to perform one of three methods designed, they hoped, to *reduce* the level of lead hazard for children, though presumably *not to totally eliminate it*. These three methods, which cost between $1,650 and $7,000, involved interventions such as scraping and vacuuming walls, repainting surfaces, and adding sealants.[4]

To find homes to undergo these various levels of repair, as one of the researchers put it, "We were basically looking for the two-story, six-room row house in Baltimore City with 8 to 10 windows in a structurally sound condition."[5] Once they found such a dwelling, if it was occupied, they would then see if its current tenants included children in the age range they wished to study, and if the family had no immediate plans to move.

In the case of a currently rented apartment, the researchers were thus undertaking a set of measures designed to *reduce* the level of lead risk to the children living there, and hoped to check, over time, how well those measures worked. During the several years of the study, the home would be tested a number of times for lead levels in the air and on various surfaces. In addition, the children would have their blood tested for lead levels on several occasions. If the lead level was shown to be at a level that, based on current medical knowledge, indicated that the child should be treated, the child would be referred to public health agencies to get that treatment. The child's parent would be asked to complete a questionnaire at the start of the study, for which they would receive $5. In addition, every six months an additional questionnaire would be completed, for which a payment of $15 would be made.

Perhaps the most controversial aspect of the study involved the fact that some of the homes selected for the study did not have any tenants in them initially. For these homes, the researchers asked the landlords to rent the home to a family that had children in the age range being studied. It does not appear that any special inducements (e.g., discounted prices) were used to rent these properties: they were advertised in newspapers the same way the landlord might otherwise have done it, and only after a family moved in was the family approached about possibly participating in the study in the same manner that the tenants in the nonvacant properties had been approached. The parents could, of course, choose not to participate in the study.

When Does a Study Impose Only a "Minimal Risk" on Participants?

As noted above, lawsuits were ultimately brought on behalf of two children who participated in the study. The lawsuits were initially dismissed by lower courts on the theory that researchers in this type of study had no legal duty to warn parents about health hazards to which their children were being exposed. The highest state court in Maryland reversed those determinations, concluding that the cases should go to trial to determine the actual facts. Many of the issues raised related to informed consent: did the consent documents adequately inform the parents about what would be happening in the study, such as the fact that the children would be exposed to some risk of lead poisoning? Based on the documentation discussed in the court opinions, there is reason to suspect that informed consent was far from ideal. Of course, as we have discussed in preceding chapters, that is far from a unique or even uncommon circumstance in the current world of research.

But the landmark aspect of this case related to an issue that *is* unique to studies involving children: even if informed consent was obtained from the parents in full compliance with all appropriate standards, should parents be permitted to enroll their children in this study? Did they have the legal authority to enroll them in a study in which the children would be living, for several years, in an environment in which the risk of lead poisoning had not been 100% eliminated? The Maryland court, in a strongly worded ruling that was highly critical of both the researchers and the Johns Hopkins Hospital institutional review board (IRB) that had reviewed the study, concluded that the parents did *not* have such authority: "We hold that in Maryland a parent, appropriate relative, or other applicable surrogate, cannot consent to the participation of a child or other person under legal disability in nontherapeutic research or studies in which there is any risk of injury or damage to the health of the subject."

In a subsequent revision of its decision, the court clarified its conclusions, noting it wasn't really referring to "no risk," but rather risks beyond the "minimal kind of risk that is inherent in any endeavor."[6] As modified, the court was creating a rule similar to one of the four categories of permissible research on minors under the federal regulations: even if a child will not benefit from participating in a study, that study may nonetheless take place (assuming appropriate agreements to participate are obtained from the parent and in many instances the child) if "no greater than minimal risk" is presented to the child.

In analyzing the appropriateness of this study, the court drew analogies to a number of "prior instances of research subjects being intentionally exposed to infectious or poisonous substances in the name of scientific research":

[Such experiments] include the Tuskegee Syphilis Study . . . where patients infected with syphilis were not subsequently informed of the availability of penicillin for treatment of the illness, in order for the scientists and researchers to be able to continue research on the effects of the illness, the Jewish Hospital study [where chronically ill and debilitated patients were injected with cancer cells without their consent], and several other post-war research projects. Then there are the notorious use of "plague bombs" by the Japanese military in World War II where entire villages were infected in order for the results to be "studied"; and perhaps most notorious, the deliberate use of infection in a nontherapeutic project in order to study the degree of infection and the rapidity of the course of the disease in the . . . typhus experiments at Buchenwald concentration camp during World War II. These programs were somewhat alike in the vulnerability of the subjects; uneducated African-American men, debilitated patients in a charity hospital, prisoners of war, inmates of concentration camps and others falling within the custody and control of the agencies conducting or approving the experiments. In the present case, children, especially young children, living in lower economic circumstances, albeit not as vulnerable as the other examples, are nonetheless, vulnerable as well.[7]

The court went on to compare the children in this study to the canaries that miners would carry into mines as a way of warning them when dangerous levels of toxic gases had collected. It concluded that "no degree of parental consent, and no degree of furnished information to the parents could make the experiment at issue here, ethically or legally permissible."

What Risks Can Children Be Exposed to in Research?

Before attempting to more fully analyze what was taking place in the Kennedy Krieger Institute study, we need to first expand our field of view. The lead paint study is a relatively unusual one, in that it is concerned not with how to best treat a sick child, but rather how to reduce an environmental risk that might ultimately make a child sick. This type of environmental study raises issues that are somewhat different from those that must be considered in the more routine research study involving children.

The *Grimes* case introduced us to one of the four categories of research involving children that are permitted under the federal regulations.[8] Only research studies that fit within one of these four "risk" categories are permitted to take place. It is now time to list these four categories and explore what they mean by discussing a number of other common types of studies. In most instances, in addition to the requirements of one of these categories being met, a parent must "give permission" for the child to participate, and the child, if old enough to understand, must agree ("assent") to participate.[9] The four categories of studies are "minimal risk," "good choice," "learn about the child's condition," and "not otherwise approvable."

The "Minimal Risk" Study

As noted above, a study that imposes no more than a minimal risk on children is permissible. Minimal risk is defined in the federal regulations as meaning that "the probability and magnitude of harm or discomfort anticipated in the research are not greater in and of themselves than those ordinarily encountered in daily life or during the performance of routine physical or psychological examinations or tests."[10] This definition leaves a number of issues open to interpretation.

For example, different children in our society encounter different types of risks. Which type of child are we supposed to be looking at in determining if a risk is minimal? The report of the federal commission whose recommendations led to the regulations indicated that the definition should refer to the risks that a "healthy" child is exposed to, but the eventual regulations left out the word "healthy."[11] Thus, on a basic issue such as whether various types of risky tests and treatments can be considered minimal risks for a sick child who regularly gets exposed to such tests, but would be more than a minimal risk for a healthy child, there is substantial uncertainty. The federal government has given no guidance on this issue, or even on any other aspect of how to interpret "minimal risk"[12] or other vague terms used in these four categories.

A related question also frequently arises, even if we confined the definition to just healthy children: risks encountered by *which* children?[13] Different children in our society, even if they are healthy, encounter different levels of risk. Should we be looking at the sorts of risks that *every* child encounters *every* day? That *many* children encounter *every* day? That *many* children encounter *some* days? Or, is this definition supposed to refer to those risks that the particular children being recruited already are exposed to in their lives? Each of these possible interpretations can lead to vastly different determinations of what kinds of studies involve "minimal risk." For example, many parents regularly take their children on skiing trips, and our society certainly does not consider exposing children to that risk child abuse. If a study involved the same level risk of injury involved in a ski trip, is that always a minimal risk? Is it a minimal risk only if that particular child already is exposed to that level of risk (e.g., regularly goes on ski trips)?

Even the *Grimes* case raises a similar issue. Many of the children in inner-city Baltimore (and, indeed, throughout the United States) are regularly exposed to the same risks from lead paint that the children in the study were exposed to. Indeed, perhaps a majority of the children in inner-city Baltimore were exposed to such risks. Does that mean that this study should be considered a minimal risk study and approvable under this category? There is no conclusive answer to this question, given the ambiguity of the regulation.

The "Good Choice" Study

Even if a study imposes more than a minimal risk—indeed, no matter how high a risk it imposes on a child—it may still be conducted if, in essence, the child might benefit from being exposed to that risk. More particularly, a child can be exposed to interventions and procedures if, for each such element of the research, (a) the risk is justified by the anticipated benefit to the subjects, and (b) the relationship of the anticipated benefit to the risk is at least as favorable to the subjects as that presented by available alternative approaches.

Simply stated, if these criteria are met, then this is a "good choice" study: it is in a child's best interests to be in this study. This is the category that is probably most often used for approving studies that involve some change in the treatment that the child might otherwise be getting for a medical problem. We will discuss it in some detail later in this chapter.

The "Learn about the Child's Condition" Study

This category was designed to fill in a possible gap between the two categories described above, those of "minimal risk" and "good choice." It was felt by those who wrote the regulations that there might be conditions under which a child can be exposed to *more* than a minimal risk, even though being exposed to that risk would not directly benefit the child (and thus the "good choice" category would not be met). A requirement for coming under this category is that the child has a particular medical problem or condition, and the study might contribute to our understanding of this problem. Thus, it was considered appropriate to allow such a child to be exposed to this increased level of risk because the child belongs to a group that is more likely than average children to benefit from the fruits of this research. These studies are approvable only if the risk imposed on the child is only a "minor increase over minimal risk."

Of course, as we noted above, the term "minimal risk" is already extremely vague, and the federal government has done little to clarify its meaning. There is virtually no guidance other than the definition provided in the regulations. The term "minor increase" is never even defined in the regulations. Thus, we are left with the less than crystal clear requirement of determining what constitutes a *minor increase* (a vague term) over a *minimal risk* (another vague term).

Some sense of the confusion over these terms is shown by the trouble that one branch of the federal government, the National Institutes of Health, got into regarding a study that it was conducting.[14] It was trying to learn about obesity and what role insulin might play in that condition. In the study, fifty obese children and fifty nonobese children with obese parents would be put in a hospital overnight and undergo a variety of tests. During this hospitalization, for a few hours the children would be given intravenous amounts of glucose (a sugar) and insulin to see how their body reacted to these compounds. To make sure that the child's blood sugar did not go too high or too low and get into a range where it might harm the child, the blood sugar was going to be tested every five minutes. In addition, a physician was going to be constantly around the child during this part of the study.

The IRB that reviewed this study had concluded this was a minimal risk study. It based this in part on information about similar procedures that had been done in hundreds of other children, showing that the blood sugar of the children never went below a normal level. During the IRB discussion, several members noted that being in the hospital with all of this close monitoring was certainly safer than playing on a sidewalk. The federal Office for Human Research Protections, while acknowledging that determining the risk level of a study is a "subjective" matter, concluded that this was not a minimal risk study. It concluded that the procedures involving the insulin and glucose involved more than minimal risk, basing that in part on how other IRBs had evaluated similar studies. However, it gave no specific explanation of why this was more than minimal risk. Interestingly, in a very rare comment about the "minor increase over minimal risk" rule, it noted that some of the other procedures in the study might constitute *more* than a minor increase over minimal risk. Nonetheless, it did not indicate which procedures it was referring to, or why they involved more than a "minor increase."

The "Not Otherwise Approvable" Study

This is basically a catchall category for studies about "serious problems" affecting the health or welfare of children that are not approvable under any of the above three categories. A special committee is set up by the Department of Health and Human Services, and it (in addition to the local IRB) must determine whether the study presents a "reasonable opportunity" to contribute to our understanding of such a problem and that the research will be conducted "in accordance with sound ethical principles." In chapter 14, we discuss how this section was used to evaluate whether a study of a diluted version of a smallpox vaccine could be conducted.

These four rules have come under quite a bit of criticism in recent years, and properly so, in our view. Notice how, apart from the relatively rarely used "not otherwise approvable" category, they boil down to two concepts: research can be performed upon children either if it exposes the child to a low risk (categories "minimal risk" and "learn about the child's condition") or if participating in the study is a reasonable thing to do purely from the viewpoint of the child's best interests ("good choice" category). Given the basic propositions explained in part I of this book suggesting that participating in research is often risky, and often may not be in a subject's best interests, it would certainly be a wonderful thing if we could accomplish the "appropriate" amount of pediatric research under the rather benign conditions permitted by these rules. (We don't appear to be able to do that with adults: as preceding chapters demonstrated, adults are often permitted to enroll in studies that may not be in their best interests and that involve substantially greater than minimal risks.)

The question to ask is, are we actually adhering to these rules? Or are they in effect being used as a smokescreen, to give an observer the incorrect impression that almost all pediatric research is innocuous, even though much pediatric research does not in fact meet the standards imposed by the rules? To delve into these issues, we examine now several types of studies that are generally considered approvable under the regulations.

The Phase I Study

As noted in preceding chapters, the initial type of study of a new drug, after using it in animals, is a "phase I study," where people are exposed to increasingly larger and larger doses of the drug to see how large a dose can be given before significant side effects develop. While phase I studies of many drugs are often conducted in healthy subjects, in one area—cancer research—these studies are conducted on people who have a cancer that is usually uncurable. The reasoning behind this policy is that these drugs—usually some form of chemotherapy—are almost certain to have significant side effects, since they usually work by interfering with one or another of the steps by which cells divide. While cancer cells divide rapidly, and thus are particularly prone to being sensitive to such drugs, other normal cells in our bodies that divide rapidly also are commonly affected. Thus, many types of chemotherapy cause hair loss, can destroy bone marrow (which can lead to severe side effects, including death), and so forth.

Children, by a large number of measures, are different from adults in how their bodies react to a drug. One of the most important differences relates to dosing: just because we know a great deal about how much of a drug we can give to an adult before getting severe side effects, it doesn't mean we can accurately predict the appropriate dose to give children (and, more significantly, children of various ages). Thus, it is generally considered important to do phase I studies of new cancer drugs not just in adults but also in children. Waiting until we have the results from adults before we do the testing in children may somewhat reduce the risks that children are exposed to, but doing so fails to eliminate those risks.

Phase I studies of new anticancer agents in children are therefore not that uncommon. Under which of the risk categories are they being approved? Oddly enough, although the federal government presumably thinks such studies are acceptable—they are considered a mandatory step in approving a drug for use in children—no definitive guidance has ever been given regarding why such studies are consistent with the regulations. The most widely stated line of reasoning is that the phase I study would be approvable under the so-called "good choice" study category, since it is theoretically possible that the child may benefit from getting the drug.[15] After all, the child does have an untreatable cancer, and there is certainly a possibility—albeit very, very slim—that getting the drug will have an effect on the child's cancer.

Yet as discussed in chapter 9, the existing evidence about what happens to subjects in phase I trials strongly backs up the conclusion that it is the rare phase I study that should be considered a "good choice" from the subject's point of view. Matthew Miller, a young oncologist who was in charge of enrolling adults in phase I studies at Harvard's prestigious Dana-Farber Cancer Institute, has well documented how classic phase I studies are designed in a way that makes it extremely difficult for a subject to benefit. Even if a drug might end up being effective, the subject only continues to be given the dose that they were assigned when they entered the trial. They are not allowed to get higher (and presumably more effective doses), even if those doses have been shown to be tolerable by the results of later subjects who received those higher doses. Thus, in essence, these studies usually lead to suboptimal doses of a drug that, from the beginning, is a huge crap shoot regarding its possibly efficacy. Miller reluctantly came to the following conclusion about the very studies he oversaw:

> We cannot continue to claim that since the novel agents under investigation have never before been used in humans any dose is potentially therapeutic. The opposite is true. Unless and until we know whether a given drug is effective, under what conditions, for what malignancies, and at what dose, these trials remain non-therapeutic and ought to be spoken of as such.[16]

All of these comments related to being more truthful with *adults* who are thinking about participating in a phase I study. But the question we are posing now is, can it pass the test of the "good choice" category: does it not only give a possibility of benefit, but also have a "risk [imposed by taking the drug] . . . justified by the possibility of benefit"? In other words, is participating in the study a reasonable choice in terms of the well-being of the child? Should we perhaps conclude that if a child has an incurable cancer, any treatment that offers even the slimmest, pie-in-the-sky chance of possibly extending the child's life, even if that treatment is almost certain to cause the child increased suffering during her remaining few months of life, is "reasonable"? In reality, that seems to be how the regulation is being interpreted in permitting many phase I studies to take place. But that interpretation of the "good choice" category seems to go far in making it toothless, in making the word "reasonable" nearly meaningless. Under that interpretation, many treatments may be tested in studies merely on the faintest evidence that they might work, regardless of the known substantial harms. Assuming we are not content to eliminate the significance of the "reasonableness" requirement, it certainly would seem to be the very rare phase I study that meets the test of a "good choice." Even the prestigious Institute of Medicine, a nonprofit group of scholars that reviews many complicated policy issues for the federal government, could only half-heartedly conclude that perhaps the most promising phase I studies might "arguably" meet that test.[17]

Thus, we are left with a troublesome state of affairs: phase I studies in children are a recognized and accepted part of drug research, imposing substantial suffering on dying children with little if any evidence that any of them benefit, yet it is questionable whether even a small portion of these studies meet the specific criteria set up by the regulations for allowing a study to proceed.

The "Slightly Better" or "Somewhat Different" Drug

Let's now examine a very common type of study a child might be enrolled in, one that compares different drugs for treating a child's illness.

An Asthma Study

Children between the ages of 4 and 11 were invited to participate in this study. These were *not* children whose asthma was poorly controlled: to the contrary, the children had to have *stable* asthma, well controlled using one of the standard medications currently being recommended.

In order to participate in the study, a child had to gradually *stop* certain types of their current medications before the study began. In some instances (if they had been using oral corticosteroids), this would require their having stopped that medication at least 30 days before the study began.

Once the study started, there would be a one-week period in which all the children got a placebo, although an inhaled "rescue medication" would be permitted if the child had an asthma attack. Following that placebo period, the actual "treatment phase" of the study would occur for three weeks. Each child would be randomized to one of four arms. Two involved different doses of the drug being studied, which was a bronchodilator that was approved for use as an inhaled drug, but the form being used here involved a somewhat different way of delivering the drug (a "metered dose inhaler") that had not been approved by the FDA. The third arm involved a fully approved bronchodilator, and the fourth arm involved a placebo. Children in all four arms were provided with rescue medications that could be used in case their asthma got worse, although the protocol noted that "habitual use will be discouraged."

In this example—as in hundreds of other studies currently being conducted that we could equally well describe here—children with some chronic medical problem are being treated with some new medication (or perhaps merely a placebo) instead of their standard medication. And as we have previously noted, any new medication poses some degree of risk of unknown side effects, in addition to the possibility that it might be less effective than the standard care for the child's condition. Presumably, these risks mean that such studies are not approvable under the "minimal risk" category: most of us would not lightly decide to take a medication that has thus far been tested in only perhaps a hundred or fewer people, rightfully considering such risk to be substantially more than minimal.

But what about the "good choice" category, under which many such studies have likely been approved by IRBs? Are they really "good choice" studies? Recall the overall theme of this category, namely, that every single thing being done to the child in the study—including taking them off all medications for a period of time—that creates more than a minimal risk must, in essence, be good for the child. In particular, the risk must be justifiable by the anticipated benefit to the child. Is that likely to be the case? Note the common features of most such trials: the children will take the new medication for a specified period of time—perhaps a few weeks, perhaps a few months—but in general they will not be permitted to take it after the study is over, since the drug is not yet approved for use outside of the study. Thus, there is certainly a possibility that the drug, during that period, will treat the subject's symptoms more effectively than the medication the child was previously on. But the child gets that benefit only for the period of the study. Imagine, then, the case of a child that only had mild of moderate symptoms to begin with. We are comparing two things:

1. The risk of being exposed to the possible side effects of a medication that has thus far been tested in relatively few human beings, together with the risk that the medication may not work as well as the child's current medications

versus

2. The possible benefit from reducing the child's symptoms, assuming the new drug works better than standard care, for only a certain period of time (weeks or months)

In how many cases can we say that such a trade-off will meet the requirements of the regulation, namely, that entering the study is better than the child's other options (including staying on a medication that may be working quite well)? In particular, how likely is it that a temporary reduction in a child's symptoms should be viewed as outweighing the unknown risk relating to side effects of a drug that has been given to relatively few children up to now? (And this analysis ignores the additional nonminimal risk that many such studies have, as this one did, of requiring the subject to be off all medications during a "washout" period at the beginning of the study. They are receiving no treatment at all during that period, with a significant chance that their medical condition will therefore worsen.)[18]

The Big Picture

Let us now compare the various examples of studies we have discussed:

1. A study involves parents moving their family to homes that have undergone an attempt to reduce the level of lead paint contamination, costing up to $6,000. Hundreds of other families are regularly moving into similar homes that have undergone *no* such attempted improvements. The children in this study get blood tests to check for lead levels beyond those that a child would normally get from their doctors, thus providing an early detection of increasing blood levels of lead. This study is compared by the Maryland Court of Appeals to the most horrific studies in history—concentration camp inmates intentionally exposed to typhus at Buchenwald, the men in the Tuskegee study who were lied to and never told there was a cure for their syphilis—and the court condemns the study in the strongest terms, finding that it was neither ethically nor legally permissible.

2. A child with cancer is exposed, in a phase I study, to a drug that, in part due to the design of phase I studies, has close to a zero chance of benefiting the child. Its chance of producing significant side effects is substantial. Those side effects are in fact likely to cause the child to get sicker and may even hasten the child's death. The likelihood of the child's participation in the study harming the child is much greater than the likelihood of it benefiting the child.

3. A child with a chronic and life-threatening disease, relatively well controlled on current medications, is asked to stop using those medications and try, for a short period of time, a new medication that has thus far been tested in only a few children. The possible benefit to the child is a temporary improvement in symptoms (which already may be well controlled on the current medication). In terms of risks, there is a not insignificant possibility of some side effect that has not yet been detected (since the drug has thus far been tested in only a few children), plus the possibility that the drug may be less effective than the child's current medications.

As we have discussed, studies like those described in examples 2 and 3 routinely take place in this country and are assumed to be a legitimate part of research involving children. We allow them to take place on the theory that they either are "benign"—imposing no more than minimal risks on the children participating—or are actually in the best interests of the child.

Comparing these three scenarios, it is difficult to see how example 1 can be so awful, allegedly rivaling the worst cases of improper experimentation in human history, yet examples 2 and 3 can be viewed as meeting the relatively restrictive criteria stated in the federal regulations. Perhaps we should accept the obvious: if indeed examples 2 and 3 are acceptable, it is *not* because they meet the criteria of the regulations that we are allegedly applying in cases of pediatric research. Examples 2 and 3 are no more benign or in the "best interests" of the child than example 1. Ultimately, neither of those two examples is totally or even minimally risk-free or in the best interests of the children who participate.

Resolving the Dilemma

Having made this determination, what should our next step be? One option would be to *ban* the types of studies we described in examples 2 and 3 above, concluding that they are not approvable under the regulations. But there is an alternative approach: to conclude that the current regulations are inappropriately restrictive. While it would, of course, be highly desirable to conduct only studies on children that either impose only "minimal" risks (or that vague criterion of being a "minor increase" above that) or where being in the study is in the child's best interests, it may be that taking that approach is, in the end, not in the best interests of our society, or even of children as a whole. Indeed, it would be quite surprising if it were the case that we could conveniently learn almost all the important information about how to treat children's medical problems without needing to subject them to more than very low-risk studies. There's no reason to suspect that our universe is constructed in such a way. That certainly isn't true for studies in adults. Perhaps examples 2 and 3 above should be considered acceptable as means of collecting important information that will lead to better treatment of many future children, even as we recognize that they impose more than minimal risks to the subjects.

To help evaluate this issue, consider a few facts. Traditionally, it has been relatively rare for most drugs to ever be tested in children. The rather cynical reason is that drug makers had no incentive to do this. This not-so-hidden secret even made its way to network television drama, when ABC's *The Practice* told a realistic story about a girl who, after taking an antibiotic that was approved for adults but not for children, ended up with liver failure. The cross-examination of the drug company executive on the show elicited the main points: the drug company noted that the FDA-approved labeling for the drug specifically stated that "safety and effectiveness in children have not been established." Thus, the company felt that the doctor should have known not to use this drug in children. But as the opposing lawyer observed, the drug company knew that, testing or no testing, doctors would use this drug in children.

Indeed, pediatricians (just like the doctor in the television episode), together with parents and children, really don't have much of a choice about staying away from drugs that have never been tested in children. They know that, in the end, by limiting children to just those drugs that have undergone the appropriate testing, they will end up harming them by denying them very useful drugs. *Between 1962 and 1970, only two drugs received approval from the FDA for use in children.* As of 1997, the U.S. Senate itself observed that fewer than 20% of the prescription medications being sold in the United States had received approval for use in children.

From the point of view of a drug manufacturer, there wasn't any benefit to going ahead and doing the studies in children: once the drug is approved for use in adults, pediatricians can indeed prescribe the drug for a child. This is another instance of the "off-label" use that becomes permissible (meaning not in violation of FDA rules) once a drug is approved for at least one use. The drug manufacturer thus knows— particularly if the drug appears very useful in adults and treats a condition for which there are few (or no) other good treatments—that pediatricians will indeed be prescribing it for children. Thus, the drug company gets the additional sales, without needing to incur the extra expense (no doubt millions of dollars) of testing the drug on children. And, to be even more cynical, perhaps that company views it as a plus that it avoids possibly uncovering new side effects in children (or results that show it is less effective than in adults), which might discourage the use of the drug in children. (The events involving the drug Vioxx serve almost as an object lesson to drug companies of what might come from doing such studies: the fact that the drug was causing tens of thousands of people to have heart attacks and strokes was only conclusively revealed when Merck, its manufacturer, conducted a study to see if Vioxx might be useful not just for treating arthritis pain but also to treat colon polyps.[19] One has to wonder if drug companies aren't going to be far more hesitant in the future to do "extra" studies on drugs that are already blockbusters and bringing in tens of millions of dollars of profit.)

The consequences of this state of affairs were that for decades, every time a drug was used in a child,[20] in effect an experiment was taking place. The doctor was to a greater or lesser extent *guessing* about two things: (1) what dose should be given to the child and (2) whether the drug was going to be effective. She had to be guessing, because the definitive studies that would have answered these questions—the studies that we required to be done before letting adults take the drug—never had to be conducted. This state of affairs was finally changed in the late 1990s, when two measures significantly changed this picture. As part of the FDA Modernization Act of 1997, Congress created a substantial incentive for pharmaceutical companies to voluntarily test in children drugs that had been previously approved for adults: this "pediatric exclusivity" rule gave the manufacturer an extra six months of patent (or similar) protection when the appropriate pediatric testing has been done. This can result in hundreds of millions of dollars of extra profits for a drug company. Not surprisingly, drug manufacturers have rushed to take advantage of it, with more than 300 proposed studies having been submitted to the FDA, including studies involving six of the ten drugs that are most frequently prescribed in this country.[21]

While the pediatric exclusivity rule involved a "carrot" approach, two years later a "stick" approach was added. For *new* drugs, the FDA modified its regulations to implement what is known as the "Pediatric Rule": a drug manufacturer that wants to get a new drug approved for use in adults would, if it appears that the drug might be useful in treating children, be required to also test it in children. Thus, a manufacturer would no longer be able to just do testing in adults, knowing that pediatricians would use the drug in children on an off-label basis (and thus being assured of the profits from those sales without ever proving that the drug worked in children, or verifying the best doses to use). In a subsequent lawsuit against the FDA, a federal court determined that the FDA lacked the authority to create this rule.[22] Within little more than a year after that decision, however, Congress passed the Pediatric Research Equity Act of 2003, giving the FDA the authority to implement the Pediatric Rule.[23] That action in effect makes any further proceedings in the lawsuit irrelevant.

From the viewpoint of society, the history leading up to these rules and Congress's action clarifies the relatively stark question at issue: which is better, (a) having millions of children take medications under circumstances where, each time the doctor prescribes it, he is unsure of the dose and of whether or not the medication is effective, or (b) doing the needed testing in children to determine effectiveness and appropriate dosing levels? Pursuing the second course means that a much smaller group of children—thousands, as opposed to millions—will be exposed to the unknown risks. The difficult question is, can we achieve that goal while at the same time assuring that the children in those studies are exposed only to relatively minor risks. As the preceding discussions in this chapter suggest, the answer appears to be no.

This doesn't mean that we should stop doing much of the pediatric testing we are already doing. Rather, we should be more upfront in specifying criteria under which we will permit studies to take place, instead of wrongly claiming adherence to regulations that allegedly assure that risks to children in studies are always low or are counterbalanced by benefits to the child. A more honest set of regulations might, for example, specify that a drug could be tested in children only after having undergone a certain amount of successful testing in animals and a certain amount of successful testing in adults. The regulations should not wrongly imply—or tell the parents considering enrolling a child—that children's participation in the study would expose them only to a "minimal risk."

14

Can Children Be Enrolled in Studies That Are Bad for Them?

In chapter 13, we attempted to show that the current regulations are somewhat hypocritical in suggesting that almost all of the studies being conducted today are either "good" for the children who participate or else impose at most very minor risks. The real world doesn't work that way: the fact that important studies may be bad choices for the subjects is as true for children as for adults. Yet failing to conduct an adequate amount of research will, in the end, hurt children overall as a group. Thus, as a policy matter, the right choice involves conducting an appropriate amount of research, even if it involves exposing some children to significant risks with no offsetting benefits. But what about the well-being of the children in such studies? Can we conduct such research and yet still be true to our underlying legal concepts?

Is It Good for the Children?

In Kansas City, there is a children's advocacy organization called the Partnership for Children. In April 1997, it launched its #1 Question Campaign, with the intent of getting "every individual and organization to use the question—'Is it good for the children?'—as a litmus test for decisions."[1] Our discussions thus far suggest that, for children as a group, it probably is very much in their interest to have appropriate levels of research done. Doing so will likely prevent countless cases of improper use of inadequately tested drugs.

But as we have also shown, doing that research is probably not in the best interests of at least some of the children who would need to be enrolled in the required research studies. Thus, assuming we as a society think this is a reasonable trade-off, we confront the issue of whether a parent has the legal authority to enroll a child in a research study that imposes more than a minor risk to the child's health, with no offsetting benefit. Assume that the current regulations were rewritten to still impose a limit on the nonbeneficial risks to which a child could be exposed (assuming a parent consented) but that those more honest rules recognize that such risks would not always be "minimal" or a "minor increase" over that level. Would such a rule be legal? Do the laws of this nation allow parents to enroll their children in such "non-therapeutic" studies?

The *Grimes* court clearly said the answer is "no":

> What right does a parent have to knowingly expose a child not in need of therapy to health risks or otherwise knowingly place a child in danger, even if it can be argued it is for the greater good? . . . Children, it should be noted, are not in our society the equivalent of rats, hamsters, monkeys and the like. . . . We hold that in Maryland a parent . . . cannot consent to the participation of a child in nontherapeutic research or studies in which there is any risk of injury or damage to the health of the subject.[2]

This answer conclusively resolves this question, at least for the moment, in the State of Maryland. But it is worth returning to it, and to the court's reasoning.

For implicit in that reasoning is the notion that the law requires parents to always be doing things that are in the best interests of their children. And the plain and simple fact is that the law requires no such thing. Yes, there are things that parents do to their children that can be so bad that the law interferes and categorizes it as child abuse. But those are the exceptions to the general rule, namely, that parents actually have a great deal of legal authority to make decisions in a way that won't always be in the best interests of the children. There are probably very few parents who actually base every decision in their lives on the answer to the question, "Is it good for the children?" Parents have lives of their own, too, and are entitled—legally and ethically—to make lots of decisions based in whole or in part on whether or not it is good for *their own* lives and not just those of their children.

And these decisions that might be "bad for the children" can even include decisions that might impose more than minor risks on the health of their children. Many people smoke at home even though they have children. There is growing evidence that this imposes substantial health risks on those children. Apart from an unusual court decision from time to time, in general this nation's laws do not require the government to be checking for these situations and threatening to remove children from the homes of parents who smoke.

Or consider the circumstances of the lead paint problem at issue in the *Grimes* case. At least some of the families currently living in lead-contaminated homes probably have enough disposable income such that they could arrange to live in homes that are totally lead-free. Perhaps a particular set of parents uses that money to go to the movies or a restaurant from time to time, having the children stay home with a babysitter. Is their choice to do that illegal? Clearly not. The law doesn't micromanage the lives of families in that way. Parents can impose lots of risks on children, for lots of arbitrary, perhaps even silly reasons, and the law will not interfere. It is only when those risks become inappropriately high—when they meet the definition of child abuse—that society deems it appropriate to take action.

Thus, we might well ask: if it is acceptable for parents to expose children to substantial (albeit below a certain level) health risks for a variety of arbitrary reasons, why should a much narrower rule—namely, no risks beyond "minimal" risks—apply when the issue is whether a child can be enrolled in a research study? One would think that such an endeavor, which serves the important social purpose of advancing the well-being of children in general, would be more acceptable than the many other, less well-justified reasons for which we allow parents to expose children to risks. It should especially be acceptable where a branch of the government with the authority to regulate this type of activity has specifically provided guidance on the appropriate level of risk (i.e., the federal regulations dealing with research involving minors).

Interestingly, in justifying the rule it announced, the *Grimes* court cited virtually no broad legal authority regarding what parents can do with their children. Almost all of its discussion was concerned with a narrow topic, prior court decisions involving kidney donation by a child. Court approval is indeed generally required in such circumstances, and appropriately so: giving up a major bodily organ is a big deal and imposes the sort of high-level risks that would normally trigger the rules about what constitutes child abuse. But it is hard to see how that specific circumstance provides much support for a broad rule that parents can't enroll children in nonbeneficial studies involving more than minimal risk, without court approval. Indeed, we don't even require such approval in other types of "donations" by children, such as a bone marrow donation. This explains why in a number of instances parents with a dying child needing a bone marrow transplant have encountered relatively few legal roadblocks in conceiving and giving birth to a child that is a genetically matching donor and then having the new child donate bone marrow.[3]

Admittedly, there should indeed be rules establishing the upper limits on the risks to which a child can be exposed and to which a parent's consent is acceptable. But the *Grimes* court's conclusion that minor risk is the appropriate line to be drawn, and that court approval is needed to conduct any nonbeneficial studies that involve a greater risk, appears not to be supported by legal precedents.

The Riskier Study—and the Importance of Informed Consent

In thinking about the possible need to expose subjects to studies with more-than-minimal risks that are not counterbalanced by possible benefits to the subjects, it is worth examining the current federal regulations again. There are two provisions that explicitly allow for such studies to take place. We have already discussed one of these, the provision that allows studies with no direct benefit to the subjects to take place if the study is about a disorder or condition that the subject has and the risk level is no greater than a "minor increase over minimal risk" (the "learn about the child's condition" study, discussed in chapter 13).

The more interesting provision is perhaps section 407 of the regulations,[4] which places no upper limit at all on the amount of risk to which a subject can be exposed. This section is designed to allow for approval of studies that are not approvable under any of the other three categories of pediatric research described in chapter 13, yet that may allow a better understanding or treatment of a "serious problem affecting the health or welfare of children." Such studies cannot be approved merely by an institutional review board (IRB). They also must be reviewed by a panel of experts— a so-called "section 407 panel" convened by the federal government. After reviewing the findings of that panel and allowing for the public to comment on the study, the Secretary of Health and Human Services must determine that the study will indeed contribute to the understanding of such a "serious problem." It is a very unusual circumstance when section 407 is employed; until the year 2000, only a couple of studies had ever been evaluated under this category. In the last several years, there has been a significant increase in the number of studies evaluated under this provision, but there are still only a few a year.

Given the rarity of the use of this provision, an examination of some of the studies that get selected for such close scrutiny might lead one to question whether the regulations are really sifting out the truly high-risk studies that deserve such special attention. For example, in April of 2003 a section 407 panel was convened to evaluate a study entitled "Alcohol, Sleep, and Circadian Rhythms in Young Humans."[5] In this study, sixty-four teenagers (ages 15 and 16) who already had "experience" with drinking alcoholic beverages would come to a sleep laboratory for four overnight sessions. During some of these sessions, the subject would drink an amount of alcohol not to exceed the amount they would have gotten in three "standard" drinks, based on their body weight. They would undergo various tests designed to determine how this affects their performance (e.g., using a driving simulator machine at the lab) and would have their sleep monitored by being hooked up to the usual sorts of machines in a sleep laboratory. Apparently, getting the three drinks was considered "more than minimal" risk (perhaps due to being illegal). Of course, hundreds of studies approved every year without needing a section 407 panel, as discussed above, pose much greater health risks when they alter a child's medications or even require them to stop taking them.

One study evaluated under section 407 in 2002 clearly was out of the ordinary, however, and it merits further scrutiny.[6] In the post-9/11 world, with particular concern about the weapons of mass destruction that Iraq might possess, there had been a great deal of interest in protecting U.S. citizens against a possible smallpox attack. The federal government evaluated a number of proposed plans designed to do this and eventually adopted a campaign to vaccinate a large number of health care workers. Part of that plan involved having the ability to quickly vaccinate members of the public—perhaps even a high percentage of this country's population— if indeed a biologic attack with smallpox ever became a reality.

One issue that came up in implementing this plan is that smallpox vaccine was no longer being made, since smallpox has been assumed to have been eradicated. The only existing vaccine was a 20-year-old stockpile being kept by the Centers for Disease Control and Prevention. This vaccine, known as Dryvax, contains live vaccinia virus, which is a close relative to the variola virus that causes smallpox. At that time there were enough doses in storage to vaccinate about 15 million people, assuming people got the same dose that was used decades ago. However, someone came up with a bright idea: perhaps it would be possible to dilute the vaccine and not significantly reduce its effectiveness. If that was possible, our stores of vaccine could in effect protect far more than 15 million people. A study was designed and quickly conducted in which adults received vaccination with various dilutions of the vaccine. That study demonstrated that even a one-to-ten dilution produced an effective immune response in about 98% of adults. Thus, were there to be an emergency requiring vaccination of large numbers of people, we know that adults can be given a dose that is one-tenth of what used to be employed.

The question that quickly followed was, what about children? Due to the biologic differences between adults and children, there was some uncertainty about whether dilution would also work in children. Again, a study was designed. Forty children two to five years of age would be given either an undiluted dose of the vaccine or a dose diluted one to five. They would be closely observed to see if there are any side effects, and blood would be drawn on several occasions. This federally funded study was to take place at three medical centers and, of course, had to be reviewed by the IRBs for those institutions. At two of these centers, the IRBs found that the study did involve more than minimal risk (since the vaccine is known to cause a variety of side effects, and in a tiny percentage of cases it can lead to death), but that it was approvable under the "good choice" category of the regulations described in chapter 13: there was a reasonable possibility that the child might benefit (in particular, receiving a vaccine that is effective against smallpox), that the benefit outweighed the risks, and that participating in the study was as good an option as any that were available outside the study.

However, at the third proposed location, Harbor-UCLA Medical Center, the IRB essentially deadlocked on the issue of whether this study met the criteria for the "good choice" category. Some IRB members noted that since there hadn't been any cases of smallpox anywhere in the world for years, they really couldn't determine that being vaccinated against smallpox was a significant benefit to a child, particularly without knowing more about the risk that the United States might be subjected to a smallpox attack. The IRB did ultimately reach agreement that this seemed to be an appropriate study to refer to the Office for Human Research Protections (OHRP) under section 407: that it concerned a "serious problem" affecting the health of children and wasn't otherwise approvable under any of the other three risk categories. OHRP agreed that it was appropriate to evaluate this study under section 407 and convened a panel of experts.

For the first time ever, OHRP made the recommendations of each of the ten experts public, posting them on its web site. All of the panelists who discussed the risk issue appeared to agree that it posed not only more than a "minimal risk" but also more than a "minor increase over minimal risk." Almost all of the panelists agreed that it should be approvable under section 407 (and indeed, two of them thought it would be approvable under the "good choice" category).

On the FDA's web site, several hundred comments were received from members of the public.[7] The great majority of the comments appeared to be highly critical of the study, objecting to the notion of using healthy children as guinea pigs in this circumstance, particularly given the uncertainty that anyone is about to be exposed to smallpox.

Less than two months after receiving the comments from the public, OHRP issued a relatively brief letter noting that "bioterrorism plans have evolved" and that, under the new plans, "the potential to use diluted Dryvax in children will no longer exist."[8] As a result, since there were no plans to use Dryvax in children, there was no justification for the study to take place. The letter didn't explain what the change in plans was, but it apparently was due to the fact that a new vaccine, one not based on a live virus and thus likely to have fewer side effects, was currently being tested in other countries. It remained unclear when that new vaccine might be available.

Two thoughts about all of this: first, barely two months after the government's determination that we didn't need to conduct this study, this nation went to war with Iraq. The avowed reason for the war was to eliminate the threat posed by that nation's weapons of mass destruction. A CIA report prepared in 2002 indicated that agency's "high" level of confidence that Iraq possessed smallpox.[9] Thus, assuming one's level of cynicism about the truth of the stated reasons for the war isn't that high, it would seem that the threat of a smallpox attack against this nation should have been rather high: there was at least the possibility that Saddam Hussein would have done his best to strike a huge blow against the United States, given that this would likely be his last chance to make his mark in history.

And, during this time period, the new smallpox vaccine was still not available. So, had such an attack materialized, and had there been a need for immunizing large numbers of Americans, what would we have done with the children? Would it have been appropriate to just give millions of them the reduced dose, not having the extra assurance that it was effective at that dose?

In chapter 13, we tried to show how thousands of children are regularly enrolled in studies that likely are not in their best interests and that may pose significant health risks to them. And for what purpose? Often, merely to let a particular drug company get its share of the market for treating some medical problem, coming up with some "me too" drug that might only be a minor improvement (if that) over existing treatments.

There's not necessarily anything wrong with that. But if we are willing to accept that as part of our system, should we perhaps ask why it ended up that the Dryvax study never took place? Surely having that extra bit of information about how well the diluted drug works in children is as important as having that third medication to treat allergies, that fifth drug to treat heartburn. And were the risks to the children all that great? They would be getting the same vaccine that years ago all of us used to get. The most serious risk, that of death, occurs approximately once in every million vaccinations in children. The risk that this—or even any of the more likely less severe side effects—would happen in any of the forty children in the trial would be extraordinarily low. A child would face twice as large a risk of death when riding on a 100-mile automobile trip to grandma's house and back.[10] It may not even be that bad an argument to claim that the risks in this study are in the "minimal risk" range and that this study was therefore approvable as a minimal risk study. And yet, although we went to war over the issue of the smallpox and related threats, it was determined that this study was not needed.

Second, in several places in this book, we've discussed how the manner in which informed consent is obtained—giving the subject lists of risks, benefits, and alternatives—fails to provide a key piece of information, namely, the relationship between the risks and benefits and whether being in a study is a "good choice" or "bad choice." We have shown that many studies that one might otherwise think are beneficial to the subject may indeed be significantly bad for most subjects, assuming they are mainly concerned about their own health.

A study that gets approved under section 407 has an interesting property: it in essence has *the official imprimatur of both the government and a panel of experts* that it is one of the "bad choice" studies. After all, a study is approvable under section 407 only after it has failed to meet any of the other three categories; therefore, there has to be more than minimal risk and inadequate offsetting benefit to the subjects. Thus, it is interesting to note that this fact is probably never disclosed to the parents of prospective subjects. Indeed, while many of the members of the expert panel made various suggestions on how to revise various things in the consent form that was proposed to be used in the Dryvax study, including better specifying what the risks and benefits are, none of them specifically suggested disclosing what it means to have been approved under section 407.

Had this study been conducted, something similar to the following would seem like an appropriate provision for the consent form:

> Being in this study is not likely to be in your child's best interests. In fact, both a panel of experts and the federal agency in charge of regulating research with human subjects have determined that *the risks to your child from participating in this study are greater than any possible benefits to your child.*
>
> While you can, of course, make your own decision about the risks and benefits from participating (and you may disagree with the panel's conclusions), you probably should not be enrolling your child in this study thinking that it is in your child's best interests. Rather, you should be recognizing that you are doing so because you are willing to expose your child to significant risks so that we can obtain important information that will benefit future children.

This type of truthful disclosure may discourage the great majority of parents, but there is no reason to think that we would not have been able to get forty who said yes. After all, there had actually been a great demand for smallpox vaccination among some elements of the public, and there is currently no way for a child to get vaccinated other than through this study. The parents who say yes may have placed an unusually high value on their child being vaccinated, and they are entitled to do that. But we could be confident that no deception was involved in obtaining the consent of these parents, that they were clearly told that their weighing of risks and benefits was outside the mainstream.

Do Researchers Have a Duty to Eliminate Preexisting Risks?

To end this chapter, we return to a broad issue that lies at the heart of the *Grimes* case discussed in chapter 13—one that goes beyond the issue of how to conduct research on children. Ultimately, the heart of the complaint on the part of the *Grimes* court seems to have less to do with the idea that the researchers were "imposing" a risk on the children in the study than with a very different notion: the idea that it was somehow improper or unethical or even illegal for the researchers to sit back and watch, doing nothing, as the children remained in homes where there were known lead hazards. The court would likely still have had problems with this study even if it had not involved families moving into new homes but merely observing what happened in the homes where the families were currently living. As the court observed, "The researchers and their Institutional Review Board apparently saw nothing wrong with the research protocols that anticipated the possible accumulation of lead in the blood of otherwise healthy children as a result of the experiment. . . ." But the court apparently saw a great deal wrong with this.

Notice how very different this issue is from most of the "horror stories" that the court initially raised as a comparison: concentration camp inmates in Nazi Germany being *infected with* typhus, elderly people being *injected with* cancer cells. These scenarios, and one other the court raised—comparing the children to the canaries that miners would carry into mines, to warn them if they were being exposed to toxic gases—involved someone intentionally creating a risk and exposing someone to that "new" risk. But this is not what was really happening in the Kennedy Krieger study. The risks were already there.

So, what about the true concern of the *Grimes* court: was it appropriate for the researchers to just stand by and watch, knowing the children would be exposed to the possible accumulation of lead? We already know the answer to this question from the principles developed in part I of this book. As we have demonstrated, the role of the researcher is different from that of a health care provider. At a minimum, apart from the stricter rules regarding getting informed consent, the researcher has fewer obligations to the subject than a health care provider.

Thus, to answer this question, we should first ask, what obligations would a health care provider have been under in this situation? Assume that a pediatrician was aware that the child was living in this type of housing. What obligations would that pediatrician have had to do something about this situation? The answer: probably nothing. Recall that 95% of the homes in inner-city Baltimore had this type of lead paint hazard (and the homes in the study actually had a likelihood of a somewhat lower than average risk, due to the possible effect of the interventions undertaken by the researchers). As noted, neither the federal nor the state government had any laws at the time indicating it was improper for these properties to be rented to families with young children—after all, if you were poor and lived in Baltimore, there really weren't all that many other choices. And it was not considered child abuse for the parents to be choosing to live in this type of housing.

Granted, this was an unfortunate situation. We all would have preferred that young children not be exposed to any risks of lead poisoning. But this was a fact of life in inner-city Baltimore (and many other cities in the United States). And it was not viewed as the clinical duty of the average doctor in Baltimore to eliminate this risk every time a child was exposed to possible lead poisoning. Yes, if it was determined that a child had blood lead above a certain level, the health department authorities were notified, the child began treatment, and efforts were made to reduce the child's exposure to lead. But this would happen in the study, also.

The bottom line, then, is that even the child's own pediatrician would not have been expected to do anything about the type of background risk of lead poisoning that existed in inner-city Baltimore, any more than that doctor would have been expected to make sure the child was moved to a residence in a middle-class suburb where she would not be exposed to a host of other health hazards—being shot, becoming a drug addict—that stemmed from living in the inner city. Pediatricians daily took care of thousands of children living in this type of housing and were not committing malpractice if they failed to get the children immediately moved to lead-free homes. Given this fact, and the fact that the duties of researchers, in terms of doing "what is best" for the subject, are no greater than those of health care providers—in fact, as we have already noted, they are substantially less than those duties—it would seem that there was nothing wrong in the researchers "standing by" and not taking all the steps that would be needed to fully eliminate the lead paint hazard to these children (steps that no one else in society was taking—neither the government nor the average pediatrician—nor were they expected to be taking, under applicable legal and ethical rules).

This line of analysis helps us determine in what situations it might indeed be improper for a researcher to just "stand by and watch." For surely most of us can agree with the underlying premise of the court's concern, that we do not want researchers to be taking *inappropriate* advantage of various vulnerable groups in society. The line to be drawn between what is acceptable and what is not should be similar to the one we discussed in chapter 5, in determining what sorts of risks it is appropriate to expose subjects to. Consider, for example, the Tuskegee study, where black men with syphilis went untreated for decades, never being told that there was a cure for their condition. The major ethical violation in that study was the lack of informed consent: not telling the men that penicillin would eliminate their medical problem. But there is a less obvious ethical issue: what if they had been told about the penicillin? If they could not afford the drug, would it have been acceptable to continue the study under those conditions?

Perhaps not. Suppose that at the time penicillin was readily accessible and could have been obtained for a relatively modest amount of money, but that some of the men in the Tuskegee study would not have been able to come up with even that small amount. Under those circumstances, it is likely that most of us would find it unconscionable to not find a way to get that treatment to those men, regardless of whether or not they were in a study. A doctor who stood by and did nothing to help such a patient get treatment would likely be considered highly morally suspect. But as we noted above, that was not the background situation involved in inner-city Baltimore. Neither doctors nor anyone else, for that matter, was considered to have a professional obligation to eliminate all lead paint hazards.

Ultimately, we need to recognize that the *Grimes* court was imposing an unrealistic and inappropriate view of the researcher as some sort of "guarantor" of perfect health or freedom from risk. To the contrary, as we have attempted to show throughout this book, the researcher is quite the opposite: a person who, under certain limitations, intentionally exposes people to risks for the primary purpose of benefiting people other than the research subject. That is quite a different kettle of fish.

15

Research and Reproduction

In addition to general questions about safety, almost no information is available to help doctors know what the best dose of a particular medicine is for pregnant women.
—Michelle Meadows, "Pregnancy and the Drug Dilemma,"
FDA Consumer

During the first two weeks of February 2004, each of the following events made news:

- An FDA advisory committee composed of scientific experts recommended that the agency approve over-the-counter sale of the "morning-after pill."[1] In spite of that recommendation, the FDA took the somewhat unusual step of delaying its decision. That delay was no doubt at least partly due to an "aggressive campaign" by forty-nine members of Congress, who had sent a letter to President George W. Bush noting how greater availability of this pill would lead to increases in promiscuity and venereal disease.
- A pharmacist at an Eckerd's drug store in Texas refused to fill a prescription for the morning-after pill for a woman who had been raped. The pharmacist claimed that it violated his moral beliefs, in that he shouldn't be forced to participate in a "chain of events that could take a child's life." He was fired.
- The U.S. Justice Department issued subpoenas to a number of prominent hospitals, seeking the medical records of women who had received abortions. The department claimed it needed the records in order to determine whether the abortions were "medically necessary." The issue had arisen in court challenges to a new federal law that banned partial-birth abortions.
- Hearings began in preparation for the murder trial of Scott Peterson in connection with the deaths of his wife Laci and their unborn child Conner. Under California law, causing the death of a fetus was considered a homicide, and thus Peterson could be found guilty of two deaths and be eligible for the death penalty. At the same time, in the U.S. Congress, the House Judiciary Committee approved a bill entitled the "Unborn Victims of Violence Act," to similarly make killing a fetus a federal crime under certain circumstances.

That bill ended up getting a second name—"Laci and Conner's Law"—and was enacted into law six weeks later.
- South Korean scientists reported that they were able to create cloned human embryos, which continued to develop longer than had previously been possible. The scientists were then able to produce stem cells from these embryos. The purpose of the research was not to create new human beings, but rather to produce innovative treatments for a variety of medical problems, such as diabetes, Parkinson's disease, and spinal cord injuries. While some cheered this breakthrough, others condemned it. Dr. Leon Kass, chairman of President Bush's Council on Bioethics (2001–2005), fearing the worst, called for the federal government to enact a ban on all types of cloning: "The age of human cloning has apparently arrived: today, cloned blastocysts for research, tomorrow cloned blastocysts for babymaking."[2]

As these stories demonstrate, one of the hot-button topics in current-day America remains how to deal with "early" forms of human life—from newly fertilized embryos to fetuses that are just days prior to being born. And within that controversial area, perhaps the most divisive issues relate to the ethics of conducting research on such entities (and thereby sometimes causing their death).

That is just one of the topics that this chapter addresses. But before we turn to the complexities of the cutting-edge science of cloning and stem cells, we first address more mundane issues relating to research involving women—sometimes pregnant and sometimes not. In many ways, these commonplace issues have much more impact on the average person than do the more controversial topics that are making the headlines.

Why Women Have Historically Been Excluded as Research Subjects

Imagine that researchers at the San Diego Zoo became concerned that some of the animals, due to spending so much time lounging around in the comfortably warm California sun, were getting too fat for their own good. So they decide to conduct a study to see if a version of the cut-the-carbs Atkins diet might work for these animals. They initially choose to do the study on elephants. Their statisticians determine that, in such a dietary study, it would be necessary to enroll about twenty animals to make it likely that the results would be statistically significant. But the researchers have a problem: they don't have twenty elephants available. So they slightly modify their study: instead of using twenty elephants, they will enroll ten elephants and ten hippopotami.

There is a good chance that this revised study is far less likely to produce a valid scientific result than the study that was initially designed. As common sense would suggest, elephants and hippopotami are very different from one another, and those differences are likely to make it unhelpful to include them in the same study. This is merely an example of the general principle of study design that we discussed in chapter 3: a good study generally makes sure that all the subjects are as similar to one another as possible, so that differences among them do not create background "noise" in the data that obscures the particular things being studied. In effect, the revised zoo study is really more like two separate studies: one in elephants and one in hippopotami, each involving ten subjects. And if the initial study, had it been done on elephants alone, was really going to require twenty animals to produce a statistically significant result, then neither of these smaller studies would meet this standard.

This hypothetical scenario is a good metaphor for at least part of the rationale behind one major theme in medical research throughout most of the twentieth century. Up until recent decades, many research studies were intentionally designed to enroll only men.[3] For a long time, this even represented the official policy of various agencies in the federal government. Rebecca Dresser, a leading lawyer-bioethicist, aptly described this state of affairs in her title for a 1992 article: "Wanted: Single White Male for Medical Research."[4] Dresser catalogued a variety of past practices. For example, studies to determine if aspirin reduced the risk of heart attack were conducted almost exclusively with men, even though heart disease was the number one cause of death in women. A major study on health and aging enrolled only men during its first twenty years, even though two-thirds of the elderly are female. Strangely enough, a pilot study looking at how obesity influenced breast and uterine cancer was conducted only on male subjects.

As Dresser correctly summed up the state of affairs as of 1992, the "failure to include women in research populations is ubiquitous." And one of the leading reasons for such a practice was a scientific one, the same one suggested by our hypothetical zoo study: men and women are biologically different in a variety of ways. Those differences are certainly not as huge as those between two different species, but nonetheless they are significant. And the differences often exist in numerous areas that have nothing to do with reproduction.

Thus, for example, hormones such as testosterone or estrogen may have an effect on the development of blockages in artery walls. If we wanted to study whether a particular new drug reduces the rate of heart attacks, it might require enrolling 1,000 men to get a statistically significant result. If women were *also* enrolled at the same rate as men, then due to the differences between the two sexes, it might be the case that 1,600 subjects would be required (800 men and 800 women) to produce the same level of statistical significance. That larger study would certainly cost a great deal more money. It would also take longer to complete, due to the need to recruit larger numbers of subjects, and thus people with heart disease would allegedly needlessly suffer due to waiting that extra time for the study to be completed.

While those arguments might seem superficially convincing—and they helped carry the day in influencing federal research policy for many years—they ultimately lead to troubling conclusions. For if indeed there were substantial differences between men and women that would affect the results of the study had both sexes been included—and that was the very reason for intentionally not including both sexes in the study—then we wouldn't know if the results of a male-only study also apply to women. In other words, we would know how to treat men for this condition, but would *not* know the proper treatment for women.

The male-only policy thus appears to discriminate against women. Indeed, if we really believed that by studying only one sex at a time we can more quickly and efficiently find answers to research questions, at the least we should have been conducting half of the studies with men only, and the other half with women only. But that was not what was happening: time and again, studies were conducted with men only, as if males were somehow the "norm" for human biology, with females representing a more complicated and perhaps abnormal biology.

Fortunately, over time, various branches of the U.S. government gradually appeared to recognize the discriminatory nature of the past practices. Beginning in the1980s, both the U.S. Public Health Service and the National Institutes of Health (NIH) issued reports questioning the exclusion of women from most research studies. Finally, in 1993, the NIH Revitalization Act was passed by Congress, which mandated that all research funded by NIH would be required to include women as subjects, unless there were good reasons for not doing so. NIH issued guidelines in 1994 implementing these new policies. It specifically noted that the increased costs for conducting a study enrolling both men and women—as opposed to men only—were not a legitimate reason for excluding women. And the FDA similarly published a 1993 position paper, acknowledging that there had indeed been "little or no participation of women" in many important studies, particularly the earliest stages of studying a new drug. It therefore adopted a new policy—somewhat less demanding than the new NIH rules—"encouraging" the inclusion of women in research studies "in the earliest phases."[5]

The Fetal Lung Maturity Study

The new federal policies have had a substantial impact on research in the United States. If nothing else, they have led to increased attention to the unique health problems of women and to the federal funding of studies specially directed at those problems (e.g., breast cancer). And, even in studies of diseases that affect both men and women, there has been an increase in the enrollment of women. In many cases, the percentage of women enrolled approaches 50%.[6] But there is one glaring exception to this state of affairs: enrollment of *pregnant* women. Pregnant women are specifically designated as a "vulnerable population" under the federal regulations, and an entire "subpart" of the regulations spells out the rules for research involving pregnant women or fetuses.[7]

To introduce the relevant issues, we turn to a relatively recent headline-making study. In the late 1980s, two doctors at the University of South Florida were conducting a study about lung development in premature babies. One of the biggest medical problems for very premature babies is that their lungs may be very underdeveloped. The University of South Florida researchers were testing the use of thyrotropin-releasing hormone (a hormone involved in regulating thyroid function) as a way of possibly increasing lung development in a fetus. In their study, pregnant women who were likely to give birth to premature infants were randomized to get either the standard drugs used in those circumstances or those drugs plus thyrotropin-releasing hormone. The women were also required to undergo one or more amniocentesis procedures, each of which imposed a 1-in-400 chance of serious complications.

Over the several years in which the study took place, about 380 women were enrolled.[8] During that period, Kay Perrin, a nurse at Tampa General Hospital where the study was taking place, began to encounter more and more women who were undergoing second and third amniocentesis procedures, generally a relatively rare occurrence. She would ask these mainly indigent, Spanish-speaking women why they were having this done, and they would answer that their doctor told them it was needed to make sure their babies would be healthy. Nurse Perrin, uncertain whether these women really understood that they were participating in a research study, ended up approaching Stephen Hanlon, a civil rights attorney who was also a friend of hers. On his advice, she tried to get the hospital to investigate. When it did nothing, she surreptitiously walked off with the log book containing the names of patients who had undergone amniocentesis, and returned it after making a photocopy.

Her subsequent letter to ten of the women who had undergone multiple amnioceteses, asking if they knew about the research study, produced a reply from Flora Diaz. Ms. Diaz eventually became the lead plaintiff in *Diaz v. Hillsborough County Hospital Authority*, a federal class action lawsuit brought in 1990 by attorney Hanlon against the hospital and the doctors who ran the study. The lawsuit alleged that in the lung development study and in thirty other studies involving pregnant women, the researchers had not obtained legally adequate informed consent. Hanlon, working pro bono, spent more than a decade on the case, and the hospital eventually settled for $3.8 million.[9]

Although, since this was a settlement, no new law was made by the case, it is nonetheless significant that the hospital was willing to settle without any of the women having actually been physically harmed. The case had been based on a somewhat controversial legal theory: that the legal system would allow money damages for a "dignitary harm"—the claim that women had been wronged (even though not physically damaged) by having things done to them without their full understanding.[10] If courts eventually adopt the dignitary harm concept in the medical research arena, it would surely lead to a rapid increase in the number of lawsuits brought against researchers. And it would hasten the impact of tort law in leading to stricter adherence to the legal rules laid out in preceding chapters of this book.

But notice that the major unique feature of this case—the possibility of substantial damages for dignitary harm—isn't limited to cases involving pregnant women. In fact, it is interesting how little of what went wrong in this case had *anything* to do with the special categorization of pregnant women as being "vulnerable." If we accept the truth of the allegations being made in the lawsuit, the women were enrolled in studies by being given complex consent forms, in many instances in a language that was not the one they best understood. They were given little further explanation about the fact that there was a research study. Some of the women allegedly were told about the study at a time that they were still "groggy" from pain medication. All of these allegations, if true, paint a picture of what would likely be a failure to get adequate informed consent even if the women had not been pregnant.

Thus, in an odd way, one of the major lessons of the *Diaz* lawsuit may be that, in terms of making sure informed consent is properly obtained, there really may not be any need to categorize pregnant women as being vulnerable. The usual protections provided by the general requirement for informed consent seem quite adequate. In fact, under the terms of the settlement, although the University of South Florida agreed to implement various changes in how it conducted research, most of those changes—including creating readability tests for consent forms and funding a program to design more readable consent forms—are not specifically directed at studies involving only pregnant women. Indeed, the suggestion that pregnant women in general are particularly vulnerable—even if there are no language difficulties, even if the women are not poorly educated, even if they have not just been given drugs that alter their ability to think clearly—might well be considered inappropriately paternalistic. It harkens back to an outdated view of a pregnant woman as a fragile creature, unable to make her own decisions, at the whim of raging hormones, and relying on others for her protection.

Recognizing that there is minimal need to provide special protections to pregnant women is one of those "Aha!" moments that allows us to perceive the true reason why the federal regulations pay so much attention to studies involving pregnant women. The underlying concern is not really about the pregnant woman, but rather about the *fetus*. Unlike the pregnant woman, the fetus is indeed vulnerable in the usual sense of that word. Like the other categories of subjects we have discussed in part III—incompetent adults and children—a fetus is not able to speak for itself. And as we noted at the start of this chapter, we live in a society where issues relating to protecting fetuses can quickly generate strongly felt opinions. Thus, it is now time to shift our focus to examining the complicated ways that our society deals with issues relating to the protection, in the research setting, of fetuses and other categories of developing human beings.

The Continuing Controversy: Excluding Pregnant Women

To address these issues, it is helpful to separately discuss two different types of studies: studies that are examining a medical problem that is not unique to pregnancy (e.g., treatment of heart attacks) and those specifically directed at pregnancy issues (including the health of the fetus). The latter group of studies obviously cannot take place if we exclude pregnant women. But what about the former group? If a study is *not* specifically directed at a pregnancy issue—if it has no special relationship to pregnancy—should pregnant women be enrolled?

Consider what happened in the fall of 2003, as the publicity about the deaths of several otherwise healthy young children from the flu caused a huge surge in demand for flu vaccine. The Centers for Disease Control and Prevention quickly issued guidelines for the public, encouraging that those at greatest risk get the remaining dwindling supplies of the vaccine. One of those high-risk groups was women who would be more than three months pregnant during any part of the flu season.[11] It was already known that the vaccine was safe for pregnant women and that taking it would produce more good than harm in protecting both the woman and, in particular, the fetus from the very serious consequences that might take place if she caught the flu.

This series of events is, in one very specific sense, rather unusual: in many instances, we actually don't know whether a particular treatment that is generally recommended for some disease should also be given to a pregnant woman with that problem. The reason for that common uncertainty is that when the research studies took place to test the treatment, pregnant women were probably not enrolled as subjects. Thus, two questions typically remain unanswered: whether the condition of being pregnant, and the changes it induces in the woman's body, also changes how the treatment works on a pregnant woman (make it less effective, change the dose that is required, or perhaps cause new types of side effects), and whether the treatment poses any harm to the developing fetus, which is often especially vulnerable to the effects of drugs. While studies are often conducted in pregnant animals to help answer these questions, the definitive answers can be obtained only by seeing what happens in humans.[12]

The FDA uses a five-letter code to categorize the possible risks to a fetus from a woman's use of a particular drug, going from A (where adequate studies in pregnant women have shown the drug to be safe for the fetus), through B and C (where there is often not that much evidence on how safe the drug is), to D (studies show risks to the fetus, but the drug may still be worth using due to its benefits to the woman), and X (adequate studies show the drug causes fetal abnormalities).[13] If you paged through a recent copy of the "bible" for drug prescribing information, the Physicians' Desk Reference (often called the PDR), you would quickly see that most drugs fall into categories B and C. And those two categories share a similar property: usually *no one really knows if using the drug will harm a fetus*. And the reason is that the studies to answer that question have probably not been conducted in pregnant women.

As we mentioned above, the federal regulations relating to the ethics of human subjects research have a specific section—subpart B—dealing with such studies. They allow an IRB to approve a study involving pregnant women or fetuses if:

- where appropriate, studies have first been conducted appropriately on animals or nonpregnant women;
- any risks to the fetus must be due solely to procedures that might directly benefit the woman or the fetus, *or else* the study must involve only a minimal risk to the fetus and the research must be directed at collecting important biomedical knowledge that cannot be obtained by other means; and
- the risk must be the least possible needed for achieving the objectives of the study.[14]

These regulations, while somewhat restrictive, recognize that a pregnant woman may choose to participate in a study that has the prospect of benefiting her own health, even if it involves a risk to the fetus's health. That conclusion is consistent with the interpretation of the U.S. Constitution under *Roe v. Wade* and subsequent Supreme Court cases: the health of the woman, who is entitled to all of the protections entitled to a "person," outweighs the protections given to a fetus, which is not yet entitled to the protections given a "person."[15]

Although the ethics regulations thus permit researchers studying a particular drug to enroll pregnant women, in fact that rarely happens. Here is a comment about current practices that appeared in the FDA's own publication in 2001: "Unless research focuses on a pregnancy-related condition such as labor induction, drugs typically aren't studied in pregnant women because of the fear of exposing the woman to an experimental drug and harming the fetus."[16]

Pharmaceutical manufacturers and other researchers are loathe to take the risk that a fetus might be harmed by a new drug and that they would then be sued.[17] It remains the case that, in drug studies that are *not* specifically about the conditions of pregnancy, pregnant women are routinely excluded.

So strong has been the concern about a fetus possibly being injured by inadvertent exposure to a drug in a study that, for many years, the official policy of the FDA was that even a woman who was merely *capable* of becoming pregnant—in technical language, a "woman of child-bearing potential"—could not be enrolled in the initial studies (phase I and early phase II) of a drug.[18] Under that FDA policy, a woman of child-bearing potential was defined in extremely broad terms, to include essentially "all premenopausal women physiologically capable of becoming pregnant, include women on oral, injectable, or mechanical contraceptives, single women, celibate women, and women whose partners had been sterilized by vasectomy." None of the women fitting into this group would be permitted to enroll in early drug studies. (E.g., a nun could not enroll in such a study.) The only time such women would be allowed access to an unapproved drug would be if it was being studied as a life-saving or life-prolonging treatment for a medical problem.

This rule was changed only relatively recently—in 1993—when the FDA noted that the consequence of the earlier rule was that, in many studies, few women were being enrolled, and thus little information was being collected about the effect of many drugs on women (including women who were not pregnant).[19] As noted above, if indeed female physiology in many instances differs from that of men, then the effect of this practice was to discriminate against women. In the 1993 pronouncement, the FDA recognized that its earlier ban had been having an inappropriate consequence and was inconsistent with other laws banning discrimination against women. It acknowledged that it could be appropriate to enroll women who are capable of being pregnant even in early studies of a new drug, though proper measures should be taken—including pregnancy testing before enrollment, requiring the use of an acceptable method of contraception (including abstinence),[20] and counseling women about the possible adverse consequences of getting pregnant while being in a drug study. It did not require that such women be enrolled in early studies, but merely removed its earlier ban.

Many "early-stage" studies of new drugs have responded to these changed rules, and it is common to see them permit enrollment of a woman who is capable of becoming pregnant, as long as she agrees to use an acceptable form of contraception.[21] But the general attitude regarding enrolling women who actually are pregnant remains fairly negative. Most researchers—particularly drug companies—are very strict in following the FDA's admonition to make sure no woman in the study is pregnant at the start of the study or becomes pregnant during the study. In most consent forms for drug studies, you will find a paragraph similar to the following: "There have been no studies of drug X in pregnant women. Treatment with this medicine may involve unforeseeable risks to the mother or the unborn baby if exposed before birth. For this reason, if you are a woman who is breast-feeding, pregnant, or trying to become pregnant, you will be excluded from this study."

Note that this policy is not limited to studies where there is a specific reason for suspecting that a drug will be harmful to a fetus. Merely "not knowing" if the drug will cause such harm is considered a sufficient reason for excluding the pregnant women. No one—not the FDA, not the NIH, and certainly not the companies that conduct and sponsor many of these studies (who fear being sued if a woman does become pregnant and gives birth to a fetus with a medical problem that may or may not be related to the drug being studied)—has concluded that it is appropriate to enroll pregnant women in such studies.

What does this mean for a pregnant woman with a medical problem in deciding how to treat that problem? She will rarely be in the situation of the pregnant women deciding to take the flu vaccine, who were dealing with a product that had been proven to be safe for the woman and the fetus. Rather, she is far more likely to be asked to take a drug in category B or C, with minimal information about its safety for the fetus. So, in effect, the woman has to roll the dice and make a difficult decision about whether treating her medical problem—a newly diagnosed cancer, for example—is important enough to impose a largely unknown risk on her fetus. In effect, each time a woman is asked to make such a decision, she is embarking on her own medical experiment. Indeed, the main way in which we currently learn about the risks to a fetus from new drugs is by collecting information about what happens to each such woman who decides to use a drug while she is pregnant. This information is placed into a "pregnancy registry": instead of there being a planned study of what the drug does to a fetus, this ad hoc information is used.[22]

Studies about Pregnancy and Fetuses

Although this state of affairs poses a very real problem for a pregnant woman who has a medical problem and must decide what treatments she wants to take, it is important to note that does not mean that the current practices, as described above, are improper. Unfortunately, there is a very real dilemma here. Obtaining additional information to give to *future* pregnant women might in many instances require having *current* pregnant women agree to impose additional risks on the fetuses they carry. (We see again an instance of the main theme of this book: good studies may often be bad choices for the subjects.) Given the horrible things that can happen to a developing fetus by being exposed to the wrong drug at the wrong time—the history of thalidomide babies with their deformed arms and legs comes to mind—it is unlikely that we would be able to convince many women to even enroll in such studies. And in many instances, the benefit from that additional knowledge may not even be worth asking current women to expose their fetuses to these risks.[23] The medical problem being studied may not affect that many women, or it may permit treatment to be delayed until the pregnancy has ended. Perhaps, in the end, it is therefore not that unreasonable to exclude pregnant women from the "average" study of a new drug.

But as we noted above, there *are* some medical problems that do disproportionately affect women or fetuses. And conducting those studies would therefore perhaps present a different balance between risks and benefits. Let us therefore turn to the second category of studies that we mentioned above—where the very purpose of the study relates to pregnancy. That purpose might be to study a particular medical problem of pregnant women, for example, a randomized trial comparing two drugs to treat preeclampsia, a condition of elevated blood pressure that can threaten a pregnant woman's health. Or the purpose might be to treat a medical problem of the fetus. The study involved in the *Diaz* lawsuit that we discussed above, where women likely to give birth to premature infants were randomized to get standard care or that care plus a drug that might speed the fetus's lung development, is a good example.

The federal regulations permit both types of studies. We quoted the applicable portion of the Common Rule earlier in this chapter. In essence, the rules permit a study to take place that involves doing things that impose risks on a fetus, as long as there is a possibility of benefit to either the fetus or the woman from doing those things. Also, even if there is no possibility of benefit to either the fetus or the woman, a study can be conducted if it involves only minimal risks to the fetus.

Given the controversy that almost any discussion about fetal interests tends to generate in the United States, these rules are actually surprisingly reasonable. When it comes to a study that has a possibility of directly benefiting a pregnant woman, that study is permissible. Period. The regulations do not even impose any requirement to somehow balance the amount of benefit to the woman against the level of risk imposed on the fetus. For example, there is no need to demonstrate that the possible benefits to the woman's health "outweigh" the risks imposed on the fetus. As noted above, the failure to include any such balancing test is consistent with the legal interpretation of a woman's rights in the wake of *Roe v. Wade* and subsequent cases, which puts the health interests of a woman (legally a person entitled to substantial protections) above that of a fetus (legally a nonperson).

The regulations nonetheless do, in some circumstances, tip the balance in favor of protecting the interests of the fetus. Imagine a study that was intended to collect information about a medical problem affecting pregnant women, but where participation did not produce any direct benefit for the research subjects. For example, women with preeclampsia might be asked to allow certain types of monitoring devices to be placed inside their uterus. Since the study does not actually benefit the women, this study would be permissible only if the risk to the fetus was minimal. In this respect, the regulations appear to give a fetus protections that in some sense are greater than those accorded children. Children can be enrolled, in some circumstances, in studies that impose greater risks—"a minor increase over minimal risk"—yet there is no similar category for research on a fetus.[24] One might think that the rules should be just the opposite: given the greater protections accorded under the law to a pregnant woman as opposed to a fetus, there is an argument for allowing fetuses to be exposed to greater risks than we expose children to, when the research is about learning information important to the health of future pregnant women. Nonetheless, considered as a whole, the regulations are far more reasonable than one might expect.

The Cutting Edge: Stem Cells

Up to now, we have confined our discussion to developing fetuses that are already inside a woman's uterus. But the biggest controversies these days involve the research that is being conducted on the very earliest stages of a developing embryo, only days old, in a dish in a laboratory. A difficult question is raised: how should our society be treating this miniscule ball of cells, not visible without a microscope, having no nervous system and unable to feel pain or to think, but having the potential, if implanted in a woman's uterus, to eventually grow into a unique human being? Before attempting to answer that question in the research setting, it is helpful to see how our society answers that question in the only slightly less contentious setting where no research is involved.

Consider the following two scenarios:

1. A man brandishing a gun robs a convenience store. As he makes his getaway, he violently pushes aside a woman who is in her third month of pregnancy. As a result of the trauma, the pregnancy shortly thereafter ends in a miscarriage.
2. A man brandishing a gun breaks into a clinical laboratory that provides services to infertile couples undergoing *in vitro* fertilization. After robbing several of the employees, he runs out, knocking over and breaking a vessel containing several hundred frozen embryos that were being saved for use by such couples.

A good gauge of how seriously our society judges these actions is to explore their criminal consequences.

The first scenario is very similar to the set of circumstances that led the federal government in 2004 to pass "Laci and Conner's Law," mentioned at the beginning of this chapter. In several states, and now under this federal law (assuming all of its complicated conditions are met), the death of the fetus will, in essence, be treated in the same manner as if it were the death of a child. This is part of a development in the law that has been gaining ground over the past several years in some states, with the imposition of greater and greater penalties on actions that lead to the death of a fetus. These laws can have substantial consequences. Scott Peterson's conviction for killing his pregnant wife made him eligible under California law for the death penalty (since he had effectively committed a multiple murder). Had his wife not been pregnant, he could not have received the death penalty for killing her.

To some extent, these laws are pushing the limits of what the Supreme Court said about the status of a fetus in *Roe v. Wade* and subsequent cases. As we have already stated, no fetus is considered a "person" under the U.S. Constitution. Thus, a fetus clearly has lesser rights than those of us who have been born. Moreover, the Supreme Court acknowledged that the government's interest in protecting the life of a fetus that had reached the stage of being viable (approximately 20 weeks old) was greater than its interest in protecting previable fetuses. A state could therefore ban abortions if the fetus has reached the stage of viability (unless the woman's life or health was at stake), but if the fetus is not viable, the state's authority to prevent a woman from getting an abortion is greatly limited. These rulings might suggest that it is inappropriate to consider the death of a previable fetus as equivalent to that of a person. Nonetheless, the few courts that have thus far considered these issues have upheld state statutes criminalizing the death of a fetus, even if it is not viable.[25]

On the other hand, the second scenario, where the robber destroys several hundred embryos, is treated very differently under the law. It appears that currently no state (with the possible exception of Louisiana)[26] or the federal government has said that causing the death of an embryo sitting in a laboratory dish or test tube (an *in vitro* embryo)—one that has not yet been implanted in a woman's uterus—is equivalent to killing a human being and deserves equal punishment. Indeed, to the extent there is any law about the status of such embryos, they are usually treated as a special category of property and not as human beings whose deaths trigger the criminal law.[27] While it is sometimes said that the embryos deserve "special respect," that type of language has thus far done little to alter the treatment of such embryos, at least when they aren't being used in research. Thus, when a now-divorced man and woman would go to court fighting over what happens to the frozen embryos that were created in happier days (as part of an attempt to conceive a child), what concerns the court are the interests of the two parties. There is little reference to the best interests of the embryo. The man and woman are free to have the embryos destroyed, if they want. And, unlike the complicated set of laws dealing with abortion—where a variety of provisions have been adopted to make it hard for women to get that procedure—states have not done much of anything to prevent the destruction of these embryos.[28] Thus, at heart, our legal system—at least outside of the research context—does indeed treat these embryos in dishes in a very different way than the fetus developing inside a woman's uterus.

With that as background, we now turn to the science behind the controversy over stem cells.[29] Most of the cells in the body of a human being are relatively specialized. They are designed for a particular purpose—to be part of someone's skin or kidney or bone—and when they divide and form other cells, those new cells will be able to perform only that same purpose. In contrast, when a sperm fertilizes an egg, and that fertilized egg begins to divide, the cells at that point are relatively unspecialized. As more and more cell divisions take place, they will over time become more and more specialized. But at that very early stage, within the first several days after fertilization, each cell has the theoretical capability, by being given the right type of "instructions" as it divides and creates successor cells, to eventually lead to virtually any other type of specialized cell. Moreover, until they are given those instructions, these cells can keep dividing to produce more and more unspecialized cells like themselves, and thus for months or even years can lead to a "line" of cells that scientists can study.

If we could eventually fully control the process by which these cells become specialized, and direct these "stem" cells to form exactly the types of cells we'd like, we might open up new ways of treating numerous medical problems. We might grow clusters of islet cells, the insulin-producing cells destroyed in childhood diabetes, and implant them into the bodies of these children. We could perhaps insert the stem cells into the brain of a person with Parkinson's disease and direct them to transform into the dopamine-producing cells that are missing. We might similarly try to repair the spinal cords of people who suffer from paraplegia or quadriplegia after spinal cord injuries. And we might even be able to grow whole new organs—kidneys, livers, lungs, hearts—to replace the defective or aging organs that cause a huge variety of common medical problems.

It is not only in the early stages of a developing embryo that there are such stem cells. Even in adults, there are some cells (adult stem cells) that retain a degree of flexibility in their future development. And there are similar such cells in a more developed fetus (fetal stem cells). Thus, some have suggested studying adult stem cells or stem cells obtained from the tissues of aborted fetuses. But these other types of stem cells appear to be less flexible, less able to be fully molded to form all types of tissues, than the cells of a very early embryo. Many scientists therefore believe that the greatest potential comes from the use of embryonic stem cells.

Unfortunately, in order to study embryonic stem cells, an embryo probably needs to be destroyed to create each different "line" of stem cells. At the time this is done, the embryo is only a few days old, barely visible to the naked eye as a tiny dot, and is composed of only a hundred or so cells. These cells are all very nonspecialized—that, after all, is why they are so valuable—and the embryo thus possesses no type of early brain development or even any nerve cells and is not capable of feeling any pain while it is being destroyed. Nonetheless, it is the precursor for what would develop into a unique human being, if it were implanted in a woman's uterus and she were allowed to carry it to term.

The question therefore arises: should our society permit the destruction of an embryo in order to help us learn more about using stem cells to help treat future patients? More particularly, since there are two primary ways that we would obtain the embryos for this research, this question can be asked about both of these situations. The first situation involves brand-new embryos being created for research purposes. In other words, a woman might be asked to donate an egg, and a man might donate some sperm, and the sperm used to fertilize the egg and create an embryo. Both the man and the woman would know that the embryo was to be used for research purposes and that it would be destroyed when the stem cells were removed. They would have consented to that. To the extent some people believe that it is significantly wrong to destroy an embryo, this situation appears particularly troublesome, since these embryos were both created and destroyed solely for research purposes.

On the other hand, there might be no need to create new embryos. It just so happens that there are lots of embryos—at least several hundred thousand of them—already in existence, floating in freezers in laboratories throughout this country. Often, when a husband and wife are unable to get pregnant due to a variety of medical problems, one solution is to use *in vitro* fertilization. This involves giving the woman hormones to cause her body to produce several eggs, then removing those eggs from her body and combining them with her husband's sperm so that several fertilized eggs are created. Some of the eggs are then inserted into her uterus in the hope that they will implant in the wall and she will become pregnant. The extra ones are frozen, to be used in a future attempt in case the first try doesn't result in a successful birth or if they want to have a second child. Eventually, the couple may end up with the number of children they wanted, or they may decide to stop trying *in vitro* fertilization. In either event, there may be leftover embryos sitting in the freezer, and the question arises of what to do with them. Although some of them can be "adopted"—some other couple with fertility problems may not be able to produce their own eggs and sperm and may need a fertilized egg—this is likely to happen to only a very small percentage. Thus, the great bulk of these extra embryos will likely eventually be destroyed, with the consent of the husband and wife.

Assuming that would be the case, should those couples be given the option of donating them to research, so that some good comes of their destruction? This possibility seems less controversial than that of creating new embryos solely for research purposes. After all, these embryos were created for legitimate, non-research-related purposes: to allow the couple to have a child. And the embryos themselves derived a benefit from being created: they had a chance to end up being implanted in the woman's uterus and to be allowed to eventually (if everything went well) be born. Once the decision has been made to not use them for that purpose, and instead to destroy them, it is not clear why destroying them as part of research is somehow less ethical than just destroying them because no one wants to allow them to eventually grow into a fetus and then be born.

Oddly enough, in spite of all the controversy that this type of research has generated, the Common Rule is relatively clear about these issues: the embryos are *not* considered to be human subjects. These regulations do apply to research involving fetuses, as we discussed above, but a fetus is defined to be "the product of conception from implantation until delivery."[30] As long as an embryo is just sitting in a lab in a dish and hasn't yet been implanted in a woman's uterus, the regulations don't prohibit any particular activities that might be "harmful" to such an embryo, including destroying it as part of an attempt to create stem cells. Nor do they have anything to say about attempts to create new embryos for such a purpose.[31] Thus, the regulations are actually quite consistent with the general way that the U.S. legal system has been treating these entities—recall the example of the robber knocking over the beaker of frozen embryos—considering them more like property (albeit a special type) than beings worthy of special protections.

Moreover, even the somewhat controversial "resolution" of this issue by President George W. Bush is, to at least some extent, consistent with these other rules. President Bush spoke to the nation in an unusual televised speech on August 9, 2001.[32] He first discussed whether or not embryos should be considered "human life," presenting the views of some who answered yes and some who answered no.[33] Without specifically stating whether he had concluded that these embryos are human life, he then went on to discuss the issue of using the preexisting embryos to create stem cells, again presenting arguments that had been given on both sides of the issue.[34] After having stated both sides of these issues, he went on to give his resolution of the problem: he authorized federal funds to be used for research on the approximately 60 existing lines of stem cells that had already been developed. As he noted, although embryos had been destroyed in creating these cell lines, there was nothing that could be done to undo that fact, and thus he felt it was appropriate to make use of those stem cell lines.

Whether or not someone agrees with his conclusions, a key point to note is that the president's decision relates *only* to federal funding of stem cell research. He did not ask Congress to enact a ban on privately funded research in this area, whether it involved using preexisting embryos or even the creation of new ones. While the president's decision has clearly made many researchers unhappy, in many ways it represents a middle-of-the-road compromise. He did not say that using embryos created for the purpose of *in vitro* fertilization, or even creating new embryos for research, is so clearly immoral that there can be no legitimate differences of opinion on this issue. If that were his view, he should presumably do more than just prevent the U.S. government from *funding* such research: he should have asked for a ban on such uses of embryos. But he did not do that. His resolution of the issue is very similar to the status quo with regard to abortion: the federal government does not fund abortions, yet women have a constitutionally protected right to get an abortion (at least prior to the fetus becoming viable). He is acknowledging that there is a great deal of controversy about the moral status of human embryos and that controversy supports a public policy that does not strictly adhere to the views of one or another polar viewpoint.

Since President Bush's announcement, large segments of the scientific community have indicated that the stem cell lines available under the his guidelines have significant limitations (including the fact that they could likely never be implanted in people, due to having been exposed to mice cells).[35] And as of mid-2004, it had been determined that there were only about fifteen usable stem cell lines meeting the president's requirements, not the sixty-odd he suggested. Given that the prohibition on federal funding is the only major limitation to either using preexisting embryos or creating new ones just for research purposes, it was likely inevitable that private funding would indeed fill much of this gap. On February 29, 2004, Harvard University announced the creation of a multimillion dollar center that would be involved in creating and studying stem cells. In March of 2004, Harvard researchers published an article in the *New England Journal of Medicine* describing how they established seventeen brand-new lines of stem cells, working from frozen embryos that had initially been created for purposes of *in vitro* fertilization.[36] This research was described as a "tour de force" of top-notch science,[37] and the researchers indicated that the stem cell lines would also be made available free of cost to other researchers.

Unless the federal government steps in with new legislation, the next likely battleground over stem cell research will take place in state legislatures, which—absent binding federal laws—are free to write their own laws regarding what type of research can take place within their borders. While some states are banning this research,[38] we are now beginning to see just the opposite phenomenon: states that are eager to embrace the high-tech research dollars that might come with being a stem-cell-research-friendly environment. New Jersey has created a stem cell institute that will be funded with $50 million of taxpayer money, and in California a ballot initiative was passed under which up to $3 billion would be available for stem cell research.[39]

Cloning

No discussion of stem cells is fully complete without mentioning cloning. While cloning certainly raises its own legal and ethical problems, it also has a direct connection to the controversy over stem cells.

The cloning process—technically called somatic cell nuclear transfer—was developed by the scientists who created the sheep named Dolly in 1997. In very simple terms, they took an egg cell from a sheep and removed its nucleus, so that there was no longer any DNA inside it (and thus no genetic instructions telling the cell how to develop). The scientists then merged the egg cell with a cell from the body of the sheep they wanted to clone. This could be any cell in that sheep's body—a so-called somatic cell—other than a reproductive cell, such as a sperm or egg cell. Somatic cells have a full set of chromosomes, all the DNA needed to code for a unique individual animal, as opposed to the reproductive cells, which only have half a set of chromosomes. The researchers discovered, somewhat to the surprise of many, that by tinkering a bit with the resulting cell, such as exposing it to electrical current, the cell would begin to divide, and it would behave as if it were an egg cell that had just been fertilized by a sperm. If allowed to continue to divide, and placed in the uterus of an adult sheep, this cell would continue to develop—if nothing went wrong—into a fetus that was nearly genetically identical to the sheep whose body cell was used.[40]

What can cloning be used for? There are two very different possible purposes: *reproductive* cloning and *therapeutic* cloning. Reproductive cloning is the far more controversial of these two, involving the use of the cloning process to create a human being. Consider the possibilities:[41] An infertile couple might use cloning to produce a child that is genetically related to one of them. Parents might create a clone of a child that has died. A couple with certain genetic problems that would otherwise affect a child might use cloning to create a healthy child. Parents might use cloning to create a child with certain desirable characteristics (e.g., great beauty, allowing the child to become a supermodel).

Several federal advisory panels have recommended that research on reproductive cloning be banned, either permanently or at least for the near future. The U.S. Congress has also debated various bills to enact a ban, and there appears to be a consensus in favor of a ban. The main thing that has thus far prevented a bill from passing is that the bills have thus far also included bans on therapeutic cloning, a practice that is far less controversial (as we discuss below).

The biggest concern with reproductive cloning is that the cloning process doesn't actually work very well. For cloning to work, the genes in the nucleus—which came from a "developed" cell—have to be "reprogrammed" so that they are ready to cause the cell to behave like a growing embryo. The surprising thing is that by exposing those genes to the cytoplasm of the egg cell, and supplying an electrical current, many of the genes apparently *do* get reprogrammed. But there are thousands of them, and the fact that cloning is very hit-and-miss is likely due to some of these genes not being reprogrammed. And, even if enough of them are reprogrammed so that a live human being is born, there is always the possibility that the failure to get complete reprogramming might lead to future defects as the child grows up. This might explain what happened to the first clone, Dolly, who died at a relatively young age and had severe arthritis problems. The uncertainty about the health of a possible cloned child leads many people to oppose the use of cloning to produce such a child.

There are also a number of other arguments against reproductive cloning. Some contend that even if the child were healthy, the fact that he or she was genetically identical to some other person might create emotional problems for the child. And there are arguments that this type of method for creating a human being—given that it allows the selection of the entire genetic makeup of a child—is a troubling step toward a fundamental alteration in how our society views children. We would be moving, so the argument goes, in the direction of treating children as "projects" that can be genetically shaped to the will of their parents.[42]

For all of these reasons, it seems reasonable to predict that, though there is currently no federal ban on reproductive cloning, such a ban is very likely to be passed. Even without such a ban, there already exists a long-standing federal policy that prevents federal funding of cloning research. This ban has its origins in the 1970s, when regulations forbade funding of research about *in vitro* fertilization (combining an egg and sperm in a laboratory) without the approval of a special ethics board. Although that board eventually proposed rules under which such funding might take place, the board was disbanded before the rules got approved. Eventually, in 1996, Congress enacted a ban on the use of federal funds for "the creation of a human embryo or embryos for research purposes, or research in which a human embryo or embryos are destroyed, discarded, or knowingly subjected to risk of injury or death greater than that allowed for research on fetuses *in utero*."[43] This language would appear to cover most research about any form of human cloning. Thus, at least from a federal funding viewpoint, the rules relating to cloning research are even stricter than those applying to stem cell research.

In contrast to reproductive cloning, research involving therapeutic cloning is a practice that has a great deal of support. In particular, many people perceive therapeutic cloning as serving a very important medical purpose, one linked to the promise of stem cells. As we discussed above, stem cell research may well lead to treatments or even cures for many medical problems. Those treatments will often require implanting in a person's new tissues or organs that have been created by manipulating stem cells. But the immune system of our bodies is designed to destroy "foreign" tissues. Thus, even if we were able to attain many of the goals suggested by the use of stem cells, a problem would still remain. People receiving new tissues or organs grown from stem cells would need to receive potent antirejection drugs, the same drugs that are given to people who now get transplanted organs. These drugs are designed to weaken a person's immune system and, as a consequence, often have their own substantial (and even life-threatening) side effects.

Therapeutic cloning provides a possible solution to this problem. Imagine a man whose kidneys have failed. We could take one of his cells, merge it with a woman's donated egg cell that has had its nucleus removed, and then allow the resulting "clone" to begin to divide for a few days until it reaches the stage at which stem cells can be extracted. Those stem cells could then be grown into a kidney. Since these cells possess the genetic makeup of the patient, his immune system would not reject the kidney, and he would not be required to take any antirejection drugs. In effect, it would be as if he were receiving a kidney almost identical to the ones that he was born with.

Unlike reproductive cloning, therapeutic cloning does not involve any attempt to create a human being. It therefore avoids almost all of the arguments used to condemn that practice. Indeed, the arguments against therapeutic cloning to a large extent duplicate those against creating new embryos for the purposes of producing stem cells, since essentially the same procedure is taking place in both situations. As noted above, those arguments have not led the federal government to ban the creation of such embryos: the federal government merely refuses to fund such research.

The same sensible solution seems appropriate with regard to therapeutic cloning. This is already the status quo.[44] The major argument being made against this resolution of the issue is the type of "slippery slope" argument that Dr. Leon Kass, former chairman of President George W. Bush's bioethics council, has made, which we quoted near the beginning of this chapter: "The age of human cloning has apparently arrived: today, cloned blastocysts for research, tomorrow cloned blastocysts for babymaking." But Kass seems wrong in thinking that there is no way to prevent therapeutic cloning—with its huge potential to provide treatments to a number of major medical problems—from leading society down the road to creating cloned children.

Indeed, the very body that he chaired, the President's Council on Bioethics, has determined that this slippery slope is not a problem.[45] It recommended that Congress ban "attempts to conceive a child by any means other than the union of egg and sperm," and also prohibit "the use of human embryos in research beyond a designated stage in their development (between 10 and 14 days after fertilization)." These recommendations, while banning reproductive cloning, allow for both stem cell research and research on therapeutic cloning. They also give a degree of "special respect" to embryos in banning research on embryos that have developed beyond those first 14 days.

We began this chapter with stories making headlines in early 2004 that demonstrate how highly divided our nation is with regard to these issues. And thus it is refreshing to close by describing a set of recommendations that are surprisingly sensible. Perhaps there is indeed hope that the future of this area may involve more reasoned analysis and less heat.

Part IV

The Role of Money

16

Should Research Subjects Be Paid?

Show me the money!
—Jerry Maguire

The idea of paying research subjects for their participation in a study remains a controversial one. In this chapter, we first explore the issue of paying subjects for contributing a part of their body—such as tissue or blood—to a study, and then turn to the more general question of whether subjects should be paid for their services. As we show here, paying subjects generates far more controversy than it should—and actually serves a number of valuable purposes, including helping people to distinguish between "good choice" and "bad choice" studies.

John Moore's Body

In 1976, John Moore was diagnosed with the "hairy cell" form of leukemia (a type of cancer of cells in the bone marrow), so named because of the numerous hair-like appendages that form on abnormal cells.[1] He was referred to UCLA Medical Center for treatment and underwent a variety of diagnostic procedures there, including tests of his blood and bone marrow. Dr. David W. Golde, who was in charge of his treatment, soon discovered that Moore's medical problem was especially interesting in an unexpected way. Leukemia is a type of cancer in which certain cells in a person's bone marrow keep dividing in an uncontrolled way. It just so happened that the cancerous cells in Moore's body also secreted a substance known as a lymphokine, a protein that plays an important role in regulating the human immune system. At the time Moore was being treated, it was difficult for researchers to produce lymphokines in the laboratory. Thus, Moore's cancerous cells appeared to be especially useful: they could be put into dishes in a laboratory and the cells resulting from their

211

continual divisions (a so-called "cell line") kept alive for long periods of time and used in essence as a way to produce significant amounts of lymphokines.

Dr. Golde and his colleagues allegedly quickly recognized the value of Moore's cells and undertook a series of procedures designed to make sure they had enough of the cells to manufacture lymphokines. Thus, in October of 1976 they told Moore that his spleen should be removed and that if he failed to undergo the surgery his life would be in danger. Moore agreed to the surgery and underwent a splenectomy in that month. Over the next six years, Dr. Golde had Moore return (from his home-town of Seattle) to UCLA Medical Center several times, and each time the doctor collected samples of his blood, skin, and bone marrow. In each instance, Moore was advised that it was necessary that Dr. Golde himself do these procedures and that they could not be performed by doctors back in Seattle. In January of 1981, Dr. Golde and a colleague filed a patent application on behalf of themselves and the Regents of the University of California, relating to the cells they had cultured from Moore's tumor. Dr. Golde subsequently negotiated agreements with biotechnology compa-nies relating to the use of the cell lines, which resulted in his acquiring millions of dollars worth of stock.

During this period, John Moore was not told anything about the research that was taking place using his cells. When he learned what had taken place, he sued Dr. Moore, UCLA, and the biotechnology companies, making a variety of claims. His case made its way through a variety of lower courts, each evaluating various mo-tions made by the defendants to dismiss it, until it reached the California Supreme Court, which wrote a landmark opinion about this series of events. That court ad-dressed the issue of whether, assuming the true facts about what happened were as Moore stated them to be, Dr. Golde and his colleagues at UCLA had done anything wrong. In particular, two separate legal arguments were addressed by the court.

The first argument was that the researchers' failure to tell Moore about the re-search breached a "fiduciary" duty they owed to him and meant that they had there-fore failed to get appropriate informed consent to treat him. The court found in favor of Moore on this argument. It correctly noted that a "physician who treats a patient in whom he also has a research interest has potentially conflicting loyalties."[2] That physician-researcher might well end up, while trying to advance the research (and earn the big bucks from a successful new product), doing things to the patient that are not in the patient's best interests. As the court noted, under the "reasonable patient" test for determining what information should be given to a patient in ob-taining informed consent, a reasonable patient would indeed want to know about this "profit motive" that might be motivating his doctor. Thus, the doctor was le-gally required to let the patient know about this conflict of interest.

The second argument was that the doctors had effectively stolen Moore's cells. The technical legal term for this was "conversion," but it amounts to very much the same concept as theft. Under this theory, the cells from Moore's body were his prop-erty, and thus no one would be able to use them without getting his permission. It is same argument that we regularly apply to other things people own. If, while Moore was in the operating room having his spleen removed, Dr. Golde had taken Moore's car keys and used his car to drive around town, that would clearly have been an improper "conversion" of the car. The question posed by the case was whether Moore's cells were any different than his car: in particular, does he perhaps not "own" his cells in the same way he owns his car, and thus not have a legal right to tell someone else not to use them?

The California Supreme Court noted that no court had ever specifically ruled that a person had an ownership interest in portions of his or her own body, and it ruled against Moore on the conversion claim. It noted that there are many specific laws relating to the disposition of human tissue and body parts and that such narrow laws should guide the decision on whether or not people have an ownership interest in their body parts or tissues. Those laws did not specifically create such an ownership interest, and the court declined to "extend" the existing law to create such a right. One of its major reasons for reaching that decision was on policy grounds. It noted that biologic materials play a critical role in medical research and that allowing people to assert an ownership interest in their tissues could seriously disrupt a great deal of important research.

In a concurring opinion, Justice Arabian was even more eloquent in highlighting the problems that might stem from concluding that people have an ownership interest in their own bodies: "Plaintiff has asked us to recognize and enforce a right to sell one's own body tissue *for profit*. He entreats us to regard the human vessel—the single most venerated and protected subject in any civilized society—as equal with the basest commercial commodity. He urges us to commingle the sacred with the profane. He asks much."[3]

In evaluating whether the *Moore* court was correct in rejecting the ownership claim, it is interesting to look at what has happened in the world of biotechnology in the fifteen or so years since the case. In numerous ways, the "business" of using human tissues has boomed. There has been an explosion in the number of university researchers owning or working for companies, each trying to get their share of the millions that might come from patenting the new "hot" gene. Indeed, the ties between the university world and the for-profit world have become so great that the resulting conflicts of interest are seen by many as a major problem for the integrity of research.

The extent to which tissue has become a big business was revealed by a controversial series of articles in the *Orange County Register* in April of 2000, dealing with what happens to tissues taken from bodies that are "donated" after people die.[4] As the series noted, businesses earned hundreds of millions of dollars from using these tissues, even though federal law theoretically makes it illegal to profit from such materials.[5] Many of the uses were probably not those that families had in mind when they were asked to donate the body of a loved one: "Families are led to believe they are giving the gift of life. They are not told that skin goes to enlarge penises or smooth out wrinkles, or that executives of tissue banks—nonprofit groups that obtain body parts—routinely earn six-figure salaries. The products are rarely life-saving as advertised."[6]

As the series of articles detailed, a person's dead body could end up producing thousands of dollars in profits—theoretically, up to $220,000, if all of the tissues could be used. And none of that money goes to the family of the deceased, who have agreed to "donate" the body.

Sharing the Profits with Subjects

Regardless of whether the *Moore* court was correct in rejecting the conversion theory, it did at least recognize that patients need to be told if their doctors are doing things with their tissue that might help the doctors earn large financial profits. The same sort of disclosure should apply to the setting where someone is explicitly being asked to participate in a research study (unlike what happened in *Moore*, where the research was hidden). As we showed in chapter 7, a researcher, in getting informed consent, is under a duty to disclose information that a reasonable research subject would want to know under those circumstances. Given that more and more subjects are being asked to contribute tissue in research studies, it seems appropriate to regularly be telling those subjects in what ways the researchers or sponsors of the study are contemplating using the tissue to generate profits.

A recent lawsuit highlights how important this issue is becoming. Canavan disease is a rare but fatal genetic disorder that mainly affects Jews whose ancestors came from Eastern and Central Europe, a group that includes more than 90% of American Jews.[7] Approximately one in forty such Jews is a carrier of the defective gene that leads to the disease. Due to the lack of an enzyme called aspartoacylase, the sheathing that surrounds nerve cells in the brain begins to degenerate in children with the disease. Symptoms begin when an infant is only a few months old. Affected children cannot crawl, sit, or talk. They may have seizures or become mentally retarded or blind. They will almost always die by the age of ten.

Beginning in 1987, a group of parents of such children got together to promote research about Canavan disease. One of the leaders of the group, Daniel Greenberg, contacted Dr. Reuben Matalon, then a researcher at the University of Illinois at Chicago, and convinced him to begin working on the disease. Greenberg and others worked actively to find families affected by Canavan disease and to get them to donate tissue to Dr. Matalon's studies. Those efforts eventually bore fruit, for in 1993 the researcher was able to isolate the gene that caused the disease, often a first step toward developing treatments. Unbeknownst to the families, Miami Children's Hospital Research Institute, where Dr. Matalon was then working, applied for and was awarded a patent on the genetic sequence for the defective gene. This patent allowed the institute to charge others for using that sequence for a variety of purposes, including in prenatal testing, doing further research on the gene, or even developing a treatment for the disease.

The institute did in fact develop a test for the disease and began charging a royalty to anyone in the country who wanted to use the test. When the parents learned about this, they were very disturbed to hear that other laboratories and medical centers were being forced to pay to use the information that had been produced, in part, by their volunteer efforts. A front-page story in the *New York Times*, entitled "Sharing of Profits Is Debated as the Value of Tissue Rises; Patients Increasingly Ask: What about Me?" recounted some of their concerns.[8] Greenberg was quoted as being "disappointed and disheartened and disgusted" about what happened. Had the parents known that the results of the research were not going to be made freely available to everyone, they might have gone to a different researcher in the first place. The *New York Times* article quoted a number of experts who also pointed out the hypocrisy involved in the current system, where everyone involved seems to be out to make a profit, yet somehow the subjects are supposed to be volunteering their time and effort, in addition to donating their tissues.

The families ended up suing the institute and Dr. Matalon on a number of legal theories, including lack of informed consent, breach of fiduciary duty, unjust enrichment, and also the conversion argument rejected in the *Moore* case. A federal district court rejected most of these theories—including the conversion argument—but held that a trial should be held on the issue of whether the defendants had been "unjustly enriched" by working with the parents to develop the genetic test and not telling them about the intent to patent the results.[9] Although this was formally a different legal argument than the one accepted in *Moore*—the *Moore* court found a breach of the fiduciary duty owed by a doctor to a patient, but in this case the court found there was no such duty owed by the researcher to the subjects—it nonetheless may (and should) lead to a similar result: that researchers who contemplate profiting from the results of a research study are under a duty to let the subjects know about this possibility.

Beyond Disclosure

Of course, even if such a duty to disclose exists, it doesn't necessarily give subjects a great deal of power. The consent form need merely disclose that the researchers will possibly profit from using the subject's tissues, and that the subject will not be given any of those profits. (That is what most consent forms currently say, though in vaguer and more confusing language.) At that point, subjects have to choose whether this aspect of the study bothers them enough to discourage them from enrolling. On their own, they are unlikely to be able to convince the researchers to change the policy on not giving them a share of the possible profits from using the tissue. Indeed, in spite of negative publicity such as the front-page *New York Times* story mentioned above, it is extraordinarily rare for researchers to ever agree to give subjects a share in such profits.

To some extent, the attitude of the research field toward allowing subjects to share in these profits reflects a broader theme, one that in a variety of ways discourages financially compensating subjects for their services. And thus we turn now to explore that broader question: *when, if ever, can subjects to be paid for their services?* To address this question, we'll begin with a hypothetical scenario far from the world of research. Imagine that you picked up your morning newspaper, and in an article about upcoming negotiations between police and fire fighters and New York City administrators, you read the following comments by the negotiators representing the best and the bravest:

> Regarding the proposed new pay scale for our members, we are concerned that the city may be paying new recruits too much. After all, these recruits are young people who often are relatively poor—many come

from minority groups—and thus the higher starting salaries may coerce them into taking this job. We know that this job involves very substantial health risks—death is a possibility that confronts our members daily—and we want to make sure that these impressionable new recruits are not inappropriately influenced by a large amount of money in deciding to embark on this career path. Thus, it may be necessary, on ethical grounds, to limit the starting salary, even though we are aware that the city is offering to pay them more money.

Of course, you are not about to encounter such a statement any day soon.

How odd, then, that in the world of human subjects research, the concerns expressed by our mythical negotiators are indeed a reality. As we noted at the start of this chapter, paying someone to participate in a research study continues to be controversial. Leading regulatory bodies require that such payments be carefully scrutinized to make sure that they are not too high. The federal regulations declare that "economically disadvantaged persons"—presumably a technical term for poor people—is a group, like pregnant women, children, and prisoners, that is "vulnerable" to undue influence, and that institutional review boards (IRBs) must make sure they are protected from undue influence.[10] Unlike those other categories of vulnerable subjects, however, the regulations fail to specify what IRBs should be doing to protect poor people.

The FDA is more explicit and has an entire policy statement on payments to research subjects.[11] While acknowledging that payments to subjects can be used as a "recruitment incentive" (as opposed to a "benefit" to subjects), particularly where health benefits to subjects are remote, the agency nonetheless cautions that such payments must not be "coercive or present undue influence."[12] Similarly, a leading international standard for research states that the amount and method of payment should be reviewed to make sure they do not create "problems of coercion or undue influence."[13] While this alleged problem is frequently highlighted, the authorities give very little guidance on what makes a particular payment coercive or an undue influence.[14]

Do we really need to worry about payments to subjects being coercive? In general, offering someone an additional opportunity to earn some money is not the sort of thing we view as being coercive. Coercion more typically takes place when someone threatens to do something bad to you unless you do the desired act: "Pay us the million dollars or your kidnapped daughter gets killed."[15] Creating an additional opportunity that we can choose to accept or reject is not commonly thought of as coercive. The fact that it is an exceptionally good opportunity—that we might get paid a lot more than we were expecting—probably just means that it is our lucky day, not that we are being coerced.[16]

Indeed, if we are looking for "coercive" situations in the research setting, there is a much more logical candidate than the payment issue: permitting subjects to get access to an unapproved drug only by being in a research study does indeed seem coercive. Either participate in the study, and get a 50% shot at being given the new drug (and a 50% chance of placebo), or else don't get any chance at the new drug.

This is much closer to the classic coercive "your money or your life" threat, where someone is being denied something they might otherwise be entitled to—why shouldn't the person be allowed to get the drug outside of the study?—than refusing to give someone money unless they do something to earn it (by participating in a study). Yet few are suggesting getting rid of that clearly coercive element (nor do we).

In spite of the lack of very good explanations on why payments to subjects are so likely to be so problematic, there remains a great deal of concern about these allegedly coercive payments. A recent survey of payment practices among sponsors of research studies indicated a wide variety of payment policies. While almost all of those responding at least sometimes paid subjects, nearly two-thirds of them had no written policies or guidelines about this issue.[17] This issue is so controversial that the nation's leading medical journal, the *New England Journal of Medicine*, felt it necessary to devote valuable pages to an article defending a less-than-startling conclusion: that it is acceptable to pay subjects based on the number of hours they spend participating in the research, using the "fairly low" hourly rate that an unskilled laborer receives.[18] In other words, research subjects should get paid similar to what they would get if they were working the cash register at McDonald's.

The reason the authors recommend this rule is that it is unlikely to create any of the dreaded "undue inducement"—and they are certainly right about that. If we pay our research subjects the minimum wage or something very close to it, then even the very poor are likely to have many other ways to earn this same amount (e.g., taking minimum wage jobs, of which there are usually quite a few). We do not have to worry about poor people being "coerced" into entering studies due to the payment. But let us examine another claim that the authors of this article made: that this type of approach to payment is "just." What is it, exactly, that makes it quite so just?

If we were talking about a study that involves essentially no health risk—for example, drawing a tube of blood from a healthy volunteer and then performing some tests on it in a laboratory—then it does indeed seem as if the hourly rate for unskilled laborers is appropriate. But, of course, that is not the sort of study that raises any difficult issues, or that implicates the tragic choices that lay at the heart of the issues discussed in this book. Let us instead consider a study where subjects are assuming some not insignificant health risks, any one of the "bad choice" studies that expose them to risks without an equivalent possibility of benefit. Is it "just" to say that these people should be paid at the same rate as the checkout clerk at McDonald's? Are they participating only for their time and effort?

The clear answer is no. It is not their "time and effort" that is important. Rather, it is their *willingness to expose themselves to health risks*, the sorts of risks that most of us are generally not willing to be exposed to, absent some sort of appropriate inducement. And, as we have already shown, many research studies, as currently designed, do not have any such inducement. Thus, we need to ask: under other circumstances, would people be paid additional amounts when we are asking them to assume health risks above and beyond the time and effort that a particular job requires? Is it not more just to pay a person who assumes such risks more than a person who performs identical tasks but is not subject to such risks?

While we don't have any specific data on this question, the appropriate answer seems to be "yes." People in our society who expose themselves to high levels of risks to their health deserve to be paid in a way that recognizes those risks: to fail to do so is unjust. There is a reason why firefighters and the police were considered among the heroes of 9/11: the health risks that they daily assume to protect all of us had been highlighted in an exceptional way. These uniformed officers certainly felt there was a connection between the risks they take and the amount they should be paid. Indeed, during salary negotiations in 2002, the New York City uniformed officers held a rally demanding larger raises, expressing "anger and disbelief" that the city had so soon forgotten "the sacrifices they made rushing to fires, cutting crime and responding to the horrors of Sept. 11."[19]

Why is it that when firefighters and police officers expose themselves to risk, they are entitled to payments recognizing that level of risk, yet paying research subjects to assume risks (beyond those that will directly benefit them) is improper? One argument for this distinction relates to the difference between the "active" role that the firefighter takes, as opposed to the "passive" role that the research subject takes.[20] But this is not a distinction that we recognize in other situations. We hope that people who engage in risky jobs are paid more than those who are not exposed to such high risks, regardless of the source of the risk. American civilian personnel who have taken jobs performing various administrative tasks in postwar Iraq are "passively" exposed to huge life-or-death risks due to the hazardous environment there. They are likely getting paid more than their counterparts in America who are doing exactly the same administrative tasks but in a much safer environment. And if they are not being paid more, then they *should* be: not to do so is unjust.

Finally, it is interesting to note that if indeed the defenders of either paying the subjects nothing or paying them merely at a minimum wage rate were true to their beliefs, they should be objecting to an extremely common practice: giving free medical care as part of a research study.[21] This country remains one of the few civilized nations that does not provide access to free health care for its citizens. Approximately 40 million Americans are without any health insurance for at least part of the year. For such an uninsured person, or a person of modest income who cannot afford the deductibles or copayments imposed by their health insurer, the prospect of getting zero-cost treatment for a medical problem can be a huge incentive to enroll in a research study. Given the cost of health care, the payments they in effect receive for participating in the study (by getting this free care) can be in the thousands of dollars, far more than an hourly payment at a minimum wage. And perhaps the biggest practitioner of this free care practice is the federal government itself, since studies conducted at the elite research centers of the National Institutes of Health are traditionally without cost to the subjects.

So, if we were sincere about dealing with the alleged problem of paying subjects too much in a study, we should be taking action against the "free care" studies. But we don't. Perhaps the reason we don't is a cynical one: if we didn't provide this incentive, we would get far fewer subjects enrolling in these studies. Or perhaps the reason is less cynical: by having these studies take place in this manner, these subjects at least get the opportunity to get free medical care. Thus, in a sense, the studies are helping to remedy the ethical quagmire of this nation's failure to adopt a health plan that covers everyone. But if that is our reasoning, it is hard to see why it shouldn't extend to other forms of substantial payments to subjects—certainly it would be an equally good thing to remedy poverty by allowing people to earn money by choosing to participate in a research study.

Sending the Right Signals to Research Subjects

There is an important additional argument in favor of paying subjects amounts that bear a relationship to the risks that they are undertaking. This argument has nothing to do with fairness. It instead relates to issues we discussed in part II regarding informed consent and the need to make sure subjects understand why they are being asked to participate in a study.

When someone pays you to do something, a clear message is being sent: you are *providing a service* to that person. You are receiving the money because what you are doing is valuable to the person who pays you. In general, as a task gets more demanding, you will be paid increasing amounts of money. That is the way compensation generally works.

Thus, when someone goes to a doctor and gets some sort of medical treatment, the doctor does not pay them, since the patient is not providing a service to the doctor. Quite the opposite: the patient is receiving a service and is expected to pay the doctor. Indeed, a patient would find it very odd to be paid by his doctor. In contrast, when a subject is participating in a study, that person is now providing a service to the researcher. The fact that they receive a payment, the very oddness of that in the context of being treated for an illness, sends an important reinforcing signal to the subject. It highlights in a very visible way how much things have changed from the usual doctor–patient relationship. The person who might otherwise have not fully appreciated the differences between being a patient and being a research subject might take notice of this and ask himself: "Hold on a second, why is my doctor giving me money? What is it I am doing for him that makes him willing to pay me?"

And beyond the wakeup signal sent by the mere fact of the payment, the *amount* of the payment sends an additional signal, helping to clarify which studies are not just bad choices but really bad choices. Studies with minor risks should involve minor payments. In contrast, studies with significant risks should involve larger payments: those larger payments will not only more fairly compensate the subjects for undertaking the risks but also make sure they understand, before signing up for the studies, the extent to which participation involves being exposed to additional risks. Consider a study such the one discussed in chapter 6, where patients with colon cancer were asked to consent to being randomized to keyhole surgery, and a possibly higher risk of cancer recurrence, one not fully balanced by the possible benefits from participation. They were being asked to undergo a type of surgery that colorectal surgeons as a group considered too risky to perform on anyone outside of a research study. It would be very reasonable to pay these subjects an amount in the hundreds or even thousands of dollars for participating in this "bad choice" study. Even if they tended to gloss over much of what was in the consent form, this large payment might make them finally wake up and ask, "Why is someone paying me so much merely to be treated for my cancer?"

The Justice Argument

The bottom line is relatively straightforward: if in the research setting it is so bad for people to be exposed to particular risks, then we should be banning the studies that involve these inappropriate risks. But, on the other hand, if we have already decided that the risks are reasonable—and presumably we have, if we are allowing a study to take place even if the subject is not being paid anything—then why is it any worse to pay people to participate (even a great deal of money, perhaps, if that is justified by the risks)? As we have shown, the claim that such payments are coercive is wrong. Quite the contrary, they more likely represent fair compensation for the risks that the subjects are assuming for the benefit of all of the rest of us.

There is, however, a separate and perhaps more relevant argument for not allowing "high" (or perhaps even moderate) payments to subjects. That argument relates to the requirement that we conduct research in a "just" manner. The "justice" issue was one of the three principles for the ethical conduct of research announced in 1979 in the *Belmont Report*, which created the foundation upon which most of the federal regulations have been constructed.[22] Throughout most of this book, we have been concentrating on evaluating the risks and benefits of a study in terms of what participation might mean to a particular subject. But the justice issues opens up the scope of the discussion and asks us to look beyond a particular subject to the universe of all people who might be participating in a study. As the Belmont Report puts it, justice is about the "fairness of distribution." The justice issue has been explicitly incorporated in the federal regulations by a requirement that IRBs, in reviewing a study, make sure that selection of subjects is "equitable."[23]

There are two very different ways that this fairness issue pops up in human subjects research. One involves making sure that the *benefits* of research are fairly distributed among different groups in our society. Thus, if a particular group has relatively less research conducted with regard to its medical problems, then in effect an injustice has taken place, and it will suffer due to the relative lack of information about its special problems. We discussed one example of this phenomenon in chapter 15, noting how for many years relatively little research was performed on women. Similar justice issues exist with regard to other groups that may have distinct medical problems due to genetic, economic, social, or other differences, such as various ethnic minorities.

This aspect of the justice issue—making sure that a particular group is not denied the benefits of research—is separate from the problem raised by the payment issue. Rather, that issue raises a concern about how our society distributes the *burdens* of research. In other words, not only might a particular group be denied its fair share of the benefits of research, it might be subjected to more than its fair share of the harms that can take place from participating as research subjects. Thus, for example, it would be considered unjust if, in order to prove the efficacy and safety of a drug that would primarily be used by Americans, the clinical trials took place in underdeveloped nations because Americans would be unwilling to consent to the risks involved in the study. Similar issues arise if certain categories of Americans, such as particular racial groups or ethnic minorities, appear to be overrepresented as participants in studies (particularly those that provide the subjects with relatively few benefits).

The federal regulations are specific in noting that an IRB should, in determining whether subjects have been selected equitably, pay particular attention to issues relating to the enrollment of people who are "economically disadvantaged."[24] No further guidance is provided about how IRBs are to implement this requirement or what exactly it means. One possible interpretation is that it would be inequitable if poor people were overrepresented as a percentage of people participating in research studies. Note that this conclusion shouldn't automatically follow: if indeed subjects were being paid a large enough amount to fully compensate them for the risks they undertook, would it be a bad thing that mainly poor people were enrolling in such studies? That conclusion is far from obvious.

Nonetheless, for the sake of argument, let us assume that it would indeed be inequitable if poor people were overrepresented as subjects in studies. Accepting that conclusion, it still does not lead us to the result that we should be minimizing payments to subjects. Even if payments are kept very low—for example, at a minimum wage rate—poor people are likely to find such payments more of an inducement than the more well-to-do. So, the likely result would be that we would end up with predominantly poor people as subjects anyway, but they would be getting relatively low amounts of money for their services. Indeed, segments of our society that are sometimes relatively hard pressed for money—college students and the retired elderly —in many instances already make up an above-average share of those who enroll in certain types of studies, particularly the nontherapeutic ones.

If in fact we are concerned that poor people should not be overrepresented as study subjects, then we should be doing what we do with other populations, such as ethnic minorities and racial groups. For those categories, federally funded studies are required to keep track of what percentage of subjects are from each group and to take appropriate efforts to make sure that no particular group is overrepresented. We can certainly do the same thing with regard to poor people: if a study is enrolling too high a percentage of poor people, the investigators should be required to turn away some of the people in that category and to make efforts to recruit more well-to-do people. And perhaps, if they cannot recruit adequate numbers of the nonpoor, then that will tell us that the study is too risky and that it should not be conducted at all.

In the end, if our concern is that we have representation from all income levels in most studies, there are more straightforward ways of doing that than inappropriately reducing the compensation paid to subjects. It is ironic indeed that, in pursuit of "justice," we might continue to pay poor people amounts that seriously undervalue the contribution they make to society when they participate in research studies. Somehow, that policy seems more *un*just than just.

17

Compensating Researchers
Dealing with Conflicts of Interest

In chapter 16, we examined the issues raised by paying research subjects to participate in studies. While paying *subjects* very large amounts of money is controversial and still relatively uncommon, allowing *researchers* to earn substantial amounts of money from their research activities—as we saw in the discussion of what happened to John Moore—is quite common and is even encouraged by government policies. Only in the past few years, however, have a growing crescendo of voices raised questions about the conflicts of interest that such financial interests are creating.

The initial trigger for much of the reexamination of the role of money on the researcher side was what took place in the study that led to the death of Jesse Gelsinger. We briefly mentioned that study at the beginning of this book, and it is now time to examine it in more detail, with particular attention to conflicts of interest. As we will attempt to suggest, the recent attention to financial conflicts may be inappropriately condemning many arrangements that are relatively benign while largely ignoring some more common arrangements that are far more problematic. In both instances, the result is a failure to help people distinguish between the "good choice" and "bad choice" studies that they are asked to participate in.

Money and Genes at Penn

Jesse Gelsinger had been born with a genetic disease known as ornithine trans-carbamylase (OTC) deficiency. His liver was not able to make enough OTC, a key enzyme that is needed by the body to eliminate the ammonia that is the by-product of metabolizing food. Severely affected babies soon slip into a coma and die within the first few years of life. But some people affected with the disease have a milder version, and they can sometimes live relatively normal lives. Jesse had this milder version of OTC deficiency. Although the disease had at times brought him near the brink of death, over time he was treated with various medications that managed to keep the worst consequences in check. As he approached his eighteenth birthday in September of 1999, the disease was under relatively good control.

In recent years, there has been a great deal of interest among medical researchers about possible ways to treat genetic diseases. One of the most promising approaches, often referred to as "gene therapy"—though it is at present more promise than true therapy—involves altering the DNA of a virus so that it contains copies of the undamaged gene whose defect causes a particular disease, and then exposing a subject to a large amount of the virus. The hope is that the good copies of the gene will be transferred to many of the cells in the subject's body and that the good gene will then begin functioning in those cells.

The University of Pennsylvania was one of this nation's leading centers for this type of research. It had successfully recruited Dr. James M. Wilson, a renowned gene therapy researcher, appointing him as the John Herr Musser Professor of Research Medicine and making him the director of Penn's Institute for Human Gene Therapy. One of Dr. Wilson's interests was OTC deficiency, and in 1999 his laboratory was conducting a phase I study of gene therapy for that disease. As we have noted in other chapters, phase I studies are the earliest stage in evaluating a possible new treatment, and in general there is an extremely low likelihood that a subject will benefit from participating in such a study. The main purpose is to see how large a dose of the treatment can be given to people before it starts to produce unacceptable side effects.

The study was intentionally designed to enroll subjects who were legally adults (older than the age of majority, which is eighteen in Pennsylvania) so that the subjects could consent on their own to participating in the study. The decision to enroll these subjects—who would likely only have a mild form of the disease—was attributed to Arthur Caplan, the nation's leading bioethicist and a Penn faculty member who was a paid adviser to the researchers. His belief was apparently that if the research was performed on the very young children with the severe form of OTC deficiency—children who would not be expected to live very long and thus exposing them to research risks might be considered less likely to cause great harm than someone with the milder form of the disease—the parents of these children might not be able to give adequate informed consent, due to their emotional distress about the child's medical problem.[1]

Thus, within days after reaching age eighteen and legally becoming an adult, Jesse Gelsinger signed a consent form allowing him to enroll in the phase I study at Penn. He was given the virus on September 13, 1999. Four days later he was dead, after many of his organs failed to function, presumably as a result of some type of reaction to the virus. Subsequent investigations into what happened indicated that a variety of "wrong" things had taken place in the study—among them, allowing Jesse to participate with an ammonia level higher than allowed in the study protocol, not reporting to the FDA side effects experienced when the virus was tested in monkeys and previous human research subjects, and not stopping treatment of earlier subjects as required by the protocol when they experienced certain levels of side effects—though it is not clear that any of these problems had a relationship to what caused Jesse's death.

Fallout from the Penn Study

There was a great deal of fallout as a result of Jesse Gelsinger's death. His father brought a lawsuit against the University of Pennsylvania, Dr. Wilson, and the other researchers, which was quickly settled for an undisclosed amount of money, presumably in the millions. The FDA began an investigation into the study[2] and ended up prohibiting Dr. Wilson from conducting research on human subjects, detailing a variety of ways in which he had failed to "fulfill his obligations as the clinical investigator" in charge of the study.

But perhaps the aspect of the study that has had the most significant continuing impact on the field of human subjects research relates to the financial relationships that were revealed. Years before these events, Dr. Wilson had founded a biotechnology company, Genovo, Inc. That company was providing about 20% of the budget for Dr. Wilson's laboratory. In turn, it would be entitled to the exclusive right to sell any products that were developed out of that research. In other words, if Dr. Wilson's work at Penn led to a treatment for OTC deficiency or other diseases and that treatment could be patented, Genovo would get the profits from marketing the treatment. Dr. Wilson continued to own substantial stock in the company, and the University of Pennsylvania also owned stock.[3] When Genovo was purchased by another company, even after the stigma caused by the events that led to Jesse Gelsinger's death, Dr. Wilson ended up getting stock options worth $13.5 million, while the university's interest was worth $1.4 million.

In the wake of these events, regulators began paying a great deal of attention to the sorts of financial conflicts of interest that existed in the Penn study. Up until recently, there have been relatively few legal restrictions preventing researchers from having an ownership interest in a company or technology whose value might dramatically increase depending on the results of the study that the researcher is in charge of. The FDA, for studies that came under its jurisdiction, and the U.S. Public Health Service, for certain federally funded studies, had rules requiring disclosure of certain financial interests or payments to the government, but these rules have properly been described as "vague and inconsistent."[4] The Department of Health and Human Services (DHHS) had begun paying greater attention to this issue and attempting to give more specific guidance to institutional review boards (IRBs) and the institutions where research takes place. In 2001, it issued a document that was described as "draft interim guidance" on financial conflicts, which in turn was replaced with a final version in 2004.[5]

The DHHS guidance document is perhaps most noteworthy for the number of issues it does *not* resolve. It discusses the three major ways of dealing with financial interests that had previously been raised by commentators—(1) *eliminating* the financial interests, (2) *managing* the conflicts they create, and (3) *disclosing* the conflict to subjects—and provides a number of questions that IRBs and institutions should think about in dealing with financial conflicts. But the DHHS document gives very little concrete guidance. It doesn't say that one of these methods is ever better than the others, nor does it require any particular method to be used in particular circumstances. In the end, the document comes down to mainly being a long list of things to think about.

DHHS's difficulty in coming up with very specific guidance is not that surprising, since the conflict of interest problem is not that easily dealt with. The only "complete" solution would involve selecting the first of the options mentioned above, namely, eliminating the financial interests that are the source of the problem—in other words, preventing researchers from having significant financial interests in the research that they are conducting. But not only would that be a big change, it would be conflicting with government policies from recent decades that have been going in just the opposite direction.

Prior to 1980, it was actually very rare for universities and their professors to own the sorts of financial interests that existed in the Penn study. But in 1980, Congress passed the Bayh-Dole Act,[6] which allows universities and scientists to patent discoveries made with federal research dollars and keep the money they make. Congress was concerned that new drugs and medical devices that were discovered with government money would not be taken to market because the government did not itself fund market development and private investors would not fund development unless they could get the patent rights. Once universities and scientists could patent discoveries made with federal grants, they shifted their research direction toward patentable products. Scientists could become rich if they discovered a patented product. Universities would also share in the wealth. New biotechnology departments were created and were funded at the expense of other departments because biotechnology promised patent wealth.

How to Resolve the Ownership Problem?

Thus, to a large extent, the sorts of financial interests that created the conflicts in the Penn case exist precisely because Congress believed that they served a useful purpose. And, in fact, they have accomplished much of what they were intended to do: there is indeed now a great deal of growth in the field of biotechnology. Researchers are highly motivated to create products that are likely to help treat medical problems affecting thousands or even millions of people. Thus, before we move to make changes that might reduce or even eliminate the positive results of this law, we need to evaluate more carefully the negative aspects of these incentives and see if the good outweighs the bad.

Such incentives presumably might encourage a researcher to pay insufficient attention to protecting the well-being of subjects, as researchers strive to produce study results that will lead to their perhaps becoming wealthy. But a key question needs to be answered: to what extent are these incentives substantially different than those that existed *even if the researcher did not possess any financial interest in the product being studied?* The Penn study provides an appropriate example for examining this question. Dr. Wilson was one of the world's leading experts in the developing field of gene therapy. He had spent years of his life trying to make this successful, and he had a huge amount at stake, including his very substantial academic reputation. Indeed, he probably had far more motivation due to his desire for academic success—including perhaps a not unrealistic dream of getting a Nobel Prize—than due to the possibility of getting wealthy as a result.

Seen in that light, it is far from clear that the financial relationships created by giving researchers ownership interests in possible products dramatically alter the incentives that researchers already had. And, again, it is worth noting that such incentives should not be assumed to be entirely bad ones. We *want* researchers to do cutting-edge work, to produce breakthrough discoveries. We *want* the best minds in our society to go into medical research. And we therefore create appropriate incentives for them to do this, by enabling them to move upward in academia, to attain prestigious positions, and yes, to sometimes earn a great deal of money as a result. In most instances, these incentives produce good results: they encourage behaviors that our society very much desires.

Admittedly, those same incentives may lead some researchers to try to cut corners, and to perhaps do things that inappropriately risk the well-being of research subjects, but that is hopefully an anomaly. In any event, *those researchers will still have substantial incentives to cut corners even if they had no ownership interest in what they were studying.*[7] The federal government's Office of Research Integrity regularly publishes on the Internet instances in which researchers at some of this nation's best institutions have faked data or done other unethical acts to alter their study results.[8] These instances appear to rarely be related to ownership interests; rather, they are due to the more mundane but omnipresent pressures on researchers to produce good results so that they can get more grants, keep their jobs, and move upward on the ladder of academic success.

And if we wanted to eliminate those incentives, there are straightforward ways to do it: *don't allow the researcher who comes up with a particular idea to be the one who conducts the study that tests that idea.* Such a policy could be adopted as a general rule, if we wanted to, and not merely in those instances where the researcher has a financial interest. But if we are unwilling to take that step, we should not kid ourselves that we are accomplishing very much by removing the financial incentives and yet permitting incentives that are often far more significant. Nor should we deceive prospective research subjects by suggesting that, by removing ownership interests, we have somehow produced a state of affairs where researchers, now free of conflicts, will be making decisions based only on the best interests of the subjects.

Consider again the events that led to the death of Jesse Gelsinger. There is little reason to think that the financial interests had anything to do with the specific "wrong things" that were considered to have taken place in the study. For example, some of the steps taken in enrolling Jesse in the study appeared to violate procedures required by the protocol. But there's no specific evidence linking these decisions to Dr. Wilson. More likely they were made by more junior members of the research team, all of whom in any event had substantial career incentives (apart from anything financial) to be part of the group that created a successful method of gene therapy.

Moreover, protocol violations are not uncommon in day-to-day research. If other studies were examined with the degree of scrutiny applied to the Penn study, a variety of similar violations would probably be found in numerous studies, many due to mere inadvertence. There were certainly inadequate disclosures in the consent form used in the Penn study, but as we have shown in this book, such failings are commonplace in research these days, and there is no need to attribute it to the effect of the stock ownership. And regarding the financial interests of the university itself, it seems unlikely that administrators at one of this nation's most prestigious institutions, who regularly deal with amounts in the many millions of dollars, would have been pressuring researchers to cut corners because of the possibility that Penn's rather modest share of the company ($1.4 million) would then be worth more.

One of the other major complaints about the study was that the researchers had not been notifying the federal government of all of the bad things—adverse events, in technical terms—that had happened to previous participants in the study. But as subsequent events demonstrated, this was not at all uncommon. Following Jesse Gelsinger's death, the National Institutes of Health (NIH) sent out a reminder to researchers that they were supposed to promptly be reporting adverse events in gene therapy studies, and that penalties would be imposed if they failed to do so. During the four-month period following that notice, from February to June of 2001, NIH received 921 adverse event reports for such studies, more than the total that had been submitted during the preceding ten years.[9] Clearly, failure to submit adverse events was a common practice. And it seems unlikely that most of this improper conduct by researchers nationwide had anything special to do with financial conflicts of interest.

Thus, the rationale for eliminating these types of ownership interests is far from clear. If it is to be done, the case still needs to be made that doing so will produce more good than bad. The events surrounding the death of Jesse Gelsinger do not appear to make a compelling case. So, we are left to examine the other two proposed solutions to these financial conflicts of interest: *managing* them and *disclosing* them.

Managing a conflict involves putting into place protections that prevent the researcher or the institution from acting in an improper manner. This can involve a number of things. One possibility, as noted above, is not permitting the researcher to be the one doing the research—he would have to allow others, with no financial interests, to run the study. Or, other independent reviewers may be used to, in effect, look over the shoulder of researchers, so that they know that they cannot get away with actions that are improper. While all of these are reasonable steps to take—they would actually resolve the problem, if rigorously implemented—they obviously involve costs in terms of resources, money, time, and effort. In deciding which of these are appropriate to implement in a particular case, we still need to have better information on the scope of the problem: to what extent are such financial interests actually causing researchers to behave improperly?

The only evidence we currently have are a few well-publicized instances in which subjects had bad outcomes in studies where researchers had interests in the treatments being studied,[10] and even in those instances—as we have shown in the Penn study—there is little clear evidence that the financial interests altered anyone's behavior. It would not be worthwhile to throw a great deal of money at a problem without being more certain that this really is indeed a problem. At the least, a great deal more empiric investigation into the extent of this apparent problem should be done before enacting possibly costly "remedies" that may themselves cause more harm than good.

Finally, what about the option of *disclosing* this type of conflict to a subject thinking about entering the study? This is certainly a good thing to do, and easily accomplished. It would not take much work to add a brief paragraph in the consent form mentioning, for example, that the researcher (and the university, if that is also the case) owns stock that may be worth millions of dollars if the research is successful. But, interestingly, it is far from clear what message a subject should take from reading such a paragraph. Consider the following two hypothetical studies involving possible treatments for a thus far incurable cancer:

1. A researcher has developed a new compound that has had promising results in treating similar tumors in rats. He has given patent rights to a new company he created that, due to investments by venture capitalists, is worth millions of dollars.
2. A researcher has developed a new compound that has similarly had promising results in treating tumors in rats. Although he has given patent rights to a new company he created, the stock is worth very little. Venture capitalists are very uncertain about the eventual results from this compound and have been unwilling to invest in the company.

From a subject's viewpoint, one of the most important things about a study is usually the likelihood that the new treatment being tested is actually going to work well. And the fact that sophisticated investors are willing to bet millions of dollars on a new treatment by investing in a company with rights to it is something that a reasonable research subject might well view as very positive: it independently validates the work of the researcher, giving additional evidence that the study is worth participating in. That positive signal may be far more important to the subject than the possible negative connotation that, because of the financial interest, the researcher is going to inadequately protect the well-being of the research subjects. Thus, we again see that the existence of ownership interests has both good and bad effects and that there is a need to separately evaluate these two consequences before deciding how to deal with these financial interests.

The Fee Problem

Thus far, the issue of researchers owning valuable interests in products or companies had been the one topic that has generated the most discussion. Yet there is a very different type of practice, which likely affects far more research subjects than the ownership issue, that may be much more problematic for the well-being of subjects. To understand why, we need to again look at the nature of the incentives created by the particular practice and to evaluate how they are likely to alter behavior in a good or bad way.

The practice in question involves the usual way that multicenter studies are conducted. Such a study is designed and put together at a central location (e.g., a drug manufacturer or a university research center), but the actual enrollment of subjects and performing of the study procedures are in essence contracted out to take place at a number of locations around the country, often at university medical centers or the private offices of physicians. And the study will commonly involve payments to the personnel that conduct the study at these other sites. In particular, there will usually be payments to the doctors who are involved in enrolling and treating the subjects, to compensate them for their time and effort. The payments will often be a specified amount of money per subject in the study, and that amount, depending on what is required of the physician-researcher, may be several thousand dollars. For a doctor who is enrolling patients in a number of different studies, these payments can, over an entire year, add up to tens or even hundreds of thousands of dollars, constituting a large part of their compensation.

These amounts are clearly significant enough to create real incentives on the part of some doctors to enroll subjects in studies.[11] But, more important, this is a *new* incentive, one that did not exist prior to the creation of the payment. Compare this situation to the "ownership" problem discussed above: in those scenarios (e.g., the Penn case), we had researchers who, regardless of any financial interest, already have usually invested a great deal of time and effort in the research, and its success may be crucial to their future career advancement. The addition of the financial elements likely is not a major change to the incentives they already have (including the negative incentive of wanting to cut corners or fake results). In contrast, in multicenter studies, the doctors being hired to conduct the studies at the various satellite locations have nothing invested in the particular study; in most cases, they were probably not even aware of it until someone sent them a protocol and asked them if they were willing to participate.

Thus, such payments create what is essentially a brand-new incentive on the part of these doctors to enroll subjects in the study. And that incentive can have highly negative consequences, since the doctors may, given the money at stake, try to inappropriately suggest to subjects that being in the study is a good thing for them. (This would not be that difficult to accomplish, given how common the therapeutic misconception on the part of subjects is, as discussed in chapter 2.) In the year 2000, the Office of Inspector General (OIG), the investigative arm of the DHHS, produced a report on the growing pressures to recruit subjects in research studies sponsored by private companies.[12] It found a number of factors that were leading to this increasing pressure. The costs of getting a drug to market have dramatically increased in recent years, now often rising into the hundreds of millions of dollars, pushing drug manufacturers to do all they can to speed drug approval. The companies are testing more drugs, and the research studies are increasing in complexity, both of which have led to a demand for growing numbers of research subjects.

This had led to the mantra from drug manufacturers of "more, faster, better" recruiting of subjects. Drug and other manufacturers now are getting more and more subjects from the offices of private doctors, often bypassing the major university research centers where most research used to take place, since the universities tend to have more regulatory policies in place that might slow down recruiting and conducting the research. Institutions that are unable to quickly recruit adequate numbers of subjects might be dropped from consideration as a site for future studies, thus risking the loss of substantial amounts of money.

The OIG report documented a variety of questionable practices, from "finder's fees"—where a doctor may be paid a fee to merely supply a name of a patient who might qualify to be in a study—to a variety of bonus payments that are made to those who can recruit substantial numbers of subjects, and who can do so under tight time limits. The report noted one instance in which researchers were initially paid $12,000 per subject, but when the company sponsoring the study was told that this amount barely covered their costs, the company offered a $30,000 bonus to any site that enrolled six subjects, and then offered an additional $6,000 for each subject after the sixth. The use of the bonus arrangement—instead of merely increasing the payments to $18,000 per subject—was designed to create a special pressure to enroll higher numbers of subjects.

And, lest there be doubt that these payments are influencing how doctors behave, the OIG report documented how physician-researchers are actually *advertising* to the companies who pay for the studies to make sure that they are getting enough of these "business" opportunities. The report noted that such advertisements are now both numerous and prominent, and it provided an example:

> Looking for Trials!
>
> We are a large family practice office with 4 physicians and 3 Physician Assistants. We have two full time coordinators and a computerized patient data base of 40,000 patients. . . . We are looking for Phase 2–Phase 4 trials as well as postmarketing studies. We can actively recruit patients for any study that can be conducted in the Family Practice setting.[13]

As the report explains, these and similar practices seemed questionable, at the least: "[T]he consent process may be undermined when, under pressure to recruit quickly, for example, investigators misrepresent the true nature of the research or when patients are influenced to participate in research due to their trust in their doctor."[14]

Perhaps most noteworthy was the report's observation that IRBs rarely reviewed many of these compensation arrangements, in part because they had been given no guidance from either of the major federal agencies in this area, the Office for Human Research Protections (OHRP) and the FDA, about what sorts of payments are or are not acceptable. But that approach often makes it hard for an IRB to take action against a particular practice. An IRB that banned bonuses at its institution will not have any specific provision of the regulations, or any federal guidance, to back up its actions. And other IRBs, maybe even at competing medical centers in the same city, would likely have allowed these payments. The result is that the IRB ends up denying money to researchers at its institution, and doing so in a way that makes it look as if it is being arbitrarily too restrictive in interpreting the regulations.

The OIG report correctly concludes that OHRP and the FDA should alter this situation by giving specific guidance. In particular, it said there should be guidelines about whether bonus payments can be made for recruiting and whether doctors can receive fees for merely referring patients as candidates for a research study. Adopting clear guidelines on these issues would certainly create a fair playing field in which all institutions are effectively bound by the same clear rules. And by doing that, it would remove the stigma that an IRB otherwise might get at its institution by trying to do the right thing in interpreting the regulations on its own.

Unfortunately, four years later there was still no answer from the federal government about the acceptability of these practices. Although the 2004 guidance document on financial interests tells IRBs to examine "incentive payments," the only guidance it gives is to ask whether such payments are "reasonable."[15] It would seem that many of the bonus payments and finders fees are appropriate candidates for being banned, regardless of whether or not they are reasonable. The incentives they create are troublesome, and there is little evidence that they are needed to serve any important purposes. But the proper way to deal with this, as the OIG suggested, is for the federal government to establish clear rules, instead of leaving IRBs with the pressure of struggling with the lack of definitive guidance.

Payments for Services

The OIG report confined itself to a relatively narrow category of payments to researchers, namely, the types of bonuses and finder's fees discussed above. It specifically noted that it was not commenting on a very routine—and indeed, essentially noncontroversial—practice, namely, paying physician-researchers for the extra time and effort they need to spend in conducting the research study.[16] Physicians are paid for their time and effort in most privately sponsored studies and in almost all government-sponsored studies. Although these commonplace payments were not addressed by the OIG report, it is interesting to see what happens if we evaluate them in terms of the incentives they create.

These types of payments have generally been considered acceptable because they are measured against the standard we use for other types of payments: the doctors can only be paid amounts that represent a fair payment for the time and effort they are putting into the study. Thus, for example, a study that merely requires a doctor to spend an hour to examine each subject could not pay the doctor $5,000—that would be an unreasonably high fee for an hour of her time and would create an unduly great incentive on her part to enroll people in the study. If she is regularly paid $250 an hour for her time in examining patients, then that would be the appropriate amount of compensation.

And, unlike the bonus payments and the finder's fees, these payments more clearly appear to serve a legitimate goal. Most people expect to be compensated for their time and effort. If we want doctors to be conducting a valuable part of a research study at their institution (or using time that would otherwise be spent on their private practice, earning money for each patient treated), they will likely expect to be paid for their assistance in helping the study reach completion. There is no reason for them to be volunteering their time when the people running the study (either a private company, e.g., a drug manufacturer, or perhaps researchers at NIH or at some other university in the case of federally funded studies) are getting paid for their work. Thus, if we didn't pay the doctors at a reasonable rate, these multicenter studies would never get done, since the doctors would have no incentive to participate. This is a rather compelling justification for allowing these types of payments.

But we are not done with the analysis. Just because these payments are legitimate, and thus should not be banned, doesn't necessarily resolve the issue of whether they create some inappropriate incentives that might perhaps require management or disclosure. Consider a key aspect of these payments: the mere fact that someone is being paid at a reasonable rate for the services they provide does not mean that offering them the payment might not create a strong incentive for them to accept that offer. An example can help explain this simple point: imagine that a doctor earns on average $200 an hour when he is seeing patients. But, as is true for many doctors, it is a competitive world out there, and he can't get as many patients as he'd like. Thus, there are times during the week when he isn't earning anything since he is not seeing patients.

A representative from a pharmaceutical company comes along, telling him about a research study regarding a particular medical problem that several of his patients already have. He currently sees these patients for an hour a month, on average. If they were in the study, there are lots of additional tests and procedures to perform and a substantial amount of paperwork to be completed: instead of one hour a month, each of the patients would generate ten hours a month of work. And the pharmaceutical company would be paying him the usual $200 an hour for that work. By enrolling someone in the study, he changes that person from someone who generated $200 a month of income to someone who now generates $2,000 a month. While he is not getting paid any more per hour than he otherwise would get, the $1,800 difference is nonetheless very real extra income for him, since he is now getting paid for portions of his work week that previously generated no income. And imagine what these numbers might look like as we multiply them by the number of patients he enrolls in the study. And as a further multiplier, there are likely other studies that he might have patients enroll in. Thus, even apart from the "clearly bad" bonus and finder's fee payments, it is not surprising that doctors are competing with each other to place advertisements like the one we reprinted above, begging companies sponsoring studies to let them conduct the studies at their medical offices.

This example demonstrates that, even though we may not want to ban these payments, they certainly have the possibility of creating exactly those same bad incentives that the OIG was worried about in the context of bonuses and finder's fees.[17] A physician's desire to get these very substantial amounts of money could equally well cause them to "misrepresent the true nature of the research" and inappropriately lead patients "to participate in research due to their trust in their doctor." What remedial measures might be taken to counteract this possibility? In contrast to its effect in the "ownership" situation, disclosure to subjects would likely send a relatively clear message to the subject.

But for disclosure to be meaningful, it can't merely be some vague statement whose meaning is rather cryptic, such as, "There are some financial relationships between the researchers and the company that is conducting this research." Appropriate disclosure should be done in a manner that clearly indicates to the subject what the conflict might be, such as:

> If the researcher treated you outside of the study with either standard care or with the new treatment that is being evaluated in this study, she would earn substantially less money than she gets by enrolling you in this study. If you enroll in this study, she will be receiving additional payments of $_____ beyond what she would get if you were not in the study. These payments are designed to compensate her fairly for the additional time and effort she must spend in conducting the study. Nonetheless, you may want to think about the effect of these additional payments in evaluating the advice she gives you about enrolling in the study.

If nothing else, such a statement gives patients another opportunity to recognize that research is different and to perhaps think again about whether they want to be in the study, instead of reflexively accepting what a doctor tells them as good advice. This is another chance for them to overcome that all-too-common therapeutic misconception and to make a more reasoned evaluation of whether being in this study is a "best choice" for them.

Selectively Targeting Inappropriate Incentives

Our main point in this chapter has been to suggest that not all financial elements that create conflicts of interest are bad. Even where the possibility of an undesirable incentive is created, that incentive may in the end not change how people behave, because they already have other reasons to behave in that undesirable way. We need to be concentrating on those financial elements that are most likely to change someone's behavior (in the "wrong" direction) and take appropriate action against them. And there are more than enough of those that merit such action, including the payments to investigators discussed in the preceding section.

As a final example of the need to carefully evaluate each category of financial arrangement, consider the appropriateness of federal government regulatory personnel having interests in products being developed by private companies. In general, we apply a higher conflict of interest standard to the actions of most federal employees, being fearful that the enormous power wielded by the federal government makes it a very desirable target for manipulation by private companies. And the NIH, controlling the award of billions of dollars of federal research funds and setting the agenda for much of the medical research that takes place in this nation, would seem to be an agency that should be particularly scrupulous in avoiding financial conflicts, and even the appearance of such conflicts.

Thus, it came as something of a surprise to many when, in a December 2003 article, the *Los Angeles Times* disclosed that hundreds of researchers at the NIH—

including some of the highest-level personnel of that agency—had substantial financial relationships with private companies, such as drug manufacturers, that regularly dealt with the NIH.[18] In later hearings before a congressional subcommittee investigating this states of affairs, NIH Director Dr. Elias Zerhouni disclosed that, since 1999, 527 employees of the agency had been paid by outside companies as consultants.[19] Moreover, 94% of the highest-paid employees were exempt from having to publicly disclose these types of payments, even if they came from drug companies or other private entities.

The *L.A. Times* article described, among many other things, a study at the NIH's National Institute of Arthritis and Musculoskeletal and Skin Disease, in which a subject died in 1999 following complications from an experimental drug made by the German pharmaceutical manufacturer Schering AG. Dr. Stephen I. Katz, the scientist in charge of that branch of the NIH, was a paid consultant to Schering, having collected at least $170,000 from the company. As the *L.A. Times* noted, although the NIH could have chosen to stop the study following this death or issue warnings to doctors using the drug for other purposes—"steps that might have threatened the market potential for the drug"—it did neither.[20] And the money Dr. Katz received from Schering was only a small part of the more than $475,000 he received from companies, including $140,000 from one that received $1.7 million in grants from that NIH branch.

Dr. Katz's situation was only one of a number of examples that the article described:

- A director of the NIH Clinical Center, which is where the government conducts its own studies with human subjects, received hundreds of thousands of dollars in fees and stock proceeds. While being paid as a consultant for a subsidiary of a particular company, he co-wrote an article "highlighting" a technology developed by the parent company.
- A director of a major laboratory at the National Institute of Allergy and Infectious Diseases had collected more than $1.4 million in fees and stock options from companies, and one of those companies was collaborating with his laboratory.
- A top NIH diabetes researcher had written a letter to the FDA stating that a particular product has only a "very minimal" risk of causing liver failure. The letter failed to indicate that he was a paid consultant for that company. A subject in a study he was conducting later died from liver failure, and experts determined that the drug likely did cause that subject's death.

These examples, and others in the *L.A. Times* article, raise concern that these high-ranking NIH officials may be exercising their enormous power in a way that is inconsistent with the special duty they have to the public. Their role is distinctly different than that of Dr. Wilson at Penn or other private researchers: the NIH personnel have in effect chosen to work for the public, accepting both the benefits and obligations that come from working for this premiere institution. They should be expected to adhere to the high standards we demand of such workers.

Subsequent events demonstrated the broad public recognition of how inappropriate these payments and stock ownership interests were. Within six weeks of the initial newspaper article, in the face of growing criticism, the NIH director announced at a congressional hearing that top NIH scientists would no longer be permitted to accept consulting fees or stock options from drug companies.

As this example demonstrates, we should certainly be wary of financial arrangements that create conflicts of interest. But the key thing to keep in mind in the future will be the need to appropriately evaluate each such category of relationship and determine to what extent it creates inappropriate incentives that might outweigh any positive outcomes from allowing the relationship to exist. A broad-brush approach, condemning all financial ownership interests and all payments to researchers, is likely to do far more harm than good.

Part V

The Challenge for the Future

18

Where Do We Go from Here?

The Paradox of Pediatric Cancer Research

In 1974, Charles Fried—then a professor at Harvard Law School, later to go on to become the Solicitor General of the United States and a justice on the Massachusetts Supreme Judicial Court—published a slim volume entitled *Medical Experimentation: Personal Integrity and Social Policy*. At the time he was writing, people were being enrolled in randomized studies without being told of that fact. In studies in England and Denmark, for example, women with breast cancer were randomized to receive either a "simple" mastectomy or a more radical surgical procedure. Fried noted that the women apparently knew neither that they were participating in a study nor that the type of surgery they received was chosen by, in essence, the flip of a coin.[1]

Fried spent most of his book articulating the legal duties owed by a doctor to her patient, and concluded that patients should be told about such studies and allowed to choose whether or not to participate. But he recognized that implementing this disclosure requirement might create a substantial problem for society: "If the rights in experimentation I have just mentioned were to spell the end of all experimentation, were to make [randomized clinical trials] and other kinds of experiments impossible, the cost would be enormous. We would have to think again."[2]

Fried's influential book concluded with an examination of whether, if subjects had to knowingly consent to participate in research studies, there would indeed be the unfortunate outcome of too little research taking place. He decided that, for a number of reasons, the picture was not so bleak and that an appropriate amount of research would likely still be conducted.

Thirty years later, the world of human subjects research has dramatically changed. We live in a country with a substantial system for protecting research subjects, involving both federal regulations and state laws. In almost all instances in which participation in a study involves a possible change in someone's medical treatment, prospective subjects *will* be given a consent form and *will* be given at least some information about the risks, benefits, and alternatives to participation.

And Fried's somewhat controversial prediction has been proven correct: even though people are being regularly informed that participation in a research study may involve choosing their treatment by randomization, the sky has not fallen. Millions of people each year choose to enroll in research studies. While it is likely that our society would benefit from even more participation in research,[3] nonetheless there have not been calamitous results from letting people volunteer to be in research, as opposed to the previous practice of sometimes hiding that fact from them and involuntarily enrolling them.

In this book, we have tried to illustrate how far the system of protections afforded subjects has evolved since the "nondisclosure" practice that Fried wrote about. We have highlighted protections—particularly regarding informed consent—that the law appears to require but that are not routinely being implemented. Thus, it seems appropriate to revisit Fried's question, applying it to those disclosure standards that modern tort law would seem to require (and future lawsuits will likely enforce). Will implementing those stricter disclosure standards—giving subjects the information that would enable them to adequately distinguish between studies that are "good choices" and "bad choices" for them and thus let them make more meaningful choices about participating—prove a major barrier to conducting an appropriate amount of medical research?

As noted in our introduction, we, like Fried, remain optimistic that research studies can be conducted in a way that is consistent with the law and with ethics, yet without providing a serious barrier to the search for knowledge. Indeed, we expect that greater adherence to the legal standards would provide the public—which has seen enough headlines about research misconduct—with greater assurance about the integrity of human subjects research, and might well lead to increased willingness to participate.

To further explore whether that optimism is appropriate, we end this book with an examination of what is perhaps one of the greatest success stories of modern medical research: the world of pediatric oncology. Amazing breakthroughs have taken place during past decades, and many childhood cancers that were previously viewed as fatal are now routinely cured. No doubt part of this success story relates to the unique nature of pediatric cancer and how cancer in children is more treatable than cancer in adults. But a major part of the story surely also is attributable to the fact that so many research studies involving children are very successful in enrolling subjects.[4]

The contrast with the world of adult cancer research is particularly startling.[5] Among adult patients with cancer, relatively few patients choose to enter the studies for which they are eligible. Admittedly, there are a variety of reasons that might explain the low enrollment: childhood cancers are rare and thus these patients are treated in specialized centers where research studies are already being conducted; the specialists who care for these children are very familiar with these studies; there have been many studies taking place on the types of cancers (leukemias and lymphomas) that are most common in children, among other arguments.[6] But even given those explanations, it is surprising how very few adults with cancer choose to participate in research studies: only 2.5%. For adults 70 or more years of age, the percentage is even lower, less than 1%.[7] Given the poor treatment available for most adult cancers, one would think that even the slim chance of lucking out and getting some magic bullet in a research study would be a relatively attractive one. But the numbers speak for themselves; apparently, it isn't nearly attractive enough.

In contrast, the world of pediatric oncology research appears to present almost the flip side of the picture. Substantially more than half of all children with cancer end up getting most of their treatment as subjects in a research study. This is a puzzling statistic. After all, many pediatric cancers are far more curable than those in adults. And we all recognize that parents, who effectively (and legally) play the major decision-making role in putting their children in these studies, are surely steadfast in doing what is best for their own children: they are likely not intentionally choosing to be altruistic, to be enrolling their child in a study just because it may benefit future children, even though it may not be in their child's best interests. Thus, presumably these parents have concluded that it is in the child's best interests to be in most of these studies, that these are "good choice" studies.

Some questions seem to need answers: are these parents correct in having concluded that being in these studies is in their children's best interests? Have pediatric oncologists somehow found the Holy Grail of research designs, creating large numbers of studies where participation in most cases *is* in the best interests of the subjects? And if that is not the case, why are so many parents enrolling their children in these studies? We attempt to give some possible answers to these questions further below. But to provide a backdrop for that analysis, we first detour to explore a framework for thinking about a question we first posed in chapter 1: what things might a society legitimately do to make sure enough people enroll in research studies?

The Only Henniker on Earth

In January of 1997, ABC's *Nightline* television show dedicated one night to a dilemma confronting the people of Henniker, New Hampshire.[8] This quaint town of only 4,000 residents dates back to the 1700s, priding itself as being "the only Henniker on Earth." The town's web page describes it as "a wonderful small town nestled in the foothills of southwestern New Hampshire."[9]

But in early 1997, in a page out of *The Music Man*, there was trouble-with-a-capital T brewing in Henniker. And that trouble came in the form of a drugstore. For at the entrance to town, there was a lovely wooded lot that everyone drove past as they came into Henniker. The owner of that lot was proposing to sell it so that Rite Aid could build a pharmacy there. At the time, there was "not a chain store in sight" in town, as Ted Koppel noted during the *Nightline* episode. There was, however, the Henniker Pharmacy. This century-old establishment was the last of the old-fashioned drug stores left in town. In the back, it had a lunch counter, where regulars each had their own mugs. In the basement was a toy store. If you didn't have enough money to pay for a prescription, the owner would put it on your tab. In many ways, this was a real-life version of *It's a Wonderful Life*.

And there was a fear among the people of Henniker that if the Rite Aid was built, the Henniker Pharmacy would be driven out of business. Losing the Henniker Pharmacy would be another step toward making Henniker less unique, no different than thousands of other cookie-cutter towns across America. The decision on whether to allow the Rite Aid to be built was to be made by the town planning board in a few months.

As Ted Koppel often used to do on *Nightline*, he ended the show with a final thought of his own. Having detailed the attempts of the people of Henniker to preserve their town's special qualities, he wondered whether all the attention given to the upcoming planning board vote wasn't misdirected:

> These stories tend to be more complicated than they seem, but even so, there's one aspect to keeping "the only Henniker on Earth" safe from the Rite Aid behemoth that eludes me. If, in the final analysis, most people in Henniker made clear their intention to keep patronizing the Henniker Pharmacy and if they were truly determined not to patronize the Rite Aid, if and when it's built, then the Henniker Pharmacy would survive and eventually the new Rite Aid would go out of business.
>
> But experience seems to have convinced the folks at Rite Aid that no matter what people say, eventually they bring their business to whichever store offers the best merchandise at the lowest price. If the people of Henniker are different, it remains within their power to prove that. No one can force them to buy at Rite Aid and no one can force them to stay away from the pharmacy that they and their forbears have been patronizing for more than 100 years now. It is still their choice.

Ted Koppel is a *very* smart man—but this was one of those rare circumstances where he had it wrong. The residents of "the only Henniker on Earth" were absolutely right: it was vitally important to have the planning board veto the Rite Aid application. For once the Rite Aid was there, it was in each person's best interests to shop at that Rite Aid, *regardless* of how they felt about preserving the unique aspects of Henniker. (As the people at Rite Aid knew: "If you build it, they will come.") Even if someone was the most devout supporter of the Henniker Pharmacy, that individual's actions in choosing to shop there versus the Rite Aid would have little effect on whether or not that pharmacy survived. Ultimately, that would depend on where *everybody else* chose to shop. On the other hand, the dollars saved by shopping at the Rite Aid go directly into that individual's pocket. So, it would make sense for that person, acting rationally, to shop at the Rite Aid, once it has been built.

The Prisoner's Dilemma

The people of Henniker had been smart enough—smarter than Ted Koppel in this instance—to recognize they were dealing with a phenomenon that is considered one of the most common yet vexing scenarios to plague human behavior. It is best described as a problem in game theory—the previously little-known field that Nobel Prize winner John Nash, of *A Beautiful Mind* fame, helped to develop. Indeed, the first description of the "most famous game of strategy in all of social science"—commonly called the Prisoner's Dilemma—was inspired by Nash's work. Here is how Sylvia Nasar referred to it in her book (on which the movie was later based):

> [T]he police arrest two suspects and question them in separate rooms.
> Each one is given the choice of confessing, implicating the other, or
> keeping silent. The central feature of the game is that no matter what the
> other suspect does, each (considered alone) would be better off if he
> confessed. If the other confesses, the suspect in question ought to do the
> same and thereby avoid an especially harsh penalty for holding out. If
> the other remains silent, he can get especially lenient treatment for
> turning state's witness. . . . The irony is that both prisoners (considered
> together) would be better off if neither confessed—that is, if they
> cooperated—but since each is aware of the other's incentive to confess, it
> is "rational" for both to confess.[10]

As Nasar summarizes, "[w]hen each person in the game pursues his private interest, he does not necessarily promote the best interest of the collective."

The Prisoner's Dilemma had been devised by Albert Tucker, a Princeton mathematician and colleague of the then-young John Nash, to demonstrate that Nash's work was not as useful as many thought. Nash's great breakthrough had been the idea that, in many games of strategy, the best outcomes would involve the players making choices that led to a particular type of stable outcome (later to become known as a Nash equilibrium). But as Tucker noted, in the Prisoner's Dilemma, the Nash equilibrium would involve both prisoners confessing—clearly not an optimal outcome for either of them, since they both would have been better off if neither had confessed. Thus, it seemed that Nash's solution to this type of strategic situation—which involved each player choosing on their own what was best, without any coordination between them—was not a good one.

Since this game was first described in 1950, people have realized that it also applies to many other situations that commonly occur in daily life: the arms race between nations possessing nuclear bombs, factories spewing pollution into the air or waterways, cows grazing on a public pasture, traffic on a rush-hour highway, to name a few. And, as we have noted, the situation of the residents of Henniker, New Hampshire. In all of these scenarios, *absent some attempt to coordinate the behavior of a group of parties* (individuals or companies or countries), each participant, doing what is best for him or her individually, will behave in such a way that an outcome is reached that relatively few people would want.

This, of course, is very similar to the scenario that arises in the world of research involving human subjects.[11] As we have shown in previous chapters, in many cases it will not be in a person's best interests to enroll in a research study. Many good studies can be bad choices for most self-interested people. Thus, if a person behaves rationally and in a nonaltruistic manner—and, in particular, is not very willing to expose herself to health risks in order to help others—the person will often, if told the truth about what participation in the study involves and what her other alternatives are, choose *not* to participate in the study.

But this is a game in which we *all* have a stake. You, the reader, are a human being, and absent a dramatic change in the laws of this universe, you will at some future date develop a medical problem, a problem that might have been treatable had sufficient research taken place. We would all benefit, to at least some extent, from making sure that sufficient research takes place. Charles Fried, in his now-classic book, contemplated what might happen if the Prisoner's Dilemma posed by human subjects research was allowed to go unaltered. He painted a lemming-like "calamitous picture" in which "individuals, choosing rationally in their own self-interest one by one, have collectively chosen a disaster which engulfs them all."

That disaster surely does not have to take place, nor, as we noted above, did Fried think it would. For there is a solution to the Prisoner's Dilemma, as what happened in Henniker demonstrates: if allowing all individuals to choose what is individually best for them leads to a bad outcome (the equilibrium point predicted by John Nash) for the nation as a whole, then it is often appropriate for society—within accepted limits—to *impose* restrictions on individual behavior so as to cause the desired outcome. Thus, to deal with nuclear proliferation, countries enter into nonproliferation agreements; air and water pollution is reduced by passing laws that impose fines on companies that pollute; to prevent cows from overgrazing on a commonly owned pasture, property rights are created that allow people to buy and own pieces of that pasture. In the Henniker situation, those restrictions came in the form of the action by the town planning board. It had the authority to limit the autonomy of some of the players—in particular, Rite Aid and those residents who wanted to shop at a new, cheaper drug store—and thus to produce an outcome that they hoped was the preferred one for most residents of the town.

Pediatric Oncology Revisited

But just as took place in the Henniker scenario, there are ways that a society deems acceptable and not acceptable for "solving" a Prisoner's Dilemma scenario—for making the sorts of decisions that restrict the autonomy of particular individuals in order to promote things that are good for broader segments of society. In the case of the proposed drug store, the rules relating to such decisions were well established. There was a long-standing delegation of this authority to the town planning board, and that board then engaged in accepted practices for making sure that everyone got an opportunity to give their views to the board before it then deliberated and reached its decision.

Let us now return to the scenario that opened this chapter, the striking success story of research in pediatric oncology, and see how that field has apparently resolved its Prisoner's Dilemma. Consider, as a representative example, a recent prominent study published in the *New England Journal of Medicine*, one that was accompanied by an editorial highlighting the great successes in treating childhood cancers.[12] The study involved comparing two different combinations of chemotherapy drugs for Ewing's sarcoma, a highly malignant type of bone tumor. Half of the children in the study would be randomized to get the combination of four drugs that was considered standard care for Ewing's sarcoma. This combination had substantially improved survival of patients compared to treatments used in earlier decades, but nonetheless the cancer would often eventually return.

The other half of the subjects would get those same four drugs but would also be given two additional drugs. One of those additional drugs was ifosfamide; during the 1980s it had been used in smaller studies as a way to treat patients with Ewing's sarcoma whose cancer had returned after initial treatment with the usual four-drug combination. As the designers of this new study described it, in those previous studies ifosfamide had produced "remarkable responses."

Like most research studies involving children with cancer, there was not a major problem recruiting subjects. Indeed, the researchers commented that "[e]nrollment was higher than expected." Why were they so successful in getting parents to enroll their children in this study? More generally, why is it that the percentage of such parents consenting to participation is twenty-five times or more greater than when adults with cancer are asked to participate?

It is certainly not obvious that participation in this study—or many other pediatric cancer studies—is such a good choice for the child. As we have previously discussed, when any new treatment comes along, there is a degree of uncertainty about it. Adding additional drugs to existing chemotherapy can often increase side effects, and those side effects can be deadly. On the other hand, the new treatment being evaluated in this study appeared very promising (recall those "remarkable results" from the earlier studies). And pediatric researchers had a relatively good track record for testing new treatments that often were indeed proven to be better than standard care.

These considerations suggest that making a decision about participation in the study—and being randomized 50–50 between standard care and standard care plus the two new drugs—would likely have been a difficult choice for many parents. Some might have been reluctant to risk exposing their children to anything new and would have chosen to stick with the tried-but-true combination that constituted standard care. If the parents wanted their child to get standard care, there would have been little reason to enroll the child in the study.[13] Other parents might have concluded they had no good reason for preferring one treatment to the other and thus chosen to have their children participate in the study and get randomized.

The most interesting question relates to those parents who, after reviewing the information provided to them, believed that the new combination *was* worth trying and presented an even better option than standard care. As we have discussed in preceding chapters, wanting to get the new treatment is a common preference of many subjects. It often represents very reasonable behavior, depending on what is known about the risks and benefits of the new treatment as compared to those of standard care. Thus, there is an obvious question to ask: why would they enroll their child in the study—with only a 50% chance of getting that combination—*as opposed to getting the promising new treatment outside of the study?* All of the drugs used in this study were on the market and could have been used by any doctor. Indeed, as the editorial in the *New England Journal of Medicine* noted, "this trial was based on drugs and methods that had all been available for many years before the study began."[14]

One possible explanation for the high enrollment in this and other pediatric oncology studies suggests itself: the parents were not told about the option of getting the new treatment outside of the study. Indeed, as we discussed in chapter 10, it is quite common for consent forms not to disclose that a new treatment can be obtained outside of the study. As we noted in that chapter, failing to disclose this piece of information should generally be considered wrong, a deceptive act taken to induce people to enroll in the study.

But, oddly enough, the failure to tell parents about the option of getting the new treatment outside of the study may not be quite so inappropriate in these cancer studies. Why? Because in these studies, the parents actually *might not have had* that option. They probably could *not* obtain the new treatment for their child without the child participating in the study. And the reason is that pediatric oncologists have gotten together and informally agreed among themselves not to provide new unproven treatments outside of a study. Here is how the *New York Times* described this arrangement, one that has rarely been written about: "Doctors, of course, can voluntarily regulate themselves and those in one tiny specialty, pediatric cancer, have done so. These doctors have agreed to provide experimental procedures only to patients who participate in valid research."[15]

In effect, this relatively small and close-knit group of doctors has reached an informal agreement among themselves that restricts the choices open to the parents, for the explicit purpose of making sure more children will enroll in research studies. In essence, this is the restriction on individual autonomy that "solves" the Prisoner's Dilemma presented by research on childhood cancers. It changes a study that might have been viewed as a "bad choice" by some parents into a clear "good choice."

Given that circumstance, the high enrollment rate in pediatric oncology research studies becomes less surprising. Imagine a mother and father being told about their options for their child, who has a highly malignant cancer. They are told that existing treatments are only sometimes effective. They can choose to treat their child with standard care, which is described to them as "basic" treatment.[16] Or they can participate in a randomized study, in which there is a 50% chance of the child getting that basic treatment but also a 50% chance of getting some new treatment that appears very promising. And based on previous research studies in this field, new treatments for childhood cancers have often been proven to be much better than existing treatments. At least some parents—and probably a substantial percentage of them—will conclude, after comparing the risks and benefits of standard care to those for the new treatment, that getting the new treatment for their child is their first choice. And with the options of either getting standard care or being in the study as the only choices presented to them, it is quite rational for such parents to choose to enroll their child in the study.

Thus, the fact that a majority of parents enroll their children in such studies is not surprising. It probably has little to do with parents becoming unusually altruistic and willingly enrolling their own children in "bad choice" studies as a way to help future children. Many of the parents likely enrolled their child in the study as the only way of getting access to the new treatment. And in the case of the Ewing's sarcoma study, that choice would have ended up being a good one (though it certainly could have worked out quite the opposite). As the *New England Journal of Medicine* editorial observed, the new treatment provided "substantial" superiority over standard care: "a 28 percent improvement in five-year event-free survival and an 18 percent improvement in five-year overall survival among patients with non-metastatic disease." This was another breakthrough in "one of the great success stories of modern medicine," the attempt to cure pediatric cancers.

Who Gets to Impose Limits on the Choices of Patients?

The success of pediatric oncology research speaks for itself. Restricting the choices of patients (or, in this case, their parents as decision makers) can alter incentives and "solve" a Prisoner's Dilemma, producing a solution that is better for society. As the *New York Times* noted, describing the consequences of the unwritten agreement among the oncologists to not provide unproven treatments outside of a study: "In that specialty, the availability of a pool of test subjects assures that new ideas for treatments are rapidly tested, allowing them to be adopted nationwide if they work, or tossed aside if they prove useless. As a result, the advances in this field have been phenomenal, far outracing anything seen in adult medicine."

That solution is not, however, without its costs. Consider the Ewing's sarcoma study (though we could equally well pick many other examples of pediatric oncology research studies). As noted, some of those parents—perhaps many—would have opted for directly giving their child the new treatment outside of the study, had it been available. But they were not even offered that option. Some of those children enrolled in the study, were then randomized to standard care, and ended up dying of their cancer. Given the advantage that the new treatment was ultimately shown to have over standard care, it is likely that some of these children would have at least been put into remission and had many more years of life, had they received the new treatment.

The lives of these children thus represent the real "costs" of the decision by pediatric oncology doctors to *not* offer new treatments outside of studies. That decision by them will, in the long run, likely lead to huge benefits for society as a whole: the children who end up living longer will greatly outnumber those who are denied a treatment that their parents would have chosen and that might have benefited them. But that consequence doesn't alter the tragic fact that *some* children had to die sooner in order to save those future lives. Even though that takes place in the name of the greater good for future children, it nonetheless highlights the momentous nature of the choice being made here when treatment options are foreclosed.

And even though many may conclude that the pediatric oncology doctors have made an appropriate choice, the results of which speak for themselves, a question still remains: *who gave those doctors the authority to make that rather awesome choice?* Doctors, in all but a very few circumstances, are expected—both legally and ethically—to do what is best to treat their current patients. Our society hasn't authorized them in this particular circumstance to make decisions about who lives and who dies. Most of us, as patients, would be very surprised if our doctor were to tell us that she was intentionally refusing to offer us a form of treatment—one that she agrees would be a reasonable choice for us—because she instead wants to help out future patients (by having us enroll in one medical study or another in which we would have only a 50% chance of being selected to receive the treatment deemed best for us). Charles Fried, in writing his book thirty years ago, long before this practice existed, declared that such behavior would be "inhuman."[17]

And the actions of the pediatric oncologists go beyond this: not only have a majority of these doctors individually decided to take such actions, but they have entered into an agreement that is intended to *prevent* some of their colleagues from doing what they believe is best for the individual patients that they are treating.[18] When the *New York Times* wrote about this agreement, it observed that doctors can "voluntarily regulate themselves." But this is not the usual type of voluntary regulation. Most such "agreements"—for example, an "agreement" that a new procedure should be the standard of care for a particular medical problem—end up benefiting all patients. The agreement among the pediatric oncologists is very different: it ends up subordinating the well-being of some present patients to that of future patients.[19]

And it does so for the purpose of strongly encouraging patients to enter research studies. Is it appropriate that pediatric oncologists, as a group, should be permitted to make such a choice, to create such an agreement changing the behavior of their members? Each physician-researcher, acting on his own, has a conflict of interest in proposing that a patient enter a research study. That is why the federal regulations were written: to manage those conflicts and to make sure that, when patients enroll in research, they have chosen to do so voluntarily, having accepted the change in their role that takes place in going from being a patient to being a research subject.

But if each individual physician has a conflict of interest in trying to get research done and isn't permitted to take actions to in effect force subjects into studies, what is it that permits a *group* of physicians to try to do that very thing? Nothing in the law, at least as it is currently written, seems to clearly indicate that groups of doctors are permitted to do this. Compare their actions to the planning board in Henniker, New Hampshire, which was an entity *whose very purpose* was to make decisions that would bind everyone in the town so as to produce an outcome that best serves the community's interests.

Up to now, the law has not specifically empowered doctors to band together to deny patients appropriate treatments for the specific purpose of encouraging enrollment in research studies. To the contrary, the federal regulations, and the ethical principles on which they rest, would seem to disallow such behavior. Their purpose is to assure that people generally enroll in research studies in a fully voluntary manner. At first glance, then, these doctors seem to be behaving in a manner that at the least raises serious ethical and legal questions.[20]

To provide an appropriate comparison, consider again the events (discussed in chapter 10) that took place after doctors began to believe that the use of high-dose chemotherapy followed by bone marrow transplantation offered the best chance for women with metastatic breast cancer. We know now that they were wrong and that this treatment was no more effective than low-dose chemotherapy. But at the time, it was perfectly reasonable for many a woman to choose the new, very promising (though yet unproven) high-dose treatment, even in spite of its high toxicity and the likelihood it would cause her substantial suffering and might itself cause her death, given that the alternative—the standard low-dose chemotherapy—was known to provide little chance of curing her cancer.

Suppose that the doctors who treated breast cancer had voluntarily gotten together and refused to provide the high-dose treatment except in randomized studies that gave a woman only a 50% chance of getting the new treatment. One of these women might well have said to her doctor, "You tell me that the current standard treatment, low-dose chemotherapy, is unlikely to cure my cancer. And you admit that the new treatment, high-dose chemotherapy, is very promising and would be my best choice. We both agree that would be my best choice. Yet you won't give it to me?" The doctor would have to admit that he and his colleagues have chosen, in a sense, to sacrifice her best interests to the goal of answering the research question.

Had the oncologists treating breast cancer taken such a step, they would likely have been subjected to the same type of criticism that was thrown at the "evil" insurance companies, some of which were similarly trying to encourage women to enroll in studies by denying payment for costs of the treatments outside of a study. We could imagine a judge making the same hand-wringing remarks about the actions of these doctors that were made about the actions of the insurance companies: "The court will have to live with the haunting thought that Ms. Smith, and perhaps others, may not ultimately receive the treatment they need and deserve." And the fault, in this case, would be the very doctors who had ethical and legal obligations to do what was in the best interests of those very patients.

Legitimizing the Hard Choices

Yet these hypothetical adult oncologists would be doing exactly the same thing that the pediatric oncologists have chosen to do. In the case of the pediatric oncologists— who are currently behaving in a manner that may violate both law and ethics—the outcome of their agreement speaks for itself. The results of research in pediatric oncology have been, as we quoted from the *New York Times*, "phenomenal, far outracing anything seen in adult medicine." Those results come at a cost—some children likely died as a result—but that cost may well be an acceptable one. Indeed, had adult oncologists done the same thing, and never offered the high-dose chemotherapy except in research studies, the poor results of that treatment would have been known years earlier, and tens of thousands of women would have been spared the major discomfort of undergoing bone marrow transplantation for no good purpose.[21]

What lesson should we take from this? That perhaps it is about time for our society to revisit the dilemma of medical research. This chapter has tried to show that "solving" a Prisoner's Dilemma scenario often requires restricting the choices individuals would otherwise be free to make. But precisely because we live in a nation that places a high value on preserving individual choice, our laws are relatively stingy in allowing such restrictions. And surely the ability to get access to the health care we want (and that might be best for us) is one of the most important elements of our autonomy. Such restrictions can have life-or-death consequences for many individuals.

Our society, however, already recognizes that there are *legitimate* ways to restrict autonomy when doing so serves important public interests—including the interest of advancing medical research. Perhaps the best example is the authority given to the FDA with regard to new drugs that have not yet been approved for use in the treatment of any disease. In general, it is rather hard for individuals to get those drugs outside of a research study. Thus, if patients correctly perceive the new drug as promising greater benefits than standard care, benefits that outweigh the risks, they have a substantial incentive to participate in a research study. In effect, the FDA, with its explicit legal authority to make sure that drugs are approved for marketing only after appropriate research has been done, plays the same role as the town planning board in the Henniker situation. It is the legally authorized entity with the power to solve the Prisoner's Dilemma. And it does that by restricting individual choice, by preventing patients from getting unproven drugs outside of research studies.

But right now, as we noted earlier in this book, there are many types of new treatments over which the FDA has no authority. It cannot prevent doctors from using these treatments outside of a research study. And no one else explicitly has such authority either.

Perhaps we are not doing enough research these days. Perhaps there should be greater restrictions on the ability of patients to get access to some unproven treatments, in order to encourage participation in such research. One option for accomplishing that would be to expand the FDA's authority so that it can restrict use, outside of a study, of a much wider range of innovative treatments. Another option might be to specifically legitimize a system by which members of the medical profession, in some organized manner (perhaps similar to what the pediatric oncologists have been doing), can create such restrictions. There are many similar hard questions to be answered, and it is time to begin thinking about them.

The Future

We began this book with a quotation from a landmark work, *Tragic Choices*, that a society should be judged by how it determines that "suffering shall come to some persons and not to others." And at its heart, that it is what this book has been about. Our nation already has in place a system that conducts a certain amount of medical research. Some people end up in research studies; others do not. For some diseases, research is quickly accomplished; for others, answers to important questions are long in coming. All of these events have very real consequences for determining which people live and which others die. Whether or not we've realized it, this set of rules has already been determining, for many years, some aspects of who ends up suffering and who doesn't.

The question remains to be asked: how will *our* society be judged? This final chapter shares a common theme with many of the preceding chapters: that there are right and wrong ways to encourage more participation in research. Among the legitimate ways might be changing the laws and—in a fair, open and even-handed manner after due deliberation—restricting access to certain treatments that are still undergoing testing. Sometimes a much more modest intervention may be sufficient, such as increasing the amount of money that can be given to someone for participating in research.

Up to now, too much of our current system has contained remnants of a disturbing notion: that to have the appropriate amount of research, we need to deceive many patients when they are being asked to participate in clinical trials. We hope that, if nothing else, this book exposes that harmful attitude to the light of day and shows that it is not just unworthy of our society, but also wrongheaded. We *can* be honest with those people who are contemplating enrolling in studies. We *can* be more honest with the public in describing the things that we need to do to make sure research takes place. There are proper ways to be honest and yet still have a robust system of research.

Until such time as our system for regulating research becomes truer to its own avowed aspirations, the information provided in this book will, we hope, at least enable readers to better distinguish, on their own, the "good choice" and "bad choice" studies. We end with the quotation that began chapter 2: "[T]he issue in medical experimentation is the risking of lives to save other lives."[22] But as we have tried to argue, while the world of research presents hard choices for our society, we are the better for directly addressing those choices and recognizing their consequences.

Notes

Introduction

1. David J. Rothman, *Strangers at the Bedside: A History of How Law and Bioethics Transformed Medical Decision Making* 15 (New York, Basic Books 1991).
2. In addition to being the principal author of chapter 17, Ed Richards, who is an authority on the use of governmental powers to improve the public's health, has been involved in the planning and writing of the book from the beginning. Jerry Menikoff is the author of all of the other chapters.
3. Charles Fried, *Medical Experimentation: Personal Integrity and Social Policy* 156 (New York, American Elsevier 1974).

Chapter 1

1. *See, e.g.,* Anna Mastroianni and Jeffrey Kahn, *Swinging on the Pendulum: Shifting Views of Justice in Human Subjects Research*, 31(3) Hastings Center Rep. 21 (2001).
2. Jane Brody, *Ferreting for Facts in the Realm of Clinical Trials*, New York Times D7, October 15, 2002.
3. Children's Oncology Group: About Cancer Clinical Trials, *available at* www.childrensoncologygroup.org. (This web site was revised in 2004 and no longer addresses this issue, but you can view the earlier version by going to www.archive.org and using the above URL.) The web site goes on to note that "for children with cancer, participation in clinical trials significantly increases survival rates."
4. Jeffrey M. Peppercorn et al., *Comparison of Outcomes in Cancer Patients Treated within and outside Clinical Trials: Conceptual Framework and Structured Review*, 363 Lancet 263 (2004).

5. Amy Argetsinger, *Smallpox Vaccine Studies Swamped with Volunteers*, Washington Post B1, October 27, 2001.

6. Henry Beecher, *Ethics and Clinical Research*, 274 New Engl. J. Med. 1354 (1966).

7. Christopher K. Daugherty et al., *Quantitative Analysis of Ethical Issues in Phase I Trials: A Survey Interview Study of 144 Advanced Cancer Patients*, 22(3) IRB 6 (2000).

8. *Id.* at 11. For additional analysis on why subjects enroll in research studies, *see, e.g.*, Advisory Committee on Human Radiation Experiments (ACHRE), Final Report at 738–41 (1995), *available at* tis.eh.doe.gov/ohre/roadmap/achre/index.html; Steven Joffe et al., *Quality of Informed Consent in Cancer Clinical Trials*, 358 Lancet 1772 (2001); Martin H. N. Tattersall, *Examining Informed Consent to Clinical Trials*, 358 Lancet 1742 (2001); Sarah J. L. Edwards et al., *The Ethics of Randomised Controlled Trials from the Perspectives of Patients, the Public, and Healthcare Professionals*, 317 Br. Med. J. 1209 (1998) ("The finding that so many people participate out of self interest needs exploring. . . . Given equipoise and freely available treatments, gain is not a realistic aim prospectively in late phase trials."). *See also* the references in chapter 10, note 33.

9. *See* Stephanie Strom, *Extreme Philanthropy: Giving of Yourself, Literally, to People You've Never Met*, New York Times, sec. 4 at 3, July 27, 2003 (noting that the number of altruistic organ donors is increasing, although it is still very small).

10. Nuremberg Code, Trials of War Criminals before the Nuernberg Military Tribunals under Control Council Law No. 10 (1949), *available at* www.hhs.gov/ohrp/references/nurcode .htm. Among those principles was a requirement that a research study not be too risky for the subjects, and that subjects should be enrolled in studies only with their informed consent.

11. For the history of various aspects of human research, *see, e.g.*, Susan E. Lederer, *Subjected to Science: Human Experimentation in America before the Second World War* (Baltimore, Johns Hopkins University Press 1997); David J. Rothman, *Strangers at the Bedside: A History of How Law and Bioethics Transformed Medical Decision Making* (New York, Basic Books 1991); National Bioethics Advisory Commission, 1 Ethical and Policy Issues in Research Involving Human Participants, Appendix C (2001), *available at* www.georgetown.edu/research/ nrcbl/nbac/pubs.html; Cynthia McGuire Dunn and Gary Chadwick, *Protecting Study Volunteers in Research* at 1–14 (Boston, CenterWatch 1999); Robert J. Levine and Louis Lasagna, *Demystifying Central Review Boards: Current Options and Future Directions*, Appendix A: Historical Perspectives and Regulations, 22(6) IRB 1, 4 (2000).

12. ACHRE Final Report, *supra* note 8. Judicial opinions relating to the three cases described in the text are Central Intelligence Agency v. Sims, 471 U.S. 159 (1985) (the MKULTRA study); *In re* Cincinnati Radiation Litigation, 874 F. Supp. 796 (S.D. Ohio 1995) (the Cincinnati study); Bibeau v. Pacific Northwest Research Foundation, 1999 U.S. App. LEXIS 38092 (9th Cir. 1999) (the prison study, also discussed at pp. 424–28 of the ACHRE Final Report).

13. U.S. Department of Health, Education and Welfare, Report of the National Commission for the Protection of Human Subjects of Biomedical and Behavioral Research, The Belmont Report: Ethical Principles and Guidelines for the Protection of Human Subjects of Research (1979), *available at* www.hhs.gov/ohrp/humansubjects/guidance/belmont.htm.

14. The Common Rule specifically refers to the set of federal regulations that establish the system by which institutional review boards (IRBs) review research studies to make sure they are in compliance with certain standards. Although the same set of regulations has been implemented by each of a number of federal agencies that fund research, people most typically cite 45 CFR part 46, the regulations of the U.S. Department of Health and Human Services, which are administered by the Office for Human Research Protections. Although the Common Rule is often used to refer to the full set of these regulations, formally it should

be used only to refer to subpart A. There are additional rules in subparts B–D that apply to special categories of "vulnerable" subjects. For more details about the history of the Common Rule, *see, e.g.,* National Institutes of Health (NIH), Final Report: Evaluation of NIH Implementation of Section 491 of the Public Health Service Act, Mandating a Program of Protection for Research Subjects at 2 (1998).

15. It must be noted that not all research studies in this nation are subject to the Common Rule. In general, one or another version of that rule will apply to (a) studies that are federally funded, (b) studies that are conducted at an institution that has chosen to apply those rules to all human subjects research at that institution and not just to federally funded research, or (c) studies involving products regulated by the U.S. FDA (namely, drugs, devices, or biologics), which enforces its own version of the Common Rule.

16. *See* 45 CFR part 46, subpart A. The IRB has to have at least five members from a variety of backgrounds, including at least one member who is primarily concerned with scientific issues, one who is concerned with nonscientific issues, and one who is not affiliated with the institution where the research will take place (45 CFR § 46.107). The IRB must review the study before it can begin and then must perform "continuing review" at least once a year, or more frequently if the risks of the study merit closer scrutiny (45 CFR § 46.109(e)).

17. 45 CFR § 46.111(a)(1)–(2). More specifically, the regulation reads:

> Risks to subjects [must be] minimized: (i) By using procedures which are consistent with sound research design and which do not unnecessarily expose subjects to risk, and (ii) whenever appropriate, by using procedures already performed on the subjects for diagnostic or treatment purposes, [and]
>
> Risks to subjects [must be] reasonable in relation to anticipated benefits, if any, to subjects, and the importance of the knowledge that may reasonably be expected to result.

18. 45 CFR §§ 46.116, 117.

19. For a discussion of other instances in which unfortunate things happened to subjects in research studies, *see, e.g.,* Susan Levine, *The Story of Patient #10*, Washington Post F1, July 31, 2001 (five of ten subjects who carried the virus that causes hepatitis, but were not even currently sick, ended up dying as a result of a toxic reaction to a new drug they were given); Sharon Begley and Donna Foote, *Trials—and Errors*, Newsweek 38, August 6, 2001 (describing several other scenarios in which subjects participating in research studies ended up being seriously harmed by the treatments they were given); Bradley D. Freeman et al., *Safeguarding Patients in Clinical Trials with High Mortality Rates*, 164 Am. J. Respir. Crit. Care Med. 190 (2001) (an additional 150 deaths took place in subjects assigned to the treatment arms in three studies, as compared to those assigned to placebo); and Bloomberg News Special Report, *Drug Industry Human Testing Masks Death, Injury, Compliant FDA,* November 2, 2005, *available at* www.bloomberg.com/apps/news?pid=specialreport&sid=aspHJ_sFenls&refer=news.

20. It is certainly the case that the field of human subjects research has already come under scrutiny from many other aspects. Among the numerous reports and articles examining it are, *e.g.,* Institute of Medicine, *Integrity in Scientific Research: Creating an Environment That Promotes Responsible Conduct* (2002); Institute of Medicine, *Responsible Research: A Systems Approach to Protecting Research Participants* (2003); National Bioethics Advisory Commission, Ethical and Policy Issues in Research Involving Human Participants, Vols. 1, 2 (2001); Donna Shalala, *Protecting Research Subjects: What Must Be Done?* 343 New Engl. J. Med. 808 (2000); Office of Inspector General, Department of Health and Human Services, Institutional Review Boards: A Time for Reform (1998).

21. *See* Charles Fried, *Medical Experimentation: Personal Integrity and Social Policy* 157 (New York, American Elsevier 1974) (evaluating the possibility that the requirement of full disclosure to prospective subjects might cause many research studies to be impossible to conduct).

22. Rebecca Dresser, *The Ubiquity and Utility of the Therapeutic Misconception*, 19 Soc. Phil. Policy 271, 288–90 (2002).

23. Robert A. Burt, *Where Do We Go from Here?* in Stuart J. Youngner et al., eds., *The Definition of Death: Contemporary Controversies* 339 (Baltimore, Johns Hopkins University Press 1999).

Chapter 2

1. Although the title on the cover of the magazine is as stated in the text, the actual story inside appears as Michael D. Lemonick and Andrew Goldstein, *At Your Own Risk*, Time 46, 51, April 22, 2002.

2. Steven Joffe et al., *Quality of Informed Consent in Cancer Clinical Trials*, 358 Lancet 1772 (2001).

3. Dale Keiger and Sue De Pasquale, *Trials and Tribulations*, Johns Hopkins Magazine, February 2000 (emphasis added).

4. Department of Health and Human Services, News Release, *HHS Names 11 to Secretary's Advisory Committee on Human Research Protection*, January 3, 2003.

5. R. P. Kelch, *Maintaining the Public Trust in Clinical Research*, 346 New Engl. J. Med. 285 (2002). On a similar theme, *see* comments of a noted expert in research ethics, Charles Weijer, *Placebo Trials and Tribulations*, 166 CMAJ 603 (2002) ("Clinician investigators must reaffirm their commitment first and foremost to the well-being of their patients"). An accompanying editorial, *The Better-Than-Nothing Idea: Debating the Use of Placebo Controls*, 166 CMAJ 573 (2002), characterized this as the view that "the physician's duty to the research participant *qua* patient is paramount."

6. *See, e.g.,* 45 CFR § 46.111(a)(6). *See also* Office of Human Subjects Research, NIH, Information Sheet No. 3, *Criteria for Institutional Review Board (IRB) Approval of Research Involving Human Subjects*, Item 2(e), *available at* ohsr.od.nih.gov/info/sheet3.html.

7. For another example of mixed messages, in addition to those noted in the text, in the wake of the controversy that followed Jesse Gelsinger's death, the American Society of Gene Therapy apparently felt it necessary to provide some form of reassurance to the public. Within a year of his death, it therefore requested its members to adopt a policy for gene therapy research studies under which the "best interests of the patients *must always be primary*" (emphasis added); Vida Foubister, *Gene Therapy Group Adopts Stringent Rules on Financial Ties*, American Medical News, May 8, 2000 (emphasis added).

8. Consider this quotation from a recent letter to the federal government by its own distinguished advisory panel on human research: "Research invariably consists of multiple interventions or procedures; by definition, some or all of them must be 'nonbeneficial' or 'nontherapeutic.'" Letter to Irene Stith-Coleman, Office for Human Research Protections, from Mary Faith Marshall, Chairman, National Human Research Protections Advisory Committee, conveying recommendations regarding proposed amendments to regulations relating to the protections of pregnant women and human fetuses, dated September 4, 2001, *available at* www.hhs.gov/ohrp/nhrpac/documents/oct01c.pdf.

9. Jay Katz, *Human Sacrifice and Human Experimentation: Reflections at Nuremberg*, 22 Yale J. Int. L. 401, 402 (1997) (emphasis added). *See also* National Bioethics Advisory Com-

mission, *Ethical and Policy Issues in International Research*, Vol. 1 at 48 (2001); Robert J. Levine, *Ethics and Regulation of Clinical Research* 10, 192–94 (2d ed., New Haven, Yale University Press 1986) (discussing loss of ability to have individualized decision making by a doctor as "one of the burdens imposed on the patient-subject in a clinical trial"); Robert J. Levine, *Clinical Trials and Physicians as Double Agents*, 65 Yale J. Biol. Med. 65 (1992) ("Conflicts between the roles of physician and researcher are inevitable and, in some circumstances, incorrigible"); Jay Katz, *Human Experimentation and Human Rights*, 38 St. Louis L. J. 7 (1993); Jesse Goldner, *An Overview of Legal Controls on Human Experimentation and the Regulatory Implications of Taking Professor Katz Seriously*, 38 St. Louis L. J. 63 (1993); Robert Steinbrook, *Protecting Research Subjects—The Crisis at Johns Hopkins*, 346 New Engl. J. Med. 716, 716 (2002) ("When people are enrolled in a study, there is an inherent tradeoff between the potential importance of the information that may be gained and the potential risk to the subject"); Franklin G. Miller and Howard Brody, *A Critique of Clinical Equipoise*, 33(3) Hastings Center Rep. 19 (2003); Franklin G. Miller and Donald L. Rosenstein, *The Therapeutic Orientation to Clinical Trials*, 348 New Engl. J. Med. 1383 (2003); Pilar N. Ossorio, *Pills, Bills and Shills: Physician-Researcher's Conflicts of Interest*, 8 Wid. L. Symp. J. 75, 95 (2001) ("The researcher . . . is primarily interested in developing generalizable knowledge. This supercedes her interest in advancing the well-being of individual research subjects. . . . By its very nature, research on human beings involves knowingly and intentionally exposing them to interventions that may diminish rather than enhance their health and well-being"); Grimes v. Kennedy Krieger Institute, Inc., 782 A.2d 807, 851 (Md. 2001); Department of Health and Human Services, *Protection of Human Subjects*, 66 Fed. Reg. 3878, 3879 (2001) ("One commentator objected to the distinction between 'therapeutic' and 'nontherapeutic' research as illogical, because, by definition, the purpose of research is always to contribute to generalizable knowledge. The commentator noted that this distinction confuses therapy with research. *The Department concurs with this comment and has modified the final rule to eliminate language implying that the purpose of research is ever therapeutic*") (emphasis added). As the author of a leading textbook on the design of research studies has noted,

> "*Individual ethics*" means that each patient should receive that treatment which is thought to be most beneficial for his condition. This is the clear aim of good clinical practice. . . . [M]ost people instinctively feel that we should pay exclusive attention to individual ethics. However, I feel that if this were to be the case then properly designed clinical trials could no longer exist and there would be no constructive framework for meaningful progress in therapy. In particular, a total commitment to individual ethics would appear contradictory to the use of randomization, blinding and placebos.

Stuart J. Pocock, *Clinical Trials: A Practical Approach* 104–05 (New York, Wiley 1983). *See also* the references in note 19 *infra*, relating to the concept of therapeutic misconception. For a contrary view by a highly influential scholar, *see* Benjamin Freedman, *A Response to a Purported Ethical Difficulty with Randomized Clinical Trials Involving Cancer Patients*, 3 J. Clin. Ethics 231 (1992). The view promoted by Freedman, that participating in an appropriately designed research study cannot be bad for any subject, appears to find its most prominent supporters among his fellow Canadians and, to some extent, from codes of ethics outside of the United States, such as the Declaration of Helsinki.

    10. Complaint in Gelsinger v. University of Pennsylvania, *available at* www.sskrplaw.com/links/healthcare2.html.

    11. It is interesting to note the recent popularity of not referring to people who enroll in research studies as "subjects" but instead as "participants," on the theory that a subject

passively allows things to be done to himself, while a participant plays an active role. *See, e.g.*, Petra M. Boynton, *People Should Participate In, Not Be Subjects of, Research* (Letter), 317 Br. Med. J. 1521 (1998). Of course, changing the terminology will likely have little effect unless significant substantive changes are made that do in fact give research subjects more control over what happens to them. For that reason, we will generally use the traditional (and more correct, in our view) term "research subjects" throughout this book, though sometimes the term "participants" will be used to improve readability.

12. The Ellen Roche study was similar to that of Jesse Gelsinger. Ellen Roche was a perfectly health young woman. The researchers were *intentionally* having her inhale a compound that they *expected* to damage her lungs. They did not expect to do much damage, and they expected that the minor damage would quickly go away. They were wrong. Perhaps, using 20/20 hindsight vision, we can argue that they might have been better able to guess that the study imposed an inappropriate risk to Ms. Roche. But it is only in hindsight that we have such perfect vision. As *Time* magazine noted, "In the end, nobody could say that strict compliance would have saved Roche." *See* Lemonick and Goldstein, *supra* note 1 at 53. The welfare of Ms. Roche was not paramount, and it couldn't be paramount no matter how we revise the study, because the very *purpose* of the study was to *expose* her to a risk. If we truly wanted to keep her welfare paramount, there was an easy answer: don't let her enter the study. More simply, we shouldn't be letting the study take place if that was truly our guiding principle.

13. Guido Calabresi and Philip Bobbitt, *Tragic Choices* 17 (New York, Norton 1978).

14. For example, in one of the leading studies of the history of "human experimentation," Yale scholar Susan Lederer never appears to make a distinction between these two categories. Both subjects participating in research and those getting experimental care outside of research are lumped together under the heading of "human experimentation." Professor Lederer's work correctly reflects the long-standing history of this confusion. Susan E. Lederer, *Subjected to Science: Human Experimentation in America before the Second World War* (Baltimore, Johns Hopkins University Press 1997).

15. For discussions of the special role that the AIDS community played in the shift toward viewing clinical trials as a positive thing for particular interest groups, *see, e.g.*, Rebecca Dresser, *When Science Offers Salvation: Patient Advocacy and Research Ethics* (New York, Oxford University Press 2001); Steven Epstein, *Impure Science: AIDS, Activism, and the Politics of Knowledge* (Berkeley, University of California Press 1996).

16. The FDA's rules for when a drug manufacturer can allow such compassionate use are relatively vague. *See* FDA, *Treatment Use of Investigational Drugs*, in Information Sheets: Guidance for Institutional Review Boards and Clinical Investigators, 1998 Update, *available at* www.fda.gov/oc/ohrt/irbs/drugsbiologics.html#treatment. To provide a drug in this manner, there must first be "sufficient data" to show that the drug "may be effective" and that it does not have "unreasonable risks." The are also four additional requirements that must be met: "1) the drug is intended to treat a serious or immediately life-threatening disease; 2) there is no satisfactory alternative treatment available; 3) the drug is already under investigation, or trials have been completed; and 4) the trial sponsor is actively pursuing marketing approval." The FDA does not require drug manufacturers to make unapproved drugs available on a compassionate use basis; it is solely at the manufacturer's discretion, and policies differ widely among companies. Allowing such compassionate use will often create a dilemma for a drug manufacturer, since doing so may discourage people from participating in the ongoing research studies needed to prove effectiveness and safety.

17. For more on the battle over Erbitux, *see, e.g.*, Stacey Schultz et al., *The Drug That Could Have Been*, U.S. News & World Report 18, August 19, 2002; Abigail Alliance v. McClellan, No. 03–1601 (RMU) (D.D.C. August 30, 2004). For discussions about compassionate use

availability of drugs generally, *see, e.g., Compassionate Use,* 60 Minutes, May 6, 2001; Hearings before the House Government Reform Committee, *Experimental Drugs for the Terminally Ill,* June 20, 2001.

18. *See, e.g.,* Robert J. Levine, *Ethics and Regulation of Clinical Research* 8–9 (2d ed. New Haven, Yale University Press 1986).

19. Paul S. Appelbaum et al., *False Hopes and Best Data: Consent to Research and the Therapeutic Misconception,* 17(2) Hastings Center Rep. 20, 20 (1987). *See also* Paul S. Appelbaum et al., *The Therapeutic Misconception: Informed Consent in Psychiatric Research,* 5 Int. J. L. Psychiatry 319 (1982); Charles W. Lidz and Paul S. Appelbaum, *The Therapeutic Misconception: Problems and Solutions,* 40(suppl.) Med. Care V-55 (2002); Rebecca Dresser, *The Ubiquity and Utility of the Therapeutic Misconception,* 19 Soc. Phil. Policy 271 (2002); National Bioethics Advisory Commission, Ethical and Policy Issues in International Research, Vol. 1 at 48 (2001).

20. *See, e.g.,* John D. Lantos, *The "Inclusion Benefit" in Clinical Trials,* 134 J. Pediatr. 130 (1999); B. Schmidt et al., *Do Sick Newborn Infants Benefit from Participation in a Randomized Clinical Trial?* 134 J. Pediatr. 151 (1999); S. J. L. Edwards et al., *Ethical Issues in the Design and Conduct of Randomised Controlled Trials,* 2(15) Health Technol. Assess. 29–36 (1998); D. A. Braunholtz et al., *Are Randomized Clinical Trials Good for Us (in the Short Term)? Evidence for a "Trial Effect."* 54 J. Clin. Epidemiol. 217 (2001); TROUT Group, *How Do the Outcomes of Patients Treated within Randomized Control Trials Compare with Those of Similar Patients Treated outside These Trials?* February 15, 2001, *previously available at* hiru .mcmaster.ca/ebm/trout (readers can find a copy at the Internet Archive, www.archive.org). But as the Harvard researchers who reviewed the literature on this issue demonstrated, thus far this is no good evidence that this "inclusion benefit"—or any other benefit from participating in cancer clinical trials—produces better outcomes for the participants. *See* Jeffrey M. Peppercorn et al., *Comparison of Outcomes in Cancer Patients Treated within and outside Clinical Trials: Conceptual Framework and Structured Review,* 363 Lancet 263 (2004). *See also* Gina Kolata, *Study Devalues a Popular Idea on Evaluating Medical Trials,* New York Times A19, January 23, 2004.

Chapter 3

1. Ilene K. Gipson, *Anatomy of the Conjunctiva, Cornea and Limbus,* in Gilbert Smolin and Richard A. Thoft, eds., *The Cornea: Scientific Foundations and Clinical Practice* 3–24 (3d ed. Boston, Little Brown 1994); Henry F. Edelhauser et al., *Physiology,* in *id.* at 25–46.

2. S. Arthur Boruchoff and Richard A. Thoft, *Keratoplasty: Lamellar and Penetrating,* in Smolin and Thoft, *supra* note 1 at 645–57.

3. *See The Tampa Trephine,* USF Health Sciences Update, Spring 1995; Anne DeLotto Baier, *Corneal Transplant Device Uses Fewer Sutures,* 6(39) USF Health Sci. News (1994).

4. U.S. Patent No. 5,584,881 issued December 17, 1996, to J. James Rowsey.

5. Final Report for the University of South Florida Technology Deployment Center, December 30, 1999, *available at* www.research.usf.edu/ed/reports/TDC_Final_Report_Digest .pdf.

6. Letter from Office for Human Research Protections (OHRP) to University of South Florida, relating to studies involving the Tampa Trephine, September 28, 2000, *available at* www.hhs.gov/ohrp/detrm_letrs/sep00f.pdf.

7. Edward T. Pound, *Federal Rules for Research on People Often Fail,* USA Today 1A, February 26, 2001.

260 Notes to Pages 28–29

8. Letter from the OHRP to University of South Florida, relating to studies involving the Tampa Trephine, November 17, 2000, *available at* www.hhs.gov/ohrp/detrm_letrs/nov00f.pdf.

9. Letter from OHRP, *supra* note 8.

10. Complaint in Cassidy v. Rowsey, Fla. 13th Jud. Cir. Ct. (2000).

11. Pound, *supra* note 7.

12. *Id.*

13. We use the term "nonstandard" care for this purpose throughout this book to avoid the confusion created by many of the other descriptive terms that are commonly used in this scenario, such as new, experimental, innovative, and untested. The *Belmont Report* began by distinguishing between practice and research:

> For the most part, the term "practice" refers to interventions that are designed solely to enhance the well-being of an individual patient or client and that have a reasonable expectation of success. . . . When a clinician departs in a significant way from standard or accepted practice, the innovation does not, in and of itself, constitute research. The fact that a procedure is "experimental," in the sense of new, untested, or different, does not automatically place it in the category of research.

Department of Health, Education and Welfare, Report of the National Commission for the Protection of Human Subjects of Biomedical and Behavioral Research, The Belmont Report: Ethical Principles and Guidelines for the Protection of Human Subjects of Research (1979), *available at* ohrp.osophs.dhhs.gov/humansubjects/guidance/belmont.htm. *See also* Robert Levine, *The Boundaries between Biomedical or Behavioral Research and the Accepted and Routine Practice of Medicine*, in *id.*, Appendix, Vol. 1 at 1-1 (1979).

A recent example of the use of an "innovative procedure" involved a new technique for lengthening the intestines of a child who has too short an intestine ("short bowel syndrome"). The standard procedure to correct this was very difficult to perform and often did not work. The new procedure involved making a number of slits along the child's intestines, and then stapling them back together in a way that made the intestines much longer. The doctors who devised it first tested it on animals, where it appeared to be successful. When the procedure was performed on 2-year-old Alex Malo at Children's Hospital in Boston, it was presented to his mother as risky but nonetheless a very reasonable choice given how poor his other options were. "[F]rightening as it was, she believed the surgery was her son's best chance at survival." Denise Grady, *Brainstorm to Breakthrough: A Surgical Procedure Is Born*, New York Times A1, August 4, 2003. Although this study was reviewed by the hospital's institutional review board (IRB), it is not clear whether any research procedures were taking place, or whether the IRB reviewed it due to an internal policy to have all uses of innovative procedures be reviewed by the IRB regardless of whether there were any procedures taking place primarily for research purposes.

A recent judicial opinion distinguishing the innovative use of an antibiotic from research is Ancheff v. Hartford Hospital, 799 A.2d 1067 (2002). For other discussions of the difference between getting treated with nonstandard care, as opposed to having your treatment altered for research purposes, *see, e.g.*, Karine Morin, *The Standard of Disclosure in Human Subject Experimentation*, 19 J. Legal Med. 157, 165–68 (1998), and the articles cited in note 1 in chapter 4. *See also* Dieter Giesen, *Civil Liability of Physicians for New Methods of Treatment and Experimentation: A Comparative Examination*, 3 Med. L. Rev. 22 (1995) (discussing need to distinguish, for European law purposes, concepts of therapeutic treatment, therapeutic experiments, and research experiments; these concepts correspond to categories different from those established in this book, since Giesen's category of therapeutic experiments includes both activities that have no research component and those that take place in the context of a research study).

14. A more technical definition appears in the Common Rule: "Research means a systematic investigation, including research development, testing and evaluation, designed to develop or contribute to generalizable knowledge." 45 CFR § 46.102(d). The key points in this definition are a *systematic* investigation designed to produce *generalizable* knowledge. Here is how the *Belmont Report* distinguishes research from medical care:

> The purpose of medical or behavioral practice is to provide diagnosis, preventive treatment or therapy to particular individuals. By contrast, the term "research" designates an activity designed to test an hypothesis, permit conclusions to be drawn, and thereby to develop or contribute to generalizable knowledge (expressed, e.g., in theories, principles, and statements of relationships). Research is usually described in a formal protocol that sets forth an objective and a set of procedures designed to reach that objective.

Belmont Report, supra note 13.

15. However, as the discussion later in this chapter demonstrates, it is not merely what is in the doctor's mind that separates the two categories. The applicable intent, for one category or the other, gets expressed in terms of specific actions and binding commitments by the doctor. Thus, if Dr. Rowsey was providing the Tampa Trephine procedure outside of a research study, he was of necessity making a legally enforceable commitment (under tort law) to his patients that this was the best treatment for them.

16. Charles Fried, *Medical Experimentation: Personal Integrity and Social Policy* 57 (New York, American Elsevier 1974).

17. Council on Ethical and Judicial Affairs, American Medical Association, Code of Medical Ethics: Current Opinions with Annotations, § 2.03, 6 (1996–1997 ed.). *See, e.g.,* Mark A. Hall, *Rationing Health Care,* 69 N.Y.U. L. Rev. 693, 703–07 (1994); Project of the ABIM Foundation, ACP-ASIM Foundation, and European Federation of Internal Medicine, *Medical Professionalism in the New Millennium: A Physician Charter,* 136 Ann. Int. Med. 243 (2002) (designating the "principle of primacy of patient welfare" as one of the three fundamental principles of medical professionalism).

A doctor is also described, under the law, as having "fiduciary" duties to a patient. For a discussion of the relatively limited role that the concept of being a fiduciary plays in determining the duties owed by a doctor to a patient, *see, e.g.,* William J. Curran et al., *Health Care Law and Ethics* 187–88 (5th ed., New York, Apsen Law and Business 1998) ("Fiduciary law can be thought of not so much as a separate source of distinct legal duties but instead as a legal status that heightens or alters ordinary contract and tort law duties. . . . Classifying physicians as fiduciaries is a simple matter; it is much more difficult, however, to say precisely what obligations result. Fiduciary law is far from a seamless web. There is no integrated body of principles or precise doctrine that applies uniformly to all forms of fiduciary relationships"); Marc A. Rodwin, *Strains in the Fiduciary Metaphor: Divided Physician Loyalties and Obligations in a Changing Health Care System,* 21 Am. J. L. Med. 241 (1995). Whatever the confusion regarding the legal consequences of a doctor being in a fiduciary relationship with a patient, there is obviously a great deal more confusion when that concept is applied to the relationship between a researcher and a subject. Indeed, it is not even clear if that relationship should be described as a fiduciary one. *See, e.g.,* Greenberg v. Miami Children's Hospital Research Institute, 2003 U.S. Dist LEXIS 8959 (2003) (finding there was no such relationship between a researcher and the parents who acted as the decision makers for children in a study). We do believe that there is indeed a type of fiduciary relationship between a researcher and a subject, and much of our analysis in this book is specifically directed at evaluating how contract and tort law is modified to apply to that relationship. Thus, while throughout this book we do not refer to the fiduciary concept very much in discussing the legal rights applying to the researcher–subject relationship, we are in effect performing the same type of analysis that might be applied if someone was specifically applying fiduciary principles to that relationship.

For a discussion of the few limited exceptions to the general principle that a doctor's allegiance must be primarily to her patient, *see* note 10 in chapter 4.

18. Jay Katz has written extensively on this issue. *See, e.g., Ethics and Clinical Research Revisited: A Tribute to Henry K. Beecher,* 23(5) Hastings Center Rep. 31, 36 (1993):

> The astronomical increase in clinical research has, in practice, not led to a clear demarcation between therapy and research, bioethical theories notwithstanding. This vital distinction remains blurred when physician-investigators view subjects as patients, and then believe that patients' interests and not science's are being served by participation in the randomized clinical trials that are so commonly conducted in today's world. . . .

See also Franklin G. Miller and Donald L. Rosenstein, *The Therapeutic Orientation to Clinical Trials,* 348 New Engl. J. Med. 1383, 1383 (2003) ("[various] research-based interventions pose risks to participants that are not compensated for by medical benefits but that are justified by the potential value of the knowledge to be gained from the trial"); Steven M. Grunberg and William T. Cefalu, *The Integral Role of Clinical Research in Clinical Care,* 348 New Engl. J. Med. 1386, 1386 (2003) ("The performance of clinical research has always been acknowledged to entail an essential conflict between the individualization of patient care and the standardization of the scientific method").

19. *See, e.g.,* citations in note 9 of chapter 2.

20. We assume he is appropriately getting the permission—formally, informed consent—of the subjects, an issue that we discuss in detail in part II. For other discussions of how being in a research study can involve things that are not in the direct best interests of a person, *see, e.g.,* Paul S. Appelbaum et al., *False Hopes and Best Data: Consent to Research and the Therapeutic Misconception,* 17(2) Hastings Center Rep. 20 (1987); Rebecca Dresser, *The Ubiquity and Utility of the Therapeutic Misconception,* 19 Soc. Phil. Policy 271, 272–73 (2002); Jay Katz, *Human Experimentation and Human Rights,* 38 St. Louis L. J. 7 (1993); Jesse Goldner, *An Overview of Legal Controls on Human Experimentation and the Regulatory Implications of Taking Professor Katz Seriously,* 38 St. Louis L. J. 63 (1993).

21. The editor of one of the world's leading medical journals, *Lancet,* has described the randomized trial as the "study design that is central to establishing evidence for or against interventions in clinical practice." R. Horton, *The Hidden Research Paper,* 287 JAMA 2775 (2002).

22. *See, e.g.,* Benjamin Freedman, *A Response to a Purported Ethical Difficulty with Randomized Clinical Trials Involving Cancer Patients,* 3 J. Clin. Ethics 231 (1992).

23. *See, e.g.,* Arthur Schafer, *The Randomized Clinical Trial: For Whose Benefit?* 7(2) IRB 4 (1985); Charles Fried, *Medical Experimentation: Personal Integrity and Social Policy* 50–56 (New York, American Elsevier 1974); Samuel Hellman and Deborah S. Hellman, *Of Mice but Not Men: Problems of the Randomized Clinical Trial,* 324 New Engl. J. Med. 1589 (1991); Franklin G. Miller and Howard Brody, *A Critique of Clinical Equipoise,* 33(3) Hastings Center Rep. 19 (2003); Robert M. Veatch, *Indifference of Subjects: An Alternative to Equipoise in Randomized Clinical Trials,* 19 Soc. Phil. Policy 295 (2002); Robert M. Veatch, *Should I Enroll in a Randomized Clinical Trial? A Critical Commentary,* 10(5) IRB 7 (1988).

24. *See, e.g.,* Fried, *supra* note 23 at 52–53 ("But, when a particular patient is involved, with a particular set of symptoms, a particular diagnostic picture and a particular set of values and preferences . . . then one may doubt how often a physician carefully going into all of these particularities would conclude that the risks and benefits are truly equal").

25. A new drug generally goes through three types of studies in order, called phases I, II, and III. As discussed in chapter 2, a phase I study involves only a small number of subjects and is designed merely to determine how large a dose can be given before unacceptable side effects take place. The next type of study, phase II, involves a larger number of subjects and begins to examine whether the drug is effective. The largest type of study, phase III, involving hundreds or thousands of subjects, generally takes place only after there has been at least some evidence of effectiveness (and safety) demonstrated in the earlier, smaller trials. Thus, some commentators who study the behavior of research subjects have found it puzzling that subjects will enroll in these "late phase" studies with the idea that this is in their best interests, even though, since they are being randomized, "gain [to them] is not a realistic aim" of their participation. *See* Sarah J. L. Edwards et al., *The Ethics of Randomised Controlled Trials from the Perspectives of Patients, the Public, and Healthcare Professionals,* 317 Br. Med. J. 1209, 1211 (1998).

26. For a discussion of some empirical evidence that being denied the individual care of a doctor and instead having care determined by a protocol may be better for some patients, *see* S. J. L. Edwards et al., *Ethical Issues in the Design and Conduct of Randomised Controlled Trials,* 2(15) Health Technol. Assess. 29–35 (1998).

27. This example is taken from Robert J. Wells et al., *Ethical Issues Arising When Interim Data in Clinical Trials Is Restricted to Independent Data Monitoring Committees,* 22(1) IRB 7 (2000). The informed consent issues raised by this example are discussed in chapter 8.

Chapter 4

1. Robert D. Truog et al., *Is Informed Consent Always Necessary for Randomized, Controlled Trials?* 340 New Engl. J. Med. 804, 804 (1999). For related discussions about the distinction between innovative care (outside of a research study) and being a participant in a research study, including some proposals to have the provision of innovative care subjected to rules similar to those that govern research, *see, e.g.,* Robert J. Levine, *The Boundaries between Biomedical or Behavioral Research and the Accepted and Routine Practice of Medicine,* in Report of the National Commission for the Protection of Human Subjects of Biomedical and Behavioral Research, The Belmont Report, Appendix, Vol. 1 at 1–1 (1978); John Robertson, *Legal Implications of the Boundaries between Biomedical Research Involving Human Subjects and the Accepted or Routine Practice of Medicine,* in *id.,* Vol. 2 at 16–1; Nancy M. P. King, *The Line between Clinical Innovation and Human Experimentation,* 32 Seton Hall L. Rev. 573 (2002); Nancy M. P. King, *Experimental Treatment: Oxymoron or Aspiration?* 25(4) Hastings Center Rep. 6 (1995); John Lantos, *How Can We Distinguish Clinical Research from Innovative Therapy?* 16 Am. J. Pediatr. Hematol. Oncol. 72 (1994); Jon Tyson, *Dubious Distinctions between Research and Clinical Practice Using Experimental Therapies: Have Patients Been Well Served?* in Amnon Goldworth et al. (eds.), *Ethics and Perinatology* 214 (New York, Oxford University Press 1995); Iain Chalmers and Richard I. Lindley, *Double Standards on Informed Consent to Treatment,* in Len Doyal and Jeffrey S. Tobias, *Informed Consent in Medical Research* 266 (London, BMJ 2001).

2. The most significant exception is the compassionate use rules, discussed in chapter 2 at note 16. Other exceptions include the following: (1) in an emergency, when there is no

time for a protocol to be approved, the FDA may authorize the drug to be used for a patient who is in a life-threatening situation and there is no standard acceptable treatment; (2) cancer drugs that are being evaluated in phase III studies (described later in this chapter) can be given to patients after FDA approval of a protocol filed under a process called a "Group C Treatment IND"; and (3) a special procedure that has been created for allowing access to promising drugs that are being studied to treat AIDS/HIV and related diseases. The AIDS/ HIV procedure is described as a "parallel track" to expand access to the new drug at the same time that the clinical trials are still taking place. *See, e.g.,* FDA, *Treatment Use of Investigational Drugs,* in Information Sheets: Guidance for Institutional Review Boards and Clinical Investigators, 1998 Update at 54 (1998), *available at* http://www.fda.gov/oc/ohrt/ irbs/drugsbiologics.html#treatment; Steven R. Salbu, *The FDA and Public Access to New Drugs: Appropriate Levels of Scrutiny in the Wake of HIV, AIDS, and the Diet Drug Debacle,* 79 B.U. L. Rev. 93 (1999).

3. *See, e.g.,* Michael H. Cohen, *Complementary and Alternative Medicine: Legal Boundaries and Regulatory Perspectives* 73 (Baltimore, Johns Hopkins University Press 1998).

4. *See, e.g.,* Jerry Menikoff, *Law and Bioethics: An Introduction* 356–57 (Washington, D.C., Georgetown University Press 2001).

5. U.S. v. Rutherford, 442 U.S. 544, 556–59 (1979) (citations omitted). This Supreme Court opinion only decided the correct interpretation of the authority that Congress had granted to the FDA. It did not decide the issue of whether that grant of authority might violate the U.S. Constitution: whether the 14th Amendment to the Constitution, and the substantive due process "liberty interests" relating to controlling certain aspects of our lives, perhaps gives people the right to use, *e.g.,* safe drugs regardless of whether they have been proven to be effective. While the Supreme Court has never directly addressed this issue, a number of lower federal courts have issued opinions rejecting such Constitutional protections. *See, e.g.,* Mitchell v. Clayton, 995 F.2d 772 (7th Cir. 1993).

6. *See, e.g.,* Cohen, *supra* note 3 at 109–19; Kathleen M. Boozang, *Western Medicine Opens the Door to Alternative Medicine,* 24 Am. J. L. Med. 185 (1998).

7. Spead v. Tomlinson, 59 A. 376 (N.H. 1904).

8. *In re* Guess, 393 S.E. 2d 833 (N.C. 1990).

9. Guess v. Board of Medical Examiners of North Carolina, 967 F.2d 998 (4th Cir. 1992).

10. There are only a few well-recognized situations where the law permits a doctor to intentionally do things that may not be in the best interests of a patient, and these generally involve furthering important public health goals, such as the mandated reporting to a state health department that a particular patient has a communicable disease. And even such actions remain highly controversial in our modern world, where we almost revere individual autonomy. When AIDS was first discovered, many states passed laws to prohibit doctors from revealing to anyone—whether the health department or even spouses who unknowingly were risking their lives every time they had sex—that any patient was HIV positive. This initial response to the new crisis was later described as *AIDS exceptionalism:* instead of balancing the interests of the patient against the well-being of other members of society, as was historically done in dealing with similar sexually transmitted diseases, we gave the patient's interests absolute priority. Our current laws regarding AIDS no longer take such an "exceptional" approach, but we still see similar conflicts in other areas. As the SARS virus spread, the *New York Times* highlighted an article by a leading physician-author, commenting on what, decades earlier in a world where tuberculosis was killing millions, would have been a nonissue: that it is acceptable to quarantine people against their will to prevent them from spreading a contagious disease. *See* Abraham Verghese, *Viral Terrors: Fighting SARS*

Can Impinge on Civil Liberties as Much as Countering Al Qaeda Does—and That's OK, New York Times Magazine 15, 16, April 20, 2003.

11. Sometimes the standard of care may itself require that patients be given a choice. For example, there might be uncertainty whether, for a breast tumor of a certain size, removing the whole breast produces any greater survival than removing just the area of the tumor; it might be the case that the standard practice for doctors is to discuss this issue with patients and to let them choose between the two types of surgery.

In addition, sometimes the standard of care may allow physicians to make certain choices. Under a doctrine know as "two schools of thought" or "respectable minority," the law may recognize that there is more than one acceptable way to treat a particular condition, and it would not be malpractice for a doctor to follow a form of treatment that is accepted by a sufficiently large and well-respected group of doctors. *See, e.g.*, Parris v. Sands, 25 Cal. Rptr. 2d 800 (1993); Jones v. Chidester, 610 A.2d 964 (Pa. 1992); William J. Curran et al., *Health Care Law and Ethics* 332–35, 340 (5th ed., New York, Apsen Law and Business 1998).

12. *See, e.g.*, Jackson v. Burnham, 39 P. 277 (Colo. 1895) (a physician who "sees fit to experiment with some other mode" of treatment does so "at his peril"); Owens v. McCleary, 281 S.W. 682 (Mo. 1926) (use of injection to treat hemorrhoids; the law does not tolerate "experimentation" on the part of a physician); George J. Annas et al., *Informed Consent to Human Experimentation: The Subject's Dilemma* 1–25 (Cambridge, Mass., Ballinger 1977); Karine Morin, *The Standard of Disclosure in Human Subject Experimentation*, 19 J. Legal Med. 157, 196–98 (1998).

13. *See, e.g.*, Barry R. Furrow et al., *Health Law* 290 (2d ed. St. Paul, Minn., West Group 2000) ("Physicians often argue that their deviation from a standard of care is clinical innovation . . . Courts have resisted such arguments. Such experiments are acceptable to the courts typically when conventional treatments are largely ineffective or where the patient is terminally ill and has little to lose by experimentation with potentially useful treatments"); William J. Curran et al., *supra* note 11 at 340 ("Is strict liability an appropriate standard for medical experimentation? Early decisions generally held "yes," but most modern courts say "no," holding that doctors are bound by a standard of reasonable experimentation"); Annas et al., *supra* note 12 at 5, 9–11; Morin, *supra* note 12 at 196–98. For a very early case that appeared to accept such a rule, *see* Fortner v. Koch, 261 N.W. 762 (Mich. 1935) (noting that "experimentation" must be done with the consent of the patient and "must not vary too radically from the accepted method of procedure"; facts of the case involved physician who was negligent in not doing tests that would have shown that syphilis was cause of patient's swollen knee).

14. Brook v. St. John's Hickey Memorial Hospital, 380 N.E. 2d 72 (Ind. 1978). For a case that does a poor job in discussing these concepts, *see* Karp v. Cooley, 493 F.2d 408, 423–24 (5th Cir. 1974) (in a lawsuit against Dr. Denton Cooley over implantation of the first artificial heart, the court holds that there was no evidence of a departure from standard care and thus no claim for improper "experimentation").

15. As the *Brook* court stated:

> Too often courts have confused judgmental decisions and experimentation. Therapeutic innovation has long been recognized as permissible to avoid serious consequences. The everyday practice of medicine involves constant judgmental decisions by physicians as they move from one patient to another in the conscious institution of procedures, special tests, trials and observations

recognized generally as effective in treating the patient or providing a diagnosis of a diseased condition. Each patient presents a slightly different problem to the doctor. A physician is presumed to have the knowledge and skill necessary to use some innovation to fit the particular circumstances of each case.

Brook v. St. John's Hickey Memorial Hospital, *supra* note 14 at 76.

16. Brook v. St. John's Hickey Memorial Hospital, *supra* note 14 at 76, note 1.

17. Tunkl v. Regents of Univ. of California, 383 P.2d 441 (Cal. 1963).

18. The form read: "The hospital is a nonprofit, charitable institution. In consideration of the hospital and allied services to be rendered and the rates charged therefore, the patient or his legal representative agrees to and hereby releases . . . the hospital from any and all liability for the negligent and wrongful acts or omissions of its employees, if the hospital has used due care in selecting its employees." *Id.* at 442.

19. *See, e.g.*, Barry R. Furrow et al., *Health Law: Cases, Materials and Problems* 368 (3d ed. St. Paul, Minn., West 1997). For discussions of the possible benefits from changing the law and permitting patients to enter into agreements with health care providers that might, among other things, alter the required standard of care, *see* Clark C. Havighurst, *Health Care Choices: Private Contracts as Instruments of Health Reform* (Washington, D.C., AEI 1995); Paul Weiler, *Medical Malpractice on Trial* 93–113 (Cambridge, Harvard University Press 1991); Richard A. Epstein, *Medical Malpractice: The Case for Contract*, ABA Res. J. 87 (1976).

20. *See, e.g.*, *Under the Knife*, Dateline NBC, November 8, 1999.

21. Here is the way a court recently described a somewhat more clear-cut scenario:

Nor is this a situation where the doctor fully informs the patient about an overtly negligent procedure with no possible benefits to the patient, and then performs that procedure. For example, were a doctor to inform the patient that he would be performing a certain surgery and that he would be leaving the scalpel in the patient's body after the surgery, even if a patient may have ignorantly agreed to this procedure, the doctor's actions would still fall below the standard of care, constituting negligence.

Heinrich v. Sweet, 308 F.3d 48, 70 (1st Cir. 2002).

22. The document read:

It is clearly understood by all parties to this instrument that no representations have been made to any of us regarding the success of the attempted transplant, and we fully understand that said transplant is in the nature of an experiment and is being performed in the hope of saving the life of the Recipient. . . . [W]e fully realize that we are signing a complete release and bar to any further claims which we may have resulting in any way from the attempted transplant. . . .

Colton v. New York Hospital, 414 N.Y.S. 2d 866, 870–71 (Sup. Ct. 1979).

23. Schneider v. Revici, 817 F.2d 987 (2d Cir. 1987).

24. Indeed, selenium is currently being studied in major research protocols as a possible treatment for prostate cancer.

25. A similar scenario occurs where a member of the Jehovah's Witness faith, which teaches that it is against God's will to accept blood transfusions, agrees to a life-saving surgical treatment but forbids the doctor from providing any transfusions during or after the surgery, even if the patient's blood loss becomes life-threatening. Doing that particular type of surgery without the possibility of a transfusion might be a very risky thing, and probably not even appropriate to suggest to a patient who was not a member of that faith. Nonethe-

less, given the special restrictions imposed by the patient who is a Jehovah's Witness, restrictions that our society accepts as legitimate and legally protected, the doctor could then provide whatever treatment is most reasonable given those restrictions. The doctor, under those circumstances, would not be committing malpractice in performing the surgery.

26. As noted in chapter 3, there are claims by various patients, backed up by some of the conclusions of the people who investigated his practices, that in fact some or all of the patients did not receive such "full disclosure" and in fact might not have even been informed that the procedure being performed was a departure from standard care.

27. There is an additional argument to be made: that given the newness of this procedure, Dr. Rowsey was under a duty to his later patients to be collecting data about the procedure each time he performed it—in other words, that he should at least have been doing some type of "records review" research. His failure to do this might be viewed as imposing an unreasonable risk on the second, tenth, etc., patient who underwent the procedure. *See, e.g.*, Leonard H. Glantz, *The Law of Human Experimentation with Children*, in Michael A. Grodin and Leonard H. Glantz, eds., *Children as Research Subjects: Science, Ethics, and Law* 103, 121–22 (New York, Oxford University Press 1994) ("if the person performing the novel procedure a hundred times is not interested in evaluating [it] but simply intends to continue to perform the procedure in the unproven belief that it is beneficial to patients, such a situation may not come under the definition of research. However, this may be very questionable medical practice"); Belmont Report, *supra* note 1 ("Radically new procedures . . . should, however, be made the object of formal research at an early stage in order to determine whether they are safe and effective").

Chapter 5

1. Modern codes of research ethics no longer employ the principle of the second clause: a researcher's willingness to be a subject won't permit a "higher" standard of risk to be imposed on subjects. On the other hand, forcing researchers to undergo the same risks that subjects are exposed to might even in modern times be an intriguing way to help make sure that risks are below an acceptable level. For the story of the major role self-experimentation has played in the development of major medical breakthroughs, *see* Lawrence K. Altman, *Who Goes First? The Story of Self-Experimentation in Medicine* (1987).

2. J. Couzin, *New Rule Triggers Debate over Best Way to Test Drugs*, 299 Science 1651 (2003).

3. The assumption behind this analysis is that there is no way to resolve the efficacy issue by, *e.g.*, exposing the subjects to a very low dose that would not harm them very much. If the latter were possible, then such a less risky study would likely be ethical.

4. J. Kaiser, *Academy Panel Mulls Ethics of Human Pesticide Experiments*, 299 Science 327 (2003); Denise Grady, *Debate Erupts over Testing Pesticides on Humans*, New York Times A18, January 9, 2003. A professor of neurology and nuclear medicine, speaking on behalf of Physicians for Social Responsibility, a group opposing the use of people to study pesticides, is quoted as saying that such studies are improper because they "violate the doctor's oath to 'do no harm.'" *Id.* That objection can of course be made with regard to most research involving human subjects, not just the pesticide studies.

A former U.S. EPA official, later a professor at Johns Hopkins University, observed that such studies had been common in the past but declined in the 1980s due to difficulty in obtaining "ethicists' approval." *Id.* It is far from obvious that these studies should be considered to be more problematic than the other types of studies described in this chapter and elsewhere in this book. Giving a healthy person large doses of a new drug in a phase I study may well involve equal or greater risks of harm. The fact that pesticides are known to harm plants may well make the idea of having a human consume small quantities appear very harmful, but it is not clear that the evidence demonstrates that the risk is any greater than that permitted in other types of studies that are deemed acceptable.

5. Donald Y. M. Leung et al., *Effect of Anti-IgE Therapy in Patients with Peanut Allergy*, 348 New Engl. J. Med. 986 (2003).

6. Beverly Merz, *Studying Peanut Anaphylaxis*, 348 New Engl. J. Med. 975 (2003).

7. Jane Brody, *Ferreting for Facts in the Realm of Clinical Trials*, New York Times D7, October 15, 2002. A similar comment has been made by Richard L. Schilsky, who is both an associate dean at the University of Chicago School of Medicine and chairman of a large national consortium that conducts research studies known as the Cancer and Leukemia Group B Cooperative: "It's hard to see how patients could make a mistake participating in a clinical trial." Sandra G. Boodman, *Trials: For the Sake of Others*, Washington Post HE01, January 27, 2004.

8. It is worth noting that the public is again being sent a mixed message regarding this circumstance. In chapter 2, we quoted from a *New England Journal of Medicine* article describing how the Association of American Medical Colleges arrived at new financial conflict of interest guidelines in the wake of the death of Jesse Gelsinger. Consider these additional excerpts from that article, which is talking about what happens in research studies:

> [Financial conflicts of interest] are particularly difficult to justify and require careful and completely transparent management, since they may threaten the primacy of the doctor–patient relationship. . . .
>
> One cannot work simultaneously as an inventor-entrepreneur and a physician or other health care provider and maintain the trust of patients and the public. To attempt to do so is to challenge the primacy of the doctor–patient relationship.

See R. P. Kelch, *Maintaining the Public Trust in Clinical Research*, 346 New Engl. J. Med. 285, 285, 287 (2002). While these comments are directed at conflicts of interest in particular, they nonetheless send an incorrect message: that somehow, in the context of a research setting, the "doctor–patient relationship" remains primary.

9. For an explanation of which studies must comply with the Common Rule, *see* chapter 1, note 15.

10. *See, e.g.,* Robertson v. McGee, 2002 U.S. Dist. Lexis 4072, 9–10 (N.D. Ok. 2002). Similarly, there is no private right of action under the Nuremberg Code or other international agreements. *See, e.g.,* White v. Paulsen, 997 F. Supp. 1380 (E.D. Wash. 1998) (rejecting right of action under Nuremberg Code); Hoover v. West Virginia Department of Health and Human Services, 984 F. Supp. 978 (S.D. W. Va. 1997), *aff'd*, 129 F.3d 1259 (11th Cir. 1997) (same); and Robinett v. U.S., 1995 U.S. App. LEXIS 21691 (Fed. Cir.) (rejecting right of action under federal regulations). *See also* Grimes v. Kennedy Krieger Institute, Inc., 782 A.2d 807, 849 (Md. 2001) (noting that the "breach of obligations imposed on researchers by the Nuremberg Code, might well support actions sounding in negligence in cases such as those at issue here"; the court's language, though somewhat vague, is consistent with the argument that the code does not itself create a right of action, but it may in effect establish duties for researchers that state tort law recognizes in allowing negligence actions).

11. Our goal in this chapter is to demonstrate the rules that determine what types of studies are or are not acceptable. As a result, we are not specifically interested in laying out the exact rules that will permit a person injured in a research study to successfully sue the re-

searchers for having breached their duties. The answer to that question involves resolving major questions not just relating to the nature of the duty, which we discuss in this chapter, but also relating to more technical legal questions, such as how soon after the injury must a subject bring the lawsuit (formally, determining the statute of limitations), are there any limitations on the amount of damages, will class actions be allowed, and so forth. These complicated and detailed rules will need to be worked out by courts and legislators over time, as we develop a better understanding of the dividing line between research and clinical care. But the first step in the process must be distinguishing the fundamental difference between legal duties established by the researcher–subject relationship and those established by the doctor–patient relationship, as we attempt to do in this chapter. For a discussion of the various issues that will arise in litigation over alleged researcher malpractice, *see, e.g.,* R. L. Jansson, *Research Liability for Negligence in Human Subject Research: Informed Consent and Researcher Malpractice Actions,* 78 Wash. L. Rev. 229 (2003); E. Haavi Morreim, *Medical Research Litigation and Malpractice Tort Doctrines: Courts on a Learning Curve,* 4 Houston J. Health L. Policy 1 (2003); Michelle M. Mello et al., *The Rise of Litigation in Human Subjects Research,* 139 Ann. Int. Med. 40 (2003); Anna C. Mastroianni, *HIV, Women, and Access to Clinical Trials: Tort Liability and Lessons from DES,* 5 Duke J. Gender L. Policy 167, 172–76 (1998).

12. The circumstance that a doctor's interaction with a patient may be subjected to different sets of legal rules depending on the role of the doctor is not unique to this scenario. Thus, *e.g.,* in many states, a doctor examining a person as part of a preemployment physical examination will not have the same legal duties to that person that would exist if the doctor and the person being examined had entered into a "usual" doctor–patient relationship. *See, e.g.,* Reed v. Bojarski, 764 A.2d 433 (N.J. 2001) (describing the general rule, though noting that New Jersey does not follow that general rule and does impose legal duties on doctors even when they are in relationships with "nontraditional" patients); Neil J. Squillante, *Expanding the Potential Tort Liability of Physicians: A Legal Portrait of "Nontraditional Patient" and Proposals for Change,* 40 UCLA L. Rev. 1617 (1993).

There is relatively little case law specifically discussing the legal duties between researchers and subjects. *See, e.g.,* Grimes v. Kennedy Krieger Institute, Inc., *supra* note 10 at 841 (noting that researchers had a duty to subjects based on the nature of the agreements between them and also based on the nature of the relationship between the parties, including duties to "(1) design a study that did not involve placing children at unnecessary risk; (2) inform participants in the study of results in a timely manner; and (3) to completely and accurately inform participants in the research study of all the hazards and risks involved in the study"). The *Grimes* case is discussed in greater detail in chapter 13, regarding the rules for research involving children. Other cases recognizing, to a greater or lesser extent, a distinct researcher–subject duty include Payette v. Rockefeller University, 643 N.Y.S. 2d 79 (N.Y. App. Div. 1996) (recognizing that a negligence lawsuit where a woman is injured in "nontherapuetic" research study does not come under the statute of limitations that applies to malpractice actions); Vodopest v. MacGregor, 913 P.2d 779 (Wash. 1996) (allowing negligence action by a research subject against a researcher in a "nontherapeutic" study and invalidating release from liability that the subject was required to sign); Greenberg v. Miami Children's Hospital Research Institute, 2003 U.S. Dist. LEXIS 8959 (S.D. Fla. 2003) (where donated tissue was used to develop a test for Canavan disease, and that test was patented; the court concluded that although that a fiduciary relationship did not exist between the subject and researcher, there was a collaboration between them and thus an unjust enrichment cause of claim had been stated); and Heinrich v. Sweet, 308 F.3d 48 (1st Cir. 2002), discussed in note 15, *infra.*

13. Charles Fried acknowledges this in his classic work, *Medical Experimentation: Personal Integrity and Social Policy* (New York, American Elsevier 1974), which critiques the then-existing system under which subjects were often enrolled in randomized studies without ever being told their medical care was being determined by randomization or that they were in a study. Fried's remedy for that situation is for the subject to be told what will happen to them and for that person to consent to this arrangement: "The law of conflict of interests and of fiduciary relations clearly provides that the fiduciary may not pursue activities that . . . do in fact conflict with the exercise of his judgment as a fiduciary . . . without the explicit consent of his client." *Id.* at 34

14. It should be noted that these altered legal standards apply only to things that are done primarily for research purposes. Just because a person is in a research study that involves recording information from his medical records doesn't mean that a doctor is not subject to the usual malpractice rules in performing the patient's needed surgery. A helpful question to ask is, has this part of the patient's care been modified from what it would have been if they were not in the study? If the answer is yes (including a change in how the type of treatment is chosen, e.g., by randomization), then the special research rules should apply. Thus, *e.g.*, a doctor may generally treat all his patients with a nonstandard treatment approach. Imagine that he then asks some of these patients to participate in a study to evaluate that approach and that this study involves collecting existing data from the patients' clinical records and also having the patients undergo an extra x-ray. The use of the nonstandard treatment is not itself one of the research procedures in this study, since the patients were already getting it regardless of participation in the study. Thus, it is not subject to the lesser legal duties relating to research: the doctor is providing that treatment as part of clinical care, and it would need to meet the "best interests for the patient" rules described in chapter 4 for providing nonstandard care to a patient.

15. In finding the existence of a duty to research subjects, the *Grimes* court paid special attention to the federal regulations, in addition to other ethical standards, such as the Nuremberg Code, and also the contents of the consent form that the parents of the children had signed. *See Grimes, supra* note 10 at 843–46, 849. *See also* Heinrich v. Sweet, 308 F.3d 48, 66–68 (1st Cir. 2002). Dr. Sweet was a Harvard physician and researcher who during the 1950s and 1960s enrolled subjects with brain tumors into studies where they were given radioactive boron. It was later determined that the treatment was not effective. There have been multiple judicial opinions in the series of lawsuits these studies generated. Most recently, a federal appellate court rejected a jury verdict that found Dr. Sweet negligent. The court looked to existing regulatory standards, including testimony by the recent head of the federal Office for Human Research Protections (OHRP), Dr. Greg Koski, to conclude that Dr. Sweet had followed the appropriate standards of care as existed during the 1950s and 1960s. The court specifically noted that in determining the standard of care, one must be "influenced by" the fact that a research study was being conducted.

16. 45 CFR § 46.111(a)(1). This means that all procedures should be consistent with good research design. Researchers will sometimes criticize institutional review boards (IRBs) for inappropriately looking into issues relating to the scientific design of the study. But such researchers fail to recognize that, as the Common Rule correctly requires, scientific design must be a key issue in terms of a study being ethical. If a study is poorly designed, then it is less likely to produce meaningful results. In effect, then, all of the risks that the subjects will be exposed to will be for naught. Thus, the bottom line is that a poorly designed study is likely to be unethical. The interaction between study design issues and the protection of human subjects recently became the subject of a highly public dispute between the editor-in-chief of the *New England Journal of Medicine* and OHRP regarding actions OHRP took

that led to the suspension of a large federally funded multicenter study about the best way to give fluids to patients in intensive care units. *See* Jeffrey M. Drazen, *Controlling Research Trials,* 348 New Engl. J. Med. 1377 (2003); Robert Steinbrook, *How Best to Ventilate? Trial Design and Patient Safety in Studies of the Acute Respiratory Distress Syndrome,* 348 New Engl. J. Med. 1393 (2003); Robert Steinbrook, *Trial Design and Patient Safety—the Debate Continues,* 349 New Engl. J. Med. 7 (2003).

In addition, to the extent it is appropriate, procedures used in the study should be those that a subject would already undergo for nonresearch (*i.e.,* diagnostic or treatment) purposes.

Some commentators have also proposed a "mirror image" of this rule, namely, a need to maximize the benefits to the subjects. *See, e.g.,* Ezekiel J. Emanuel et al., *What Makes Clinical Research Ethical?* 283 JAMA 2701, 2706 (2000).

17. 45 CFR § 46.111(a)(3). The issue of equitable selection of subjects, and its relationship to the *Belmont Report* principle of "justice," is discussed at the end of chapter 16.

18. 45 CFR § 46.111(a)(6).

19. 45 CFR § 46.111(a)(7).

20. 45 CFR § 46.111(b). There are certain categories of subjects that are deemed to be vulnerable, including children, prisoners, pregnant women, mentally disabled persons, and people who are economically or educationally disadvantaged. Protections discussed in detail in part III of this book are those to be accorded mentally disabled adults (chapters 11 and 12), children (chapters 13 and 14), and pregnant women (chapter 15).

21. 45 CFR § 46.111(a)(2).

22. This rule is to a large extent a successor to one of the provisions of the Nuremberg Code, which states: "The degree of risk to be taken should never exceed that determined by the humanitarian importance of the problem to be solved by the experiment." Nuremberg Code, Trials of War Criminals before the Nuernberg Military Tribunals under Control Council Law No. 10 (1949), *available at* www.hhs.gov/ohrp/references/nurcode.htm.

23. The version adopted by the Department of Health, Education and Welfare (HEW) read: "The risks to the subjects are so outweighed by the sum of the benefit to the subject and the importance of the knowledge to be gained as to warrant a decision to allow the subject to accept these risks." This was an early version of 45 CFR § 46.111(a)(2), as discussed in Robert J. Levine, *Ethics and Regulation of Clinical Research* 63 (2d ed. New Haven, Yale University Press 1986).

24. Levine, *supra* note 23 at 63. Levine, who was a participant in the set of events leading to this new rule, notes how the National Commission for the Protection of Human Subjects of Biomedical and Behavioral Research rejected the early language, since it forced an IRB to "assume a paternalistic stance by constraining an investigator from offering what [the IRB] considers unfavorable harm–benefit ratios to subjects." The commission recommended language that was more generous to researchers and was less protective of subjects. That language was ultimately adopted and formed the current version of section 111(a)(2) of the Common Rule.

Some might read the language that was finally adopted as making a more substantial change from the earlier version and instead requiring that there be two separate balances, *both* of which must be satisfied for a study to be ethical, *i.e.,* benefits to subjects are reasonable in relationship to risks to subjects, *and* benefits to society are reasonable in relationship to risks to subjects.

As we note later in this chapter, we will err on the side of interpreting the regulations to require greater protection of subjects and assume such a stricter rule is indeed in existence, although the history of the provision doesn't seem to support this stricter rule. Even with this assumption, a study is still not required to have a favorable risk–benefit relationship in terms of the welfare of the subjects.

25. Given that it is, in general, difficult to evaluate the third element of the equation—the benefits to society—the federal regulations do often lead, in practice, to a requirement that there must be some "reasonable" relationship between the risks and benefits to a subject. *See, e.g.*, Emanuel et al., *supra* note 16 at 2705. It is likely that few IRBs would approve a study where there are *huge* risks to the subjects (*e.g.*, a certain substantially increased risk of death) and *minimal* direct benefits to them.

26. It is worth noting that this rule also does *not* distinguish between studies that are purely nontherapeutic and those that are testing something that might treat a subject's medical problem. Nor does it distinguish between studies on healthy volunteers and those involving people that have a medical problem. The same rule applies to all of these different types of studies. Some scholars recommend, in evaluating risks and benefits, that there be a separate analysis of procedures that might benefit a subject (so-called therapeutic procedures) and of those that clearly will not benefit a subject. *See* Charles Weijer, *The Ethical Analysis of Risk*, 28 J. L. Med. Ethics 344 (2000). In particular, it has been suggested that therapeutic elements of a study should be balanced *only* against risks to subjects (*i.e.*, benefits to society are ignored), whereas the nontherapeutic elements should undergo a separate distinct analysis. This approach is also recommended by the National Bioethics Advisory Commission, in Ethical and Policy Issues in Research Involving Human Participants, Vol. 1 at 76–80 (2001). This approach does not appear to be consistent with the wording of the current federal regulations. As the discussion in chapter 6 demonstrates, many types of studies that are currently approvable would not be permitted under this approach, since it eliminates possible benefits to society as a factor in the equation in evaluating an element of a study that offers the possibility of a benefit to a subject (a possibly therapeutic element).

Precisely because of this change in the relationship, and the obvious confusion it can cause on the part of patients, some have argued for not permitting a person's personal physician to conduct research involving that person: there would be different people occupying the distinct roles of physician and researcher. *See, e.g.*, Fried, *supra* note 13 at 160–61; Franklin G. Miller and Donald L. Rosenstein, *The Therapeutic Orientation to Clinical Trials*, 348 New Engl. J. Med. 1383 (2003).

27. These are, of course, apart from informed consent problems. Note how these two rules are almost mirror images of the rules we established for departures from standard care in the nonresearch setting (*see* chapter 4, text at note 22). The distinction between negligent design and negligent failure to adhere to an appropriate design has been mentioned in some lawsuits involving research. *See, e.g.*, Grimes v. Kennedy Krieger Institute, Inc., *supra* note 10 at 841; Heinrich v. Sweet, *supra* note 15 at 70. In *Heinrich*, the court contrasts a situation where a doctor tells a patient he will perform a surgery a certain way, and then ends up leaving a scalpel inside, with the situation where the doctor tells the patient from the outset that he wants to leave a scalpel inside. The court notes that both scenarios would constitute torts, but in different ways. Under the two rules stated in the text, the first situation would be failure to appropriately follow a valid plan, whereas *intending* to leave the scalpel inside would be an improper plan.

28. For discussion of the Wan case and other examples of this type of researcher misconduct, *see, e.g.*, E. Rosenthal, *New York Seeks to Tighten Rules on Medical Research*, New York Times B4, September 27, 1996; B. Sloat and K. C. Epstein, *Overseers Operate in Dark: Ethics Panels Only Manage Cursory Reviews of Research*, Plain Dealer 1A, December 18, 1996; Robert Helms, *Guinea Pig Zero: An Anthology of the Journal for Human Research Subject* 77–81 (New Orleans, Garrett County Press 2002); Letter to Jacqueline M. Halton from FDA, April 14, 2003 (subject with neuroblastoma given doses of antibody 25 times higher than listed in protocol, after which he died), *available at* www.fda.gov/foi/warning_letters/g3946d.htm.

29. *See, e.g.*, Queensland Health Consent Form for Bronchoscopy, *available at* www.health
.qld.gov.au/informedconsent/ConsentForms/medical/bronchoscopy.pdf; British Thoracic
Society, *British Thoracic Society Guidelines on Diagnostic Flexible Bronchoscopy*, 56(suppl. 1)
Thorax i1 (2001). Presumably, however, relatively healthy people such as Nicole Wan would
be less likely to suffer most of these complications.

30. Vodopest v. MacGregor, 913 P.2d 779 (Wash. 1996).

31. The proposal was submitted after the participants had already begun the breathing
exercises. The IRB noted that it could not approve a study that had already begun, thus it
ended up approving the activities that would take place after the training, namely, the actual trek up the mountain.

32. *See, e.g.*, 45 CFR § 46.116 ("No informed consent, whether oral or written, may include any exculpatory language through which the subject or his representative is made to
waive or appear to waive any of the subject's legal rights, or releases or appears to release
the investigator, the sponsor, the institution or its agents from liability or negligence").

33. Of course, we should not forget that there are informed consent issues here also, which
can constitute separate torts. If the protocol was written in version 2, yet the subjects were
told that they would be treated the moment they developed any symptoms (version 1), then
the subjects had not given consent to what was actually going to happen to them.

34. Payette v. Rockefeller University, 643 N.Y.S. 2d 79 (N.Y. App. Div. 1996).

35. The Ellen Roche case was mentioned in the text at note 19 in chapter 1. An external
committee that reviewed the Ellen Roche study concluded that while a variety of things may
have been done improperly, it may well have been the case that the design of the study was
acceptable. In other words, it might indeed have been acceptable to expose someone to the
risks that Ellen Roche was exposed to; had the defects been corrected and the study conducted properly, a subject's death would then be viewed as an unfortunate outcome from
the conduct of a study that met all the appropriate regulations. Report of External Review
Committee to President of Johns Hopkins University, August 8, 2001, *available at* www
.hopkinsmedicine.org/external.pdf (noting at one point that if results of earlier studies had
been known, then this risk could have been disclosed to subject, thus indicating it could have
been acceptable to nonetheless conduct the study). *See also* J. Glanz, *Clues of Asthma Study
Risks May Have Been Overlooked*, New York Times A1, July 27, 2001.

Chapter 6

1. For examples of references to the concept of clinical equipoise in various types of quasi-
authoritative guidance, *see, e.g.*, FDA, *Exception from Informed Consent for Studies Conducted
in Emergency Settings*, in Information Sheets: Guidance for Institutional Review Boards and
Clinical Investigators, 1998 Update, *available at* http://www.fda.gov/oc/ohrt/irbs/except
.html; FDA, *Workshop on Clinical Trial Requirements*, 65 Fed. Reg. 50544 (2000); NIH, Institutional Review Board Guidebook: AIDS-HIV Related Research 5–31 (1993).

2. There are some important exceptions, relating to "low-risk" studies, which we discuss later in this chapter. Thus, *e.g.*, a study in which a subject with a medical problem that
has a known effective treatment is randomized to get no treatment (*e.g.*, a placebo) would
generally violate the clinical equipoise rule, yet many such studies are considered ethical.

3. Benjamin Freedman, *Equipoise and the Ethics of Clinical Research*, 317 New Engl. J.
Med. 141 (1987). To quote Freedman:

> [In] testing a new treatment B on a defined patient population P for which the
> current accepted treatment is A, it is necessary that the clinical investigator be

in a state of genuine uncertainty regarding the comparative merits of treatments A and B for population P. If a physician knows that these treatments are not equivalent, ethics requires that the superior treatment be recommended. . . . I call this state of uncertainty about the relative merits of A and B "equipoise."

Id. at 141. Although Freedman derives the concept from an earlier work by Charles Fried, Fried was discussing equipoise for a very different reason. He was critiquing the actions of researchers who, in the 1970s, were using the existence of equipoise as a justification for not telling subjects that they were in a research study. *See* Jerry Menikoff, *Equipoise: Beyond Rehabilitation?* 13 Kennedy Inst. Ethics J. 347 (2003).

Freedman spends much of his paper distinguishing what he calls *theoretical* equipoise (later referred to by others as the uncertainty principle)—an individual clinician's personal determination that there is no good reason to conclude one treatment is better than the other—from *clinical* equipoise—where there is a dispute among medical professionals as a group regarding which of the two treatments is better. He correctly concludes that the concept of theoretical equipoise is a relatively useless concept. Indeed, even in clinical practice, just because a particular physician has a preference for one treatment that has led that doctor to no longer be in theoretical equipoise regarding two treatments, a preference that is not supported by the type of evidence that would lead other professionals to prefer that treatment, this is not a reason for the physician not to tell a patient about the availability of the other treatment. Thus, the lack of theoretical equipoise on the part of a researcher is similarly no reason to not allow a patient to participate in a study comparing two treatments that are in clinical equipoise. *See, e.g.,* Don Marquis, *How to Resolve an Ethical Dilemma Concerning Randomized Clinical Trials,* 341 New Engl. J. Med. 691 (1999); Paul B. Miller and Charles Weijer, *Rehabilitating Equipoise,* 13 Kennedy Inst. Ethics J. 93 (2003).

For additional discussions of the role of clinical equipoise and related concepts in determining the ethics of randomized trials, *see, e.g.,* Don Marquis, *Leaving Therapy to Chance,* 13(4) Hastings Center Rep. 40 (1983); Samuel Hellman and Deborah S. Hellman, *Of Mice but Not Men: Problems of the Randomized Clinical Trial,* 324 New Engl. J. Med. 1585 (1991); Eugene Passamani, *Clinical Trials—Are They Ethical?* 324 New Engl. J. Med. 1589 (1991); Benjamin Freedman, *A Response to a Purported Ethical Difficulty with Randomized Clinical Trials Involving Cancer Patients,* 3 J. Clin. Ethics 231 (1992); J. A. Chard and R. J. Lilford, *The Use of Equipoise in Clinical Trials,* 47 Soc. Sci. Med. 891 (1998); Fred Gifford, *Freedman's "Clinical Equipoise" and "Sliding-Scale All-Dimensions-Considered Equipoise,"* 25 J. Med. Phil. 399 (2000); Deborah Hellman, *Evidence, Belief, and Action: The Failure of Equipoise to Resolve the Ethical Tension in the Randomized Clinical Trial,* 30 J. L. Med. Ethics 375 (2002); Robert M. Veatch, *Indifference of Subjects: An Alternative to Equipoise in Randomized Clinical Trials,* 19(2) Soc. Phil. Policy 295 (2002); Franklin G. Miller and Howard Brody, *A Critique of Clinical Equipoise: Therapeutic Misconception in the Ethics of Clinical Trials,* 33(3) Hastings Center Rep. 19 (2003); and Lynn A. Jansen, *A Closer Look at the Bad Deal Trial: Beyond Clinical Equipoise,* 35(5) Hastings Center Rep. 29 (2005).

4. By "better," he is referring to the sort of summing up of good and bad consequences from the treatment that would usually go into a determination of whether one medical treatment is recommended over another. *See* Benjamin Freedman, *A Response to a Purported Ethical Difficulty with Randomized Clinical Trials Involving Cancer Patients, supra* note 3. Thus, *e.g.,* if it were shown that a surgical procedure that removed a cancer from a person's leg and allowed the leg to be saved was very slightly less likely to cure the cancer than amputating the leg (*e.g.,* 89.9% of the time vs. 90% of the time), the leg-sparing procedure would no

doubt still be considered the preferred treatment, given the huge difference in improved quality of life versus the very slight difference in its ability to save the patient's life.

Freedman's concept does not appear to require that, in comparing the two treatments at issue, you must factor in the *existing* amount of uncertainty regarding the benefits and risks of the new treatment. In other words, to find standard care and some new untested treatment to be in clinical equipoise, would someone have to conclude that, even given the uncertainty about the new treatment (and prior to that uncertainty being resolved), there is good reason right now to be giving patients that new treatment. If that were the standard, then it would indeed be a very demanding standard, and a great many of the research studies currently being conducted would be unethical. Since a new treatment will almost always have substantial uncertainty surrounding either risks or benefits or both, it would not be in clinical equipoise with standard care unless it had a potential to be dramatically better than standard care. Yet we regularly conduct many clinical trials of new treatments for which we have little belief in such a dramatic difference and may merely be hoping for a marginal benefit. Indeed, as discussed later in this chapter, the leading medical journals have published editorials on various new treatments cautioning doctors not to use them on patients, but only to do so in research studies. That view appears to be inconsistent with this stricter view of what clinical equipoise might require. Some commentators do appear to adopt such a stricter standard (and perhaps think it is currently being used). *See, e.g.,* Eugene Passamani, *Clinical Trials—Are They Ethical?* 324 New Engl. J. Med. 1589, 1590 (1991) ("Clinical equipoise means that on the basis of the available data, a community of physicians would be content to have their patients pursue any of the treatment strategies being tested in a randomized trial, since none of them have been clearly established as preferable"); Charles Weijer, *The Ethical Analysis of Risk*, 28 J. L. Med. Ethics 344, 354 (2000) ("equipoise requires approximate equality in treatments' therapeutic index—a compendious measure of potential benefits, risks and uncertainty. Thus, a novel treatment may pose considerably more risk to subjects as long as it also offers the prospect of considerably greater benefit. With novel interventions, the uncertainty associated with the intervention's side effects will almost always be greater than the uncertainty associated with the treatments currently used in clinical practice"); Miller and Weijer, *supra* note 3. The recommendations of the National Bioethics Advisory Commission, which adopted many of Weijer's views on the issue of assessing risks and benefits, also appear to embody this stricter view of what clinical equipoise should require. National Bioethics Advisory Commission, *Ethical and Policy Issues in Research Involving Human Participants*, Vol. 1 at 78 (2001). The commission does not appear to recognize the substantial consequences this change would have for the conduct of research, likely disallowing many types of studies that are currently permitted.

5. This evidence can come from a variety of sources. Freedman mentions that it can come, *e.g.,* from the literature, from uncontrolled experience, or from considerations of basic science and fundamental physiologic processes. Freedman, *Equipoise and the Ethics of Clinical Research, supra* note 3, at 143 (discussing theoretical equipoise, although the stated sources of information should also be relevant for clinical equipoise).

6. Marcia Angell, *The Ethics of Clinical Research in the Third World*, 337 New Engl. J. Med. 847 (1997) (emphasis added).

7. *See, e.g.,* Paul B. Miller and Charles Weijer, *Rehabilitating Equipoise*, 13 Kennedy Inst. Ethics J. 93, 113 (2003) (noting that IRBs employ the requirement of clinical equipoise to ensure that a randomized study "presents potential subjects with a favorable balance of benefits to harms"); Freedman, *A Response to a Purported Ethical Difficulty with Randomized Clinical Trials Involving Cancer Patients, supra* note 3. For arguments suggesting that equipoise does not provide such protection to subjects, *see, e.g.,* Samuel Hellman and

Deborah S. Hellman, *supra* note 3; Deborah Hellman, *supra* note 3; Robert M. Veatch, *supra* note 3.

8. In its regulations governing emergency research (discussed in chapter 12), the FDA says with regard to a particular section (section 50.24(a)(3)) that it "describes why the research intervention is in the best interests of subjects. As discussed earlier, the agency expects clinical equipoise to exist in protocols that would be approved under this section." Department of Health and Human Services, FDA, *Proposed Rules: Protection of Human Subjects*, 60 Fed. Reg. 49086, 49095 (1995). Since the actual wording of the section being described does not contain any significant requirements other than those already existing in the risk–benefit rule imposed by the Common Rule, the FDA's conclusion about participation being in the "best interests of the subjects" must be attributable to the imposition of the requirement that there is clinical equipoise.

9. S. D. Wexner et al., *Laparoscopic Colorectal Surgery—Are We Being Honest with Our Patients?* 38 Dis. Colon Rectum 723 (1995).

10. J. C. Weeks et al., *Short-term Quality-of-Life Outcomes Following Laparoscopic-Assisted Colectomy vs Open Colectomy for Colon Cancer*, 287 JAMA 321, 327 (2002) (emphasis added). The complete first paragraph of the statement reads as follows:

> The American Society of Colon and Rectal Surgeons [ASCRS] recognizes that laparoscopic colectomy may be an alternative approach to traditional resection of benign [*i.e.*, noncancerous] colonic disease. The absence of 5-year survival data makes it premature to endorse laparoscopic colon resection for cancer. If laparoscopic colon resection is performed it is important to follow traditional surgical principles and standards. It is appropriate to continue to perform all laparoscopic resections in an environment where the outcomes can be meaningfully evaluated. The ASCRS encourages the development of randomized, prospective studies to evaluate the safety, efficacy and benefits of this alternative.

American Society of Colon and Rectal Surgeons, *Approved Statement on Laparoscopic Colectomy*, 37(6) Dis. Colon Rectum, unnumbered page following page 637 (1994).

11. 45 CFR § 46.405.

12. Contrast this to the facts of another recent study, where women with breast cancer were randomized to have either just one "sentinel" lymph node under the arm removed or to have removal of all of those lymph nodes. Like the colon cancer study, removing only the one node is not likely to improve the chance of curing the cancer, and it may even increase that risk, but in this instance, that less invasive surgery may produce a lifetime benefit of decreased swelling of the arm. The possibility of this permanent, substantial benefit makes the trade-off for subjects participating in that study a far more favorable one than the colon cancer study. David Krag and Takamura Ashikaga, *The Design of Trials Comparing Sentinel-Node Surgery and Axillary Resection*, 349 New Engl. J. Med. 603 (2003). The authors specifically raise the possibility that even if the sentinel node removal produced an increased risk of the cancer returning, that might be acceptable, assuming that this procedure did indeed produce substantial changes in a woman's postsurgical quality of life. These issues are similar to those that arose in the comparison of radical mastectomy to breast-sparing forms of surgery as treatments for breast cancer.

13. This promulgation might be evidence to suggest that a doctor who nonetheless performed such surgery outside of a clinical trial might be committing malpractice.

14. N. Petrelli, *Clinical Trials Are Mandatory for Improving Surgical Cancer Care*, 287 JAMA 377, 378 (2002) ("an appropriate message regarding [small-incision surgery for colon cancer] is needed now for the professional community and the public, especially for patients

who continue to request, and on some occasions demand, the 'small incision technique to remove my colon cancer.' The message is straightforward, but enforcing it will prove difficult. Based on current evidence, [small-incision surgery] as a potentially curative procedure for colon cancer should not be performed outside of a randomized clinical trial. [This surgery] performed with the intention of curative resection of colon cancer should not be recommended in clinical practice until the efficacy and safety of [it] have been definitively demonstrated"). If this surgery should not be performed in clinical practice with "the intention of curative resection," then should we similarly assume that in the research study it isn't being done with that in mind? That would no doubt come as a surprise to many of the subjects in the study who were no doubt looking for a cure.

15. The Clinical Outcomes of Surgical Therapy Study Group, *A Comparison of Laparoscopically Assisted and Open Colectomy for Colon Cancer*, 350 New Engl. J. Med. 2050 (2004); Theodore N. Pappas and Danny O. Jacobs, *Laparoscopic Resection for Colon Cancer—the End of the Beginning?* 350 New Engl. J. Med. 2091 (2004).

16. Of course, the subjects entering such a study should have agreed to enroll only after knowing the true nature of the study: that from their individual point of view (assuming they have the preferences of a "reasonable subject"), participating was not a very good choice. Other measures could have also been implemented to make the study less disadvantageous to the subjects. For example, the initial subjects might have been people whose eye was going to have to be removed shortly afterward for other reasons (it was painful, or a tumor was growing in it, etc.). These subjects would have very little to lose if this initial testing revealed problems with the procedure. And the next group of subjects might be people who only had a couple of months to live: for them, the possibility of getting better vision a few months earlier than would occur with the standard corneal transplant might be important enough to them to warrant taking the additional risks.

17. E. M. Connor et al., *Reduction of Maternal-Infant Transmission of Human Immunodeficiency Virus Type 1 with Zidovudine Treatment*, 331 New Engl. J. Med. 1173 (1994).

18. *See, e.g.*, Peter Lurie and Sidney M. Wolfe, *Unethical Trials of Interventions to Reduce Perinatal Transmission of the Human Immunodeficiency Virus in Developing Countries*, 337 New Engl. J. Med. 853 (1997); Marcia Angell, *The Ethics of Clinical Research in the Third World*, 337 New Engl. J. Med. 847 (1997).

19. *See, e.g.*, Ronald Bayer, *The Debate over Maternal-Fetal HIV Transmission Prevention Trials in Africa, Asia, and the Caribbean: Racist Exploitation or Exploitation of Racism?* 88 Am. J. Pub. Health 567 (1998).

20. *See, e.g.*, Lurie and Wolfe, *supra* note 18.

21. It should be noted that the regulations—correctly—are usually interpreted to not permit monetary payments to a subject, or free medical care, to enter the calculation as a benefit, since otherwise we would end up concluding that such studies have a much better risk–benefit ratio for poor people than for those who are better off. Thus, we would have a policy that encouraged approving the riskiest studies for poor people but concluding that such studies would be unethical for those who are richer.

22. G. Harris, *Drug Prices: Why They Keep Soaring. Dose of Trouble: For Drug Makers, Good Times Yields to a New Profit Crunch*, Wall Street Journal, April 18, 2002. *See also* Associated Press, *Rules Are Clarified to Spur Medical Advances*, New York Times, January 31, 2003 (noting FDA's response to "a sharp decline in the development of novel treatments"); Arnold S. Relman and Marcia Angell, *How the Drug Industry Distorts Medicine and Politics: America's Other Drug Problem*, New Republic 27, December 16, 2002 (an article cowritten by two former editors-in-chief of the *New England Journal of Medicine*).

23. Imagine, *e.g.*, participating in a study of the once-a-week version of Prozac, a com-

monly prescribed antidepressant. The possible benefits—the convenience of needing to take a pill only once a week—are slight. On the other hand, if the new pill is less effective than the approved version, the negative consequences could be huge. A patient's depression might be inadequately controlled, perhaps leading to suicide.

24. The withdrawal of the pain medication Vioxx, after proof that is was causing tens of thousands of people to suffer sometimes fatal heart attacks, demonstrates one instance of this. Gina Kolata, *A Widely Used Arthritis Drug Is Withdrawn*, New York Times A1, October 1, 2004. The problem with Vioxx occurred mainly in people who had been taking the drug for long periods of time (eighteen months or longer), and most new medications are not required to undergo that type of long-term testing before approval. While we could certainly do such testing, it would delay the approval of drugs. Such a policy change would raise the question of whether the benefits from the change (in terms of preventing a few instances of harm from an undiscovered risk) would outweigh the costs (in terms of delaying access to all new drugs).

25. Lauran Neergaard, *FDA to Doctors: Read New Drugs' Fine Print*, Ventura County Star A3, December 12, 2000. *See also* Mary Duenwald, *One Lession from Vioxx: Approach New Drugs with Caution*, New York Times D5, October 5, 2004.

26. *See* note 19 in chapter 1. *See* also FDA, Center for Drug Evaluation and Research, Report to the Nation: 2003, *available at* www.fda.gov/cder/reports/rtn/2003/rtn2003-3 .HTM#Withdraw (listing drugs that have been withdrawn from the market for safety reasons in recent years; updates for post-2003 years can be found by replacing 2003 in the url with the applicable year).

27. M. E. Lippman, *High-Dose Chemotherapy Plus Autologous Bone Marrow Transplantation for Metastatic Breast Cancer*, 342 New Engl. J. Med. 1119 (2000).

28. *See* Petrelli, *supra* note 14.

29. Wexner et al., *supra* note 9.

30. C. Mavrantonis et al., *Current Attitudes in Laparoscopic Colorectal Surgery*, 16 Surg. Endosc. 1152 (2002).

31. *See, e.g.*, Sarah J. L. Edwards et al., *The Ethics of Randomised Controlled Trials from the Perspectives of Patients, the Public, and Healthcare Professionals*, 317 Br. Med. J. 1209, 1211 (1998), giving quotes on how often doctors are willing to enroll subjects in studies even though the doctors think one arm is better than the other. They note that while this is perfectly acceptable behavior, the interesting question would be whether they told the subject about their own preferences and the support for those opinions. "But would these doctors subject one of their children to randomization in such circumstances—and, if not, would they at least disclose their prior opinion on the effects of the treatments in question?"

32. We will present the "flip side" of this dialogue in chapter 10, where we deal with the situation where the doctor acknowledges that it is acceptable to give the new treatment outside of the study.

33. *See, e.g.*, Margaret Talbot, *The Placebo Prescription*, New York Times Magazine 34, January 9, 2000 ("The truth is that the placebo effect is huge—anywhere between 35 and 75 percent of patients benefit from taking a dummy pill in studies of new drugs"). The mechanism by which our mind can produce objective changes in our body is still poorly understood, but it has been found to apply to a surprisingly wide range of phenomena. A famous "wart doctor" in Zurich allegedly produced a very high rate of wart disappearance by exposing his patients to an impressive but totally ineffective machine with flashing lights and a noisy motor. And in one study, where women were trained to think about their breasts pulsating, 46% ended up requiring a larger bra size. Robert Ornstein and David Sobel, *Can the Brain Heal the Body?* Washington Post B3, May 3, 1987. A similar phenomenon of mind-

over-body may be the cause of "hysterical" illnesses, such as the skin rashes that broke out among schoolgirls in many areas following 9/11. Margaret Talbot, *The Post-9/11 Mystery Rash*, New York Times Magazine 42, June 2, 2002. *But see* Asbjørn Hróbjartsson and Peret C. Gøtzsche, *Is the Placebo Powerless? An Analysis of Clinical Trials Comparing Placebo with No Treatment*, 344 New Engl. J. Med. 1594 (2001) (finding little evidence for a strong placebo effect in a review of published studies); John C. Bailar, *The Powerful Placebo and the Wizard of Oz*, 344 New Engl. J. Med. 1630 (2001) (commentary on preceding article).

34. Note that there are already criteria, apart from the risks and benefits to the subject, requiring that the study be well designed and that it minimize the risks to the subject, as we noted earlier in this chapter. If there are other ways to collect this information, and those are less risky to subjects, then a study using placebos should not be performed. *See, e.g.*, 45 CFR § 46.111(a)(1); Robert Temple and S. S. Ellenberg, *Placebo-Controlled Trials and Active-Control Trials in the Evaluation of New Treatments. Part 1: Ethical and Scientific Issues*, 133 Ann. Int. Med. 455 (2000).

35. By "really," we mean that there is some genuine physiologic effect, apart from a placebo effect.

36. The declaration went on to note that placebos were acceptable only in studies "where no proven diagnostic or therapeutic method exists." World Medical Association, *Declaration of Helsinki, Recommendations Guiding Physicians in Biomedical Research involving Human Subjects*, 277 JAMA 925 (1997).

37. *See, e.g.*, Temple and Ellenberg, *supra* note 34; Robert Temple and S. S. Ellenberg, *Placebo-Controlled Trials and Active-Control Trials in the Evaluation of New Treatments. Part 2: Practical Issues and Specific Cases*, 133 Ann. Int. Med. 464 (2000); Robert J. Temple, *When Are Clinical Trials of a Given Agent vs. Placebo No Longer Appropriate or Feasible?* 18 Controlled Clin. Trials 613 (1997); Robert Temple, *Government Viewpoint of Clinical Trials*, Drug Inf. J. 10, January/June 1982; Ezekiel J. Emanuel and Franklin G. Miller, *The Ethics of Placebo-Controlled Trials—a Middle Ground*, 345 New Engl. J. Med. 915 (2001); P. Huston and R. Peterson, *Withholding Proven Treatment in Clinical Research*, 345 New Engl. J. Med. 912 (2001); Sharona Hoffman, *The Use of Placebos in Clinical Trials: Responsible Research or Unethical Practice*, 33 Conn. L. Rev. 449 (2001); Franklin G. Miller and Howard Brody, *What Makes Placebo-Controlled Trials Unethical?* 2 Am. J. Bioethics 3 (2002) (including responses to that article in the same issue); Benjamin Freedman et al., *Placebo Orthodoxy in Clinical Research I: Empirical and Methodological Myths*, 24 J. L. Med. Ethics 243 (1997).

38. Robert Temple is the FDA official who is generally credited as its in-house expert on placebo issues. His comments in print differ little from those of any of the other commentators who recommend a nuanced approach to placebo use:

> Placebo controls are clearly inappropriate for conditions in which the delay or omission of available treatments would increase mortality or irreversible morbidity in the population to be studied. For conditions in which forgoing therapy imposes no important risk, however, the participation in placebo-controlled trials seems appropriate and ethical, as long as patients are fully informed.

Temple and Ellenberg, *supra* note 34 at 460.

39. And there are certain kinds of studies that will appear to be at the borderline. For example, studies in which a subject is to be given a new drug often involve a "washout" period, where they are taken off the old drug. During that washout period they are essentially undergoing the same type of nontreatment that occurs in a placebo arm. There are likely to be low risks in doing this, but depending on the disease, if that risk takes place, then there

can be serious consequences. Thus, *e.g.*, can persons with mild high blood pressure be taken off their medications for several weeks, assuming their blood pressures are measured regularly and that medications will be restarted if the measurements go above certain levels? These questions pose difficult problems in drawing the line between serious and nonserious risks.

40. The Declaration of Helsinki was modified in 2002 by the addition of the following language as a footnote to paragraph 29:

> The [World Medical Association] hereby reaffirms its position that extreme care must be taken in making use of a placebo-controlled trial and that in general this methodology should only be used in the absence of existing proven therapy. However, a placebo-controlled trial may be ethically acceptable, even if proven therapy is available, under the following circumstances:
> - Where for compelling and scientifically sound methodological reasons its use is necessary to determine the efficacy or safety of a prophylactic, diagnostic or therapeutic method; or
> - Where a prophylactic, diagnostic or therapeutic method is being investigated for a minor condition and the patients who receive placebo will not be subject to any additional risk of serious or irreversible harm.

World Medical Association, *Declaration of Helsinki, Ethical Principles for Medical Research Involving Human Subjects, available at* www.wma.net/e/policy/17–c_e.html#clarification. In some ways—particularly in the first clause, discussing where its use is "necessary"—this revised position is more favorable to placebo use than the position taken by pro-placebo advocates in the United States.

For a discussion of the pro and con views prior to this amendment, *see* Troyen A. Brennan, *Proposed Revisions to the Declaration of Helsinki—Will They Weaken the Ethical Principles underlying Human Research?* 341 New Engl. J. Med. 527 (1999); Robert J. Levine, *The Need to Revise the Declaration of Helsinki*, 341 New Engl. J. Med. 531 (1999).

41. Joel E. Frader and Donna A. Caniano, *Research and Innovation in Surgery*, in Laurence B. McCullough et al., eds., *Surgical Ethics* 216, 223 (New York, Oxford University Press 1998). For a discussion of whether or not this practice should change, *see* Richard C. Cook et al., *A Debate on the Value and Necessity of Clinical Trials in Surgery*, 185 Am. J. Surg. 305 (2003).

42. *See, e.g.*, B. Fisher et al., *Five-Year Results of a Randomized Clinical Trial Comparing Total Mastectomy and Segmental Mastectomy with or without Radiation in the Treatment of Breast Cancer*, 312 New Engl. J. Med. 665 (1985).

43. Leonard A. Cobb et al., *An Evaluation of Internal-Mammary-Artery Ligation by a Double-Blind Technic*, 260 New Engl. J. Med. 1115 (1959).

44. In fact, the subjects do not appear to have even been told that they were participating in a study. That obviously affects the ethics, though not the utility of this study in showing the need for similar studies.

45. J. Bruce Moseley et al., *A Controlled Trial of Arthroscopic Surgery for Osteoarthritis of the Knee*, 347 New Engl. J. Med. 81 (2002).

46. Talbot, *The Placebo Prescription, supra* note 33, at 34.

47. For the views of critics of this practice, *see, e.g.*, Ruth Macklin, *The Ethical Problems with Sham Surgery in Clinical Research*, 341 New Engl. J. Med. 992 (1999); Peter A. Clark, *Placebo Surgery for Parkinson's Disease: Do the Benefits Outweigh the Risks?* 30 J. L. Med. Ethics 58 (2002); Charles Weijer, *I Need a Placebo Like a Hole in the Head*, 30 J. L. Med. Ethics 69 (2002). Arguing in favor of sham surgery are Thomas B. Freeman et al., *Use of Placebo Surgery in Controlled Trials of a Cellular-Based Therapy for Parkinson's Disease*, 341 New Engl.

J. Med. 988; G. R. Gillett, *Unnecessary Holes in the Head*, 23(6) IRB 1 (2001); and Sam Horng and Franklin G. Miller, *Is Placebo Surgery Unethical?* 347 New Engl. J. Med. 137 (2002).

48. *See, e.g.,* Laura Johannes, *First Cut: Sham Surgery Is Used to Test Effectiveness of Novel Operations*, Wall Street Journal A1, December 11, 1998.

49. Curt R. Freed et al., *Transplantation of Embryonic Dopamine Neurons for Severe Parkinson's Disease*, 344 New Engl. J. Med. 710 (2001).

50. Gina Kolata, *Parkinson's Research Is Set Back by Failure of Fetal Cell Implants*, New York Times A1, March 8, 2001.

Chapter 7

1. Henry K. Beecher, *Ethics and Clinical Research*, 274 New Engl. J. Med. 1354 (1966).

2. David J. Rothman, *Strangers at the Bedside: A History of How Law and Bioethics Transformed Medical Decision Making* 75–76 (New York, BasicBooks 1991).

3. Beecher, *supra* note 1, at 1360.

4. In addition to the specific studies mentioned in the following text, *see also* E. T. Pound, *Federal Rules for Research on People Often Fail*, USA Today 1-A, February 26, 2001; Michael D. Lemonick and Andrew Goldstein, *At Your Own Risk*, Time 46–55, April 22, 2002.

5. There were claims that Jesse and his parents were not told about the fact that Dr. James Wilson, chief investigator and the head of the University of Pennsylvania's gene therapy research program, owned millions of dollars of stock in a company that had the right to license therapies that came out of the study, that monkeys that had been given the compound had become ill or died, and that previous subjects in the study had suffered serious medical problems from the compound. D. Nelson and R. Weiss, *Hasty Decisions in the Race to a Cure? Gene Therapy Study Proceeded Despite Safety, Ethics Concerns*, Washington Post A1, November 21, 1999.

6. There were claims that she was not told that she was being given an experimental form of hexamethonium (an inhaled version, as compared to the oral form) that was not approved by the FDA, that this drug was not currently being used for any medical uses and had lost its approval back in 1972, and that a subject who had previously received the inhaled version had experienced significant lung injury. Robert Steinbrook, *Protecting Research Subjects: The Crisis at Johns Hopkins*, 346 New Engl. J. Med. 716 (2002); C. Cassel et al., Report of Johns Hopkins University External Review Committee, August 8, 2001.

7. Grimes v. Kennedy Krieger Institute, Inc., 782 A.2d 807 (Md. 2001).

8. Diaz v. Hillsborough County Hospital Authority, 2000 U.S. Dist. LEXIS 14061 (M.D. Fla.). *See also* Research Roundtable, *The "USF Case," available at* www.researchroundtable.com/USFcase.htm (providing additional details about the lawsuit resulting from this research study involving pregnant women).

9. Subjects were allegedly wrongly told that the vaccine had been curing up to two-thirds of the people it had been given to. Lemonick and Goldstein, *supra* note 4 at 46; complaint in Robertson v. McGee, *available at* www.sskrplaw.com/gene/robertson/complaint-new.html; Omer Gillham, *Cancer Study Case Alive*, Tulsa World A17, March 16, 2003.

10. S. G. Stolberg, *On Medicine's Frontier: The Last Journey of James Quinn*, New York Times D1, October 8, 2002; M. Lasalandra, *Suit May Jeopardize FDA OK for Abiomed*, Boston Herald 3, October 17, 2002.

11. The *Seattle Times*, having reviewed more than 10,000 pages of documents, in 2001 published an award-winning series of articles about leukemia and breast cancer studies

conducted at the Fred Hutchinson Cancer Research Center. Several of the subjects brought lawsuits against "the Hutch," including informed consent claims such as failure to let them know about the high death rates suffered by subjects in the earlier (though somewhat different) versions of the studies. With regard to another claim, a judge didn't even bother to let the issue go to a jury, finding on his own that subjects would not have enrolled in the study had they been given adequate information: the subjects had not been told that a manufacturer would not be able to supply a crucial drug designed to protect them from the toxic effects of other treatments given during the research study. D. Wilson and D. Health, *The Blood-Cancer Experiment*, Seattle Times A1, March 11, 2001; Berman v. Fred Hutchinson Cancer Research Center, No. C01–0727L (BJR) (W.D. Wash. August 8, 2002); Robert M. Nelson, *Protocol 126 and "The Hutch,"* 23(3) IRB 14 (2001).

12. The Nuremberg Code, which forms the genesis of most modern thinking about informed consent, lays down well the conceptual requirements, although it too gives few specifics. It discusses informed consent as the very first item of its ten requirements: "The voluntary consent of the human subject is absolutely essential." And that requirement—unlike any of the other nine—was followed by an additional paragraph spelling out in detail what this means:

> This means that the person involved should have legal capacity to give consent; should be so situated as to be able to exercise free power of choice, without the intervention of any element of force, fraud, deceit, duress, over-reaching, or other ulterior form of constraint or coercion; and should have sufficient knowledge and comprehension of the elements of the subject matter involved as to enable him to make an understanding and enlightened decision. This latter element requires that before the acceptance of an affirmative decision by the experimental subject there should be made known to him the nature, duration and purpose of the experiment; the method and means by which it is to be conducted; all inconveniences and hazards reasonably to be expected; and the effects upon his health or person which may possibly come from his participation in the experiment.

Trials of War Criminals before the Nuernberg Military Tribunals under Control Council Law No. 10 (1949), *available at* www.hhs.gov/ohrp/references/nurcode.htm.

13. *See* the cases discussed in footnote 10 of chapter 5. One of the more interesting related cases in this area is United States v. Stanley, 483 U.S. 669, 671 (1987). This involved the saga of Army master sergeant James B. Stanley, who apparently was given LSD as part of an army study in 1958 without his knowing it. He didn't learn that he was in the study until the Army sent him a follow-up letter seventeen years later, trying to find out what happened to the participants. He then sued the federal government, attributing many unfortunate events in his life—hallucinations, memory loss, periods of incoherence, episodes when he beat his wife and the resulting divorce—to having gotten the LSD. The U.S. Supreme Court concluded he had no right to sue, based on long-standing doctrines that make it hard for soldiers to sue the military. Justices Brennan and O'Connor dissented, noting the irony that the United States, which played a major role in creating the Nuremberg Code, effectively provided no remedy against the sorts of abuses that the Code was designed to protect against.

14. For other discussions of this issue, *see, e.g.,* George J. Annas et al., *Informed Consent to Human Experimentation: The Subject's Dilemma* (Cambridge, Mass., Ballinger 1977); Jessica W. Berg et al., *Informed Consent: Legal Theory and Clinical Practice* 249–303 (2d. ed. New York, Oxford University Press 2001); Richard W. Garnett, *Why Informed Consent? Human Experimentation and the Ethics of Autonomy*, 36 Catholic L. Rev. 455 (1996); Jay Katz, *Human*

Experimentation and Human Rights, 38 St. Louis L. J. 7 (1993); Jesse Goldner, *An Overview of Legal Controls on Human Experimentation and the Regulatory Implications of Taking Professor Katz Seriously*, 38 St. Louis L. J. 63 (1993); Karine Morin, *The Standard of Disclosure in Human Subject Experimentation*, 19 J. Legal Med. 157 (1998); Richard Delgado and Helen Leskovac, *Informed Consent in Human Experimentation: Bridging the Gap between Ethical Thought and Current Practice*, 34 UCLA L. Rev. 67 (1986); Alexander Morgan Capron, *Informed Consent in Catastrophic Disease Research and Treatment*, 123 U. Pa. L. Rev. 340 (1974); Len Doyal and Jeffrey S. Tobias, *Informed Consent in Medical Research* 266 (London, BMJ 2001) (emphasizing British law).

15. For discussions of the early cases in this area, *see, e.g.*, Annas et al., *supra* note 14 at 1–25; Morin, *supra* note 14 at 196–202.

16. There are a number of excellent accounts of the history of informed consent to medical care. *See, e.g.*, Ruth R. Faden et al., *A History and Theory of Informed Consent* 114–50 (New York, Oxford University Press 1986); Jay Katz, *The Silent World of Doctor and Patient* 48–84 (New York, Free Press 1984); Jay Katz, *Informed Consent: Must It Remain a Fairy Tale?* 10 J. Contemp. Health L. Policy 69 (1994); Berg et al., *supra* note 14 at 41–75.

17. Schloendorff v. New York Hospital, 105 N.E. 92 (1914). For an interesting discussion of why this case may be of even less historical importance than suggested in the text, see Paul A. Lombardo, *Phantom Tumors and Hysterical Women: Revising Our View of the Schloendorff Case*, 33 J. L. Med. & Ethics 791 (2005).

18. Salgo v. Leland Stanford Jr. University Board of Trustees, 317 P.2d 170 (Cal. Ct. App. 1957).

19. Another difference between negligence and battery lawsuits is that it is easier to get punitive damages in a battery action. On the other hand, in many states a battery requires an unwanted "touching" of the patient's body, whereas if a doctor's failure to get adequate informed consent leads the patient to decline a treatment (because, for example, the patient might not have realized the serious consequences of not choosing to be treated), a lawsuit might successfully be brought under negligence law even though it might have failed as a battery action. Ultimately, it probably is of lesser consequence whether the legal system viewed these actions as being brought under negligence as opposed to battery law; what mattered most was that a duty to disclose an appropriate amount of information was ultimately imposed by the law. In fact, in Pennsylvania, battery law still governs failure to get informed consent that would be treated as a negligence case in other states. *See, e.g.*, Berg et al., *supra* note 14 at 134–36.

20. Canterbury v. Spence, 464 F.2d 772 (D.C. 1969).

21. For a summary of the rules followed in every state, *see* the appendix to Ketchup v. Howard, 543 S.E. 2d 371, 381 (Ga. Ct. App. 2000).

22. Some minimal guidance comes from cases involving providing nonstandard care outside of research, where it is clear that a doctor must, at the least, disclose that the care is nonstandard. *See, e.g.*, Estrada v. Jaques, 321 S.E. 2d 240 (N.C. App. 1984); Fiorentino v. Wenger, 272 N.Y.S. 2d 557 (N.Y. App. Div. 1966) (surgeon used a "gruesome" procedure only he was employing, known as "spinal jack" operation, to treat the moderate spinal curvature of a child), *rev'd on other grounds*, 227 N.E. 2d 296 (N.Y. 1967); Ahern v. Veterans Administration, 537 F.2d 1098, 1102 (10th Cir. 1976) (rectal cancer was treated with a dose of radiation that was several times greater than that used in standard care).

A somewhat differing view, which would certainly seem wrong under current law, comes from the litigation against Dr. Denton Cooley following the first artificial heart transplant in 1969. The court applied the general rules used in Texas for informed consent to medical care, holding that Dr. Cooley only had to disclose the information that other doctors would disclose. It appears to have rejected the suggestion in the literature from that period that informed consent must be obtained "more strictly" in cases where "a novel or radical medical procedure" is employed. Karp v. Cooley, 493 F.2d 408, 419–22, 423–24 (5th Cir. 1974). For discussion of this case, *see, e.g.,* Annas et al., *supra* note 14 at 11–15; Morin, *supra* note 14 at 198–99.

A rare case involving a research subject where the court discusses the content of informed consent is Gaston v. Hunter, 588 P.2d 326 (Ariz. Ct. App. 1978). The plaintiff had participated in a research study in which the experimental drug chymopapin had been injection into her back to treat a ruptured disk. Regarding informed consent, the court observed that "when a physician contemplates a novel or investigational procedure he must inform his patient of the novel or investigational nature of the procedure." *Id.* at 351. Given that the court failed to indicate it was aware of the difference between a patient getting a new treatment and a subject participating in a research trial, the comments about informed consent were likely intended to relate to the more common, former situation. *See also* Daum v. Spinecare Medical Group, Inc., 61 Cal. Rptr. 2d 260 (Cal. Ct. App. 1997) (noting that California statutes and federal regulations required that the subject be told about experimental status of a spinal fixation device).

The great bulk of the few cases relating to informed consent to participate in a research study involve situations where the subjects were never even told they were participating in research. The court opinions generally accept that this is wrong, without providing much discussion about the nature of informed consent to research. *See, e.g.,* Anderson v. George H. Lanier Memorial Hospital, 982 F.2d 1513 (11th Cir. 1993); Barrett v. United States, 689 F.2d 324 (2d Cir. 1982); Begay v. United States, 768 F.2d 1059 (9th Cir. 1985); Blanton v. United States, 428 F. Supp. 360 (D.D.C. 1977); Central Intelligence Agency v. Sims, 105 S. Ct. 1881 (1985); *In re* Cincinnati Radiation Litigation, 874 F. Supp. 796 (S.D. Ohio 1995); Clay v. Martin, 509 F.2d 109 (2d Cir. 1975); Craft v. Vanderbilt University, 18 F. Supp. 2d 786 (M.D. Tenn. 1998); Hyman v. Jewish Chronic Disease Hospital, 206 N.E. 2d 338 (N.Y. 1965); Mackey v. Procunier, 477 F.2d 877 (9th Cir. 1973); Mink v. University of Chicago, 460 F. Supp. 713 (N.D. Ill. 1978); White v. Paulsen, 997 F. Supp. 1380 (E.D. Wash. 1998).

Although the federal government would likely in at least some circumstances have the authority to impose uniform federal standards that would override stricter disclosure and substantive rules embodied in state tort law, it does not appear to have exercised that authority with regard to the types of situations discussed in this book. This issue has arisen most explicitly in the context of medical devices. *See, e.g.,* Medtronic, Inc. v. Lohr, 518 U.S. 470 (1996) (interpreting preemption provisions of the Medical Device Amendments of 1976); Robert Pear, *In a Shift, Bush Moves to Block Medical Suits*, New York Times A1, July 25, 2004 (noting attempts of the G. W. Bush administration to change prior rules by litigation).

23. *See, e.g.,* Department of Health, Education and Welfare, Report of the National Commission for the Protection of Human Subjects of Biomedical and Behavioral Research, The Belmont Report: Ethical Principles and Guidelines for the Protection of Human Subjects of Research (1979), *available at* www.hhs.gov/ohrp/humansubjects/guidance/belmont .htm (proposing "reasonable volunteer" standard under which "extent and nature of information [disclosed] should be such that persons, knowing that the procedure is neither necessary for their care nor perhaps fully understood, can decide whether they wish to participate in the furthering of knowledge"); Ernest D. Prentice and Bruce G. Gordon, Institutional Review Board Assessment of Risks and Benefits Associated with Research, National Bioethics Advisory Commission, Ethical and Policy Issues in Research Involving Human Participants, Vol. 2, at L3 (Bethesda 2001) (discussing the reasonable volunteer standard).

24. It would be far more appropriate for the regulations to clearly apply a uniform national standard to all studies, one based on the reasonable person standard.

25. In one of the lawsuits against the Fred Hutchinson Cancer Research Center, mentioned at the beginning of this chapter, the court issued an order in which it did apply the statutory informed consent standards for health care in determining the appropriate disclosure for getting informed consent to participate in research. Berman v. Fred Hutchinson Cancer Research Center, No. C01–0727L (BJR), August 8, 2002 (order granting plaintiff's motion for partial summary judgment on informed consent claim). In that instance, however, it does not appear that the court gave any thought to whether the clinical standard should apply to the research setting. It failed to discuss this issue.

26. Burton v. Brooklyn Doctors Hospital, 452 N.Y.S. 2d 875 (N.Y. App. Div. 1982).

27. The likelihood that the research aspects of the case played an important role in the court's decision is suggested by another case from the New York appellate courts that was decided four years after Daniel won his lawsuit, Kuncio v. Millard Fillmore Hospital, 1986 N.Y. App. Div. LEXIS 48931. The children in that lawsuit also lost vision as a result of treatment with high oxygen, but they were not participating in a research study. Their parents were never informed about the controversy about oxygen use, yet the appellate court upheld a jury verdict in favor of the hospital. It is difficult to rationalize this outcome and the Burton case result unless it is due to Daniel Burton's having been in a research study.

28. *See, e.g.,* Annas et al., *supra* note 14 at 27–61; Berg et al., *supra* note 14 at 279–99; Delgado and Leskovac, *supra* note 14. For a contrary view, *see* Lars Noah, *Informed Consent and the Elusive Dichotomy between Standard and Experimental Therapy,* 28 Am. J. L. Med. 361 (2002).

29. Even one of the leading cases, Estrada v. Jaques (*supra* note 22), in spite of incorrectly characterizing what happened in that case as research (as opposed to merely providing nonstandard care), recognized this point: "The psychology of the doctor–patient relationship, and the rewards, financial and professional, attendant upon recognition of experimental success, increase the potential for abuse and strengthen the rationale for uniform disclosure."

30. In certain limited situations, discussed elsewhere in this book, there may be good reasons for not getting informed consent. For a proposal to expand that category beyond its current limits, *see* Robert D. Truog et al., *Is Informed Consent Always Necessary for Randomized, Controlled Trials?* 340 New Engl. J. Med. 804 (1999).

Chapter 8

1. This view is well stated by Dr. Jeffrey Drazen, editor-in-chief of the *New England Journal of Medicine.* In describing his editorial board's decision to not publish an article that highlighted defects in consent forms, he noted that even if the forms are defective, there may not be a need to remedy this problem: "We agree that how informed consent is conducted is critical to clinical research, but the process of informed consent includes much more than the reading of a form. The investigator interacts with the potential subject to be sure that he or she understands the nature of the risks and benefits involved." Letter to Menikoff, dated January 8, 2003. *See, e.g.,* American Society of Clinical Oncology, *Policy Statement: Oversight of Clinical Research,* 21 J Clin. Oncol. 2377, 2383 (2003) ("Review Boards should place primary review and oversight on the informed consent process, not chiefly on the informed consent document").

2. The major role of contract law in this realm is deciding when a patient and doctor have agreed to enter into a doctor–patient relationship. *See, e.g.,* William J. Curran et al., *Health Care Law and Ethics* 117–19 (5th ed., New York, Apsen Law and Business 1998).

3. Hawkins v. McGee, 146 A. 641 (N.H. 1929).

4. John Jay Osborn, Jr., *The Paper Chase* 6–9 (Boston, Houghton Mifflin 1971).

5. This statement needs to be somewhat modified given an additional fact of this case: the doctor's "guarantee" of a particular result—that the hand would be nonhairy—provides a separate reason for possible liability under contract law principles. In other words, even if the doctor had agreed to provide only the same standard care that other doctors were providing, his promise of a particular result could be viewed as part of the agreement between him and the patient and could be enforceable as part of a binding contract. Of course, in most everyday circumstances, doctors are savvy enough to know never to promise (and thus enter a binding contract to provide) a particular outcome, regardless of whether they are providing standard or nonstandard care. And even if a doctor is foolish enough to make such a promise, courts are somewhat reluctant to enforce such promises as binding contract terms, often determining that a reasonable patient should have understood that the doctor was just being optimistic and was not really guaranteeing a particular result.

6. For recent cases finding the applicability of contract law in determining that researchers can be held to the promises they make in consent forms, as if those forms created legally binding contracts, *see* Grimes v. Kennedy Krieger Institute, Inc., 782 A.2d 807, 843–44 (Md. 2001) (finding that researchers may have contractual duties to subjects and their parents as a result of promises made in the consent form: "If consent agreements contain such provisions [then] . . . mutual assent, offer, acceptance, and consideration existed, all of which created contractual relationships imposing duties by reason of the consent agreement themselves."); and Dahl v. HEM Pharmaceuticals, 7 F.3d 1399 (9th Cir. 1993), *subsequently appealed after remand and summary judgment and again affirmed*, 1996 U.S. App. LEXIS 2549, 5–6 (9th Cir. 1996) (finding that subjects in a study were contractually entitled to get 12 months of an experimental drug not yet approved by the FDA, based on the language in the consent form: "[T]he starting point for any contractual obligation is the . . . consent form.").

7. Similarly, if the patient is to get nonstandard care, outside of a research study, the consent form becomes equally important, since again there would otherwise be no documentation of what the patient and doctor had agreed to. Thus, a doctor who deviates from standard care, and provides what in chapter 3 we described as nonstandard care, is well advised to prepare a consent form that describes in detail what will be done to the patient.

8. 45 CFR § 46.116(a)(1)–(4). Other items that must be included are

(5) a statement describing the extent, if any, to which confidentiality of records identifying the subject will be maintained;

(6) for research involving more than minimal risk, an explanation as to whether any compensation and an explanation as to whether any medical treatments are available if injury occurs and, if so, what they consist of, or where further information may be obtained;

(7) an explanation of whom to contact for answers to pertinent questions about the research and research subjects' rights, and whom to contact in the event of a research-related injury to the subject; and

(8) a statement that participation is voluntary, refusal to participate will involve no penalty or loss of benefits to which the subject is otherwise entitled, and the subject may discontinue participation at any time without penalty or loss of benefits to which the subject is otherwise entitled.

45 CFR § 46.116(a)(5)–(8). In addition, the following information must be given to the subject "when appropriate":

(1) a statement that the particular treatment or procedure may involve risks to the subject (or to the embryo or fetus, if the subject is or may become pregnant) which are currently unforeseeable;

(2) anticipated circumstances under which the subject's participation may be terminated by the investigator without regard to the subject's consent;

(3) any additional costs to the subject that may result from participation in the research;

(4) the consequences of a subject's decision to withdraw from the research and procedures for orderly termination of participation by the subject;

(5) a statement that significant new findings developed during the course of the research which may relate to the subject's willingness to continue participation will be provided to the subject; and

(6) the approximate number of subjects involved in the study.

45 CFR § 46.116(b).

9. National Cancer Institute (NCI), *Simplification of Informed Consent Documents: Recommendations* (2004), *available at* www.cancer.gov/clinicaltrials/understanding/simplification-of-informed-consent-docs/page2.

10. *See, e.g.,* Paul S. Appelbaum, *Examining the Ethics of Human Subjects Research,* 6 Kennedy Inst. Ethics J. 283, 285–86 (1996).

11. *See, e.g., id.* at 284. *See also* C. A. Coyne et al., *Randomized, Controlled Trial of an Easy-to-Read Informed Consent Statement for Clinical Trial Participation: A Study of the Eastern Cooperative Oncology Group,* 21 J. Clin. Oncol. 836 (2003); James Flory and Ezekiel Emanuel, *Interventions to Improve Research Participants' Understanding in Informed Consent for Research: A Systematic Review,* 292 JAMA 1593 (2004).

12. For example, in chapter 14 we discuss the debate about a study involving testing a diluted form of smallpox vaccine in children. Imagine that the following (correct) statement was prominently featured, in large red print, on the front page of the consent form: "Experts reviewing this study have almost unanimously concluded that the risks to your child's health from being in the study exceed any possible benefit to your child." Surely such a statement would have played a major role in whether or not some parents enrolled their children in the study.

13. Alan Meisel and Mark Kuczewski, *Legal and Ethical Myths about Informed Consent,* 156 Arch. Int. Med. 2521, 2522–23 (1996).

14. Since it is produced by the federal government, this form cannot be copyrighted. Thus, we can reprint it without getting anyone's permission. Although the NCI templates have been slightly revised since 1998, a revised sample consent form has not yet been provided, so we are reprinting the most up-to-date version that exists.

15. Some of the subjects will also be getting an additional drug, tamoxifen.

16. One of the "basic elements of informed consent" is "a statement that the study involves research." 45 CFR § 46.116(a)(1). The regulations do not include any specific requirement that the prospective subject be told about how being in a research study differs from being a patient.

17. While we cannot prove to you the truth of this claim, which reflects our own experience, it nonetheless is true that current regulations do not require this information to be provided to subjects. *See also* Jesse A. Goldner, *An Overview of Legal Controls on Human Experimentation and the Regulatory Implications of Taking Professor Katz Seriously,* 38 St. Louis U. L. J. 63, 121 (1993) ("currently there is no requirement that [the definition of research] be communicated and explained to the potential subject").

Apart from what common sense tells us—that this is an extremely subtle and complicated distinction, which judges have regularly confused and which we have had to spend
many pages in this book attempting to clarify—there is also empirical evidence showing that
people are indeed confused about these categories. *See, e.g.*, Advisory Committee on Human Radiation Experiments, Final Report 734–38 (1995), *available at* tis.eh.doe.gov/ohre/
roadmap/achre/index.html.

18. *See, e.g.*, Jay Katz, *"Ethics and Clinical Research" Revisited: A Tribute to Henry K. Beecher*,
Hastings Center Rep. 23(5) 31, 36 (1993) ("This vital distinction [between research and
therapy] remains blurred . . . when subjects are insufficiently apprised that attention to their
individual needs is compromised by the need to comply with the rigid and impersonal
methodology of a research protocol").

19. An interesting example of the consequences of "stopping" rules is the recent controversy over the drug letrozole. A large study had taken place to see if letrozole was better than
placebo when given to breast cancer survivors who had already completed five years of treatment with tamoxifen. Even though it was planned that the study would continue for five
years, it was ended early—after only two and a half years—when interim analysis showed a
statistically significant reduction in the rate of breast cancer recurrence in the women who
were taking letrozole. This stopping rule had been written into the study when it had been
initially designed, so it did not appear that the researchers had any option not to stop the
study. Nonetheless, these events generated a great deal of criticism, since a reduction in the
rate of cancer recurrence might well not result in any actual increase in how long women
survived. Even the *New York Times* editorialized that it would have been better if the study
did not have the early stopping rule and had continued. In effect, that august newspaper
was acknowledging that although the participants in the study would have wanted to know
about the information regarding recurrence rates, it would have been appropriate to deny
them that information—and perhaps lead to the "earlier" deaths of some of the participants—so that better information could be learned that would be of greater benefit to women
in general. *See, e.g., Editorial, Halting a Breast Cancer Trial*, New York Times, sec. 4 at 10,
October 12, 2003; Richard A. Friedman, *Long-term Questions Linger in Halted Breast Cancer
Trial*, New York Times F5, October 21, 2003; Stephen A. Cannistra, *The Ethics of Early Stopping Rules: Who Is Protecting Whom?* 22 J. Clin. Oncol. 1542 (2004).

20. This example is taken from Robert J. Wells et al., *Ethical Issues Arising When Interim Data
in Clinical Trials Is Restricted to Independent Data Monitoring Committees*, 22(1) IRB 7 (2000).

21. In fact, to end the study early, usually a level of statistical significance higher than the
0.05 level has to be attained, such as a p-value less than 0.01 or 0.02. *Id.*

22. The 8,000 to 1 odds are obtained by comparing the likelihood that B is proven to be
better than A (2 in 100,000) to the likelihood that A is proven to be better than B (1 in 6).

23. Note that even if the new drug was not available outside of the study, there can still
be problems from revealing interim results. Imagine, *e.g.*, that the midstudy results had demonstrated that the old drug was more effective at the $p = 0.10$ level; again, we would have
people dropping out of the study (to get the old drug outside of the study) and not learn the
true relationship between the two drugs.

24. *See, e.g.*, Robert J. Levine, *Ethics and Regulation of Clinical Research* 201 (2d ed. New
Haven: Yale University Press 1986) ("I suggest that we should go on to say [to someone considering enrolling in the study] that with time there will be increasing clarity that, *e.g.*, A is
superior to B. This superiority could manifest as a decreased probability of serious harms
or an increased probability of benefits. However, for good reasons, we have designed the
[study] so that neither the investigator nor the subject will be aware of this disparity until
such time as the arbitrarily preselected criteria of significance are achieved. Thus, what I

would ask the subject to consent to is an acceptance of the standards of proof agreed upon within the community of professionals"); Arthur S. Slutsky and James V. Lavery, *Data Safety and Monitoring Boards*, 350 New Engl. J. Med 1143 (2004).

25. This consent form is one of the sample consent forms included in the pocket at the back of the National Cancer Institute's 1998 report, *Recommendations for the Development of Informed Consent Documents in Cancer Trials.* That report was produced by the Comprehensive Working Group on Informed Consent in Cancer Clinical Trials.

Chapter 9

1. A leading medical ethics scholar recently wrote an article about how hard it was, when he was himself a subject in a study, to get someone to show him a copy of the protocol for the study, which usually contains far more information than the consent form. Robert M. Veatch, *The Right of Subjects to See the Protocol*, 24(5) IRB 6 (2002).

2. Laurie Tarkan, *A Debate on Radiation in Breast Cancer*, New York Times D1, February 24, 2004.

3. Emphasis added.

4. Emphasis added.

5. National Cancer Institute (NCI), Simplification of Informed Consent Documents: Templates, *available at* www.cancer.gov/clinicaltrials/understanding/simplification-of-informed-consent-docs/page3.

6. Office for Human Research Protections, Informed Consent Checklist based on 45 CFR § 46.116, *available at* www.hhs.gov/ohrp/humansubjects/assurance/consentckls.htm.

7. NCI, *supra* note 5.

8. *See, e.g.*, Nancy M. P. King, *Defining and Describing Benefit Appropriately in Clinical Trials*, 28 J. L. Med. Ethics 332 (2000).

9. *See, e.g.*, Sam Horng, *Descriptions of Benefits and Risks in Consent Forms for Phase I Oncology Trials*, 347 New Engl. J. Med. 2134 (2002).

10. *See, e.g.*, Christopher K. Daugherty et al., *Quantitative Analysis of Ethical Issues in Phase I Trials: A Survey Interview Study of 144 Advanced Cancer Patients*, 22(3) IRB 6 (2000).

11. Ed Susman, *Phase I Trials: Looking behind the Different Perceptions of Patients and Physicians*, Oncology Times 30, August 2002. For a recent overview of how the risks of participation in phase I cancer studies have decreased over a several-year period—but not necessarily resulting in a favorable relationship of risks to benefits—*see* Thomas G. Roberts, Jr., et al., *Trends in Risks and Benefits to Patients with Cancer Participating in Phase 1 Clinical Trials*, 292 JAMA 2130 (2004); Eric X. Chen and Ian F. Tannock, *Risks and Benefits of Phase 1 Clinical Trials Evaluating New Anticancer Agents: A Case for More Innovation*, 292 JAMA 2150 (2004) (editorial commenting on Roberts article, pointing out possible errors in its analysis, and noting that "assessment of benefit to patients from participation in phase 1 trials is difficult").

12. In Manish Agrawal and Ezekiel J. Emanuel, *Ethics of Phase I Oncology Studies: Reexamining the Arguments and Data,* 290 JAMA 1075 (2003), the authors mention only the use of imatinib mesylate to treat chronic myeloid leukemia as a recent study involving substantial benefits to subjects.

13. Horng, *supra* note 9. This was followed nine months later by a similar piece from members of that NIH branch that was also designated as a "special" article. That second article reached the same conclusion and was published in *JAMA*, the other leading U.S. medical journal. *See* Agrawal and Emanuel, *supra* note 12.

The most recent review of phase I clinical trials shows that the classic phase I trial has not had any recent increases in the response rate. However, studies whose designs are not "pure" phase I format do appear to have greater benefits to subjects than previously believed. Elizabeth Horstmann et al, *Risks and Benefits of Phase I Oncology Trials, 1991 through 2002*, 352 New Engl. J. Med. 895 (2005).

14. In response to a letter to the editor about this study from one of us (Menikoff), the authors of the *New England Journal of Medicine* article indicated that they in fact viewed the "benefit is not guaranteed" language as one of the better types of disclosure, presenting it as a "good example." Christine Grady et al., *Consent Forms for Oncology Trials*, 348 New Engl. J. Med. 1496, 1497 (2003). In the subsequent *JAMA* article, members of the NIH group admitted that "the majority of participants are treated at doses that cannot produce responses in human tumors," but they again failed to provide much support for why ethics did not require telling prospective subjects the specific fact that they are unlikely to benefit. Their main argument appeared to be that since there are rare instances in which a phase I study may prove highly beneficial to most participants (they gave only one example), it is somehow inappropriate to tell subjects a piece of information that they admit is truthful—that, to use their own words, "participants face . . . little chance of benefits." Agrawal and Emanuel, *supra* note 12 at 1076, 1078.

15. Matthew Miller, *Phase I Cancer Trials: A Collusion of Misunderstanding*, 30(4) Hastings Center Rep. 34 (2000); Matthew Miller, *Phase I Oncology Trials*, in Robert Amdur and Elizabeth Bankert, *Institutional Review Board: Management and Function* 465 (Boston, Jones and Bartlett 2002). Here is what a "dream team" of some of this nation's experts on research ethics had to say about this issue:

> Ample evidence, both direct and indirect, indicates that many research subjects in these trials do not fully appreciate that they are unlikely to benefit from participation. Admittedly, many of these patients would consent to participate even knowing of the remote chance of benefit, but the research community is not thereby relieved of the obligation to take all reasonable measures to promote their understanding.
>
> The language of many consent forms encourages an illusion of therapeutic benefit, whether intentionally or not. For example, many phase I trial consent forms refer to "treatments" that will be given to subjects.
>
> All phase I consent forms should include the phrase, prominently displayed in bold type on the first page, "This medical research project is not expected to benefit you. . . .

Jonathan D. Moreno et al., *Updating Protections for Human Subjects Involved in Research*, 280 JAMA 1951 (1998).

16. The *Belmont Report*, which laid the foundation for the federal regulations governing most research in this country, indicated that subjects must be "given the opportunity to choose what shall or shall not happen to them." Department of Health, Education and Welfare, Report of the National Commission for the Protection of Human Subjects of Biomedical and Behavioral Research, The Belmont Report: Ethical Principles and Guidelines for the Protection of Human Subjects of Research (1979), *available at* www.hhs.gov/ohrp/humansubjects/guidance/belmont.htm. *See also* Nuremberg Code, Trials of War Criminals before the Nuernberg Military Tribunals under Control Council Law No. 10 (1949) (a person must "be able to exercise free power of choice . . . and should have sufficient knowledge and comprehension of the elements of the subject matter involved as to enable him *to make an understanding and enlightened decision*") (emphasis added).

17. S. J. L. Edwards et al., *Ethical Issues in the Design and Conduct of Randomized Control Trials*, 2(15) Health Technol. Assess. 37 (1998).

18. *See, e.g.*, Sarah J. L. Edwards et al., *The Ethics of Randomised Controlled Trials from the Perspectives of Patients, the Public, and Healthcare Professionals*, 317 Br. Med. J. 1209 (1998). *See also* the discussion of therapeutic misconception at text at notes 18 and 19 in chapter 2.

19. *See, e.g.*, Franklin G. Miller and Donald L. Rosenstein, *The Therapeutic Orientation to Clinical Trials*, 348 New Engl. J. Med. 1383, 1383 (2003); Robert J. Levine, *Clinical Trials and Physicians as Double Agents*, 65 Yale J. Biol. Med. 65 (1992).

20. Rebecca Dresser, *The Ubiquity and Utility of the Therapeutic Misconception*, 19 Soc. Phil. Policy 271, 291 (2002).

Chapter 10

1. This discussion of the development of high-dose chemotherapy with autologous bone marrow transplantation as a treatment for breast cancer is largely taken from the excellent article by Gina Kolata and Kurt Eichenwald, *Hope for Sale: Business Thrives on Unproven Care, Leaving Science Behind*, New York Times A1, October 3, 1999.

2. *Id.*

3. Roseberry v. Blue Cross and Blue Shield, 821 F. Supp. 1313, 1318 (D. Nebr. 1992).

4. Arrington v. Group Hospitalization and Medical Services, Inc., 806 F. Supp. 287, 291 (D.D.C. 1999).

5. Harris v. Mutual of Omaha Companies, 1992 U.S. Dist. LEXIS 21393 (S.D. Ind. 1992).

6. Fuja v. Benefit Trust Life Insurance Company, 809 F. Supp. 1333 (N.D. Ill. 1992). This decision was reversed on appeal, 18 F.3d 1405 (7th Cir. 1994).

7. Kim Barker and Carol M. Ostrom, *Experimental Cures Mean Tough Choices for Health Insurers*, Seattle Times, March 2, 1999.

8. Kolata and Eichenwald, *supra* note 1. For example, the Cleveland Clinic, one of this nation's leading research institutions, was not able to enroll a single subject in spite of "monumental efforts."

9. Denise Grady, *Doubts Raised on a Breast Cancer Procedure*, New York Times A1, April 16, 1999.

10. Denise Grady, *Breast Cancer Researcher Admits Falsifying Data*, New York Times A9, February 5, 2000.

11. Edward A. Stadtmauer et al., *Conventional-Dose Chemotherapy Compared with High-Dose Chemotherapy Plus Autologous Hematopoietic Stem-Cell Transplantation for Metastatic Breast Cancer*, 342 New Engl. J. Med. 1069 (2000). For more recent studies of this form of treatment, *see* Sjoerd Rodenhuis et al., *High-Dose Chemotherapy with Hematopoietic Stem-Cell Rescue for High-Risk Breast Cancer*, 349 New Engl. J. Med. 7 (2003); Martin S. Tallman et al., *Conventional Adjuvant Chemotherapy with or without High-Dose Chemotherapy and Autologous Stem-Cell Transplantation in High-Risk Breast Cancer*, 349 New Engl. J. Med. 17 (2003); Gerald J. Elfenbein, *Stem-Cell Transplantation for High-Risk Breast Cancer*, 349 New Engl. J. Med. 80 (2003).

12. Marc E. Lippman, *High-Dose Chemotherapy Plus Autologous Bone Marrow Transplantation for Metatstatic Breast Cancer*, 342 New Engl. J. Med. 1119 (2000).

13. Tom Paulson, *Stem Cells "Saved My Life," Says Judge*, Seattle Post-Intelligencer G4, September 9, 1999.

14. The statement of facts is largely drawn from the Plaintiff's Brief in Opposition to Defendants' Joint Motion for Summary Judgment in *Stewart v. Cleveland Clinic Foundation*.

In evaluating the motion for summary judgment, the judge was required to assume that factual disputes would be resolved in favor of the plaintiff, and we make a similar assumption in the discussion in the text. We are not claiming that this statement of the facts represents the truth of what happened, although most of what we discuss in the text does not appear to involve statements that were disputed by the Cleveland Clinic.

15. It also went on to state, "When considered together with evidence from randomized trials of an apparent survival advantage for patients given simultaneous chemotherapy and radiation therapy . . . a significant role for chemotherapy appears to be emerging."

16. *See, e.g.,* United States v. Rutherford, 442 U.S. 544 (1979); Eli Lilly & Co. v. Commissioner, 84 T.C. 996 (1985), *affirmed in part and reversed in part,* 856 F.2d 855 (7th Cir. 1988); Richard A. Merrill, *The Architecture of Government Regulation of Medical Products,* 82 Va. L. Rev. 1753 (1996).

17. The issue of compassionate use was discussed in somewhat greater detail in chapter 2 (*see* text at note 16 of that chapter).

18. *See, e.g.,* FDA, *"Off-Label" and Investigational Use of Marketed Drugs, Biologics, and Medical Devices,* in Information Sheets: Guidance for Institutional Review Boards and Clinical Investigators, 1998 Update, *available at* http://www.fda.gov/oc/ohrt/irbs/offlabel.html; J. M. Beck and E. D. Azari, *FDA, Off-Label Use, and Informed Consent: Debunking Myths and Misconceptions,* 53 Food Drug L. J. 71 (1998). Although the FDA recognizes its lack of authority to control how physicians use drugs that are on the market, it has attempted to limit off-label use by restricting the ability of pharmaceutical companies to promote such uses. Off-label use is in a sense inconsistent with the spirit and intent of the underlying laws: a drug ends up being used even though there may not be adequate proof of its safety or efficacy. In recent years, federal courts have struck down the FDA's attempts to prevent the promotion of off-label uses, concluding that pharmaceutical manufacturers have a First Amendment right to publicize the results of studies about a drug, even if the studies would not meet the FDA's standards for demonstrating that the drug really is safe and effective for a new use. *See, e.g.,* Washington Legal Foundation v. Friedman, 13 F. Supp. 2d 51 (D.D.C. 1998); Andrew Pollack, *Talking Up a Drug for This (and That),* New York Times C1, April 27, 2003.

There is a possible issue that disclosing an off-label use in a consent form might be considered by the FDA to be an improper promotion of such a use. We are not aware that the FDA has ever taken such a position, nor do we think it would want to do so: telling a prospective subject information that other federal regulations require the subject be given is very different from "promoting" a drug.

19. *See, e.g.,* S. R. Salbu, *Off-Label Use, Prescription, and Marketing of FDA-Approved Drugs: An Assessment of Legislative and Regulatory Policy,* 51 Fla. L. Rev. 181 (1999); Alison Young and Chris Adams, *"Off-Label" Drugs Take Their Toll,* Miami Herald A1, November 2, 2003; Chris Adams and Alison Young, *Drug-Makers' Promotions Boost Off-Label Use by Doctors,* Miami Herald 12A, November 9, 2003; Chris Adams and Alison Young, *FDA Oversight of "Off-Label" Drug Use Wanes,* Miami Herald 24A, November 16, 2003.

20. We address this issue in chapter 13: for various reasons, drug companies have (until recent changes in the law) traditionally avoided testing most drugs on children, so these drugs were never specifically approved for use in children. Thus, use of even very well-known prescription drugs in children may be beyond the FDA-approved uses, constituting off-label use.

21. National Cancer Institute, Simplification of Informed Consent Documents: Recommendations, *available at* www.cancer.gov/clinicaltrials/understanding/simplification-of-informed-consent-docs/page2.

22. National Cancer Institute, Simplification of Informed Consent Documents: Templates, *available at* www.cancer.gov/clinicaltrials/understanding/simplification-of-informed-consent-docs/page3. The NCI subsequently revised the language quoted in the text to make the required disclosures even vaguer (and less helpful to subjects) than they used to be, so vague that the researchers are not even required to mention what the specific alternative treatments might be.

23. National Surgical Adjuvant Breast and Bowel Project, *available at* www.nsabp.pitt.edu/ STAR/Index.html.

24. This language is taken directly from the protocol for the study, which states, at page 45, that "a consent form that has been approved by the NCI and the FDA will be provided to each clinical center as a model for preparation of consent forms for individual IRB approval." When one of us (Menikoff) presented this issue at a meeting of the National Human Research Protections Advisory Committee (NHRPAC), quoting the protocol, Dr. David LePay, who is in charge of the branch of the FDA that deals with the ethics of human subjects testing, objected to this characterization: "There is no such thing as an FDA-approved consent form. FDA doesn't approve consent forms. In fact, the regulations don't even require the submission of consent forms to FDA as part of the review package. So, that to me is kind of a non-issue." Transcript of NHRPAC meeting, July 30, 2002, *available at* www .hhs.gov/ohrp/nhrpac/mtg07–02/0730NH1.txt. While Dr. LePay is technically correct, it is nonetheless the case that the FDA will usually see (and might demand to see) the draft of the consent form proposed to be used in a study, and various divisions of the FDA will often *require* that certain changes be made in the consent form. (E.g., they will often want the risks section to specify certain things.) Thus, it remains the case that the FDA commonly sees consent forms that never mention the possibility of getting a product outside of the study, and it apparently has never chosen to exercise its authority to ask for a modification of such consent form provisions.

25. Zeneca, Inc. v. Eli Lilly & Co., 1999 U.S. Dist. LEXIS 10852 (S.D. N.Y.).

26. Hanne Meijers-Heijboer et al., *Breast Cancer after Prophylactic Bilateral Mastectomy in Women with a BRCA1 or BRCA2 Mutation*, 345 New Engl. J. Med. 159 (2001).

27. Steven R. Cummings et al., *The Effect of Raloxifene on Risk of Breast Cancer in Postmenopausal Women: Results from the MORE Randomized Trial*, 281 JAMA 2189 (1999).

28. Adele L. Franks and Karen K. Steinberg, *Encouraging News from the SERM Frontier*, 281 JAMA 2243 (1999).

29. 45 CFR § 46.116(a)(4).

30. J. E. Brody, *Round 3 in Cancer Battle: A 5–Year Drug Regimen*, New York Times F7, May 11, 1999.

31. Lippman, *supra* note 12. An excellent example of how ingrained this attitude can be among physicians is a recent *JAMA* article, where a group of Canadian physicians described how the use of a particular treatment by doctors outside of research studies increased during the time it was being evaluated in randomized clinical trials. William F. Clark et al., *Effect of Awareness of a Randomized Controlled Trial on Use of Experimental Therapy*, 290 JAMA 1351 (2003). The treatment was apheresis, which involves passing a person's blood through a machine that removes certain portions of it that are felt to possibly play a role in causing an illness. The authors of the article described this phenomenon as doctors "jumping the gun" and wrongly—indeed, unethically—providing a treatment directly to patients even though it was not yet known if it was effective. They seemed to ignore the possible conclusion that these doctors were actually making a reasonable determination of what was best for their patients: that even though it was not yet known if a particular treatment is effective, there still might be enough information to conclude it was in a patient's best interests

to try the treatment if it was relatively low risk and if the disease being treated had a bad enough expected outcome. Indeed, one of the conditions for which apheresis was being studied was thrombotic thrombocytopenia purpura, an often-fatal blood disorder. The clinical trial eventually demonstrated that apheresis produced a 50% reduction in mortality compared to an alternative treatment. Thus, many of the patients whose doctors allegedly "jumped the gun" are now alive when they otherwise wouldn't have been.

32. Benjamin Freedman, *A Response to a Purported Ethical Difficulty with Randomized Clinical Trials Involving Cancer Patients*, 3 J. Clin. Ethics 231 (1992). The concept of clinical equipoise, and its role in determining whether or not a study is consistent with the federal regulations and other rules, is discussed in detail in chapter 6.

33. *See, e.g.*, Denise Grady, *Patient or Guinea Pig? Dilemma of Clinical Trials*, New York Times D1, January 5, 1999; C. K. Daugherty et al., *Quantitative Analysis of Ethical Issues in Phase I Trials: A Survey Interview Study of 144 Advanced Cancer Patients*, 22(3) IRB 6 (2000). *See also* Amanda Gardner, *Study: Cancer Patients No Better Off in Trials*, HealthDay Rptr., January 22, 2004 (quoting Dr. Joel Horovitz, director of general surgery at Maimonides Medical Center in New York City: "I think the real reason patients enroll in a trial is that they feel their only shot is if they get access to some experimental drug that turns out to work. . . . Most of my patients want to do it because they feel that's the only shot they're going to get for themselves, not that they're going to benefit mankind").

34. *See, e.g.*, Robert D. Truog and A. Morris, *Is Informed Consent Always Necessary for Randomized, Clinical Trials?* 340 New Engl. J. Med. 804 (1999).

35. One of the rare cases discussing the issue of disclosing "alternative" treatments, though in the context of consenting to get clinical care and not in connection with participation in a research study, is Schiff v. Prados, 112 Cal. Rptr. 2d 171 (Cal. Ct. App. 2001). Three-year-old Crystin Schiff was admitted to the University of California at San Francisco (UCSF) Medical Center in January of 1993 with a rhabdoid tumor, a rare and aggressive form of cancer that was growing around her brain and spinal cord. Her parents were told by the doctors that her only option, apart from getting no treatment, was to receive aggressive chemotherapy and radiation, even though her prognosis would remain poor. She underwent the recommended treatment. At the same time, however, her parents were researching other options and came across the "antineoplaston" treatment provided by Dr. Stanislaw Burzynski, a controversial Texas physician-researcher whose work had been spotlighted on various national television newsmagazines and who had been engaged in a variety of disputes with the FDA and Texas authorities about his apparent noncompliance with federal and state regulations. The Schiffs ended up taking Crystin to Dr. Burzynski, and she began antineoplaston therapy. She died two years later, but the autopsy showed no remaining tumor, and the cause of death was due to radiation damage to her lungs from the treatment she got at UCSF Medical Center. Her parents subsequently sued UCSF, claiming, among other things, that the doctors had not gotten adequate informed consent, since they never mentioned the availability of Dr. Burzynski's treatments as an alternative. An appellate court determined that this issue did not need to go to trial, since Dr. Burzynski's treatment was illegal at the time of Crystin's treatment and thus could not have been considered an "available" treatment. *See also* Halle Fine Terrion, *Informed Choice: Physicians' Duty to Disclose Nonreadily Available Alternatives*, 43 Case W. Res. L. Rev. 491 (1993).

36. For an extended analysis of this issue, *see* Jerry Menikoff, *Demanded Medical Care*, 30 Ariz. St. L. J. 1091 (1998). One of the rare situations in which there might indeed be such a legal duty would be where the study was being conducted under emergency conditions, and the patient would not have the time or opportunity to get the new treatment from any other provider. Imagine, *e.g.*, that a study involved randomizing a patient who has just had a heart attack be-

tween a standard imaging technique or a new technique for evaluating whether the person needs immediate angioplasty. There are good arguments in favor of concluding that the researchers would have a legal duty to offer the patient the new technique outside of the study.

37. J. K. Olson-Garewal and K. Hessler, *Arizona's Cancer Clinical Trials Law: Flawed Process, Flawed Product*, 31(3) Hastings Center Rep. 22 (2001).

38. M. McCullough, *Breast Cancer Study Is Short on Volunteers*, Philadelphia Inquirer, Lifestyle Section, December 14, 1999.

39. *Merriam-Webster's Collegiate Dictionary* (11th ed. Springfield, Mass., Merriam-Webster 2003).

40. As noted elsewhere in this book, there are even special protections for vulnerable populations included in the federal regulations, several of which are discussed at length in part III. *See, e.g.*, 45 CFR Part 46, subparts B–D.

Chapter 11

1. A variety of descriptive phrases have been used to describe persons who, due to some form of mental disorder, are not competent to consent to participate in a particular research study. For example, they have been described as decisionally disabled, or as having impaired decision-making capacity, or as having a mental disorder that may affect decision-making capacity. Due to the controversy that surrounds many aspects of our society's treatment of the mentally ill, the use of some of these terms has itself generated heated debate. For sake of brevity, and without suggesting it is any better than these more descriptive phrases, in the text we simply use the term "incompetent" to describe persons who lack the necessary decision-making abilities.

2. The suicide death of Tony Lamadrid, a 23-year-old with schizophrenia who had earlier participated in a UCLA study that had subjects stopping their medications for periods of time, has resulted in a lengthy and still-ongoing court battle. J. Horowitz, *For the Sake of Science: When Tony Lamadrid, a Schizophrenic Patient and Research Subject at UCLA, Committed Suicide, It Set Off a National Debate: What Is Acceptable in Human Experimentation and Who Decides?* Los Angeles Times Magazine 16, September 11, 1994.

3. *See, e.g.*, Robert M. Nelson, *Children as Research Subjects*, in Jeffrey P. Kahn et al., eds., *Beyond Consent: Seeking Justice in Research* 49–52 (New York, Oxford University Press 1998).

4. R. A. Mulnard et al., *Estrogen Replacement Therapy for Treatment of Mild to Moderate Alzheimer Disease: A Randomized Controlled Trial*, 283 JAMA 1007 (2000).

5. At that time, the agency was still known under a prior name, the Office for Protection from Research Risks.

6. The significance of these scores, in terms of how well these people would be thinking, is discussed later in this chapter.

7. Nor had the Office for Human Research Protections (OHRP) provided any specific guidance. One of the initial questions might be whether there is a federal standard for determining competence to enroll in research, in effect a floor that must be met regardless of what state law might say on this issue. The requests for information coming from OHRP (described immediately below in the text) suggest that the agency does not believe there is such a standard. The regulations do not specifically describe such a standard, and do, in related areas (e.g., determining who gets to make a decision to enroll an incompetent subject) defer to state law.

8. Lane v. Candura, 376 N.E. 2d 1232 (Mass. App. Ct. 1978). Another leading case on this issue with similar reasoning, also coincidentally involving an elderly person facing a

decision about amputating an gangrenous leg, is *In re* Quackenbush, 383 A.2d 785 (Morris County Ct. 1978). *See generally* Bernard Lo, *Assessing Decision-Making Capacity*, 18 L. Med. Health Care 193 (1990); Thomas Grisso and Paul S. Appelbaum, *Assessing Competence to Consent to Treatment: A Guide for Physicians and Other Health Care Professionals* (New York, Oxford University Press 1998); Jessica W. Berg et al., *Informed Consent: Legal Theory and Clinical Practice* 98–109 (2d ed. New York, Oxford University Press 2001); Evan G. DeRenzo et al., *Assessment of Capacity to Give Consent to Research Participation: State-of-the-Art and Beyond*, 1 J. Health L. Policy 66 (1998).

9. *See generally* Grisso and Appelbaum, *supra* note 8.

10. Some of the questions include asking about the date (5 points given if you get every aspect of it right, including the day of the week and the season) and where the person is (another 5 points if you get it completely right). You would get 3 points if you can correctly repeat the names of three objects right after you are told them, and 2 points for being able to give the correct word for a watch and a pen after being shown these items. Copies of the tasks included on the test are widely available on the Internet. *See, e.g.*, www.fhma.com/mmse.htm.

11. 45 CFR § 46.116.

12. 45 CFR § 102(c) defines "legally authorized representative" as someone who is authorized under "applicable law." That terminology has widely been interpreted to be referring to the law of whatever state the research is taking place in. More generally, the federal regulations state that they "do not affect any state or local laws or regulations which may otherwise be applicable and which provide additional protections for human subjects." 45 CFR § 46.101(f). In other areas, even those where the research regulations do not specifically defer to state law, the federal rules only establish a floor in terms of the protections given to subjects, and the states are permitted to raise that floor to a greater level of protections. It is worth noting that there is nothing forcing the federal government to create this type of rule: it doesn't have to defer to state laws. In many areas of the law, the national government sets a uniform standard that overrides state laws; *e.g.*, the reason that people are sometimes unable to sue their HMOs is because Congress passed a law known as ERISA, which attempts to set a uniform national standard for regulating benefits given by employers to their workers, such as pension or health care benefits. Under the U.S. Constitution, if Congress has authority to regulate a particular area of conduct, then its laws take precedence over those of the states, if Congress so desires. Thus, it might make sense to conclude that, since everyone in this country benefits from research, and indeed most research these days is conducted in multicenter trials, with sites across the nation participating, there should be a single uniform standard determining when an incompetent person is permitted to be enrolled in a study.

13. M. Sheils and S. Agrest, *Who Was Karen Quinlan?* Newsweek 60, November 3, 1975; *In re* Quinlan, 355 A.2d 647 (N.J. 1976).

14. Thus, *e.g.*, in Illinois the list is as follows: (1) the spouse, (2) any adult son or daughter, (3) either parent, (4) any adult brother or sister, (5) any adult grandchild, and (6) a close friend. If there is more than one person at a single level—*e.g.*, the incompetent person is divorced, but has five children at his bedside, all willing to help make decisions for him—then decisions are made by majority vote. Ill. Ann. Stat. ch. 755, para. 40/1 et seq. This assumes that the person does not have a court-appointed guardian. If there were such a person, the guardian would be the decision maker. On these laws generally, *see, e.g.*, American Bar Association Commission on Law and Aging, Health Care Surrogate Consent Chart, *available at* www.abanet.org/aging/update.html; Diane E. Hoffman et al., *Regulating Research with Decisionally Impaired Individuals: Are We Making Progress?* 3 DePaul J. Health Care L. 547,

580–81 (2000); Jerry A. Menikoff et al., *Beyond Advance Directives—Health Care Surrogate Laws*, 327 New Engl. J. Med. 1165 (1992).

15. National Conference of Commissioners on Uniform State Laws, Uniform Health-Care Decisions Act, Prefatory Note (1993), *available at* www.law.upenn.edu/bll/ulc/fnact99/1990s/uhcda93.htm.

16. Alaska Stat. 47.30.830; Colo. R. S. 27–10.5–102; Conn. Gen. Stat. 45a-677(e); and 481 Iowa A.C. 57.35, respectively. Note the additional layer of confusion in determining whether these various terms are referring to nonstandard care provided outside of a research study, nonstandard care provided as part of a research study, or both scenarios.

17 In a very few states, there are specific statutes that automatically appoint surrogate decision makers for incompetent patients not for health care decisions, but rather for decisions relating to research. Three examples of this are California, which is discussed in the text at the end of this chapter, and Missouri and Kansas. Cal. Health & Safety Code § 24178(c) (2003); Mo. Rev. Stat. § 431.064 (2003); Act of April 16, 2004, S. Bill No. 343, 2004 Kan. Sess. Laws 109. The laws in these states are especially unusual in that in each case even though the legislature has chosen to specifically provide a list of which persons can make a decision about enrolling an incompetent person in a research study, it has *not* enacted a similar law regarding who can make decisions about clinical care for an incompetent person in the *non*research setting. One would think that the latter situation is more important (and certainly more common), and thus more in need of clarification by a statute.

18. Robert Amdur et al., *Selecting a Surrogate to Consent to Medical Research*, 22(4) IRB 7 (2000). The authors, one of whom is the first author of the leading reference work for IRBs, describe how at Dartmouth College rules for enrolling incompetent subjects are followed that knowingly are in violation of the federal regulations and state law. Interestingly, OHRP does not appear to have ever investigated these practices, in spite of the fact that *IRB* is a leading journal and thus the agency must certainly be aware of this article.

19. *See, e.g.*, Hoffman et al., *supra* note 14; Peter V. Rabins, *Issues Raised by Research Using Persons Suffering from Dementia Who Have Impaired Decision Capacity*, 1 J. Health Care L. Policy 22 (1998); Jessica Wilen Berg, *Legal and Ethical Complexities of Consent with Cognitively Impaired Research Subjects: Proposed Guidelines*, 24 J. L. Med. Ethics 18 (1996); Marshall B. Kapp, *Decisional Capacity, Older Human Research Subjects, and IRBs: Beyond Forms and Guidelines*, 9 Stan. L. Policy Rev. 359 (1998); Jason H. T. Karlawish, *Research Involving Cognitively Impaired Adults*, 348 New Engl. J. Med. 1389 (2003).

20. For the history of these regulatory efforts, *see* National Bioethics Advisory Commission, Research Involving Persons with Mental Disorders That May Affect Decisionmaking Capacity, Vol. 1 at 69 (1998); Jonathan D. Moreno, *Regulation of Research on the Decisionally Impaired: History and Gaps in the Current Regulatory System*, 1 J. Health Care L. Policy 1 (1998).

21. National Bioethics Advisory Commission, Research Involving Persons with Mental Disorders That May Affect Decisionmaking Capacity (1998).

22. *See, e.g.*, John D. Oldham et al., *Regulating Research with Vulnerable Populations: Litigation Gone Awry*, 1 J. Health Care L. Policy 154 (1998); Paula Walter, *The Mentally Incompetent and Medical/Drug Research Experimentation: New York Saves the Day for the Underdog*, 6 Health L. J. 149 (1998); Alexander Morgan Capron, *Incapacitated Research*, 27(2) Hastings Center Rep. 25 (1997). The New York State lawsuit was T.D. v. New York State Office of Mental Health, 626 N.Y.S. 2d 1015 (Sup. Ct. 1995), *affirmed*, 650 N.Y.S. 2d 173 (Sup. Ct., App. Div. 1996), *appeal dismissed*, 690 N.E. 2d 1259 (N.Y. 1997), which is discussed further in the text at the end of this chapter.

23. *See, e.g.*, Diane E. Hoffman and Jack Schwartz, *Proxy Consent to Participation of the Decisionally Impaired in Medical Research: Maryland's Policy Initiative*, 1 J. Health Care L.

Policy 123 (1998); Laurie M. Flynn and Ronald S. Honberg, *Achieving Proper Balance in Research with Decisionally-Incapacitated Subjects: NAMI's Perspectives on the Working Group's Proposal*, 1 J. Health Care L. Policy 174 (1998).

24. A detailed comparison of the three proposals is provided in Rebecca Dresser, *Dementia Research: Ethics and Policy of the Twenty-First Century*, 35 Ga. L. Rev. 661 (2001).

25. Bernadette Tansey, *UCSF Violated Patients' Rights: Doctors Improperly Got Consent for Study, Feds Say*, San Francisco Chronicle A1, July 28, 2002.

26. Cal. Health & Safety Code § 24178 (2003).

27. T.D. v. New York State Office of Mental Health, 650 N.Y.S. 2d 173 (Sup. Ct., App. Div. 1996). For criticisms of that opinion, *see, e.g.*, Stephan Haimowitz et al., *Uninformed Decisionmaking: The Case of Surrogate Research Consent*, 27(6) Hastings Center Rep. 9 (1997); John M. Oldham et al., *Regulating Research with Vulnerable Populations: Litigation Gone Awry*, 1 J. Health Care L. Policy 154 (1998).

28. T.D. v. New York State Office of Mental Health, 690 N.E. 2d 1259 (N.Y. 1997).

Chapter 12

1. *See, e.g.*, Ernest D. Prentice et al., *An Update on the PEG-SOD Study Involving Incompetent Subjects: FDA Permits an Exception to Informed Consent Requirements*, 16(1–2) IRB 16 (1994).

2. *See, e.g.*, Michelle H. Biros et al., *Informed Consent in Emergency Research: Consensus Statement from the Coalition Conference of Acute Resuscitation and Critical Care Researchers*, 273 JAMA 1283 (1995); Charles R. McCarthy, *To Be or Not to Be: Waiving Informed Consent in Emergency Research*, 5 Kennedy Inst. Ethics J. 155 (1995).

3. The change in the FDA regulations was formally announced in *Protection of Human Subjects; Informed Consent*, 61 Fed. Reg. 51498 (1996). The change was codified at 21 CFR § 50.24, Exception from Informed Consent Requirements for Emergency Research. An identical policy was adopted at the same time by the Department of Health and Human Services, although it did not require a change in the regulations (*i.e.*, in the version of the Common Rule that was administered by that agency). Departmental regulations already allowed that agency to waive the need to comply with those rules under appropriate circumstances, and so the agency merely issued a policy statement providing for the waiver of the usual informed consent rules under conditions identical to those provided in the new FDA regulations. *See Waiver of Informed Consent Requirements in Certain Emergency Research*, 61 Fed. Reg. 51531 (1996), discussed in a "Dear Colleague" letter from the predecessor to the Office for Human Research Protections, *available at* www.hhs.gov/ohrp/humansubjects/guidance/hsdc97–01.htm.

4. Gina Kolata, *Ban on Medical Experiments without Consent Is Relaxed*, New York Times A1, November 5, 1996.

5. As of this writing, there have been approximately 15 studies approved under the new rules. During early 2004, a study involving a blood substitute called PolyHeme attracted national attention and was written up in the *Washington Post* and discussed on National Public Radio. *See* Rob Stein, *An Experiment in Saving Lives: Emergency Patients Unwittingly Get Artificial Blood*, Washington Post A1, March 23, 2004; *Ethics Involved in Using Blood Substitute on Trauma Patients*, National Public Radio Morning Edition, March 11, 2004.

6. Terence D. Valenzuela and Michael K. Copass, *Clinical Research on Out-of-Hospital Emergency Care*, 345 New Engl. J. Med. 689 (2001).

7. Daniel H. Lowenstein et al., *The Prehospital Treatment of Status Epilepticus (PHTSE) Study: Design and Methodology*, 22 Controlled Clin. Trials 290 (2001); Brian K. Alldredge et al., *A Comparison of Lorazepam, Diazepam, and Placebo for the Treatment of Out-of-Hospital Status Epilepticus*, 345 New Engl. J. Med. 631 (2001).

8. Since the new rules were formally adopted in 1996, it is unclear exactly what happened in the first two years of the study, since it began in 1994. The study authors and a commentator both indicate that the study was indeed conducted pursuant to the post-1996 regulations. *See* Lowenstein et al., *supra* note 7 at 298–300; Alldredge, *supra* note 7.

9. 21 CFR § 50.24. For other discussions of the new rules, *see*, e.g., Richard S. Saver, *Critical Care Research and Informed Consent*, 75 N.C. L. Rev. 205 (1996); Sandra J. Carnahan, *Promoting Medical Research without Sacrificing Patient Autonomy: Legal and Ethical Issues Raised by the Waiver of Informed Consent for Emergency Research*, 52 Okla. L. Rev. 565 (1999); Symposium, *In Case of Emergency: No Need for Consent*, 27(1) Hastings Center Rep. 7 (1997).

10. It is noteworthy that, as discussed in chapter 6, note 8, the FDA appears to believe that these rules assure that participation in an approved study will be in the best interests of a subject. The source of that FDA belief is apparently the requirement of clinical equipoise, which, as chapter 6 demonstrates, in no way assures that participation will be a "best choice" for most (or even many) subjects.

11. The people conducting the seizure study clearly grossly misinterpreted this rule. They claimed that the fact that the researchers would learn how to better treat future patients should be viewed as a direct benefit to the subjects in the study, since they would likely have future seizures. This is clearly not what the federal regulations view as a direct benefit: such a benefit must flow from things done to the subject *in the study*.

12. Norman Fost, *Waived Consent for Emergency Research*, 24 Am. J. L. Med. 163, 178–80 (1998)

13. *Id.* at 179–80 (emphasis added).

14. *Id.* at 169.

15. These issues are discussed in detail in chapters 6 and 10, among others.

16. Norman Fost and John Robertson, *Deferring Consent with Incompetent Patients in an Intensive Care Unit*, 2(7) IRB 5 (1980). A recent very large randomized study indicates that steroids do not appear to provide any benefit after head injury. MRC CRASH Trial, *Effect of Intravenous Corticosteroids on Death within 14 Days in 10,008 Adults with Clinically Significant Head Injury*, 364 Lancet 1321 (2004).

17. Norman S. Abramson and Peter Safar, *Deferred Consent: Use in Clinical Resuscitation Research*, 19 Ann. Emerg. Med. 781, 783 (1990)

18. Specifically, 15.7% of the subjects who were assigned placebo died. The death rates for the diazepam and lorazepam arms were 4.5% and 7.7%. Alldredge, *supra* note 7 at 636.

19. Thus, early in the AIDS epidemic, leaders of the gay community soon recognized the benefits of having new drugs properly tested in well-designed research studies with placebo arms. But if you had AIDS at that time, and there were no good treatments, you'd likely prefer getting the new drug to being in a study where half the time you'd get placebo. For discussions of how the AIDS epidemic altered perceptions of clinical research, *see*, e.g., Rebecca Dresser, *When Science Offers Salvation: Patient Advocacy and Research Ethics* (New York, Oxford University Press 2001); Steven Epstein, *Impure Science: AIDS, Activism, and the Politics of Knowledge* (Berkeley, University of California Press 1996).

20. *See* Rob Stein, *An Experiment in Saving Lives: Emergency Patients Unwittingly Get Artificial Blood*, Washington Post A1, March 23, 2004; *Ethics Involved in Using Blood Substitute on Trauma Patients*, *supra* note 5. The study had the interesting feature of having created an

"opt-out" provision: a person could wear a special hospital bracelet to alert emergency personnel that they do not want to be in the study. In reality, however, it is unlikely many people would be willing to wear such a bracelet all the time just to deal with the slim possibility that they might end up in an ambulance after being a trauma victim. Asking someone to wear a bracelet in order not to be in a study seems significantly different from asking people with specific medical problems to wear identification bracelets that let emergency personnel know about those problems.

21. The argument that most people would consent to be in the study would be strongest if it was limited to people whose chance of survival without an immediate blood transfusion was *very* low (which might not have been the case in the actual study). A complete evaluation of this issue for the PolyHeme study gets more complicated given that people who are randomized to get PolyHeme in the ambulance, when saline is the only alternative, continue to get PolyHeme (for up to 12 hours) after arrival at the hospital, where blood would be readily available.

22. As discussed at the end of chapter 11, this would raise constitutional issues.

Chapter 13

1. Among the circumstances that will permit minors to make their own health care decisions are when certain life-altering events take place, such as getting married (causing a minor to become legally "emancipated"), when a particular minor is able to demonstrate a high level of maturity (a special legal category described as a "mature" minor), and specific state laws allowing consent to certain types of health care (*e.g.*, relating to sexual matters, *e.g.*, contraception). *See, e.g.*, Rhonda Gay Hartman, *Adolescent Decisional Autonomy for Medical Care: Physician Perceptions and Practices*, 8 U. Chi. L. School Roundtable 87 (2001); Jessica A. Penkower, *The Potential Right of Chronically Ill Adolescents to Refuse Life-Saving Medical Treatment: Fatal Misuse of the Mature Minor Doctrine*, 45 DePaul L. Rev. 1165 (1996). Even in those circumstances where a minor has been accorded the right to make a particular type of health care decision, the minor in many instances might not have the legal authority to consent to participate in a research study involving that type of care. *See* Leonard H. Glantz, *Research with Children*, 24 Am. J. L. Med. 213, 224–27, 230 (1998) (noting how such authority may be limited to studies where participation is in the child's best interests).

2. *See, e.g.*, John F. Rosen and Paul Mushak, *Primary Prevention of Childhood Lead Poisoning—the Only Solution*, 344 New Engl. J. Med. 1470 (2001); Walter J. Rogan and James H. Ware, *Exposure to Lead in Children—How Low Is Low Enough?* 348 New Engl. J. Med. 16 (2003).

3. Grimes v. Kennedy Krieger Institute, Inc., 782 A.2d 807 (Md. 2001).

4. *Id.* at 821–22.

5. *Id.* at 823.

6. *Per curiam* opinion on motion for reconsideration in *Grimes*, *supra* note 3 at 861–62.

7. Grimes v. Kennedy Krieger Institute, Inc., *supra* note 3 at 816–17.

8. 45 CFR §§ 46.404–407. The requirements for obtaining the permission of the parent and the assent of the child are discussed in detail in 45 CFR § 46.408.

9. Regarding the assent requirement, *see, e.g.*, David Wendler and Seema Shah, *Should Children Decide Whether They Are Enrolled in Nonbeneficial Research?* 3(4) Am. J. Bioethics 1 (2003), and accompanying responses in that issue.

10. 45 CFR § 46.102(i). For an argument that this standard could allow children to be exposed to substantial—even life-threatening—risks, see David Wendler et al., *Quantifying*

the Federal Minimal Risk Standard: Implications for Pediatric Research without a Prospect of Direct Benefit, 294 JAMA 826 (2005).

11. National Commission for the Protection of Human Subjects of Biomedical and Behavioral Research, Report and Recommendations: Research Involving Children xix (1977). *See also* National Bioethics Advisory Commission, Ethical and Policy Issues in Research Involving Human Participants, Vol. 1 at 83 (2001); Robert M. Nelson, *Children as Research Subjects,* in Jeffrey P. Kahn et al., *Beyond Consent: Seeking Justice in Research* 47, 54 (New York, Oxford University Press 1998); Lainie Friedman Ross, *Do Healthy Children Deserve Greater Protection in Medical Research?* 142 J. Pediatr. 108 (2003); Institute of Medicine, *Ethical Conduct of Clinical Research Involving Children* 121–26 (2004).

12. The Office for Human Research Protections (OHRP) itself reached this conclusion about, in essence, its own actions in a 2001 report to Congress relating to the current state of research involving children. *See* OHRP, *Protections for Children in Research: A Report to Congress in Accord with Section 1003 of P.L. 106–310, Children's Health Act of 2000, available at* www.hhs.gov/ohrp/reports/ohrp502.pdf ("consensus on [the] interpretation [of minimal risk] has not been established"). For a survey indicating that IRBs in general have difficulty interpreting the risk and benefit provisions in the regulations and end up producing conclusions that vary widely from IRB to IRB, *see* Seema Shah et al., *How Do Institutional Review Boards Apply the Federal Risk and Benefit Standards for Pediatric Research?* 291 JAMA 476 (2004).

13. *See, e.g.,* Loretta M. Kopelman, *Children as Research Subjects: A Dilemma,* 25 J. Med. Phil. 745, 750 (2000).

14. Compliance letter from OHRP to NIH, November 3, 2000, *available at* www.hhs.gov/ohrp/detrm_letrs/nov00a.pdf. A workgroup of the now-disbanded National Human Research Protections Advisory Committee attempted to categorize various medical procedures as to their level of risk. It concluded that, *e.g.,* a spinal tap (lumbar puncture) or a bone marrow biopsy (aspirate) would involve a minor increase over minimal risk. *See* Final Report to NHRPAC from Children's Workgroup, *available at* www.hhs.gov/ohrp/nhrpac/documents/nhrpac16.pdf.

15. *See, e.g.,* Eric Kodish, *Pediatric Ethics and Early-Phase Childhood Cancer Research: Conflicted Goals and the Prospect of Benefit,* 10 Account. Res. 17 (2003).

16. Matthew Miller, *Phase I Cancer Trials: A Collusion of Misunderstanding,* 30(4) Hastings Center Rep. 34 (2000). For another discussion of this issue, *see* Michelle Oberman and Joel Frader, *Dying Children and Medical Research: Access to Clinical Trials as Benefit and Burden,* 29 Am. J. L. Med. 301 (2003).

17. Institute of Medicine, *supra* note 11 at 133.

18. For a recent empirical study looking at how well children actually do in asthma studies and concluding that they are exposed to unnecessary risks, *see* M. Justin Coffey et al., *Ethical Assessment of Clinical Asthma Trials Including Children Subjects,* 113 Pediatrics 87 (2004). It should also be noted that many of these new drugs don't improve symptoms, but rather have other small benefits, such as requiring less frequent administration than existing drugs.

19. *See, e.g.,* Gina Kolata, *A Widely Used Arthritis Drug Is Withdrawn,* New York Times A1, October 1, 2004.

20. This statement excludes, of course, the small percentage of drugs that underwent pediatric testing.

21. It well may be that this change created too much of an incentive for the drug companies and is in effect giving them windfall profits. *See, e.g.,* Robert Steinbrook, *Testing Medications in Children,* 347 New Engl. J. Med. 1462, 1466–67 (2002); Sheryl Gay Stolberg, *As*

Children Help Test Medicines, Profits and Questions Are Raised, New York Times 1, February 11, 2001.

22. Association of American Physicians and Surgeons v. FDA, 226 F. Supp. 2d 204 (D.D.C. 2002).

23. Pediatric Research Equity Act of 2003, Pub. L. No. 108–155 (2003), codified at 21 U.S.C. § 505B.

Chapter 14

1. Partnership for Children, *available at* www.pfc.org/initiatives_question.shtml.

2. Grimes v. Kennedy Krieger Institute, Inc., 782 A.2d 807, 852, 858 (Md. 2001). As noted in chapter 13, the court on reconsideration modified this conclusion slightly, allowing for children to be enrolled in studies that involve the "minimal kind of risk that is inherent in any endeavor."

3. *See, e.g.*, Norman C. Fost, *Conception for Donation*, 291 JAMA 2125 (2004).

4. 45 CFR § 46.407.

5. The notice allowing public comment on this study appeared at 68 Fed. Reg. 17950 (2003). Materials relating to this study are provided in Office for Human Research Protections (OHRP), Alcohol, Sleep and Circadian Rhythms in Young Humans, Study 2—Effects of Evening Ingestion of Alcohol on Sleep, Circadian Phase, and Performance as a Function of Parental History of Alcohol Abuse/Dependence, *available at* www.hhs.gov/ohrp/children/circadian.html.

6. A variety of materials relating to this study, including the written comments of each of the ten experts who was on the section 407 panel, can be found in OHRP, A Multicenter, Randomized Dose Response Study of the Safety, Clinical and Immune Responses of Dryvax Administered to Children 2 to 5 Years of Age, *available at* www.hhs.gov/ohrp/children/dryvax.html. The announcement by OHRP that this study was being reviewed, and that members of the public could comment on it, appeared at 67 Fed. Reg. 66403 (October 31, 2002).

7. Many of those comments are still online at www.fda.gov/ohrms/dockets/dockets/02n0466/02n0466.htm and following web pages.

8. Letter from OHRP to Harbor-UCLA Medical Center, dated January 24, 2003, *available at* www.hhs.gov/ohrp/dpanel/determ.pdf.

9. Valerie Lincy and Kelly Moltz, *We Still Face the Menace of Iraq's Hidden Horrors*, Los Angeles Times pt. 2 at 19, May 22, 2003.

10. Richard Wilson and Edmund A. C. Crouch, *Risk-Benefit Analysis* 225 (Cambridge: Harvard Center for Risk Analysis 2001).

Chapter 15

1. This pill is also commonly known as "plan B," because it is used when regular contraception, so-called plan A, has failed or was not used. Plan B generally works by blocking ovulation and thus prevents fertilization of an egg, a fact that the scientists on the advisory committee had emphasized to distinguish its mechanism of action from abortion.

2. Gina Kolata, *F.D.A. Delays Morning-After Contraceptive*, New York Times A12, February 14, 2004; Marc Kaufman, *Debate Intensifies over "Morning After" Pill: As FDA Deadline Nears, Conservatives Urge President to Keep Drug a Prescription*, Washington Post A2, February 13,

2004; Joe Ryan, *Assembly OKs After-Sex Pill,* New York Daily News 26, February 3, 2004; *Paula Zahn Now,* CNN, February 16, 2004 (interview with fired Eckerd pharmacist); Josh Baugh, *Drug Refusal Decried: Denton Store Denied Morning-After Pill to Woman Treated for Rape,* Dallas Morning News 1B, February 3, 2004; Eric Lichtblau, *Ashcroft Defends Subpoenas,* New York Times A27, February 13, 2004; House Comm. on the Judiciary, Laci and Conner's Law, H.R. Doc. No. 420, pt. 1, 108th Cong., 2d Sess. (2004); Gina Kolata, *Cloning Creates Human Embryos,* New York Times A1, February 12, 2004; Woo Suk Hwang et al., *Evidence of a Human Embryonic Stem Cell Line Derived from a Cloned Blastocyst,* 303 Science 1669 (2004).

    3. For the history of excluding women from research studies, *see, e.g.,* Karen H. Rothenberg, *Gender Matters: Implications for Clinical Research and Women's Health Care,* 32 Hous. L. Rev. 1201 (1996); L. Elizabeth Bowles, *The Disenfranchisement of Fertile Women in Clinical Trials: The Legal Ramifications of and Solutions for Rectifying the Knowledge Gap,* 45 Vand. L. Rev. 877, 880–85 (1992).

    4. Rebecca Dresser, *Wanted: Single, White Male for Medical Research,* 22(1) Hastings Center Rep. 24 (1992).

    5. Department of Health and Human Services, *Guideline for the Study and Evaluation of Gender Differences in the Clinical Evaluation of Drugs,* 58 Fed. Reg. 39, 406 (1993).

    6. Karen L. Baird, *The New NIH and FDA Medical Research Policies: Targeting Gender, Promoting Justice,* 24 J. Health Politics Policy L. 531, 558 (1999) (noting that preliminary NIH data show "a fairly equitable distribution" in sex distribution of subjects for studies that can enroll both men and women; for 1997, in such phase III studies, 57% of the subjects were male and 42% female); B. Evelyn et al., Women's Participation in Clinical Trials and Gender-Related Labeling: A Review of New Molecular Entities Approved 1995–1999, Office of Special Health Issues, FDA, June 2001, *available at* www.fda.gov/cder/reports/womens_health/women_clin_ trials.htm (noting that women were participating as subjects in clinical trials of recent new drugs in "proportion to their representation in the population").

    7. 45 CFR § 46.111(b) (describing "children, prisoners, pregnant women, mentally disabled persons, or economically or educationally disadvantaged persons" as fitting into the "vulnerable" category). Subpart B of part 46, discussed later in chapter 15, deals with research relating to pregnant women and fetuses and related matters.

    8. The statements relating to what happened with Kay Perrin are taken from Peter Aronson, *A Medical Indignity,* Natl. L. J. A1, March 27, 2000.

    9. *See* Diaz v. Hillsborough County Hospital, 2000 U.S. Dist. LEXIS 14061 (M.D. Fla.) (approving consent decree); Aronson, *supra* note 8.

    10. *See, e.g.,* Alan Meisel, *A "Dignitary Tort" as a Bridge between the Idea of Informed Consent and the Law of Informed Consent,* 16 L. Med. Health Care 210 (1988); Marjorie M. Schultz, *From Informed Consent to Patient Choice: A New Protected Interest,* 95 Yale L. J. 219 (1985).

    11. Anahad O'Connor, *Noting High-Risk Flu Groups and A Few Tips on Coping,* New York Times A14, December 13, 2003.

    12. The safety of the flu vaccine for pregnant women was first demonstrated in a study published in 1973, which examined more than 2,000 women. *See* Centers for Disease Control and Prevention, *Questions and Answers: Thimerosal-Containing Influenza Vaccine,* *available at* www.cdc.gov/flu/about/qa/thimerosal.htm, *citing* O. P. Heinonen et al., *Immunization during Pregnancy against Poliomyelitis and Influenza in Relation to Childhood Malignancy,* 2 Int. J. Epidemiol. 229 (1973).

    13. The complete description of each category is as follows:

    A: Adequate, well-controlled studies in pregnant women have not shown an
       increased risk of fetal abnormalities.

B: Animal studies have revealed no evidence of harm to the fetus, but there are no adequate and well-controlled studies in pregnant women; or animal studies have shown an adverse effect, but adequate and well-controlled studies in pregnant women have failed to demonstrate a risk to the fetus.

C: Animal studies have shown an adverse effect, and there are no adequate and well-controlled studies in pregnant women; or no animal studies have been conducted, and there are no adequate and well-controlled studies in pregnant women.

D: Studies, adequate well-controlled or observational, in pregnant women have demonstrated a risk to the fetus, but the benefits of therapy may outweigh the potential risk.

X: Studies, adequate well-controlled or observational, in animals or pregnant women have demonstrated positive evidence of fetal abnormalities, and the use of the product is contraindicated in women who are or may become pregnant.

Michelle Meadows, *Pregnancy and the Drug Dilemma*, FDA Consumer, May-June 2001, *available at* www.fda.gov/fdac/features/2001/301_preg.html.

14. 45 CFR § 46.204.

15. Note that, under the quoted regulation, studies that benefit neither the woman nor the fetus—*e.g.*, those designed just to collect information without altering care—are not approvable if they impose more than minimal risk to the fetus. If the fetus was nonviable, the woman would have the right to abort it, so in this regard the regulations are more restrictive than would be required by the Constitution.

16. *See* Meadows, *supra* note 13.

17. There do not, however, appear to have been any successful lawsuits.

18. FDA, General Considerations for the Clinical Evaluation of Drugs, HEW Publication No. (FDA) 77–4030 (1977).

19. FDA, *Guideline for the Study and Evaluation of Gender Differences in the Clinical Evaluation of Drugs*, 58 Fed. Reg. 39406 (1993).

20. For an IRB's deliberations about whether it was appropriate for the sponsor of a research study to insist on the use of particular forms of contraception, *see* James R. Anderson et al., *Women in Early Phase Trials: An IRB's Deliberations*, 25(4) IRB 7 (2003).

21. For a discussion of the extent to which this change has taken place, and a claim that a 1998 FDA rule requiring new drug applications to document a drug's safety and effectiveness in both sexes means that women must be included in such early studies, *see* Gary T. Chiodo et al., *Continued Exclusion of Women in Clinical Research: Industry Winks at the FDA*, 3(5) Med. Res. L. & Policy Rep. (BNA) 180 (March 3, 2004).

22. *See* Meadows, *supra* note 13.

23. Contrast this to what is generally claimed to be true of the pediatric studies discussed in chapter 13: that by failing to do them, far more harm will come to children, as a group, than the harm that occurs to children who participate in the studies.

24. The regulations do, however, have the same type exception that appears in the child research rules (in essence creating panels similar to section 407 panels, as discussed in chapter 14), which allows for the federal government to put together a panel of experts to approve important studies about the health of pregnant women or fetuses that are not otherwise approvable under the other provisions of the regulations. 45 CFR § 46.207.

25. *See, e.g.*, People v. Davis, 872 P.2d 591 (Cal. 1994); State v. Merrill, 450 N.W. 2d 318 (Minn. 1990).

26. A Louisiana law, La. R.S. § 9:124, defining the legal status of embryos, is perhaps the state statute that goes furthest in trying to categorize such an entity as having legal rights. That provision describes an *in vitro* fertilized human egg "as a juridical (legal) person," which entitles it "to sue or be sued."

27. *See, e.g.,* Janet L. Dolgin, *Embryonic Discourse: Abortion, Stem Cells, and Cloning,* 31 Fla. St. U. L. Rev. 101, 155 ("these courts have presumed that embryos are not persons. In some cases, courts have, in effect, defined embryos as commodities despite their own protestations"); Timothy Stoltzfus Jost, *Rights of Embryo and Foetus in Private Law,* 50 Am. J. Comp. L. 633 (2002); Erin P. George, *The Stem Cell Debate: The Legal, Political, and Ethical Issues Surrounding Federal Funding of Scientific Research on Human Embryos,* 12 Alb. L. J. Sci. Technol. 747 (2002); Kayhan Parsi, *Metaphorical Imagination: The Moral and Legal Status of Fetuses and Embryos,* 4 DePaul J. Health Care L. 703 (1999).

28. The major such effort appears to be donating the excess embryos so that they could be "adopted" by another couple and implanted in the uterus of the female member of the couple. The federal government has been encouraging such voluntary programs by providing funding. *See* Naomi D. Johnson, *Excess Embryos: Is Embryo Adoption a New Solution or a Temporary Fix?* 68 Brooklyn L. Rev. 853 (2003). It seems highly unlikely that more than a small percentage of infertile couples would be eager to take advantage of this option, since it would mean that, in effect, some other couple would be raising children that, by this society's usual standards, the infertile couple would have viewed as their own.

29. Much of the information in this section is taken from the NIH primer on stem cells, Stem Cell Basics, *available at* http://stemcells.nih.gov/info/basics. For a discussion of the many issues raised by the use of stem cells, *see, e.g.,* President's Council on Bioethics, Monitoring Stem Cell Research (2004), *available at* www.bioethics.gov/reports/stemcell/index .html; National Bioethics Advisory Commission, Ethical Issues in Human Stem Cell Research, Vols. I–III (1999–2000), *available at* www.georgetown.edu/research/nrcbl/nbac/ pubs.html; Suzanne Holland et al., eds., *The Human Embryonic Stem Cell Debate: Science, Ethics, and Public Policy* (Cambridge, MIT Press 2001).

30. 45 CFR § 46.202(c). There are suggestions that the George W. Bush administration might wish to change the rules and have embryos protected also. The Secretary's Advisory Committee on Human Research Protections, a successor to the National Research Protections Advisory Committee, included in its charge a mandate to provide advice with regard to research involving embryos. Charter, Secretary's Advisory Committee on Human Research Protections, *available at* www.hhs.gov/ohrp/sachrp/charter.pdf.

31. OHRP has issued guidance on the use of stem cells. In essence, that guidance notes that if the identities of the donors of the cells are known to the investigator, then the creation of a cell line does constitute research involving a human subject—but only because the donors are the subjects (since identifiable information about them is being used). The agency notes that if no identifiers are made available to the researchers, research on a stem cell line would not meet the definition of research with human subjects. Oddly, the document did not address whether the creation of a stem cell line from a preexisting embryo, or the creation of an embryo to be used to then create a stem cell line, would be human subjects research. However, the arguments in the guidance document make it clear that, assuming no identifying information about whose tissues are being used is given to the researchers, then these activities would not meet the definition of human subjects research. OHRP, Guidance for Investigators and Institutional Review Boards Regarding Research Involving Human Embryonic Stem Cells, Germ Cells and Stem-Cell Derived Test Articles, March 19, 2002, *available at* www.hhs.gov/ohrp/humansubjects/guidance/ stemcell.pdf.

32. The text of the President's speech to the nation is provided in Remarks by the President on Stem Cell Research (August 9, 2001), available at www.whitehouse.gov/news/releases/2001/08/20010809-2.html. A summary of the criteria established by the President is provided in Office of the Director, NIH, Notice of Criteria for Federal Funding of Research on Existing Human Embryonic Stem Cells and Establishment of NIH Human Embryonic Stem Cell Registry (November 7, 2001), available at grants.nih.gov/grants/guide/notice-files/NOT-OD-02-005.html.

33. The President said:

> On the first issue, are these embryos human life—well, one researcher told me he believes this five-day-old cluster of cells is not an embryo, not yet an individual, but a pre-embryo. He argued that it has the potential for life, but it is not a life because it cannot develop on its own.
>
> An ethicist dismissed that as a callous attempt at rationalization. Make no mistake, he told me, that cluster of cells is the same way you and I, and all the rest of us, started our lives. One goes with a heavy heart if we use these, he said, because we are dealing with the seeds of the next generation.

Remarks by the President on Stem Cell Research, *supra* note 32.

Determining the answer to this question, in any event, doesn't seem to help resolve the underlying issues. The cells are certainly "alive," by almost any standard. And they are designed (programmed) to become a human being if given sufficient opportunity and if everything works out well. Whatever name we give them—human life, a precursor to a human being, a pre-embryo—we are still left with the issue of how they should be treated, and what constitute "inappropriate" treatment of them.

34. The President's observations on this issue were as follows, in part:

> And to the other crucial question, if these are going to be destroyed anyway, why not use them for good purpose—I also found different answers. Many argue these embryos are byproducts of a process that helps create life, and we should allow couples to donate them to science so they can be used for good purpose instead of wasting their potential. Others will argue there's no such thing as excess life, and the fact that a living being is going to die does not justify experimenting on it or exploiting it as a natural resource.

Remarks by the President on Stem Cell Research, *supra* note 32.

35. Editorial, *The Privatization of Stem Cells*, New York Times A24, March 9, 2004.

36. Chad A. Cowan et al., *Derivation of Embryonic Stem-Cell Lines from Human Blastocysts*, 350 New Engl. J. Med. 1353 (2004).

37. John Gearhart, *New Human Embryonic Stem-Cell Lines—More Is Better*, 350 New Engl. J. Med. 1275 (2004).

38. For a summary of state laws that limit the use of embryos in research, *see* U.S. Conference of Catholic Bishops, *Current State Laws against Human Embryo Research*, *available at* www.usccb.org/prolife/issues/bioethic/states701.htm.

39. *See, e.g.*, Laura Mansnerus, *New Jersey Faces Tough Competition for Stem Cell Scientists*, New York Times A16, January 17, 2005 (quoting a foundation administrator as noting that more money is now going into stem cell research than would have been the case if President Bush had allowed federal funding); Claudia Kalb, *Brand-New Stem Cells*, Newsweek 57, March 15, 2004; Andrew Pollack, *Measure Passed, California Weighs Its Future as a Stem Cell Epicenter*, New York Times C10, November 4, 2004. This phenomenon is very similar to what we

described in chapter 11, with some states modifying their laws to allow a greater ability to enroll incompetent subjects in research studies as a means of attracting such research.

40. We need to say "nearly" because there is DNA contained in a cell's mitochondria—a part of the cell that is involved in energy production—and that DNA will be derived from the sheep that supplied the egg cell, since the mitochondria are located outside of a cell's nucleus.

41. *See, e.g.*, President's Council on Bioethics, Human Cloning and Human Dignity: An Ethical Inquiry 75 (2002), *available at* http://www.bioethics.gov/topics/cloning_index.html; National Bioethics Advisory Commission, Cloning Human Beings, Vol. 1 at 31 (1997), *available at* www.georgetown.edu/research/nrcbl/nbac/pubs.html. For a discussion by a leading bioethicist of why it would have been wrong to try to clone his 20-year-old daughter, who died as the result of violent crime, *see* Thomas H. Murray, *Even If It Worked, Cloning Wouldn't Bring Her Back*, Washington Post B1, April 8, 2001.

42. *See* President's Council on Bioethics, Reproduction and Responsibility: The Regulation of New Biotechnologies 99–110 (2004), *available at* www.bioethics.gov/reports/reproductionandresponsibility/index.html.

43. *Id.* at 129. In addition to the ban on federal funding, the FDA has claimed that it has jurisdiction to regulate reproductive cloning, claiming that this is a "biologic" product. Some commentators have disputed the FDA's interpretation of the law. *See, e.g.*, Rebecca Dresser, *Human Cloning and the FDA*, 33(3) Hastings Center Rep. 7 (2003).

44. As noted earlier in this chapter, these embryos are not even considered human subjects under the Common Rule, and thus that rule generally does not prevent them from being created or destroyed.

45. President's Council, *supra* note 42 at 222–24. The council also properly notes that to the extent that the debate over reproductive cloning has raised issues relating to the health of children created by such technology, similar scrutiny should be applied to the many other methods of assisted reproductive technology. *Id.* at 210. Until recently, there has been minimal regulation, at either the federal or state levels, of methods of assisted reproduction. *See generally* New York State Task Force on Life and the Law, Assisted Reproductive Technologies (1998).

Chapter 16

1. Moore v. Regents of the University of California, 793 P.2d 479 (Cal. 1990). The statements in the text are based on the findings of fact made by the California Supreme Court.

2. *Id.* at 484.

3. *Id.* at 497.

4. *See* Mark Katches et al., *The Body Brokers, Part 1: Assembly Line*, Orange County Register A1, April 16, 2000; William Heisel et al., *The Body Brokers, Part 2: Skin Merchants*, Orange County Register, April 17, 2000; Ronald Campbell et al., *The Body Brokers, Part 3: Researchers*, Orange County Register, April 18, 2000; Ronald Campbell et al., *The Body Brokers, Part 4: Gatekeepers*, Orange County Register, April 19, 2000; and Mark Katches et al., *The Body Brokers, Part 5: Pioneers*, Orange County Register, April 20, 2000, all *available at* www.ocregister.com/features/body/. More recent articles raising the same issues include John M. Broder, *In Science's Name, Lucrative Trade in Body Parts*, New York Times A1, March 12, 2004 (generated by a report that an employee in UCLA's willed body program had been selling body parts for years); Annie Cheney, *The Resurrection Men: Scenes from the Body Trade*, Harper's 45, March 2004.

5. Federal law (42 USC § 274e(c)(2)) does not allow organs to be sold, but it does permit "reasonable payments" for processing organs. *See* Jerry Menikoff, *Law and Bioethics: An Introduction* 484–85 (Washington, D.C., Georgetown University Press 2001).

6. Katches et al., *The Body Brokers, Part I, supra* note 4.

7. *See* Canavan Foundation, *What is Canavan Disease?* at www.canavanfoundation.org/canavan.php, and National Institute of Neurological Disorders and Stroke, NINDS Canavan Disease Information Page, at www.ninds.nih.gov/disorders/canavan/canavan.htm.

8. Gina Kolata, *Sharing of Profits Is Debated as the Value of Tissue Rises; Patients Increasingly Ask: What about Me?* New York Times A1, May 15, 2000.

9. Greenberg v. Miami Children's Hospital Research Institute, 2003 U.S. Dist. LEXIS 8959 (2003). This case has since been settled, and thus no trial will take place.

10. *See* 45 CFR § 46.111(a)(3), 111(b). *See also, e.g.,* T. Howard Stone, *The Invisible Vulnerable: The Economically and Educationally Disadvantaged Subjects of Clinical Research,* 31 J. L. Med. Ethics 149 (2003).

11. FDA, *Payment to Research Subjects,* in Information Sheets: Guidance for Institutional Review Boards and Clinical Investigators, 1998 Update at 31, *available at* http://www.fda.gov/oc/ohrt/irbs/toc4.html#payment.

12. This language is borrowed from the FDA regulations about informed consent in general, which require that a prospective subject should be asked about enrolling in a study only under circumstances that "minimize the possibility of coercion or undue influence." 21 CFR § 50.20.

13. International Conference on Harmonisation of Technical Requirements for Registration of Pharmaceuticals for Human Use (ICH), Topic E6, Guideline for Good Clinical Practice, sec. 3.1.8, *available at* http://www.ich.org/LOB/media/MEDIA482.pdf.

14. One of the few relatively well-recognized restrictions relates to the timing of payments. If a subject's participation takes place over a period of time—many weeks or months—it is considered inappropriate to have the only payment take place at the end of the study, with no option for pro-rata payment for completing part of the study. Failure to pay the subject for partial completion creates the classic "threat" that makes something coercive: if you do not complete the study, then something bad (in this case, losing payment for the services that you have already provided) will happen to you.

15. *See, e.g.* Martin Wilkinson and Andrew Moore, *Inducement in Research,* 11 Bioethics 373 (1997); Ezekiel J. Emanuel, *Ending Concerns about Undue Inducement,* 32 J. L. Med. & Ethics 100 (2004); Andrew Hetherington, *The Real Distinction between Threats and Offers,* 25(2) Soc. Theory Pract. 211 (1999).

16. We should also distinguish situations in which the services being sought are illegal or immoral, such as the scenario of paying a married couple $1 million if the wife will have sex with the rich businessman. Admittedly, there can be situations in which a research study involves an inappropriate risk–benefit ratio from the point of view of the subjects, one that would violate the applicable provisions of the federal regulations. But if that is the case, then the study is inappropriate regardless of whether or not the subject is paid. The fee paid to a subject should not be taken into account in determining the appropriateness of the risk–benefit ratio, that is, should not be considered a "benefit" for that purpose.

17. Neal Dickert et al., *Paying Research Subjects: An Analysis of Current Policies,* 136 Ann. Int. Med. 368 (2002).

18. Neal Dickert and Christine Grady, *What's the Price of a Research Subject? Approaches to Payment for Research Participation,* 341 New Engl. J. Med. 198 (1999).

19. William K. Rashbaum, *Firefighters and Police Hold Protest for Raises,* New York Times B3, August 16, 2002.

20. As Charles Fried has put it, "A mountain climber may expose himself to risks, but he does so actively, by exercising his capacities to attain a goal he can understand and attain. The experimental subject does not hazard his physical capacities by using them." Charles Fried, *Medical Experimentation: Personal Integrity and Social Policy* 166 (New York, American Elsevier 1974).

21. Gina Kolata and Kurt Eichenwald, *For the Uninsured, Drug Trials Are Health Care*, New York Times A1, June 22, 1999.

22. For an extensive discussion of many aspects of the justice issue, *see* Jeffrey P. Kahn et al., ed., *Beyond Consent: Seeking Justice in Research* (New York, Oxford University Press 1998).

23. *See* 45 CFR § 46.111(a)(3).

24. *See id.* It is noteworthy that in many discussions of the justice issue, there is often minimal or no reference to the issue of enrolling the proper percentage of poor subjects. *See, e.g.,* Kahn et al., *supra* note 22, where this topic is barely touched upon.

Chapter 17

1. Deborah Nelson and Rick Weiss, *Penn Researchers Sued in Gene Therapy Death; Teen's Parents Also Name Ethicist as Defendant*, Washington Post A3, September 19, 2000.

2. Letter from FDA to James M. Wilson, dated February 8, 2002, *available at* www.fda.gov/foi/nooh/Wilson.htm.

3. Jennifer Washburn, *Informed Consent*, Washington Post W6, December 30, 2001.

4. Patricia C. Kuszler, *Curing Conflicts of Interest in Clinical Research: Impossible Dreams and Harsh Realities*, 8 Wid. L. Symp. J. 115, 140 (2001).

5. Department of Health and Human Services, *Financial Relationships and Interests in Research Involving Human Subjects: Guidance for Human Subject Protection*, 69 Fed. Reg. 26393 (2004).

6. Act of December 12, 1980, Pub. L. No. 96–517, 94 Stat. 3015 (1980), *codified as amended at* 35 USC §§ 200–11, 301–07. Although this act applied to all forms of research, the comments in the text are limited to its application in areas involving research with human subjects.

7. *See, e.g.,* Norman G. Levinsky, *Nonfinancial Conflicts of Interest in Research*, 347 New Engl. J. Med. 759 (2002).

8. Office of Research Integrity, Handling Misconduct: Case Summaries, *available at* ori.dhhs.gov/misconduct/cases.

9. *See, e.g.,* Dan Vergano, *Drug-Trial Deaths "Go Unreported,"* USA Today 12D, November 8, 2000.

10. In a lawsuit regarding the Fred Hutchinson Cancer Research Center studies discussed in note 11 of chapter 7, claims of inappropriate conflicts of interest were alleged, but the judge ended up determining that those charges lacked merit, and they were not given to the jury. Goldie Blumenstyk and Jeffrey Brainard, *Jury Clears Cancer Center of Failing to Tell Participants of Clinical-Trial Risks*, Chron. Higher Ed. 33, April 23, 2004.

11. *See, e.g.,* Trudo Lemmens and Paul B. Miller, *The Human Subjects Trade: Ethical and Legal Issues Surrounding Recruitment Incentives*, 31 J. L. Med. Ethics 398 (2003).

12. Office of Inspector General, Department of Health and Human Services, Recruiting Human Subjects: Pressures in Industry-Sponsored Clinical Research (2000), *available at* oig.hhs.gov/oei/reports/oei-01–97–00195.pdf.

13. *Id.* at 18.

14. *Id.* at 2.

15. Department of Health and Human Services, *supra* note 5 at 26396.

16. "It is important to distinguish the financial incentives used to encourage timely recruitment from the sponsor payments to investigators for costs associated with conducting clinical research." Office of Inspector General, *supra* note 12 at 17.

17. Any compensation payment—even in clinical care—creates some degree of bad incentives. A surgeon has an incentive to operate—instead of recommending a drug treatment—due to surgical fees. But the problem is worse in the research setting, because research involves activities that are not necessarily in the patient's best interest.

18. David Willman, *Stealth Merger: Drug Companies and Government Medical Research,* Los Angeles Times, A1, December 7, 2003.

19. David Willman and Jon Marino, *NIH Directors No Longer Drug Firm Consultants,* Los Angeles Times A1, January 23, 2004.

20. Willman, *supra* note 18. The final NIH conflict of interest policy adopted as a result of these disclosures is discussed in Evan G. Derenzo, *Conflict-of-Interest Policy at the National Institutes of Health: The Pendulum Swings Wildly,* 15 Kennedy Inst. Ethics J. 199 (2005).

Chapter 18

1. Charles Fried, *Medical Experimentation: Personal Integrity and Social Policy* 143 (New York, American Elsevier 1974).

2. *Id.* at 156.

3. *See, e.g.,* Nancy S. Sung et al., *Central Challenges Facing the National Clinical Research Enterprise,* 289 JAMA 1278 (2003) (noting that there is a growing need for increased numbers of people to participate in research, with a prediction that by 2005 19.8 million people a year will be needed for the clinical trials that are being projected by the research establishment); Roger N. Rosenberg, *Translating Biomedical Research to the Bedside: A National Crisis and a Call to Action,* 289 JAMA 1305 (2003).

4. Robert E. Wittes, *Therapies for Cancer in Children—Past Successes, Future Challenges,* 348 New Engl. J. Med. 747 (2003).

5. Dr. Eric Kodish, one the nation's leading pediatric cancer researchers, who is Chairperson of the Bioethics Committee for the Children's Oncology Group, makes this point in a graphically compelling manner in the slides he presents at talks (such as one held at the University of Kansas Medical Center in November, 2002), showing bar graphs using data from the National Cancer Institute's SEER program comparing the fact that, for cancer studied by the NCI, cancers in children generate only 1% of the cases, yet 71% of the children eligible for such studies enroll in them. Adults 50 or more years of age generate 86% of the cancer cases, yet only 1% of these people enroll in studies.

6. National Cancer Institute, Facts and Figures about Cancer Clinical Trials, *available at* www.nci.nih.gov/clinicaltrials/facts-and-figures#patients.

7. *Id.*

8. *Just Plain Folks,* ABC News Nightline, January 24, 1997.

9. www.henniker.org, *as of* January 1, 2002.

10. Sylvia Nassar, *A Beautiful Mind: A Biography of John Forbes Nash, Jr., Winner of the Nobel Prize in Economics, 1994* 118 (New York: Simon & Schuster 1998).

11. Note one difference between the generic prisoner's dilemma and research: although overall doing more research may benefit everyone in the long run, in specific instances particular individuals will be harmed by being forced to be in certain studies.

12. Holcombe E. Grier et al., *Addition of Ifosfamide and Etoposide to Standard Chemotherapy for Ewing's Sarcoma and Primitive Neuroectodermal Tumor of Bone*, 348 New Engl. J. Med. 694 (2003). The editorial in question was Wittes, *supra* note 4.

13. As noted in chapter 1, there is no good evidence that merely being in a study produces better outcomes than if you received the same treatment outside of a study.

14. *See* Wittes, *supra* note 4.

15. Gina Kolata and Kurt Eichenwald, *Hope for Sale: Business Thrives on Unproven Care, Leaving Science Behind*, New York Times A1, October 3, 1999.

16. This is the terminology that one of the leaders in the ethics of pediatric oncology research, Dr. Eric Kodish (*see* note 5 *supra*), recommended for describing the standard care arm to parents, as he discussed in a presentation at the December 2002 annual meeting of Public Responsibility in Medicine & Research, the leading research ethics organization in the United States.

17. As Fried wrote in 1974, hypothesizing about the possibility of a doctor refusing to provide such care as a means of encouraging a patient to enter a research study:

> A doctor's duties to his patient] are not satisfied if the patient knows how he is being used, but is given no choice as to his treatment. . . . Thus to leave the patient no choice but to be a subject in a [research study] is inhuman insofar as the physician deliberately withholds from the patient not information this time but *a treatment which that patient reasonably desires and which it is within the power of the physician to give.* Little more need be said to show how such a proceeding violates the imperatives of fidelity as well. The very vulnerability of the patient to his doctor creates expectations, expectations not just of truthfulness but of human treatment. . . . [I]n disappointing those expectations the possibility of a system of trust is itself undermined.

Fried, *supra* note 1 at 156 (emphasis added). A recent defense of a somewhat related proposal is provided in David Orentlicher, *Making Research a Requirement of Treatment: Why We Should Sometimes Let Doctors Pressure Patients to Participate in Research*, 35(5) Hastings Center Rep. 20 (2005).

18. Even if there is not a formally enforceable agreement, given that this is a small professional community, a doctor who chose not to adhere to this policy might well find herself shunned by her colleagues in various ways. This could obviously affect her ability to advance within her profession.

19. One of the rare circumstances in which a somewhat similar type of arrangement is currently acceptable would be the rules relating to triaging of patients during an emergency.

20. Antitrust law, which outlaws the collective action of individuals that are in restraint of trade, might be applicable to this situation. These laws can be triggered by otherwise benign-appearing behavior, such as an agreement among doctors to have an upper limit or ceiling on how high patient charges for a particular treatment can be. *See, e.g.,* Arizona v. Maricopa County Medical Society, 457 U.S. 332 (1982).

21. For a recent example presenting a somewhat similar dilemma involving common use of a controversial therapy, see Gina Kolata, *Spinal Cement Draws Patients and Questions,* New York Times 1, August 28, 2005.

22. Guido Calabresi, *Reflections on Medical Experimentation in Humans,* in Paul A. Freund, ed., *Experimentation with Human Subjects* 178 (New York, G. Brazillier 1970).

Index

Abigail Alliance for Better Access to Developmental Drugs, 21
Abortion, partial birth, 190
Advance directives, 151
African Americans, 6, 7, 169
AIDS and HIV, 20, 299
    equipoise and use of AZT in pregnant women, 67–68
Allergies, peanut, 52
Allopathic medicine, 41–42
Alternative health care, 41–42, 294
Alternatives to participating in study, 97, 124–141
    See also Nonstandard care; Off-study availability of new treatments
Altruism, myth of, 4–6
Alzheimer's disease, 146–147, 148, 152, 155–156
American Academy of Ophthalmology, 24
American Medical Association, 30
American Society of Colon and Rectal Surgeons, 64, 71
Angell, Marcia, 63
Antidepressant use in teenagers, xi
Artificial heart, 85
Astigmatism, 26–27

Atomic Energy Commission, 7
Autonomy, 7, 250

Bad choice research studies, 4, 9, 10, 11, 51–60, 61–79
    incompetent subjects, 145–146
    rarity of, 68–70
    See also Consent forms; Informed consent
Baltimore. See Lead paint study
Basic treatment, 246
Battery, 87, 283
Bayh-Dole Act, 225
Beautiful Mind, A, 243
Beecher, Henry, xii, 5, 84–85
Belmont Report, 7, 220, 290
Beneficence, 7
Benefits, of participating in research, 22–23, 96, 117–120
    to society versus those to subjects, 55–57
    and risks, 55–57
    STAR study, compared to risks, 135–137
    See also Consent forms; Informed consent

Blindness caused by oxygen use in premature infants, 90–91, 92–93
Bonuses for enrollment of subjects, 230
Breast cancer, 114, 122
  high-dose chemotherapy and bone marrow transplant, 70, 124–129
  lawsuit regarding nonstandard care, 47–49
  prevention of, xiii, 133–141
  See also STAR study
Brody, Jane, 3, 19, 53, 63
Bronchoscopy. *See* Wan, Nicole
Brook v. St. John's Hickey Memorial Hospital, 44–45, 265–66
Burton, Daniel, 90–91, 92–93
Burzynski, Stanislaw, 294
Bush, George W., 190, 207
  stem cell research, 203, 306

Canaries in mines, 169
Canavan disease, 214–215
Cancer
  adult research participation compared to children, 240–241
  See specific type; Pediatric cancer research
Cancer cells, injection into subjects, 6
Candura, Rosaria, 148
Canterbury v. Spence, 88–89
Caplan, Arthur, 18
  and gene-transfer study, 223
Capacity to make decisions
  determination of, 147–149
  distinguished from competence, 148
  role of psychiatrist in determining, 149
  See also Incompetent adults
Cardiac surgery, 116
Cardozo, Benjamin, 86–87
Celebrex, xi
Chicken soup, 62
Children in research
  assent requirement, 165
  authority to make own decisions, 300
  hepatitis, intentional infection with, 146
  "learn about the child's condition" studies, 171–172
  legally authorized representative for, 165
  minimal risk studies, 168–169, 170, 182

  minor increase over minimal risk, 171–172, 182
  nonbeneficial studies, encouragement of, 177–179
  "not otherwise approvable" studies, 172, 183–187
  off-label treatments for, 133, 178
  parental permission requirement, 165
  pediatric exclusivity rule, 179
  Pediatric Research Equity Act, 179
  Pediatric Rule, 179
  phase I studies, 173–174
  placebo use, 175
  regulations permitting enrollment in research, 165–166
  risk categories in regulations, 165, 169–172
  section 407 panels, 183–187
  See also Pediatric cancer research; Lead paint study
Childhood cancers. *See* Pediatric cancer research
Christian ophthalmology department, 27
Cholesterol, 117–118
Christian Scientist healers, 41
CIA, 7, 185
Cleveland clinic, xiii, 71, 129–130, 132, 141
Clinical equipoise. *See* Equipoise
Clinical Outcomes of Surgical Therapy (COST) study, xiii, 64–66, 70–73
Clinical trials, 21–23
  defined, xii, 3
  participation in, 3
Cloning, 205–207
  federal ban on funding research, 206
  reproductive versus therapeutic, 205
  research by South Koreans, 191
  uses for, 205–207
Coercion, 55
Colon cancer surgery, xiii, 64–66, 70–73
Colton v. New York Hospital, 46–47
Common Rule, 8, 37, 61, 254–255
  disclosures required in consent forms, 96–97
  substantive protections for research subjects, 53–57, 66
  See also Federal research regulations
Compassionate use, 21, 132, 258, 263–264
Competence, determination of, 147–149
Coercion, 216–217

Confidentiality of subjects. *See* Privacy and confidentiality of subjects
Conflicts of interest, 30
  future patients, over current patients, 248–249
  as justification for research regulations, 98
  professional standard for research informed consent, 93
  researcher career advancement, 226
  See also Financial conflicts of interest
Consent
  implied, 158
  versus informed consent, 87
  See also Informed consent
Consent forms
  benefits from participating, 117–120
  consent form versus use of form, 94–97, 285
  extra tests and procedures, 100–101
  interim results, failure to disclose, 102–104
  NCI sample consent form, analysis of, 99–104
  new information section, 102
  new treatment, effectiveness, 113–115, 130–131
  off-study availability of new treatment, 124–141
  phase I studies, 118–120
  protocol, 101–102
  randomization, 101
  reasons for not enrolling in study, nondisclosure of, 121
  research as different from clinical care, 100
  revisions to improve subject understanding, 120–123
  sample form from NCI, 105–112
  standard care, 115–117
Constitution, U.S., 196, 201
  enrollment of incompetent subjects in research, 156–157
  right to refuse care, 48
Contraception, 197
Contract law, 95–96
Conversion of a person's tissues, 212
Corneal transplantation
  experimental treatment, 26–27, 31, 43, 50
  standard treatment, 25–26, 43
Cure, 130–131

Data and safety monitoring, 55, 103
Deceit, ethics of, 10–11
Decisional capacity. *See* Capacity to make decisions
Declaration of Helsinki, 74
Diaz v. Hillsborough County Hospital Authority, 194–195
Dignitary harm, 194
Dresser, Rebecca, 192
Drugs, recently approved, risks of, 69–70
Dryvax vaccine, 183–187

Economically disadvantaged persons, 216, 221
Embryo, frozen,
  adoption of, 305
  excess of, created by in vitro fertilization, 203
  legal status of, 200–201
Emergency research, 158–164, 298
  new treatments, availability outside study, 161–163
  rationale for subjects, 160–164
  research without consent, 158, 159–160
Equipoise, 32, 123, 273–275
  difference between theoretical and clinical equipoise, 274
  FDA view regarding, 63
  limitations of, 63–70
  requirements for equipoise to exist, 62–63
  role in STAR study, 135
  role in studies comparing nonstandard care to standard care, 62–68
Equitable selection of research subjects, 55, 220
Erbitux, 21
Estrogen, as treatment for Alzheimer's disease, 146–147, 152

Federal research regulations, 8, 37, 78, 85, 86, 221
  fetus, application to, 203
  frozen embryo, application to, 203
  right of subjects to sue for breach of, 54
  See also Common Rule

Fetus
  FDA letter codes for risks of drugs to,
    196, 303–304
  federal research regulations, status
    under, 203
  killing of, as homicide, 190, 200–201
  legal status of, 200–201
  lung-maturity study, 193–195
  medical problems of, research on, 198–
    200
  personhood of, 196–197, 200–201
  vulnerability as subjects, 195
Fiduciary duty, 212
  and relationship between researcher and
    subject, 261–262
Financial conflicts of interest
  approaches to dealing with, 224–225
  compared to non-financial conflicts,
    226–227
  DHHS guidance document, 224–225
  disclosure, need to, 212
  disclosure, type of, 233
  enrollment fees paid to researchers,
    228–231
  FDA disclosure rules, 224
  in gene transfer study, 222–224
  NIH, existence among employees at,
    233–235
  ownership of interests, 225–228
  payment to researchers for services,
    231–233
Finder's fee, 230
Food and Drug Administration (FDA),
    20–21, 175, 185, 190, 193
  banning off-label uses, 141
  code categories for drug risks to fetus,
    196, 303–304
  emergency research rules, 158–164
  Jesse Gelsinger, death of 223–224
  off-label use, rules relating to, 131–133
  placebo studies, 74, 279
  post-9/11 rules, 51–52
  payments to research subjects, rules on,
    216
  pregnant women, in research, 197
  regulation of drugs, devices, and
    biologics, 39–41, 69–70
  researcher's financial conflicts of
    interest, disclosure of, 224, 230–231

  unapproved drugs, preventing use of
    39–41, 250
  women of child-bearing potential in
    research 197
  See also Compassionate use
Fost, Norman, 160–162
Fraud, 93, 124
Fred Hutchinson Cancer Research Center,
    85, 129, 281–282, 285, 309
Free medical care, as incentive, 218–219
Freedman, Benjamin, 62
Fried, Charles, 239–240, 244, 311

Game theory, 242–244
Gelsinger, Jesse, 8, 18, 60, 85, 222–224,
    226–227
  enrollment in study, rationale for, 223
  See also Financial conflicts of interest
Gene transfer research, 8, 18
Genovo, Inc., 224
Good choice research studies, 9, 10, 11,
    51–60, 61–79
  involving children, 170–171, 173–176
  See also Consent forms; Informed
    consent
Grimes v. Kennedy Krieger Institute, Inc.,
    167–169, 181–182, 187–189
Guess v. Board of Medical Examiners of
    North Carolina, 42–43

Hairy hand, case of, 95–96, 286
Hanlon, Stephen, 194
Harm, dignitary, 194
Harvard University, 3, 9
  stem cell research at, 204
HDC-ABMT (high dose chemotherapy
    followed by autologous bone marrow
    transplantation), 70
  early history of, 124–126
  financial incentives to use, 126
  judges' attitudes toward, 126–127
  lawsuits against insurance companies,
    126–127
  women in randomized studies, inability
    to enroll in, 127–128
Healthy research subjects, 52, 217
  See also Nontherapeutic studies
Henney, Jane, 69–70
Henniker, New Hampshire, 241–244

Hepatitis, intentional infection of children, 6, 146
Hexamethonium, 9, 60
High altitude sickness, 58–59
History of research with human subjects, 6–8, 254
HIV. *See* AIDS and HIV
HOGLAW, 28
Homeopathy, 41, 42
Hormone replacement therapy, xi
Hutch. *See* Fred Hutchinson Cancer Research Center

ImClone, 21
Inclusion benefit of participating in research, 22–23, 259
Incompetent adults, 145–157
  capacity to decide, 147–149
  enrollment decision making, 149–153
  enrollment in nonbeneficial studies, constitutional limitations on 156–157
  enrollment in research, justification for, 145–146
  enrollment in research, substantive limitations on 153–156
  incompetence versus lack of capacity, 148
  legally authorized representative, role of, 149–153
  New York State regulations, lawsuit regarding, 145–146, 156–157
  state laws on enrollment in research, 151–153
  studies conducted, limitations on 153–156
  terminology, 295
Incompetent subjects. See Incompetent adults; Children; Emergency research
Informed consent, 10, 83, 283–285
  distinguished from battery, 87
  federal regulations, disclosures required by, 96–97, 286–287
  financial conflicts of interest, disclosure of, 212
  good- versus bad-choice studies, disclosure of, 70–73
  historical developments of, during twentieth century, 84–88

  improvement of, through revision of consent forms, 120–123
  legal standards for, 86–93
  Nuremberg Code requirement for obtaining, 8
  obtaining, versus use of form, 94–97
  reasonable person standard, 88–89
  reasonable subject standard, 89–93
  in research, as compared to clinical care, 54, 91–93
  See also Consent forms
Innovative treatments, 260–261
  access to, 19–21
  direct access versus participation in research, 19–20
  off-study availability, failure to disclose, 124–144
  See also Nonstandard care
Institutional review board (IRB), 8, 58, 130, 168, 171–172, 187, 230
Insurance companies, 126–127
Interim results, failure to disclose, 34–35, 102–103
International research, 67–68
Investigational New Drug (IND) application, 132
Iodine, radioactive, 60, 78

Jewish old age home residents, as subjects, 6
Johns Hopkins University, 8
  See also Lead paint study
Justice, 7, 220–221

Kansas City, Missouri, 180
Kass, Leon, 191, 207
Katz, Jay, 18
Kennedy Krieger Institute. *See* Lead paint study
Keyhole surgery. *See* Colon cancer surgery
Kingsfield, Professor, 95
Klais, Daniel, 129–131, 141
Knee surgery for arthritis, 77–78
Koppel, Ted, 241–242
Koski, Greg, 17

Laci and Conner's Law, 191, 200
Laetrile, 40–41
Laparoscopic surgery. *See* Colon cancer surgery

Lead paint study
  court opinion, 168–169, 176, 181–182
  description of, 166–168
  informed consent problems, 85
  rights of parents, and exposure of
    children to risks, 168–169, 187–189
Legally authorized representative
  for children, 165
  for incompetent subjects, 149–153, 296–
    297
Letrozole, 288
Leukemia, hairy cell, 211
Licensing laws, 41, 131
Louisiana law, defining status of frozen
  embryos, 201
LSD experiments with soldiers, 6, 282
Lymphokines, 211

Malignant melanoma, experimental
  vaccine for, 85
Malpractice law, 10, 41, 283
  flawed study design, 57–60
  nonstandard care, 43–50
  and participation in research, 268–270
  protecting patients, role in, 43, 95
  study protocol, deviation from, 57–58
  suing for damages, right of research
    subject to, 54
McGregor, Rosemary, 58–59
Mental disorders. *See* Incompetent adults
Miller, Matthew, 119–120, 173–174
Mini-mental status exam, 146–147, 149
Minimum wage, as payment to research
  subjects, 218
Miranda warning, 97–99
Monitoring of data and safety of subjects,
  55
Moore, John, 211–212, 222
Morning-after pill, 190
Mountain climbing, 58–59
MKULTRA project, 7

Nash, John, 243
National Bioethics Advisory Commission
  (NBAC), 154–155
National Cancer Institute (NCI), 97, 115,
  117, 119
  consent form for STAR study, 133–135
  sample consent form, 105–112

template for disclosure of alternatives,
  133
National Institutes of Health (NIH), 65,
  146, 171, 227
  financial conflicts of interest, of
    employees, 233–235
  NIH Revitalization Act, 193
Nazis, research studies conducted by, 6,
  56, 169, 187
Negligence. *See* Malpractice law
Neutron generator, 27
New York Hospital, 46, 86, 90, 93
Nondisclosure of interim results in
  research, 34–35
Nonstandard care, 28–29, 31, 260
  contract law in permitting, 95–96
  FDA limitations on, 39–41
  legal protections given to patients, 37–
    50
  role of equipoise compared to standard
    care, 62–68
  state legal limitations on, 41–50
  See also Off-study availability of new
    treatments
Nontherapeutic research studies, 52
  therapeutic, compared with, 21–22, 272
Nuremberg Code, 6, 8, 51, 86

Office for Human Research Protections
  (OHRP), 17, 25, 28, 184, 230
  emergency research rules, 158–164
  research on incompetent adults, 146–
    147, 152
Office of Inspector General, DHHS, 229–
  231, 232
Office of Research Integrity, 226
Off-label use, 20, 131–133, 292
  in children, 133, 178
  See also Off-study availability of new
    treatments
Off-study availability of new treatments,
  19–21, 293–294
  failure to disclose, 124–141
  proposed wording for disclosure, 136
  requirement of doctor to provide, 138–
    140
  when disclosure is not required, 136–
    138
  See also STAR study

Organ donation, role of altruism, 5–6
Ornithine transcarbamylase (OTC) deficiency, 8, 222, 224
Osteoporosis drug, use to prevent breast cancer, xiii
   See also STAR study
Oxygen use in premature infants, 90–91, 92–93

Paper Chase, 95–96
Parkinson's disease
   placebo studies in early-stage disease, 75
   sham surgery studies, 78–79
Participant in research, 257–258
Paternalism, 39, 56
Patient
   best interests of, rule for nonstandard care, 44–45
   as different from research subject, 24–36
   duties of physician toward, 30
Payette, Michelle, 59–60, 78
Paying research subjects, 211–221
   based on risks assumed, 217–219
   coercion, role of, 216–217
   FDA rules regarding, 216
   as signal that study might be a bad choice, 219–220
   undue influence, role of, 216–217
Paying researchers, 222–235
   See also Financial conflicts of interest
Pediatric cancer research xiii, 3, 61, 239–241, 244–249
   agreement among oncologists on new treatments, 246–249
   high enrollment in, 240–241
   record of success of, 240–241
Peterson, Scott and Laci and Conner, 190, 200
Pharmaceutical manufacturers
   enrolling women, reluctance to 197–198
   recruiting subjects, 228–231, 232
Pharmacists refusal to fill prescriptions, 190
Phase I research studies, 5, 155, 289–290
   benefits from participation, disclosure of, 118–120
   children, enrollment in, 173–174
   See also Gelsinger, Jesse
Phases of a drug study, 263

Physicians
   best interests of current patient, acting against, 247–250, 264–265
   ethical duties toward patients, 30
   licensing of, 41–43
   off-label treatments, authority to use, 136
   role as researcher versus role as clinician, 29–30, 138–140
   See also Fiduciary duty
Placebos, 67, 278–280
   acceptable and unacceptable uses, 74–76
   children, use in studies involving, 175
   equipoise requirement in placebo studies, 73–76
   justification for use in research, 73–74
   risks to subjects from, 74–76
   surgery studies, role in, 76–79
Plague bombs used by Japanese military, 169
PolyHeme, 163–164
Pregnant women
   drug side effects for, 195–198
   exclusion as research subjects, 193–200
   flu vaccine, use by, 195–196
   pregnancy registry, 198
   premature infants, 193–195
   in studies about problems relating to pregnancy, 198–200
   in studies not about problems unique to pregnancy, 195–198
   vulnerability of, 193–195
President's Council on Bioethics, 191, 207
Prisoners, 7
Prisoner's Dilemma, 243–244
Privacy and confidentiality of subjects, 55
Procedure, research, defined, 22
Profits, from use and sale of human tissues, 213–215

Quinlan, Karen Ann, 150

Radiation experiments, 6–7
Raloxifene. *See* STAR study
Randomization, 31–33, 101
Reasonableness rule, 42–50
Recruitment of subjects, 229–230
Regulations. *See* Federal research regulations

Release of right to sue, 58–59
Representative. *See* Legally authorized
  representative
Research, definition of, 15–16, 29–30,
  261
  distinguished from clinical care, 30–35
Research studies
  design of, and risks to subjects, 57–60
  primary purpose of, 15–19
  role of, xii
  See also Clinical trials
Research subject
  best interests of, 55–57
  versus being a patient, 24–36
  equitable selection of, 55
  misunderstanding of difference from
    being a patient, 21–22, 71
  right to sue for damages, 54
  terminology used, in contrast to
    participant, 257–58
  weakened legal protections of, 51–60
Researcher, duties to subjects, 51–79, 269–
  272
Retinopathy of prematurity, 90–91, 92–93
Revici, Emanuel, 47–49
Risks from participation in research, 30–
  35, 96
  requirement to minimize, 55, 255
  role in approval of research, 8
  STAR study, compared to benefits, 135–
    136
  See also Consent forms; Informed
    consent
Roche, Ellen, 8–9, 21, 60, 85, 258, 273
Rockefeller University, 59–60
Roe v. Wade, 196, 200
Rojas, Barbara, 46
Rowsey, James, 24–29, 31, 33, 36, 37, 43,
  50, 65

Salgo, Martin, 87–88
Scandals, in research, 6–7, 85
Schiff v. Prados, 294
Schloendorff, Mary, 86–87
Schneider v. Revici, 47–49
Seizures, continuous (status epilepticus),
  159–160
September 11, 2001, 4, 7, 56, 183, 218
Sham surgery, 76–79

Smallpox vaccine research studies, 4–5,
  183–187
Somatic cell nuclear transfer. *See* Cloning
South Korea, cloning research, 191
Standard of care, 26, 43, 265
  See also Nonstandard care
Standardization of treatment in research,
  34
STAR study (Study of Tamoxifen and
  Raloxifene), 133–141
  alternatives listed in consent form, 134
  described, 133
  off-label use of raloxifene, 134
  off-label uses, arguments against
    disclosure, 135
Stem cells
  cloning to produce, 191
  creation of new embryos to produce,
    202
  destruction of embryos to produce,
    202–205
  federal regulations, 305
  funding of research regarding, 203–205
  special properties of, 201–202
  state laws regarding, 204–205
  types of, 202
Stewart, Martha, 21
Stopping rules, 102–104, 288–289
Subject. *See* Research subject
Substandard care, 51
Supreme Court, U.S., 40–41, 97, 200
Surgery. *See* Colon cancer surgery; Corneal
  transplantation; Sham surgery
Surrogate decision-maker. *See* Legally
  authorized representative

Tamoxifen. *See* STAR study
Tampa General Hospital, 194
Tampa Trephine, 24–25, 27–31, 33, 36, 66
*T.D. v. New York State Office of Mental
  Health,* 145–146
Terminally ill patients, right to unproven
  care, 40–41
Tests and procedures, extra, in research,
  22, 35
Therapeutic misconception, 21–22, 71
Therapeutic versus nontherapeutic
  research studies, 21–22
Thompson, Tommy, 17

Tissue
  ownership of, 212–213
  profits from sale of, 213–215
Tort law, 10, 86, 95
  See also Malpractice law
Transplantation, 25, 46–47
  See also Corneal transplantation
Truog, Robert, 38
Truth, reluctance to reveal, xiii-xiv, 10–11
Tunkl v. Regents of University of California,
  45–46, 266
Tuskegee study, 6, 169, 188

UCLA Medical Center, 45, 184, 211–212
Unborn Victims of Violence Act, 190
Uncertainty about medical treatments, xi, 9
Undue influence, 55
  role in paying research subjects, 216–
  217
University of Pennsylvania, 8, 60, 223
  See also Gelsinger, Jesse
University of Rochester, 8, 57
University of South Florida, 24, 28–29, 31,
  193–195
University of Washington, 58

Unjust enrichment, 215
Unproven medical care. *See* Nonstandard
  care

Vioxx, xi, 178, 278
Vodopest, Patricia, 58–59, 60
Vulnerable subjects, 55
  economically disadvantaged persons as,
  216, 221
  See also Children; Incompetent adults;
  Pregnant women; Prisoners; Fetus

Waiver of right to sue for malpractice, 45–48
Wan, Nicole, 8, 21–22, 57, 60, 78
Washout periods in studies, 279–280
Willowbrook study, 146
Wilson, James W., 223–224, 226, 234
Women
  of child-bearing potential, 197
  contraception use, as condition to
  enrollment in research, 197
  exclusion as research subjects, 191–193
  See also Pregnant women

Zerhouni, Elias, 234

9 780195 147971